# THE ENGLISH BUILDER!
## ACE YOUR ENGLISH IN 365 DAYS

## Jessie Gao

First published by Busybird Publishing 2022

Copyright © 2022 Jessie Gao

ISBN
Print: 978-1-922691-90-3
Ebook: 978-1-922691-91-0

This work is copyright. Apart from any use permitted under the *Copyright Act 1968*, no part of this publication may be reproduced, stored in a retrieval system or transmitted in any form or by any means, electronic, mechanical, photocopying, recording or otherwise, without the prior written permission of Jessie Gao.

The information in this book is based on the author's experiences and opinions. The author and publisher disclaim responsibility for any adverse consequences, which may result from use of the information contained herein. Permission to use any external content has been sought by the author. Any breaches will be rectified in further editions of the book.

**Cover image:** Busybird Publishing

**Cover design:** Busybird Publishing

**Layout and typesetting**: Busybird Publishing

**Illustrations:** Jessie Gao

Busybird Publishing
2/118 Para Road
Montmorency, Victoria
Australia 3094
www.busybird.com.au

To the English Builder,

who dares to dream,

who has a passion,

who can work hard,

who is determined,

you are remarkable!

## The Maths of Building Your Home

An essential guide to build a solid foundation for your home.

+ A how-to-guide to live your life to the fullest.

+ ♡ A useful guide to advance your career.

+ A handy guide to stimulate your bright ideas.

+ A practical guide to help you survive and thrive overseas.

---

  An ultimate guide to sharpen your English skills!

# TABLE OF CONTENTS

| | |
|---|---|
| ABOUT THE AUTHOR | 1 |
| ACKNOWLEDGEMENTS | 2 |
| PREFACE | 3 |
| IMPORTANT: HOW TO USE THE BOOK | 6 |
| **INTRODUCTION** | 11 |
| **CHAPTER 1** An English Builder | 12 |
| **CHAPTER 2** An English Practitioner | 23 |
| **PART 1 ENLIGHTEN AND EVOLVE** | 28 |
| **CHAPTER 3** A Dream Chaser | 29 |
| **CHAPTER 4** An Unbiased Self-Evaluator | 42 |
| **CHAPTER 5** A Time Management Artist | 49 |
| THE WORD – AWAY | 58 |
| **CHAPTER 6** A Brain Trainer | 59 |
| **CHAPTER 7** A Capable Money-Maker | 66 |
| **CHAPTER 8** A Relationship Nurturer | 74 |
| THE WORD – AT | 86 |
| **CHAPTER 9** An Utter Powerhouse | 87 |
| **CHAPTER 10** A Real Trooper | 95 |
| **CHAPTER 11** A Happy Person | 102 |
| THE WORD – OUT | 111 |
| DAY 100 – IDIOMS ABOUT BODY PARTS | 112 |
| **CHAPTER 12** An Emotion Expresser | 113 |
| **CHAPTER 13** A Life Adventurer | 120 |
| **CHAPTER 14** A Big Achiever | 131 |
| THE WORD – UP | 148 |
| **PART 2 LOVE YOUR PROFESSION** | 149 |
| **CHAPTER 15** A Career Planner | 150 |
| **CHAPTER 16** An Active Job Hunter | 155 |
| **CHAPTER 17** An Aussie Culture Insider | 164 |
| THE WORD – DOWN | 176 |
| **CHAPTER 18** A Dedicated Workafrolic | 177 |

| CHAPTER 19 | A Great Team Player | 183 |
| CHAPTER 20 | A Corporate Ladder Climber | 189 |
| | THE WORD – THROUGH | 206 |
| CHAPTER 21 | A Stellar Leader | 207 |
| | DAY 200 – IDIOMS ABOUT FOOD | 213 |
| CHAPTER 22 | A Job Exiter | 214 |
| CHAPTER 23 | A Passionate Entrepreneur | 219 |
| | THE WORD – IN | 223 |
| | **PART 3 THINK BIGGER** | 224 |
| CHAPTER 24 | An Essay Writer | 225 |
| CHAPTER 25 | A Health Adviser | 231 |
| CHAPTER 26 | A Modern Educator | 233 |
| | THE WORD – ON | 237 |
| CHAPTER 27 | A Technology Innovator | 238 |
| CHAPTER 28 | A Lifestyle Change Analyst | 242 |
| CHAPTER 29 | An Environmental Advocator | 248 |
| | THE WORD – OFF | 251 |
| CHAPTER 30 | A Culture Protector | 252 |
| CHAPTER 31 | A Crime Detector | 255 |
| CHAPTER 32 | A Social Problem Observer | 261 |
| | THE WORD – WITH | 277 |
| | **PART 4  SHINE BRIGHT** | 278 |
| CHAPTER 33 | An Aussie Life Starter | 279 |
| CHAPTER 34 | A Qualified Driver | 291 |
| CHAPTER 35 | A Down Under Navigator | 296 |
| | THE WORD – AROUND | 314 |
| | DAY 300 – IDIOMS ABOUT ANIMALS | 315 |
| CHAPTER 36 | A Global Traveller | 316 |
| CHAPTER 37 | A Fashionable Beauty | 330 |
| CHAPTER 38 | A Sports Enthusiast | 339 |
| | THE WORD – BACK | 352 |
| CHAPTER 39 | A Holistic Foodie | 353 |

| | | |
|---|---|---|
| **CHAPTER 40** | An Amateur Home Cook | 362 |
| **CHAPTER 41** | A Creative Hobbyist | 370 |
| | **THE WORD – OVER** | 380 |
| | **YOUR TURN** | 381 |
| | **THE END** | 383 |
| **APPENDIX 1** | COMMON BOY NAMES | 385 |
| **APPENDIX 2** | POPULAR GIRL NAMES | 387 |
| **REFERENCES** | | 389 |

# ABOUT THE AUTHOR

Jessie Gao had a happy childhood, surrounded with attention and love from parents, grandparents and relatives.

Jessie originally comes from China and has lived in Australia for over 10 years. She graduated from the University of Melbourne in Master of Management (Accounting) and volunteered at the Melbourne Museum for over 7 years.

She works in accounting and is a Certified Practising Accountant (CPA). Food makes her happy. Cooking brings her joy. She loves every second writing, painting and calligraphing. She's also a hobbyist photographer and an all-round sports enthusiast.

# ACKNOWLEDGEMENTS

I would like to thank for my parents for their unconditional love and unwavering support along the way. They have always been there for me whenever I needed them, for sure. Without my parents, I would not be standing where I am today. I love you, Mum and Dad.

Special kudos to my Uncle Wang, a successful entrepreneur, whom I deeply respect in many aspects. I'm grateful that you persuaded me to pursue further studies in Australia when I hesitated because studying abroad back then was not as popular as it is today. This book would not have been born if I had selected to stay in my hometown.

Life in Melbourne is filled with its happiness and its struggles. I deeply appreciate my best friend Sophie Zhang who has given me all sorts of help and support, especially in the tough times.

A big thanks to my wonderful workmates and all my other friends, who encouraged me all these years. I could not have done this without you.

Special thanks to Blaise van Hecke and Les Zig, my publishers, Kev Howlett, my book cover and layout designer, and Scott Vandervalk, my editor. They have been shoulder to shoulder with me, helping me to take my book to the next level and actualise my dream of publishing a book.

Most importantly, thank you, my dear readers. I will be delighted if you enjoy reading this book and if you get something valuable from it.

I met myself in Melbourne, and this book reminds me of my life journey in that city – it always will.

# PREFACE

## About me, the author

I was born and raised in Chaoyang, a small city in Liaoning province in China. I didn't start my English journey until the age of 13. In all honesty, English classes were the last thing I wanted to take from middle school through to bachelor's study back in China. I didn't love it, and it felt monotonous. But I didn't resent it. It was just that I could not see the point in learning English except in passing endless nonsensical exams. For me, English was simply a subject that I didn't quite like.

In 2010, I flew to Australia with excitement and a certain confidence in my English language because I had passed the IELTS (the International English Language Testing System) and GMAT (the Graduate Management Admission Test) exams required by the University of Melbourne. Soon, I found out that I didn't even know how to order food at McDonald's. All I could say was 'Can I get that?' by pointing out the picture on the screen up on the wall. I didn't know when ordering a burger, chips and drinks together, all I needed to say was 'I'd like an Angus beef burger meal, please.'

My pronunciation was a disaster. I asked my friend 'Are you busY?' (sounding like ZEI). This should have been easy English. He could not understand me at all. I later found out that I did not pronounce many words properly. From that experience, I learnt that when your pronunciation confuses the recipient, you can change it to 'I'm asking are you busy. B U S Y?' Spell out the letter of the words. Then communication can resume.

When volunteering at the Melbourne Museum, one of the staff members let me inform visitors who had prams to leave them in a specified area. I did, but I totally had no idea what 'prams' were at the time. If it happened again today, I would ask what a pram was right away. If you don't understand, please just ask. People are friendly and willing to help. In this way, you can boost your vocabulary on the go. Miscommunication can be avoided.

With my lousy English, I struggled with university studies and had a hard time getting a professional job and advancing my career. I had no idea how to make a wonderful life for myself in Australia. My English sucked! For a while, I was deflated. No matter how hard I worked on my English, I could not improve.

But I never stopped learning, not even today. All those years, I kept throwing myself out there, reading local newspapers and English books, watching TV programs loved by locals, grabbing interesting phrases from my workmates, and taking part in many activities with the locals in Melbourne.

As time went by, I started to use authentic and cool expressions that I found out there in the world. I started to laugh at all those stupid moments. Ahh, English is the love that creates life. English is a language that's inventive and designed to communicate with people with all your heart and all your love. I marvel at how much I've grown as a person and how amazingly life has been transformed, just by using the amazing communication tool that is English.

As an English-as-an-additional-language learner, as an overseas student with a Chinese background, as a migrant working in a global company, I understand how hard it is to reduce language barriers, to live in a foreign country and to move upwards in life. I experienced challenge after challenge! If I knew all the things in this book beforehand, I would have struggled less when I started out in Australia.

The fancy, funny and vivid expressions in this book capture, collect and summarise what I have learnt over a decade. The book is not just here to entertain you, but to open your eyes on both western and Chinese cultures, while offering general life guidance and encouragement.

With a full-time job and weekend errands, time is precious. This book was built in bits and pieces, but through it I wrote my heart out. *Sharing* is what I've learnt all these years from the successful and brilliant people around me.

This is all why I just can't wait to share this book with you.

### About you, the English Builder

Are you experiencing any of the situations below?

- I struggle with my English studies.
- I bought study materials, enrolled in online courses, joined English study groups, but I have not been able to master English.
- I am often stuck expressing my feelings and describing things when talking to westerners.
- I find it hard to fit into the western-working culture – I feel blocked from climbing the corporate ladder.
- I am preparing for IELTS or other English tests.
- I am curious about life in Australia and I'd like to be a part of it.
- I am confused about my life. (Don't worry, I'll get to this!)

We are all in the same boat. I experienced much of the above. The good news is that you've come to the right place, and that you're hopefully holding the right book.

From the moment you cracked open this book, you became an English Builder. Grow into a committed and enthusiastic English Builder, constructing your dream house block by block, brick by brick, callus by callus. You will eventually get what you have been dreaming of.

I am not a smart cookie, but I do have the courage and perseverance to stick to the end. So if I can do it, you definitely can.

It is just a matter of time.

Of course, some of the advice within does not only apply to studying English. It can help you with anything in your life, really. It could be your day job, cooking skills, hobbies, just anything else. Trust me, you will achieve something big, something that you won't regret in life.

I hope you enjoy reading this book.

Now let's take a break from me and my advice. Can you find the trick to the following sentence?

**The quick brown fox jumps over the lazy dog.**

The answer will be revealed at the end of the book.

Okay, so without further ado, let's decode the secret of the English language! Let's smash it!

# IMPORTANT: HOW TO USE THE BOOK

### Symbols

The ≈ symbol is for an approximation. It means something is similar to another thing, but not exactly the same. In the book, similar expressions that can be used in the same context are linked to the original expression by the approximation symbol (≈) and placed in square brackets [ ]. This is the essence of the book. [≈ This is what this book is about.]

In most cases, only one to five instances of alternative language for an expression are listed. But there are sometimes other similar expressions. Try collecting your own and write them down in the blank areas provided in the book. Have fun with this!

The < > symbols are angle brackets. I use them to present the origin of an idiomatic expression [≈ idiom]. They could also describe some kind of a culture shock, grammar explanation, communication trick, or even some brainstorm from me associated with a particular phrase or the particular content mentioned in a topic.

The • symbol is a bullet point. This black dot is used to introduce key items in the form of a list.

The ☐ symbol is a checkbox. This could be provided for an activity for you to tick or cross a response.

This: ⊞ is a table. A table might often consist of words or phrases of a similar nature. If there is space available in the table, write something down based on the given instructions.

This: .................... is a dotted underline. This is a space for you to write in the book. Add any words, phrases, sentences or thoughts here.

### The book's structure

As suggested in book subtitle 'Ace Your English in 365 Days', the book consists of activities for 365 days, with a 'brick' towards your house each day. Each day consists of a particular topic to learn and think about to help improve your English skills. So, you just need to lay one brick of the English language each day to build your 'house'.

The foundation of your house is laid in the **Introduction**, including the parts of speech and secret formulas to take your English to the next level. Starting with **Part 1**, at the end of every three chapters, we'll take a break, have a relaxing read with stories or facts that use the little English words, such as *away* (**Day 46**), *at* (**Day 74**), *out* (**Day 99**), *up* (**Day 136**), *down* (**Day 163**), *through* (**Day 193**), *in* (**Day 210**), *on* (**Day 223**), *off* (**Day 237**), *with* (**Day 263**), *around* (**Day 299**), *back* (**Day 337**), *over* (**Day 365**). Some of these words are often prepositions, but don't assume the words in the list are all prepositions in the way they're used each time. Identify the part of speech in the context once you've gone through that day's activity. Then celebrate each milestone!

**Part 1 Enlighten and Evolve** gets you to think about what kind of 'dream house' you'd love to build. **Part 2 Love Your Profession** navigates through your career, providing you with the ability to buy your building materials. **Part 3 Think Bigger** inspires great ideas in you and raises your awareness of being a responsible individual. This sets up your personal taste for your house. **Part 4 Shine Bright** is a bit more fun, getting you to think about the style of living you'd like in your life.

No 'brick' is exactly the same as another, though some share similar themes or topics. Each brick shares the same importance as another when building your house. This means there is really no particular reading order for the chapters. If you're new to the English language, start with Introduction. If you're new to Australia or any other English-speaking country, feel free to begin with Part 4. Are you seeking life advice? Part 1 is a great starting point. Jump into Part 3 if you want to learn how to write academic essays. Part 2 is helpful for those planning a career, looking for a job or wanting to experience the Australian workplace culture and climb the corporate ladder.

## Idioms

On Day 100, Day 200 and Day 300, you'll find three (untrue) stories with collections of interesting idioms. Some other idioms are spread across the book. The origin and meaning of some of these idioms are explained. Do some homework to find out more about those left unexplained.

## English names

People's names are randomly selected for the examples in the book. Appendix 1 contains some popular boy names and Appendix 2 contains some popular girl names. Quite importantly, English Builder, if you like, please give yourself a proper English name. Don't name yourself 'Cherry', 'Turbo', 'Batman' or 'January'. You might be inspired by a food, a car, a film character or the current month, but they could be really weird, terrible and inappropriate if you choose poorly.

## Notebook

The space in the book is limited. While some blank areas are given, I suggest that you carry a notebook with you as you go through the book. Write down phrases or sentences that you like, and add in more when you come across new expressions. The notebook can also be used to write down any ideas that spark in your head, or the answers to questions that you raise, and to reflect on your experiences. It should be a notebook that helps to record your growth in your English study journey. You could use a laptop or your mobile phone, but there are studies that indicate handwriting can improve your memory! It's really up to you which tools to use.

This book can't cover topics about everything in life, even with 365 days' worth of content! So use your notebook to build up more language bricks, not only for your first house, but eventually your second house, third house, and more.

**Curious minds**

Read actively, question things, and research to find answers on your own.

For example, you might notice a sentence in Day 1: 'I don't mind how you read this book.' In contrast, there's a sentence appearing in Day 4: 'I am an English Builder who sticks to the end.' What are the differences between these two sentences? What might you question? Ah, why is the contraction of the word ('I don't') used in the first sentence not in the second one ('I am')? Under what situations should I use a contraction?

In this book, we use a number of contractions of words to give the sense of casual conversation from the author (me) to the reader (you), emulating how some of this might be heard. Most online articles point out that you might want to avoid using word contractions in academic writing or other formal documents unless there are exceptions. For other types of writings (text messages, blogs, fiction, non-fiction and so on), it's completely okay to use them. They impart to the reader a conversational tone.

Here are some typical contractions you might encounter in English:

- it is (it's)
- it is not (it isn't)
- there is (there's)
- here is (here's)
- I have (I've)
- I am (I'm)
- I did not (I didn't)
- you are (you're)
- you cannot (you can't)
- you will not (you won't)

- she would (she'd)
- she would not (she wouldn't)
- he does not (he doesn't)
- he might have (he might've)
- we are (we're)
- we do not (we don't)
- we will (we'll)
- who had (who'd)
- let us (let's)
- of the clock (o'clock)

Always be curious. One of your very next questions might be to ask, 'What is the full form of "etc."'?

### Be innovative and experimental

A book itself is artwork. Artwork is innovative. Don't be surprised if you see some words or phrases in a table, in a list or in square brackets that are not illustrated in alphabetical order like many other English books or dictionaries do. This includes the boy and girl names in the appendixes. They are put in a random order in most cases in this book. Why?

Why should we be the same as others? English dictionaries always start words with letter *a* and finish with words ending with *z*. It's organised to be easy for you to look up for the words. But have you ever finished reading the whole dictionary? Did you lose your interest and stop at just the letter *a*?

So this book demonstrates in a different manner.

### Opinions

You don't have to agree with all of the opinions given in this book. The exercises are there merely to get you thinking. You can always ask yourself if you agree with author's opinions. If you're not sure on your opinion on a topic, take the time to shape your own view of things. Don't be swayed by the author, or even by any others. There are no standard answers for questions raised by me in this book. But I'd be happy for you to contribute your thoughts.

# INTRODUCTION

You, the English Builder, are about to build up your dream home. Excited?

Before getting right into it, let's lay a solid foundation for your home – we'll look into the nine parts of speech as an introduction. Don't get me wrong. This is not a theoretical English grammar book. But knowing the parts of speech will make you into a stronger reader, a better writer, a more authentic listener, and a clearer speaker. All of this will improve your building's structural strength.

I'll also share my secret sauce recipe for sharpening your English skills, something you'll need to apply throughout the book and along your language learning journey.

Let's start with enthusiasm!

# DAY 1
# A COMMITTED BUILDER

Hey there, fellow builders. Welcome on board! From this moment onwards, you are a committed English Builder! It is a commitment to me, and to yourself.

The very first skill that we'll learn is to write down the definition of a word in your own words. How would you define the word 'commitment'? Write your definition down below.

.................................................................................................................................

.................................................................................................................................

.................................................................................................................................

A commitment is an agreement, and an engagement to be responsible and to deliver what you have promised. In starting this book, you are committing to build your English language skills step-by-step, and to be consistent with your learning.

I don't mind how you read this book. You can read it word by word, or skim read it [≈ speed read it]. Read front to back, or back to front. Read a page per day, or finish the whole book in a month and spend the rest of the year reviewing the content.

You could read the book on the couch in your pyjamas. Maybe you'll sit on your balcony with a cup of tea and the book on a warm afternoon. Perhaps you'll read the book on your commute to work on the train. Any of these is fine, just as long as you do the reading! Just read mindfully.

But as the author, I get to set a few housekeeping rules:

- Please don't pirate this book [≈ don't copy or steal this book].
- Don't fall asleep while reading this book.
- Keep your reading consistent.
- Respect the opinions of others.
- Put in your two cents' worth. [≈ Share your opinion.]
- Keep the book in good condition (or even mint condition).

< 'Housekeeping' means to keep a place clean, neat and orderly, which creates a safe and efficient environment. Do you have your own definition of 'housekeeping'? >

< Regarding the last bullet point, please note that you don't have to keep the book in mint condition [≈ in perfect condition]. You're more than welcome to highlight, write or draw in anywhere in the book, as long as it gets you thinking, growing and improving. >

# DAY 2
# NOUN IS A THING

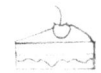

Hey there, English Builder. Are you ready? Let's start with some super easy grammar. Observe the words in the table below. Which part of speech are they?

| |
|---|
| dream, roadmap, millionaire, builder, oyster, pearl, crossroads, herd, option, sword, cost, head, question, moments, hometown, decision, tree, goals, timeline, slacker, commitment, value, personality, cucumber, faith, actor, time, train, customers, airport, application, weeds, dissatisfaction, music, exhibition, wisdom, mind, length, facts, expressions, traffic, memory, English, brain, grade, passport, money, property, chapter, formula, patterns, relationship, friendships, world, love, family, life, oat, exercises, food, baby, downtime, pressure, athlete, soul, gratitude, kindness, heart, people, friends, expectations, temperature, anger, passions, change, opportunity, feet, rules, conversation, success, achiever, astrology, idol, appearance, failure, race, patience, consistency |

Bingo! These words are all nouns (though a few could also be used as a verb) – as today's title indicated.

These particular nouns are all extracted from **Part 1 Enlighten and Evolve**. Take a close look at which nouns are presented as the singular form and which are in the plural form. A noun can refer to a person (Albert Einstein) or a place (Australia). A noun can also name a thing, such as countable things (flowers, cupcakes and tomatoes) or uncountable stuff (snow, chocolate and love). Out of these six examples the word love is the abstract noun while the rest are concrete nouns.

Today's content is a piece of cake [≈ a cakewalk ≈ a snap ≈ a cinch], right?

< The above expressions refer to something that is easy to do. Why is a piece of cake considered easy? How is a cake walking related to easy? Aha! Both idioms are associated with the cakewalk dance competition on plantations in the 19th century where African-American slaves would dance around a cake. The winners of the competition would be given slices of cakes as a prize (Koerner, 2003). The phrases developed over time into the meaning of easy, perhaps because of the graceful and elegant dance steps involved. The people who won the cake made the dance look easy (Gandhi, 2013). Who knows if this is true? But knowing the story behind a word or a phrase might make your English learning journey a fun process… maybe even a cakewalk. Just keep an open mind. >

Can you identify all the nouns in today's text other than those in the table? Circle and count them. I spotted 87 nouns in total. Did I miss any, or have I overcounted? How many nouns did you get?

# DAY 3
# ADJECTIVES DESCRIBE THINGS

Today, we'll be looking into adjectives. Adjectives are used to describe [≈ modify] nouns. Examples are **beautiful** flowers, **yummy** cupcakes, **sour** tomatoes, **powdery** snow, **gooey** chocolate and **heartfelt** love.

Observe the below adjectives from **Part 2 Love Your Profession** of this book. Can you spot any pattern to them?

> happy, future, good, qualified, huge, daily, straightforward, glad, regular, green, exciting, beautiful, sustainable, permanent, cold, hard, extensive, dynamic, best, natural, irrelevant, real, terrible, potential, empty, behavioural, formal, sharp, smart, confident, ambitious, nervous, perfect, short, tiny, slow, unwell, sick, extra, cute, epic, quiet, overcast, sensitive, big, new, serious, responsible, super, deep, agitated, polite, private, respectful, young, stupid, efficient, kind, concise, Australian, committed, helpful, essential, excellent, stellar, ruthless, speedy, trapped, comfortable, redundant, successful, complicated

Many adjectives end with -y, -able, -ful, -al, -ive, -less, -ous, -ic, -ing… In grammar, these endings are called suffixes. Did you spot any words ending with these suffixes in the table? By adding suffixes to a word, you change the function of the word, or change its meaning. For instance, the verb 'fear' can become the adjective 'fearless'; the verb 'adapt' can be changed into 'adaptable'; the adjective 'fruity' comes from the noun 'fruit'.

It's too easy [≈ easy peasy ≈ dead easy ≈ easy breezy], isn't it?

< The individual word 'peasy' may not exist in your dictionary. The full version is 'easy peasy lemon squeezy', which rhymes. An old British dish detergent Sqezy commercial is thought to be one of the origins of the idiom (Easy Peasy Lemon Squeezy, n.d.). It just means something is extremely easy. >

In my view, this book is a doozy [≈ excellent ≈ terrific ≈ fabulous]. It is perceptive, informative, entertaining, amusing, engaging, passionate, practical, powerful and influential. It is unputdownable. Now use as many adjectives as you can to give your opinion on what you've learnt today. Was it boring? Interesting? Creative? Conversational? Powerful? Nonsensical?

# DAY 4
# VERBS ARE ACTION WORDS

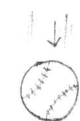

Hi builders! Nicely done! You've reached the fourth day! While you are here, let's look at verbs, those 'doing' or 'being' words. They are powerful words that tell the story in a sentence or show action. They can be used to:

- Express a physical action – 'I **speak** English every day.'
- Express a mental action – 'I **believe** I'll master English.'
- Express a state of being – 'I **am** an English Builder who sticks to the end.'

< In the example sentence in the second bullet point, 'master' is also a verb. Does it express a physical action, a mental action, or a state of being? >

Some verbs from **Part 3 Think Bigger** have been picked out and put into the table below.

> summarise, use, do, answer, see, think, avoid, improve, keep, set, act, learn, play, compete, spend, disobey, focus, relieve, transform, say, read, move, replace, grow, raise, provide, find, reduce, throw, emit, survive, generate, share, showcase, save, protect, contribute, become, comment, break, stock, respond, call, sit, flock, involve, encourage, show, keep, reduce, lose, reveal, improve, feel, develop, shake, pay, cast, strike

Here are a few of the superstar verbs: get, make, do, go, come, take, turn, bring, drop, have, feel. Observe how frequently they are used in daily life. It is not the fancy, long or complicated English words that will take you to an advanced English level. On the contrary, mastering common words is the essence of learning English.

The verb 'master' here means to understand the words completely, use them correctly, effectively, and in the right context. Now, read a short story using the verb 'drop'. Then make up a story full of other verbs on your own.

Rod dropped the ball [≈ made a mistake] at work. He came back home and dropped onto the sofa. While dropping his wallet on the coffee table, his eyes dropped to the floor. There was $100 note! 'Drop everything and help me cook dinner!' his wife yelled from the kitchen. 'Coming!' he called out. Rod then dropped his voice. 'See, that's why I dropped my hobbies a long time ago. I can't catch a break!'

Okay, let's bring today's topic to an end. Do me a favour? Go get [≈ Go grab] a few friends and recommend this book to them. Maybe you can even read some of the book with them! Fantastic! Now let's grab a drink together. Come by?

# DAY 5
# ADVERBS MODIFY VERBS, ADJECTIVES, OTHER ADVERBS

Adverbs are words that are used to describe verbs, adjectives and even other adverbs. Identify how they are used in the below paragraph.

You are behaving **extremely well** when you listen **keenly**, speak **respectfully**, read **eagerly**, write **passionately** and commit **wholeheartedly** for your English study. You are **really** good!

Now also observe some of the adverbs below that appear in **Part 4 Shine Bright**. Can you see any pattern?

> now, normally, weekly, locally, roughly, newly, once, really, basically, relatively, simply, quite, rarely, almost, regularly, beforehand, quickly, closely, predominately, tomorrow, lately, mildly, moderately, heavily, away, initially, very, largely, nowadays, primarily, totally, yesterday, gently, probably, thoroughly, regularly, definitely, always, obviously, hopefully, beautifully, unexpectedly, purely, slightly, environmentally, luckily

Aha! It appears that most adverbs end in '-ly'.

Be mindful that there are non-adverbs that also end in '-ly'. Check out the below paragraph with words ending in '-ly' not being adverbs.

Our **family** likes playing **Monopoly**. We are **friendly** and **lovely** people. If you feel **lonely,** feel free to come over. I can make strawberry **jelly** for you.

Just a **timely** reminder that we will **fly** to Paris next month. So drop by earlier.

Moreover, not all adverbs end with '-ly' [≈ many adverbs do not have an '-ly' ending]. There are some adverbs in paragraph below as an example:

Let's study **together. Why** should we live **present**? What you did **yesterday** has become history. What you will do **tomorrow** is **still** a mystery. What you are doing **today** is a gift. Work **hard now**, or cry **hard later**. Similarly, today's content is extremely easy [≈ **as** easy **as** ABC ≈ **as** easy **as** apple pie ≈ **as** easy **as** falling off a log]. Do you agree?

# DAY 6
# ARTICLES ARE SPECIAL MODIFIERS

In the last four days, we've looked at nouns, adjectives, verbs and adverbs, which make up [≈ consist of ≈ account for ≈ take up] the vast majority of all words in the English language.

The other five parts of speech are articles, interjections, conjunctions, pronouns and prepositions. These are set in stone [≈ carved on stone ≈ written on stone] and they are even easier to master! Today, we'll get to know more about articles.

An article itself is an adjective, modifying a noun. English only has two articles: 'the' and 'a/an'. 'The' is the definite article (modifying a particular or specific noun) while 'a' and 'an' are indefinite articles (modifying a non-particular and non-specific noun). 'A' is placed in front of the singular noun starting with a consonant sound whereas 'an' is used before a singular noun that starts with a vowel sound. Is this sort of grammar boring? Does the grammar confuse you? Let me explain it in an old English proverb.

**An** apple **a** day keeps **the** doctor away.

< The origin of this old-fashioned expression was 'Eat an apple on going to bed, and you'll keep the doctor from earning his bread.' It evolved into 'An apple a day, no doctor to pay' and 'An apple a day sends the doctor away' (Ely, 2013). Fact? An apple a day may not really keep the doctor away [≈ keep you out of the doctor's office], but including apples in your diet is good for you! >

'**An** apple' and '**a** day' in the sentence indicates any apple and any day will do. The letter *A* in the word of apple is a vowel sound, so the article 'an' is used. **The** doctor means your particular doctor (who you don't have to visit if you're eating healthily).

Now pick five of the below phrases to make up a story:

> a spate of burglaries, an overwhelming majority of people, a plethora of [≈ a myriad of] food options, a flurry of phone calls, a dose of laugh, a hit of caffeine, a sizeable amount of money, an egg, an idiot, an old radio, an umbrella, an hour, a unicorn, a book, a house, an English Builder

# DAY 7
# INTERJECTIONS TO EXPRESS SUDDEN FEELINGS

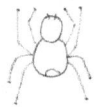

Me: Hey there, English Builder!

You: **Yo!**

Me: **Bah!** A spider on your hair! Don't move.

You: **Ew**, they're so scary!

Me: Don't worry. It's off now.

What are we doing? **Ah! Dear me!** We're learning interjections, which are used to convey the feelings of the author or the speaker. In writing, they are often followed by an exclamation mark (!) to show the emotion of the interjection. Observe the words in bold here and make a judgement on whether they are interjections based on our definition.

Me: **Hush!** People say interjections are the least important part of speech. **Phew!** I've got that off my chest!

You: **Uh-huh!** Why?

Me: They often stand alone without any connection in a sentence.

You: **Ah.**

Me: **Anyway!** You will be awarded 100 bucks for reading this book!

You: **Really? Unbelievable! Boo-yah! [≈ Yay!] OMG! [≈ Oh my god! ≈ Oh dear god! ≈ Good heavens! ≈ Good lord! ≈ Hooley dooley! ≈ Holy moly!]**

Me: Okay, okay, not really! **Holy moly!** I just want to know that pennies don't come from heaven.

< 'Holy moly' is used to express surprising or shocking feelings. It's also an example of rhyming phrases. Have a read of a short story with some other rhyming expressions. Marcus's wife, Janice, was tired of the **hurly burly** [≈ busy and noisy] city life and those **hoity-toity** [≈ arrogant] people around her. Marcus wasn't supportive of moving to the suburb. **Oh no!** Janice then left him. Marcus wasn't a **happy chappy**. **Gee!** I don't think he'd ever heard of '**Happy wife, happy life**'! >

You: **Ouch. Ahem.**

Me: By the way, I have two tickets for the Melbourne Symphony Orchestra, performing tomorrow night 7 pm. Would you like to come along?

You: **Bloody awesome! [≈ Splendid! ≈ Superb! ≈ Fantastic! ≈ Remarkable!]** I'd love to go.

Me: **Great!** Let's go to the concert together. **Whew!** It's nearly the end of the day. **Hallelujah! [≈ Woo-hoo! ≈ Whoo!]** Go enjoy the rest of your day! **Hurray!**

# DAY 8
# CONJUNCTIONS TO CONNECT

Conjunctions are words that are used to connect other words, phrases, clauses and sentences. Here are some examples of conjunctions:

> and, but, because, other than, besides, as, or, neither, yet, therefore, although, whereas, unless, until, whenever, if, though, when, nor

Today, let's play with conjunctions in a short story. These are made in bold below.

My life has been a mess **since** last week. I washed the Bluetooth earphones! My laptop fell in water! [≈ I dropped my notebook computer in water!] I stomped on my phone **and** I couldn't boot up [≈ couldn't restart] my 6th generation iPad either! All of them have gone kaput [≈ been busted ≈ been broken].

**Because** of this, I couldn't do my assignment. **Therefore**, I wanted to use the computer at the library. **While** driving there in the morning, I ran a red light. But as soon as I was there, I realised the library was closed on the weekend.

And then, tonight, I stepped on the dog poo **when** I was walking in the park.

< Here is a superstition from France: stepping on dog poo can bring you luck, **but** only when you step accidentally on it with your left foot (Croissant, 2021). If it's your right foot, sorry, that means bad luck. >

I stepped on the dog poo with my right foot. No good things have happened **yet**. But **as** I write this down, I'm feeling much better. Although things are not looking quite right, I still believe my life will soon fall into place.

I don't know **whether** you like my story or not. How are you doing with learning English or other languages so far? Please share your story with me – and highlight any conjunctions in the story.

In addition [≈ Add to that ≈ On top of that], have you been paying attention? Have you noticed that some conjunctions in the story haven't been made bold? Ah, I did that on purpose [≈ purposely ≈ deliberately ≈ intentionally]. Now go back and highlight the ones that were missed.

# DAY 9
# PRONOUNS TAKE THE PLACE OF NOUNS

Hello, it's good to see **you** again. The word '**you**' here is a pronoun, which takes the place of [≈ substitutes ≈ replaces] a noun. Below is a short list of **such**.

> I, you, he, she, it, its, we, they, me, her, hers, him, his, us, them, my, our, your, yours, their, theirs, mine, ours, myself, himself, herself, themselves, itself, yourself, yourselves, ourselves, these, those, such, few, all, nobody, anything, some, everyone, who, whom, which, whoever, whomever, whichever, somebody

Alright, let **me** break the ice [≈ break the silence] now.

< 'Break the ice' here means that **I** am the icebreaker. But **I** am not really using a hammer to break the ice. I just want to do an activity with **you** to start the conversation [≈ ease into the conversation] and reduce any tension or unfamiliarity in **our** social settings. >

Now, half close **your** eyes. Imagine the sounds made by animals in the table below.

| Cows – moo | Birds – tweet, chirp | Parrots – squawk | Penguins – chitter |
|---|---|---|---|
| Bees – buzz | Cats – mew, meow, hiss | Dogs – bark, woof, ruff | Frogs, toads – croak |
| Ducks – quack | Guinea pigs – squeak | Mosquitos – buzz, whine | Sheep – baa, bleat |

I hope **your** imagination has calmed **you** down now.

Now challenge **yourself** with a short story that has at least one pronoun in each sentence. **I** will give **you** an example:

Georgia is dating **somebody**. This guy, Alex, cares about **her** so much. **He** wasn't **himself** today. [≈ **He** wasn't **his** normal self today.] But **he** still cooked dinner for **her**. **He** isn't **anything** like **her** ex, Nick, who kept saying **he** was busy, but **he** messaged **his other** girlfriends all the time. **He** also bad-mouthed **whomever he** dated, and hid **himself** from Georgia when **their** holiday was coming up [≈ approaching]...

Now close **your** eyes. Do **you** still remember the sounds of animals that **we** have mentioned in the activity earlier? Have I made all the pronouns bold? Can **you** give the above story a happy ending? Can **someone** tell **me** whether **you** have finished reading up to here before shutting your eyes?

# DAY 10
# PREPOSITIONS SHOW RELATIONSHIPS

Prepositions are words that show relationship between a noun or a pronoun and other words in a sentence. Here are some common single word prepositions that indicate time, location or direction.

> about, out, on, off, in, of, to, for, with, at, from, by, across, into, through, after, during, without, under, around, among, behind, beyond, above, upon, towards

Now answer the yes-or-no questions below. Observe how the prepositions in bold below are paired with other words in the sentence.

- Do you grind your teeth **in your sleep**?
- Are you **on a diet**? Do you know the word diet **comes from** the Greek word 'diaita', which means 'way of life'?
- Is your house always bursting **at the seams** with people?
- Do you like setting up New Year Resolutions for yourself **on the first day** of January each year? And after a while, you give up [≈ pull out ≈ opt out ≈ abandon them]?
- Hello, **I'd like to** tell you a dirty secret! Could you please not let the cat **out of the bag** [≈ not take the lid off ≈ not lift the lid on ≈ not spill the beans ≈ keep your mouth shut]?
- Has your boyfriend or girlfriend ever **cheated on** you? Did you **listen to** your sixth sense [≈ **go with** your gut feeling ≈ trust your guts ≈ follow your natural instinct]? Do you **believe in** that quote 'once a cheater, always a cheater'?

< For the fifth bullet point above, apparently, I can only tell you the secret if you promise not to reveal it. But humourist Will Rogers said, 'Letting the cat out of the bag is a whole lot easier than putting it back in.' Do you agree? >

< For the last bullet point, human beings have five senses: taste, smell, vision [≈ sight], hearing, and touch. A sixth sense is considered the ability to sense something with your intuition. Your emotions could be your seventh sense. What is spider-sense, then? >

Hey, you don't always have to respond with 'yes' or 'no' to the questions. You can say 'yeah', 'yep', 'nope', 'nah' or 'nuh-uh', instead. What's on your mind now?

# DAY 11
## HYPHENATED COMPOUND WORDS

A hyphen (-) is a punctuation mark used to join words or parts of words together.

Today's tall tale story brims with such compound words, which are two or more words joined [≈ melded] together to create a closer meaning.

Identify the components of each word, such as noun-noun, noun-adjective, adjective-noun, adjective-adjective, verb-preposition, preposition-verb, or none of these forms, although adjectives in particular are often hyphenated words (that is, compound words). This activity also helps to review what we've learnt so far, understanding the different parts of speech for English.

My **wafer-thin** but **well-rounded great-uncle** George has **snow-white** hair. He's a **right-thinking** and **well-meaning** [≈ **well-intentioned**] person. He's owned a **large-scale** business for more than 40 years. He says it feels like it all started light years away!

< What is light year? A light year is the distance that light travels in 1 year, which is nearly 9 trillion kilometres [≈ 6 trillion miles]. It refers to a long distance or a long period of time. >

Uncle George is always humble. He doesn't like those **know-it-all** type people. His company provides **all-inclusive** service from meat production to export and **on-site** parking. All parts of animals are used in the business to make revenue, even the **by-products** such as hide, skin and blood. He cares about his employees, and those **best-performing** employees are given a big bonus each year. I always enjoy having **one-on-one in-depth** conversations with him.

As for myself, I'm **thirty-four** years old. I was born in the **mid-1980s**. I love my career. I don't see it as a **dead-end** or **high-stress** job. I started with a bit of an **all-round** role, and I later became a **full-blown** [≈ **full-fledged**] entrepreneur.

I sometimes think of myself as a **would-be** [≈ potential ≈ prospective] author, sharing my experiences and dissecting **hot-button** issues. But my newborn baby keeps me busy! I'd like to recommend *The English Builder!* book. The author is my bestie, Jessie. This is a **long-awaited** [≈ belated] book. It is a **well-informed**, **must-read** book. I believe it will be a **well-received** book too. Are you **all-in** [≈ committed fully]? If so, give me a high five [≈ up top]!

By the way, do you reckon this story sounds almost **impossible-to-believe** [≈ too **far-fetched**]?

# DAY 12
## HOW GOOD IS YOUR ENGLISH?

To start with [≈ To start ≈ To begin with ≈ Well, for a start ≈ First ≈ First off ≈ First up], what level is your English language at? Mark X in the below boxes depending where you think your English language sits.

- ☐ I'm new to English. I'm a beginner.
- ☐ My English is adequate but far from perfect.
- ☐ I'm proficient in English.
- ☐ English is my native tongue [≈ mother tongue].

If you feel like you're at the ultimate level of English, I encourage you to work on another language and become bilingual, or even a multi-language speaker!

Not only does this boost your brainpower [≈ activate brain cells], but it will also open up your world [≈ open a new window ≈ expand your view]. You will become globally minded and embrace another country's culture.

Take the above question as an example. When filling out forms, Australians prefer to cross (✗) checkboxes ☐☐☐☐, while Chinese people like ticking (✓) a checkbox.

There are over 6000 spoken languages in the world today. I have only listed 28 of them in the table below. Pick up one or two of these languages and become a master. Are you intrigued [≈ keen to do this]?

| Italian | German | Japanese | Arabic | Russian | Bengali | Vietnamese |
| --- | --- | --- | --- | --- | --- | --- |
| Thai | Turkish | Hindi | Spanish | Portuguese | Filipino | Chinese Mandarin |
| French | Lahnda | Korean | Turkish | Cantonese | Persian | Mongolian |
| Latin | Greek | Dutch | Malay | Danish | Swiss | Indonesian |

If you are a non-native English speaker and you can understand at least 10% of today's content, I define you as an English Builder, someone who is at a higher level of understanding than the basic level. Even if you are at an intermediate or advanced level, there is always room for improvement [≈ you can always sharpen your English skills] with grammar, buzzwords, phrases, idioms, culture, and so on.

To acquire any language, confidence should always come first. Believe in yourself. You can do it! Never doubt your abilities. With this weapon (that is, confidence!) at hand, I'll teach you how to take your English to the next level. Many secrets of English follow!

# DAY 13
# SECRET SAUCE RECIPE – READ EXTENSIVELY

Here you go. Here's the secret sauce recipe to improve your English:

**To better your English skills = Practise + Practise + Practise + Practise…**

All this really means is to employ the language as often as you can. I know, it sounds full of crap [≈ nonsense ≈ I'm talking rubbish]! It is not really a recipe for a secret sauce. It is an open secret that everyone knows by heart. But not everyone readily applies it.

Today, we're looking at reading practice.

Increase your reading time of anything with English in it. Read best-selling books, online news, magazines, and textbooks. Read whatever and whenever you can. The more you read, the better your comprehension will get. The good news is that you do not have to study seriously. You can even study English on the go [≈ on the move].

If you are not living in an English-speaking country, you still can:

- Set up English as your mobile phone language. [≈ Change your phone's default language setting to English.]

- Read user manuals [≈ user guides ≈ instructions] from your newly purchased all-in-one desktop, wireless printer, or even the rice cooker.

- If there are any English words on it, take a close look at the labels on an imported wine bottle or on any food labels.

If you live in Australia, observe the language around you.

For example, notice nearby signs while riding the train or bus: *On request these seats must be vacated for use by passengers with special needs. [≈ Please vacate this space for use by passengers using a wheelchair or mobility aid.] Penalties apply if you do not comply.*

The majority of Australians follow the rules on public transport. You can select not to follow the rules, but once you are caught out [≈ get busted] by an authorised officer, the fine is heavy. Think twice before you do. The point here is to immerse yourself in reading English words – any English words – you are doing it right now! Good on you!

# DAY 14
# SECRET SAUCE RECIPE – KEEP WRITING

You know the secret now: use language as much as you can. To improve your writing, you basically need to write, write and write. Get the flow of the work going in your mind.

Reading is one of the best ways to learn writing. Check out the headlines below from three different newspaper sources:

- 'Airbnb partygoers trash home in Hawthorn East' – *The Age*
- 'Luxury rental home trashed during party brawl' – *Herald Sun*
- 'Girl gang bashed elderly man at Hawthorn East Airbnb' – *9News*

The news was reported on 1 July 2018. Different phrases were used in each of the headings. The same story was reported: partygoers, a gang of girls, caused lots of damage on Airbnb rental property. A brawl broke out. A man was attacked. The party went wild and was out of control.

It is always much easier to read English than to write on your own. Confucius (Kongzi 孔子) says, 'I hear and I forget. I see and I remember. I do and I understand.' So use your own words to write down what happened in Hawthorn East.

.................................................................................................

.................................................................................................

.................................................................................................

See, even reading these short, concise and simple headlines can expand [≈ boost ≈ double or triple] your vocabulary and help to upgrade your writing skills.

There are also other great ways to approach writing, such as:

- Reading journals, blogs, Twitter posts [≈ tweets], postcards, emails, texts… then writing them in English.
- Comparing your writing with other better quality writing.
- Hiring an expert to revise [≈ refine ≈ twist ≈ tune up] your writing.
- Taking advantage of modern technology. If you bump into new words, fun phrases or interesting expressions, put them down on your notebook or your mobile phone notes. Revisit and force yourself to use them in the right context.

Two words: just write. Every day. Day-to-day, step-by-step, you will end up with a proficient knowledge for writing English.

# DAY 15
# SECRET SAUCE RECIPE - LISTEN ALL THE TIME

Please memorise this secret by heart: to improve your English language use, you need to immerse yourself [≈ submerge yourself] for hours on end [≈ for many hours] in the language.

For those saying they can become fluent in English in 3 hours, 10 days, or 1 month, I don't buy it. I cannot even guarantee that you'll really master English after a year even after reading my book. (Of course, you can't improve your listening skills by simply reading, including just reading my book!)

Have you heard the rule of 10,000 hours? This means that 10,000 hours of deliberate practice is needed to make you an expert in a field.

So to understand what people are saying, you need to listen. A lot!

Listen to English textbooks on tapes, podcasts, audiobooks, TED Talks, *Q&A* or news from ABC, BBC, VOA – any material will do.

The most effective way to learn is to get yourself engaged in a conversation with locals. They talk ten times faster than a textbook on tape! While watching an English movie, drama or sport, you can tune up by using subtitles on a smart TV.

The International Phonetic alphabet for English pronunciation is also useful. Pay attention to pronunciation, including native speakers' tones and the rising and falling intonation and pauses. The key here is to open your ears [≈ activate your ears ≈ cock your ears ≈ listen carefully and actively]!

Whenever you are listening to any English sounds, be 100% in it. Become a good listener.

Let's finish off by 'listening' to the weather forecast from a meteorologist on the radio:

Today's temperatures are spot-on for Victoria. Twenty-four degrees in Melbourne right now. Warm and sunny in Adelaide too, temperature to be jumping up to 32°C very soon. New South Wales is cloudy and windy. Thunderstorms are underway across the state. Gusty and humid in Canberra. Rain developing. Western Australia, widespread fog in the morning, partly cloudy during the day. Tasmania 12°C, showers, easing later on today. Up to Brisbane, 100–300 mm heavy rainfalls with destructive wind [≈ damaging wind]. To the west, inland, it's dry and hot in Darwin, 34°C. The heatwave will last for a couple of days. See you tomorrow.

< When a fog is extremely thick, you can say it's a pea soup fog. When it's humid and hot outside, you can say it's sauna-like. What can you say if it's very windy or too cold? >

< Examples of extreme weather [≈ severe weather] phenomena include tornadoes, hurricanes, cyclones, blizzards, avalanches, floods, ice storms, dust storms and droughts. >

# DAY 16
# SECRET SAUCE RECIPE - SPEAK, SPEAK, SPEAK

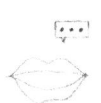

I'll reinforce the secret sauce recipe one last time. To gain skill in the English language, you have to put yourself out there, using it as much as possible. Practice makes perfect, and this leads to mastery.

This also applies to your speaking skills. To perfect them, just open your mouth and speak. And speak confidently. Repetition is the key here.

You may struggle with the actual words to say. Simply interpret any unknown word by expressing its function, feature or how it looks. For example, you are after food wrap [≈ plastic wrap] at the supermarket. But you don't have the name on your lips. You go to ask sales assistant, 'Excuse me. I'm looking for something. Er… I don't know the word. We use it to wrap the food to keep it fresh.' Sometimes, confident body language may just help.

Sometimes you will make mistakes or come across awkward and embarrassing situations. A conversation might end awkwardly because of your weird accent. You feel that you made an ass of yourself [≈ made a faux pas] in public since you couldn't speak English fluently.

< 'Faux pas' is a French word. Faux means false and pas refers to dance step. Many years ago, when people made a noticeable mistake in the dancing in social gathering that kings and queens held, they would feel embarrassed, and they made a faux pas. A faux pas nowadays means an embarrassing mistake in a social setting (Jones M. , n.d.). >

Come on. No-one will bite you, beat you or kill you for this, or even notice it much really. Instead, we learn quicker from mistakes. Don't run away. Don't be shamed about it at all. Don't even feel frustrated or disappointed. Laugh at yourself [≈ Poke fun at yourself ≈ Tease yourself a little] and move on. Such a moment marks progress, a step further.

Don't be shy and nervous. If you just clam up [≈ stop talking], how are you going to improve your English? Just keep practising as much as you can, and as long as you can! Anytime, anywhere. Have fun! Practise until one day you can communicate in English freely [≈ speak English unthinkingly ≈ speak English automatically ≈ speak English unconsciously ≈ speak English on autopilot ≈ speak English without even thinking about it].

It will eventually become second nature [≈ instinctive ≈ habitual ≈ subconscious ≈ automatic ≈ a knee-jerk reaction].

# PART 1 ENLIGHTEN AND EVOLVE

In Part 1, you'll 'design' your own home. What type of house are you dreaming to build and live in? What's the house's structure and layout? What's the budget for the house? Do you dream of a luxury and stylish home in a tranquil suburb? Do you dream of a cosy home tucked away up in the mountains or a beautiful home facing the sea? And how will you build this house from basically nothing?

Throughout this 'design' process, dare to dream. You'll furnish yourself with knowledge and gain insight and experience on all sorts of things that life offers or is yet to offer (enlightenment). You'll keep growing into a better version of yourself (evolve). Eventually, you'll have a fabulous house like no other.

Keep in mind: you're the owner of this house, so make sure it will be a house that you love.

Let's get started!

# DAY 17
# DREAM BIG

Hello everyone! Do you dream of something more in your life? Here, to 'dream' doesn't refer to images or stories occurring in your mind while you're asleep.

To 'dream' in today's topic means to have ambition and aspiration. It is a state of life that you desire and that you need to chase after [≈ take charge ≈ go after ≈ pursue] your dream as hard as you can. It's a fantasy that sticks in your mind all the time until it becomes true.

Before you start to dream, think about your dreams when you were younger. You may have wanted to become a scientist, a doctor, or to be a pilot, flying in the blue sky... Have you fulfilled any of these dreams yet?

But now you're grown up. So, what are your dreams [≈ what do you dream about ≈ what are your burning desires]? Write them down. [≈ Draw a blueprint of your dreams. ≈ Chart your path. ≈ Create a dream roadmap.]

- I dream one day of becoming a master of English.
- I'll carry out my dream to travel to more than 100 countries.
- I'm a dream chaser. I crave winning the Oscars.
- I'm a dreamer and wannabe. I'll become a millionaire to help people in need.
- Climbing Mount Everest one day is what I dream about.

- 
- 
- 
- 

Go wild. Dare to dream big. We all have infinite potential. But don't build castles in the air [≈ don't build castles in Spain]. You can dream about talking to 100 CEOs and becoming a CEO yourself. But dreaming of meeting up with former US President Donald J Trump in person might be unrealistic [≈ idealistic ≈ elusive ≈ not attainable].

Take out a blank piece of paper, or your notebook. Get your pen ready. Write a letter to your future self with the dreams you have now. Record today's date and the dates that you believe your wonderful dreams can be accomplished by. Put the letter aside for now. Carry these dreams in your heart. Great work!

# DAY 18
## WHY DREAM BIG?

Hey English Builders! Did you have trouble discovering your dreams yesterday? That is okay. We all have those days. You don't have to dream now. You could go through the book first before coming up with your dreams and aspirations.

But if you are certain that you dream of nothing, and you prefer to enjoy the stability, certainty and comfort that life has offered to you, why not? I respect your choice. Whatever you do, the Earth still spins, the sun still comes up in the morning, and the ocean still has tides. However, I encourage you to dream, especially in your 20s. Why?

We all come to this world with purpose. Dreams and aspirations are like a vision, guiding you to a better life. Without such a dream, you will move aimlessly [≈ drift around] and be unfulfilled and miserable later on in life.

Why should you dream big then?

Life is short, folks. You only live once. [≈ You only get one life to experience.] I just don't want you to settle for less [≈ for mediocre]. Live the life that you are capable of. The truth is you have the potential to create a better life for yourself. Do you want it? Do you really want it? Do you want it as bad as you want to breathe?

If your answer is *yes*, take the chance to live big. Stay hungry, stay foolish. Keep hunting [≈ Keep looking] for that life. During the bumpy journey, you may stay in limbo, enduring the instability or discomfort. You could also learn things the hard way. But when you are young, the world is your oyster.

< When you open an oyster, you can find a beautiful pearl. 'The world is your oyster' means that you have many opportunities (the pearl) and world is open to you. >

One day, you'll reach the brightest star. You'll settle down, staying comfortable with your significant other, and you'll have no worries about your financial situation, and do the things you love, and feel peaceful in mind. How does that sound to you? A penny for your thoughts?

# DAY 19
# AT A CROSSROADS

At some points in your life, you will hit a crossroads, where you stand in the middle of a range of choices. Decisions on which road to take must be made. These are big and important decisions for sure, and this can seem daunting.

A decision tree is a visualisation tool that can give you a better picture of all the possible roads ahead of you. Say you're about to graduate from high school. What are you going to do when you finish school? Let's draw a decision tree.

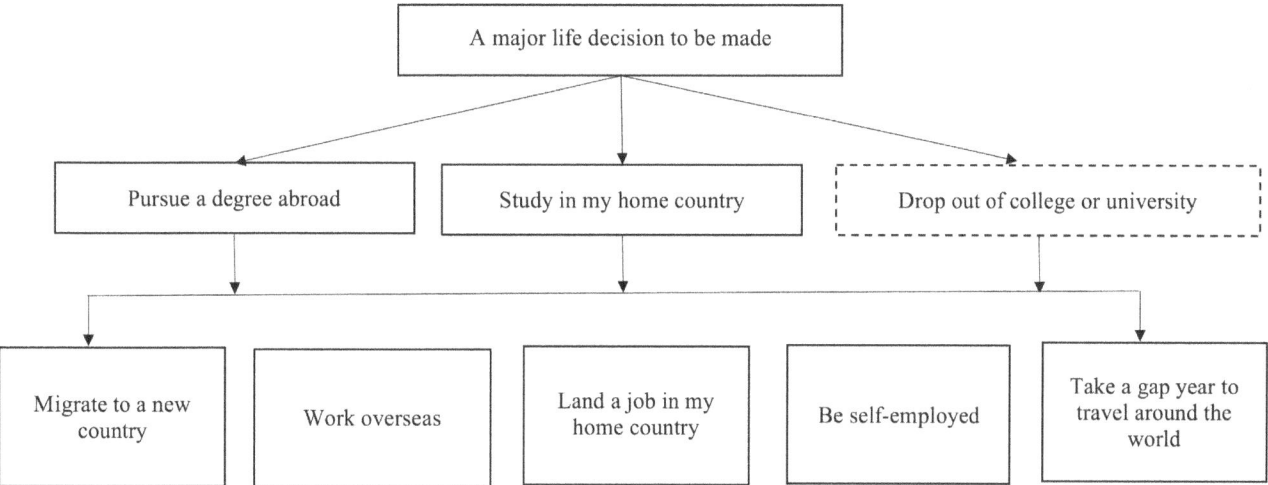

Clearly, you can turn right for studying overseas, go straight into gaining a degree in your homeland, or turn left with school unfinished and start a business of your own, or even other enticing choices.

Alas, you're stuck with too many choices. These choices are crucial junctions [≈ watershed moments ≈ turning points] in life that you don't want to mess up.

Understandably, each direction on this roadmap can seem attractive and full of challenges. Whichever direction you choose, you'll pass by even more roads, be them smooth asphalt roads, cement roads, rough gravel roads or muddy earth roads.

There is no black and white [≈ There is no wrong answer] in making these kinds of life decisions. But make a decision of your own, not because of any expectations and preferences from others. You don't have to follow the herd [≈ don't have to do what others are doing].

< The idea of herding behaviour is where a herd of animals starts to move in one direction and the rest of the herd follows. >

How to make the best decision on your roadmap? We'll discuss further [≈ discuss in depth] in the next 6 days.

# DAY 20
# WEIGH UP YOUR OPTIONS

How exciting! Today, I'm going to give you a set of magic scales to help you make the best choice in your life. I'll start with the example of starting a new life in another country. Bear in mind, every choice, every coin has two sides [≈ there are pros and cons ≈ there are positive and negative points ≈ there's Yin and Yang ≈ it is double-edged sword].

< A double-edged sword can cut both ways, which could hurt both the person who attacks and who is attacked. So the metaphor means something has both advantages and disadvantages. >

First, make a list of all possible advantages and disadvantages.

| Options | Advantages | Disadvantages |
| --- | --- | --- |
| Continue life at home [≈ Live where you were born ≈ Stay close to your parents ≈ Live with your parents in your hometown] | + Strong family bond and close friendships<br>+ Enjoy the comfort of home<br>+ Have a sense of belonging<br>+ Take care of parents as they get older<br>+ Save on rent and bills | − Too comfortable<br>− Get stuck in routine<br>− Lack of excitement<br>− No privacy from parents<br>− No independence |
| Go overseas [≈ Lead a life in a new country ≈ Leave home country ≈ Study abroad or work in a foreign country ≈ Become an overseas student or be an expat] | + Embrace different cultures<br>+ Experience exciting adventures<br>+ Expose yourself to local language and international events<br>+ Different career opportunities<br>+ Make new friends with different backgrounds<br>+ Form new perspectives on the world<br>+ Become independent more quickly | − Culture shock<br>− Communication barriers<br>− Safety concerns<br>− Challenging to begin<br>− Feel homesick and lonely<br>− Financial pressures<br>− No deep friendships |

Once you've listed all your options, go through each of them again. Rate each of the advantages and disadvantages. Which advantage matters to you most? Rate each advantage using a scale of importance: from 1 (the least important) to 10 (the most important). What disadvantages do you like least? Rank each disadvantage using a scale of dislike: from −10 (strongly dislike) to −1 (slightly dislike).

Sum up each side. Which option scores higher? Are the weights still in equilibrium? Or is your scale tipped? Go with the option with the heavier side.

# DAY 21
# TRADE A TO GET B

Hold on a second. Before you make a final decision, I want you to understand three types of costs for decision-making from an economic perspective. These are:

- **Opportunity cost [≈ Alternative cost]:** The loss of an opportunity when an alternative is chosen.
- **Sunk cost:** The costs that have already been incurred and cannot be recovered.
- **Prospective cost:** The future costs that may be incurred if an action is taken.

Based on these concepts, identify the type of costs in each of the below examples:

- Money spent on an air ticket to fly to a new country could have been used to buy a fine-dining restaurant experience many times over at home.
- Tuition that you paid for your university course can't be taken back once the course is complete.
- It's expected that you'll incur high living costs once you start a new life in a new country.

This doesn't have to be applied in money terms. It can be applied to any decisions that you need to make:

- Go out with the guy who loves you more, or date the guy who you love more?
- Hold onto your current relationship or move on?
- In holiday seasons, go travelling to see the world instead of [≈ rather than] staying at home to relax and enjoy comfort? Or should you do it the other way around?
- Give up your career to take care of the kids? Is it worth it?
- Trade a relatively low salary package for a less stressful job?

Wherever you go, there are many choices. There are hundreds of suburbs you can choose to live in, thousands of schools to enrol at, millions of jobs to find, billions of companies to work for, zillions of guys to date. But you can only pick one (for now). You can only be one person doing one thing at a particular location at any given time of your life. You can't have your cake and eat it, too. [≈ You can't have everything.] You have to sacrifice one thing to get another thing.

< Are you confused about the proverb of 'you can't have your cake and eat it too'? Why can't I own the cake then eat it? Aha, the proverb actually means that you can't retain or possess the cake once you've consumed it. >

To get your choice of B, all other options (A, A+, A++, etc.) become closed off to you and certain costs will be incurred. So make the most of your decisions. You may end up with B *and* C, or possibly D *and* E. Make sure your careful choice becomes the best thing that's ever happened to you.

# DAY 22
## TAKE THE PLUNGE

Even with the three decision-making tools I've given to you over the last three days, do you find yourself still indecisive [≈ in two minds ≈ wishy-washy ≈ hesitating ≈ suffering from indecision] with where to go?

< Someone who is 'wishy-washy' can't make up their mind on what they want to do. If an apple juice is wishy-washy, it's thin and watery. >

If you're still hesitating, for example, whether to study overseas, ask yourself what your worries or concerns are on making this decision. Are you fretting about the uncertainty? Are you dismayed at any risks? Are you gun-shy about making the wrong call? Are you scared of an unknown future: What if I failed degree? What if I couldn't survive in the new environment? Here comes the fourth tool for your what-if questions. List them and analyse the probability of each worst-case scenario that could happen. Is it certain, almost certain, highly likely, probable, probably not, highly unlikely or impossible?

I reckon the chances of bad things happening are extremely low. If you're in two minds about pursuing study in a new country, you won't know if you'll succeed or fail if you don't try at all. And even if you fail, you could return home to your motherland. No big deal. The point would be that at least you tried.

So put these questions out of your head. Stop worrying. Be brave and unafraid. Don't fret. [≈ Don't flinch. ≈ Don't boggle. ≈ Don't let the fear to tie you down. ≈ Squash your fear.] When you are young, you are footloose and fancy-free. You have nothing to lose.

The questions you should really ask are: What would I do if I weren't afraid? Will I be regretful if I don't attempt something? One of the most common regrets from people on their deathbeds is that their dreams were unfulfilled because of decisions they had made or not made.

So my advice to you [≈ a piece of advice ≈ little gem of advice ≈ a tip for you ≈ a word to you ≈ let me tell you ≈ take it from me]: listen to your heart. Dare to make unconventional decisions. Take the risk. Take the plunge. Take a chance (it could just be a once-in-a-lifetime opportunity) and have a crack. You never know what awaits you!

If you're still not sure [≈ uncertain], don't make the decision just yet. Do your research. Reach out to other people for advice. [≈ Seek wise counsel.] I'm happy to share my overseas success story with you over the next 2 days of activities.

# DAY 23
## EXCITING MOMENTS IN AUSTRALIA

From the moment I earned myself an airplane ticket to Australia, I gained a new perspective of the world [≈ saw the world at a whole other level ≈ saw the world through a new set of eyes].

The saying 'the grass is always greener on the other side of the fence' refers to what others have always seems to be better than what you have. We have a similar expression in Chinese: 'The moon is rounder in foreign countries than in China.' ('外国的月亮比中国的圆') This is probably true. The moon on some nights in Australia seems huge, brighter and rounder.

In Australia, seeing people wearing shorts and thongs and sweaters in wintertime doesn't make you feel weird. Don't be surprised if you spot people walking barefoot on the streets. Basically, wear whatever you like, and no-one will judge you, even if you are nude. We even have a naked bike ride in Melbourne, and a naked restaurant!

In summer, people in Australia wear sunglasses but no-one uses umbrella to prevent the strong sunshine. It is the opposite in China. The Chinese call the bottom-most floor [≈ the floor at ground level] the first floor while Australians refer it as the ground floor. In Australia, the first floor is the floor above the ground floor. University campuses don't have fences that prevent the public from going in, whereas universities in China do have fences, and the public can't go in without permission.

Over time, I've made friends from all over the world (from Australia, UK, Chile, USA, Singapore, Sri Lanka, Pakistan, Vietnam, Russia, India, you name it). I've learnt each accent and got to know my friends' traditions, customs, foods, beliefs and etiquette. I've gained a global mind-set [≈ mind-shift], becoming more tolerant and caring, and seeing things from multiple perspectives.

I participated in quite a few interesting volunteer activities. I tried out being a waitress and a tutor before I started my accounting job. I travelled around and showed off photos of various Australian natural wonders on social media.

I would say the last 12 years has opened up a whole gamut of new experiences for me [≈ broadened my horizon ≈ deepened my experiences]. I fell in love with Melbourne. This is the city of dreams. I've done a 180-degree turn and I'm living my dreams.

< When you made a big change in life, you're said to have turned your life 180 degrees. If someone makes a 360-degree turn, this is a complete circle, meaning they come back to where they started. >

# DAY 24
# GET READY MENTALLY IN AUSTRALIA

Wait! My story doesn't stop here. I have to acknowledge that to live abroad [≈ to live by the ocean] is not always easy as it looks. It can be tough, extremely tough. Really? Hell yeah!

How can I forget days like this:

- To receive high scores [≈ secure high distinctions ≈ get flying colours] for my Master's degree, I spent tons of time in the library, hitting the books [≈ studying intensely].

- The high university tuition was a burden. Rent was not cheap either. The financial stress was beyond imagination. This forced me to make countless phone calls and inspect many houses just to get a relatively cheap place to live in (but cosy and close to the university campus). I ended up sharing a small two-storey house with other six flatmates from different countries.

- When I first started out in Australia, the exchange rate for 1 Australian dollar (AUD$) was roughly 6 Yuan (元) RMB [≈ renminbi (人民币)] (CNY ¥). Everything felt pricey. I rarely ate at restaurants or cafés unless I needed to be social with friends.

There were days when I missed Mum and Dad back home. And my hometown food, the restaurants, the weather and my friends. I felt all this when I was sick, when I got lost in the suburbs and no-one was around, when I was blamed by my boss for the language barrier…

I sometimes cried myself to sleep. I was homesick, fragile, stressed, helpless and frustrated. I could just have stayed at home, enjoying a comfortable lifestyle in my early 20s. I was left wondering why I was even there.

As time went by [≈ As time passed ≈ As time marched on ≈ As time wore on], I found I was surviving [≈ getting through] and I had created my own life. All these experiences have made me into a resilient person who likes challenges and who now stays positive. And because of that, you are holding this book.

If given a second chance, I would do the same (that is, living in a totally different country [≈ in a completely new country]) and would not have changed a thing.

# DAY 25
## YOUR FINAL DECISION

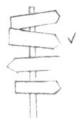

Have you got an idea what living overseas might look like from listening to my stories? Have you made up your mind whether to go and live overseas?

The fifth decision-making tool that I'm handing over to you is to ask the right person for the right advice. Should you ask a divorced person whether to get married? Would you enquire with someone who has never invested in property if you should invest in property? Might you ask someone who can't swim if you should learn to swim? The answers that you will get are probably like this: it's risky, and it isn't even worth trying out and you will suffer and fail.

So the right person should be someone who has the relevant experience and has succeeded, and someone who is willing to advise objectively.

Having said that [≈ Enough said ≈ In saying that ≈ Suffice to say that], use the five tools that you've learnt to make decisions of your own, then go with your heart.

Give serious thought about your future life. It is YOUR life after all. Whatever you choose [≈ select ≈ elect ≈ decide] to do, you will be the only one who lives with it. The choice that you make should leave you with no regrets.

Don't be rash. Never cut down a tree in the wintertime.

< Why shouldn't you cut down the tree in the winter? The quote is from Robert Schuller. He sawed a dead tree down in winter for firewood. He was sure the tree was dead. However, the new shoots sprouted out the next spring (Mangold, 2011)! The story indicates that you shouldn't make the important decisions in your low time. Be patient and wait until spring. >

Whatever your final decision is [≈ Whatever path you choose ≈ Whichever road you go down], you will move forward [≈ go ahead]. You are the one in control of your life. [≈ Your life is in your hands.] In the end, you need to navigate and create your own beautiful story.

For those who were lost in identifying your wonderful dreams, have you figured them out yet? Write them down now or do so whenever you are ready.

..................................................................................................................................

..................................................................................................................................

..................................................................................................................................

Protect these dreams and keep them to yourself [≈ keep them under your hat ≈ keep them under wraps].

# DAY 26
# 12-MONTH GOALS

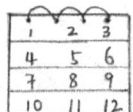

I'm glad that you have discovered your dreams. Awesome! Let's set up some specific goals for the following 365 days, which should keep you on the right track, bringing you closer to these lofty dreams.

Say your dream is to further [≈ resume] studies overseas. You can make that happen in a way so that you don't miss out on a wonderful life. Below is an example of what you might need to do to get set up:

| Area | 12-month goal | Action required |
| --- | --- | --- |
| Personal development | Work on my English. | Read *The English Builder!* every day. |
| | Get offers from overseas university. | Prepare for English tests. |
| Financial | Save my monthly income. | Stop buying unnecessary clothes. |
| | Learn to manage cashflow. | Read financial books and put their tips into practice. |
| Relationships | Find the love of my life. | Go out and meet new people. |
| | Pay for my parents [≈ folks] to travel. | Buy air tickets and book hotels. |
| Health | Lose weight. | Go jogging at least three times a week. |
| | Get adequate rest. | Put away the phone before bedtime. |
| Fun | Try something new (e.g. solve a Rubik's Cube). | Watch online videos on how to manipulate the Rubik's Cube. |
| | Improve my accuracy in archery. | Find a coach to learn how to aim better and shoot for the target. |

Do you see any problems with setting the above goals? Bingo! These goals are great, but some are vague or too broad. The goals need to be specific and measurable. If you're planning to lose weight, do you aim to lose 1 kg for the whole year, or 1 kg per month? You also need to give your goals a timeline.

Another improvement is to put 'I will' in front of the first verb of each goal. For example, I will save $100 per month. This will reinforce that you will make it, which is more powerful than 'want' or 'would like' or nothing at all.

To achieve one goal, multiple actions might be required. Note down [≈ Write down ≈ Jot down] all actionable and specific steps.

Now take out a blank piece of paper or your notebook. Write down your goals for the next 12 months that align with your ultimate dreams. Come back to this piece of paper or your notebook to periodically check your progress. Cross out any goals that you've completed. Identify where refinement or adjustments are needed. Set or adjust goals for the next year. Visualise your dreams. Work on your goals.

# DAY 27
## START BY DOING

In **Day 26 12-Month Goals**, you developed your action plan for the year. With this plan, and the goals you set up, you can start to get ahead. Well done!

Dreams are only dreams without action, no matter how wonderful they are. Now, everything is down to [≈ boils down to ≈ rides on] the action you actually take. This is easier said than done. Often, you will make endless excuses for not being able to do what you have planned, or delay action over and over again.

Have you ever given an excuse similar to that in the below table?

| Classic excuse | How to overcome the excuse |
| --- | --- |
| I don't have the time. | You can always make time. Start with 5 minutes per day. |
| The time is not right. | Time should never be an issue. You don't have to be 100% ready to start doing. There will never be a perfect time if you keep waiting. You may not want to wait until your 80s. |
| It is above my abilities. | You will never know without taking action. |
| I'm too old to start. | Assume you're 50 years old this year. It will take 4 years to complete the degree that you want. By then, you'll be 54 years old. But it's also true that you'll be 54 after 4 years regardless of whether you started study or not. So you're never too old to learn, or too old to start! Just take action now. |

Putting your plans into action [≈ Setting the wheels in motion] is not an easy job [≈ is not easy]. It requires consistent self-discipline, passion and determination.

If you choose to sit there only daydreaming, your dreams will remain dreams forever. Come on, you can do it. No excuses. Less lip, more action.

Start writing if you want to be an author. Begin to code if you aim to be a software developer. Commence your environmental projects if you desire to do good for the planet. Talk English and read English if you dream of taking that global trip. Just do it. Start now [≈ Take action, right now ≈ Roll up your sleeves and get cracking ≈ Pull your socks up], without any delay.

Every effort invested will help you to attain your goal.

# DAY 28
# DON'T BE A SLACKER!

A slacker is someone who is lazy, tardy, unmotivated, and slow to act. They put in less effort than they should. You can also call them a goof-off, a deadbeat or a sluggard. Their personal lifestyle could be something like this:

- Wakes up late [≈ Sleeps in ≈ Oversleeps] all the time. No-one can drag them out of the bed [≈ They don't jump out of bed] early in the morning.
- Goes back to bed again after being up for a while in the morning almost every day.
- Always puts off washing dirty dishes.
- Slacks off at work most days.
- Leaves things until the last minute: doesn't study for exams or doesn't stick to deadlines for reports.

They know they shouldn't put off what should be done today until tomorrow. Some even feel guilty for not getting things done on time. But they just can't beat their procrastination [≈ can't remove their laziness ≈ can't stop dragging their feet ≈ can't overcome their sloth ≈ can't quit stalling].

Worry no more. Here comes a magic pill to help cure each of abovementioned laziness:

- It only takes a millisecond to get out of bed. You only need to overcome this fraction of a second. Getting to sleep earlier or forcing yourself to get up to turn off the alarm [≈ hit the snooze button] that is out of reach could help.
- Set a routine: get up, make your bed, get dressed, exercise, eat breakfast, and drink coffee. You'll forget about bed for the rest of the day.
- It takes no more than 10 minutes to wash dishes. Why not get this in now?
- Set specific goals. Get yourself motivated.
- Leaving things until the last minute is always stressful. Get it done early so you can enjoy the pleasure of relaxation earlier. Why not?

Laziness only creates short-term happiness. It won't make you into a qualified English Builder. It won't help lead you to the wonderful life that you're dreaming of.

To achieve your dreams, you need to apply yourself diligently. Be industrious. [≈ Become a hard-working person.] You will become accustomed to being diligent. Ready, set, go! [≈ Get ready, get set and get going!]

# DAY 29
# GIVE IT YOUR ALL

Dreams are fancy, like a fairytale. It's always easy to have fairytale dreams, but most of the time the road to achieve them could be long and tough. Make it or break it? It's up to you. [≈ It's your call. ≈ You call the shots. ≈ You are the one who makes the call.] The question is: do you really want to reach the brightest star, stars such as Sirius, Canopus, Arcturus, Rigel, Vega, Capella or Procyon?

If your answer is a big yes, give it your all [≈ give every ounce of yourself]. It means to make greatest possible effort, to give as much as you possibly can, and to do whatever it takes to get there. It is a commitment.

If you give nothing [≈ don't give anything], you are only dreaming. If you don't give your 100%, you're unable to reach for the stars. If you don't, when you get older, you might blame yourself and ask, 'Why didn't I try harder?' Regrets. So shoot for the sky and give everything.

The answer to how is quite simple: work hard [≈ strive hard].

No, that's not enough. You need to work extremely hard [≈ work immensely hard]. Are there any other similar expressions for 'being very industrious'?

Of course there is! Repeat after me: 'I'll work tirelessly. [≈ I'll work relentlessly. ≈ I'll work day and night. ≈ I'll break my back. ≈ I'll put in blood, sweat and tears. ≈ I'll fight through thick and thin. ≈ I'll fight tooth and nail.]'

< The idiom 'fight tooth and nail' has a long history, which comes from wild animals fighting. They have to fight with everything they've got (teeth and nails) because they have no weapons. So it means to try very hard to get something that you want (What Does Fight Tooth and Nail Mean?, n.d.). >

Fight to the death for your dreams. But I'm not really asking you to fight to exhaustion and death. I only need you to put in the maximum effort towards your dreams.

Marvellous! Ramp up your efforts. Apply yourself. Knuckle down. Go into overdrive. And soldier on! Eventually, you will make it! (Even if it does take years.) But it's only a matter of time [≈ it's only a matter of when]. You will live your dream going forward.

# DAY 30
## TELL ME ABOUT YOURSELF

Hello builders! Before we start on a journey of self-evaluation, can you please tell me a bit about yourself [≈ give me an introduction ≈ introduce yourself]?

Relax. We're not having a professional job interview today. Share anything about yourself – your bio, tidbits about yourself, or random obscure facts, extraordinary stories, or even your boring side, maybe even your favourite flavour of ice cream.

Let me start first.

My name is Jessie. I am originally from China. [≈ I was born and raised in China. ≈ I grew up in China.] (😪 *Sleepy face* Boring!) I love sports, food, reading, and more. (🥱 *Yawning* Is there a more interesting side to you?)

I'm not a good singer. [≈ I can't sing well. ≈ I can't sing properly. ≈ I can't sing in tune. ≈ I can't carry a tune. ≈ I have no ear for music. ≈ I'm tone-deaf. ≈ I'm off-key when singing. ≈ I'm pitchy.] I treat it as my 'specialty' now. Every time I sing, everyone in the room is rolling on the floor with laughter.

I also have fears. I'm afraid [≈ petrified] of dogs and cats. I have a phobia of heights [≈ I have a strong fear of heights]. I start sweating by just thinking about standing at the top of the mountain. I'm paranoid about bugs and spiders. I faint [≈ I black out ≈ I pass out] at the sight of blood. Uh-oh.

Now it's your turn. Grab yourself an audience of at least one and introduce yourself. Once you've done this, I have some more challenging homework for you. Prepare a self-introduction for both formal and causal occasions. Talk to yourself in front of a mirror. Practise until you can say it freely [≈ without thinking]. Then sell yourself in 25 words or less.

Thanks for joining today's warm up! Before we start a self-assessment tomorrow, let's wrap up with some 'self' related words.

| Self-knowledge | Self-judgement | Self-impose | Self-evaluation | Self-fulfilling |
| Self-affirmation | Self-worth | Self-destruct | Self-conscious | Self-discipline |
| Self-talk | Self-help | Self-educate | Self-reflection | Self-esteem |
| Self-management | Self-defence | Self-importance | Self-medicate | Self-assurance |

# DAY 31
# CULTIVATE SELF-AWARENESS

How well do you know yourself? Let's begin a self-discovery journey. Take a moment now. Have a think about what you are good at and what you are not. Jot this down.

**What are your strengths?**
- My greatest strength is my multi-language skills.
- Being patient is my strong point.
- I have great people skills.
- I'm a good communicator and team player.
- ................................................................
- ................................................................

**What are your weaknesses?**
- Creativity is my weak point. [≈ Creativity is not my strong point.]
- I don't have much patience. [≈ My patience is shot. ≈ I'm impatient.]
- I struggle with numbers. [≈ I'm not good at dealing with numbers. ≈ I'm no good at numbers.]
- I see delegation as a handicap.
- My Achilles' heel is that I'm not assertive.
- ................................................................
- ................................................................

Let's face it. We all have our foibles [≈ weaknesses]. We have to accept ourselves, warts and all. We are one of a kind. [≈ We are unique. ≈ We are special. ≈ We are distinctive. ≈ We are not copies of anyone else.]

Be self-aware. Increase your self-awareness [≈ self-knowledge]. Diagnose yourself. Play to your strengths. Use them. Wield your strengths. Don't overvalue yourself. [≈ Don't be self-righteous. ≈ Don't overplay your hand.]

Be fully aware of your shortcomings and speak openly about them. This is one of my disadvantages, but I'm willing to improve it. You don't have to downplay yourself [≈ look down upon yourself ≈ discount yourself ≈ belittle yourself].

Stay true to yourself. Be yourself. Be authentic. Be proud of yourself all the time.

# DAY 32
## DISCOVER YOUR CORE VALUES

Self-awareness is not just about being conscious of what you are good at or what you are lousy at. You should know yourself in all aspects better than anyone else. This includes knowing your core values.

So, what are core values? A core value is a belief that you view as being important in life. Let's list some values that you could have. Add any others that you can think of in the blank area below.

> health [≈ fitness], family, love, happiness, kindness, success, money [≈ wealth], optimism, positivity, perseverance, environmentalism, friendship, honesty, integrity
>
> ...............................................................................................
>
> ...............................................................................................
>
> ...............................................................................................
>
> ...............................................................................................

What are the most important values in your life? [≈ What values are the pillars of your life? ≈ What are your top personal values?] And why?

My most important values in life [≈ The pillars of my life ≈ My top personal values] include fitness and family, while wealth is my least important value [≈ wealth is at the bottom ≈ wealth comes the last]. No amount of money can buy health. In some cases, health can deteriorate to the point that you can't get it back [≈ you can't undo the damage to health ≈ the damage to your health is irreversible]. No matter how rich you are.

No-one else in the world can love you the same way as your family. Money? Nah, you don't come to this world with it, and you go without it.

< 'The most' and 'the least' are examples of superlative adjectives, describing something or someone that has a quality to the greatest or least degree in one group. But you don't have to always use superlative adjectives to describe the 'best of the best': that is, a cut above the rest, app of the day, photo of the month, joke of the year, stands-outs, editor's picks, highlights of the 2018 World Cup, etc. >

There are no right or wrong answers. A core value is always a personal choice.

# DAY 33
## EXPLORE YOUR PERSONALITY

Let's continue with the self-diagnosis journey. Pick any of the below positive character traits to describe yourself.

> aspirational, approachable [≈ amiable], bold, ballsy, charming [≈ charismatic], cheerful, caring [≈ considerate], cordial, candor, chipper [≈ dynamic ≈ bubbly], dedicated, diplomatic, decisive, empathetic, even-handed, friendly, funny, faithful, generous, hearty, inquisitive, joyful, kind, lenient, magnetic, neat [≈ tidy], observant, open [≈ open-minded], philanthropic, patient, polished, punctual, quick, rejuvenated, resilient, sociable, trustworthy [≈ trusty], upbeat, versatile, witty, warm, youthful, zealous

Whether you admit it or not, no-one is perfect [≈ no-one is flawless ≈ no-one is impeccable ≈ we all have character flaws].

Now, please be honest with yourself. Circle the below personality traits that tend to be considered negative.

> abrasive, aggressive, arrogant, batty, bossy, crisp, calculating, cheeky, cold, devious, extravagant, extreme, feisty, flighty [≈ frivolous], finicky, fussy, intimidating, irresponsible, jealous, moody, muddle-headed, naïve, offensive, opinionated, pompous, phoney, possessive, quarrelsome, rough, rude, superlative [≈ over-the-top], sloppy, sneaky, touchy, unpredictable, untrustworthy, vain, vague, yellow-bellied

If your positive and negative traits are not mentioned in these tables, write them down in the table below.

| Positive personality trait | Neutral or negative personality trait |
|---|---|
|  |  |

Be mindful that there is absolutely no right or wrong answer for your personality. If you dislike your undesirable traits, you can always make a plan to improve them until your ideal self is formed. No big deal. Remember this mantra by heart: You are prefect the way you are. Be proud. You are fabulous!

# DAY 34
## I'M AN INTROVERT

I want to share this activity with those who classify themselves as an introvert, including myself. I'm not anti-social. But I have a quiet nature. [≈ I'm a person with a few words.] I prefer time to myself. [≈ I gain energy when I'm alone.] But I'm nervous [≈ I'm nervy ≈ I'm frightened ≈ I'm a bundle of nerves ≈ I'm flustered ≈ I'm flapping] when speaking in public [≈ talking publicly ≈ speaking to a crowd].

Here are some of my physical reactions:

- My face turns beef red. [≈ I blush.]
- I'm tongue-tied. [≈ I'm unable to articulate. ≈ I stammer.]
- My heart races. [≈ My heart pounds. ≈ My heart quickens. ≈ My heart leaps. ≈ My heart jumps fast. ≈ My heart races a million miles an hour.]
- I have sweaty palms. [≈ I have clammy hands.]
- I have butterflies in my stomach.
- I have a stomach cramp.
- I get cold feet.

For years, I've been wondering why I'm crap at social situations like this. Why am I an introvert? Why is it a nerve-wracking and stomach-churning experience for me? [≈ Why does it make me tense?]

I realised that I didn't have to feel this way. Public speaking is a skill that everyone can practise. To overcome the nervousness, all I needed to do was to handle myself well [≈ control myself ≈ contain myself ≈ gather myself ≈ pull myself together ≈ get a grip on myself]. Be as cool as a cucumber!

I admit that I still need more practice with mindfulness and being calm, collected, unfazed and unflappable under such circumstances.

But I'm now happy to put myself out there if I need to. I'm also happy to acknowledge and announce that I'm a typical introvert. I'm proud of who I am. Although our society appears to favour extroverts, we introverts have our own strengths (being a good listener, great observer, thoughtful partner, deep thinker, compassionate friend…) that extroverts might not have. Who says that we can't be exceedingly excellent!

# DAY 35
# YOUR PAST, PRESENT AND FUTURE

Let's proceed with our last self-reflection activity. In your notebook, write down a few things about yourself – any achievements, dreams, anything you're proud of, or anything you've yearned for years – anything big or small. Try using all 12 English verb tenses for this.

Here's an example:

| TENSE | PAST | PRESENT | FUTURE |
|---|---|---|---|
| **SIMPLE** | I won the first place in the rope skipping competition in primary school. | I love reading. | I will become a Broadway actor. |
| **CONTINUOUS** | I was eating healthy and exercising regularly. | I am training hard, shaping my body and taking care of my looks every day. | I will be pursuing my dreams. |
| **PERFECT** | I had spread my ideas through a TED Talk. | I have finished my law degree. | I will have found my perfect match. |
| **PERFECT CONTINUOUS** | I had been travelling for years. | I have been buckling down on my English study. | I will have been performing charity work. |

Make sure you understand the differences between these 12 tenses. Most importantly, I hope you now have a big smile on your face, now that you've explored your capabilities and dreams.

Steve Jobs said, 'You can't connect the dots looking forward; you can only connect them looking backwards. So you have to trust that the dots will somehow connect in your future. You have to trust in something – your gut, destiny, life, karma, whatever.'

Please trust yourself with absolute confidence. When you look back many years later, you'll find the dots you connected. It could be your actions from past simple, past continuous, past perfect or past perfect continuous tenses.

# DAY 36
## HAVE FAITH IN YOURSELF

You've now seen a holistic version of yourself in this chapter. I need you to trust yourself in every aspect of your life.

I understand that you might have some past experiences that could drain your confidence [≈ make you lose confidence ≈ dent your confidence]. For example, you might feel something like:

- No matter how hard I tried, I couldn't catch up with those who were academically smarter than me.
- At school, my classmates laughed at my small eyes and thick curly hair.
- My family couldn't afford fancy stationery and toys when I was young.

So you started to doubt yourself [≈ second guess yourself]:

- I was such a big loser because I couldn't do things well.
- I felt insecure about my appearance.
- I was not affluent.

The first thing that I need for you to do is to stop all this negative talk. You are becoming what you say. If you say, 'I can't', in the end you really can't. If you keep saying 'I'm ugly', you will become bald and have wrinkles years later. If your inner dialogue says 'I'm poor', you will end up living with little money.

English Builders, when you lack confidence [≈ you're low in confidence ≈ your self-confidence is short], please talk yourself up. You might say any of this to yourself:

- I can do better next time.
- I love myself, my body and my appearance.
- I've started saving. I'll become rich.

Reinforce these sentences in your mind: I'm confident. [≈ I believe in myself. ≈ I can do it.] I'm the best!

If you don't trust yourself, who else can? Do others seem to have that admirable, rock-solid or limitless self-confidence? It's because they've worked on it for years. You can do this as well! I feel it in my bones. [≈ I believe it strongly.]

Why? Remember this: The chances of you being born [≈ you coming out being you] were about 1 in 400 trillion. You're a miracle! So I'd like to congratulate you on being born [≈ that you were a newborn baby] _____ years ago with unique genes, different from everyone else in the universe.

< Hey, be careful when filling in your age in blank above. The western system counts your age from the time of your birth. In China, we also have nominal age system, of which your age is counted from the time of your mum's pregnancy, and it increases 1 year on the Chinese New Year. >

So there's no reason that you should not feel brilliant and confident inside and out!

# DAY 37
# RUN WITH TIME

We are all racing against the clock. Let's assume we each live up to 100 years and 1 year has 365 days. (Leap years don't count.) Therefore, we only live on this planet for 36,500 days. That means, our days are numbered. Time flies. [≈ Time ticks away. ≈ Time trickles away.] Whichever stage of your life that you're at right now, you're living your youngest day.

Now let's hear a piece of advice from a lovely lady who is 2 months short of her 101st birthday. Observe the bold font text below. What function does this text play in the sentences?

**A century ago**, I was born. I loved bedtime stories from my mum: '**Once upon a time** [≈ **A long time ago**], there were three little pigs…' **In my 20s**, I never thought about what the time was. Or maybe I just had ample time. **Until one day**, I realised the years had rolled by [≈ passed by], one by one. I couldn't stop time moving forwards. I started to be time-poor. So, what did I do with the time?

**Now in the blink of an eye** [≈ **in the bat of an eye** ≈ **in the wink of an eye** ≈ **in the twinkling of an eye** ≈ **at the speed of light**], I've lived over a century. **Over the course of my life**, I've been brave enough to do whatever I wanted to do. I am very happy.

Young people, please don't kill the time by watching the clock [≈ don't sit around watching the clock ≈ don't become a clock-watcher ≈ don't sit there and twiddle your thumbs ≈ don't tread water ≈ don't squander your time ≈ don't goof around ≈ don't faff about].

Time is just so precious [≈ priceless]. No-one can keep it. We're all in the same boat. It's mine, it's yours, and it is free to use. How to spend it is up to you. You can spend 4 hours a day on playing electronic games, going for a spontaneous trip with friends, or sweating at the gym. But those 4 hours in your life will be gone forever. You can't have it back. So you can't afford to waste it. Every second counts.

The bold font text includes adverbs of time from a grammar point of view. They are usually placed at the end of a sentence. For example, I spent 4 hours reading the book **yesterday**. But by putting it in the beginning of a sentence ('**Yesterday**, I spent 4 hours reading the book.'), you can emphasise the time.

# DAY 38
## STRUCTURE YOUR TIME WISELY

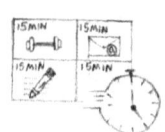

Since there is no time to waste for everyone, and everyone gets only 24 hours a day, that means we only have 1440 minutes a day or 86,400 seconds. On average, you spend one-third of your time sleeping. Not too much left, huh?

But if you plan ahead and use your time well, you can get the most out of it.

During orientation day at Melbourne University, we were handed [≈ distributed ≈ given ≈ dished out] a student diary. This type of diary gives you the chance to make to-do lists. To-do lists can help to set reminders for all things that need to be dealt with (and their priority). Nowadays, there are heaps of time management apps available to help better manage your day.

Dwight David Eisenhower's principle on time management is popular. That is, get the most important and urgent matters done first, followed by the important but not urgent tasks. Delegate tasks that are not important but urgent. Delete [≈ Eliminate] unimportant and non-urgent tasks.

< Eisenhower served as the 34th president of the United States between 1953 and 1961. His principal stems from his quote: 'I have two kinds of problems, the urgent and the important. The urgent are not important, and the important are never urgent.' >

< Talking about the presidents of the United States: George Washington became the first president in 1789. Joe Biden is the 46th president – his inauguration was in 2021. How many years have passed? Can you list the names of all other presidents? >

You can also use your money to buy yourself time. Don't be afraid of delegating professional tasks to others [≈ entrusting professionals to do the jobs]. Hire a gardener, a cleaner and a child-carer to help you out. Getting your husband to share housework and paying your kids to offer a hand are not bad ideas either.

Another trick is to make the most of any waiting time you may have. You might have idle time while waiting at train stations, bus stops, airline terminals, queues for restaurants – these times are not meant to be wasted. Use the time to check out your emails, catch up on missed phone calls, reply to text messages, listen to podcasts, and read news and books. In the next few days, I'll teach you how to keep on top of things and free up more time.

# DAY 39
## STAY FOCUSED

Attention, please! One way to create more time is to stay focused on [≈ concentrate on] things that you are engaged with. This ensures your productivity is maximised within the time given, and you may end up doing more things in the day.

Let's find out some solutions to two scenarios that could happen to any of us.

Scenario 1: While others are talking, your mind wanders [≈ your brain is somewhere else ≈ you tune out ≈ you zone out]. 'I'm sorry. What were you just saying?' Ah, time just wasted.

Solution: Live in the moment. [≈ Embrace the present moment.] Be fully present. [≈ Be 100% in it.] The moment you catch yourself drifting off, switch attention back quickly. If you keep getting distracted, just push the conversation to another time.

Alrighty, now take a break. Come back in 5 minutes with a fresh mind to check out the second scenario. This is also a technique to keep yourself preoccupied [≈ in the zone] on a new task, increasing work effectiveness.

(5 minutes later…)

Scenario 2: When doing homework, you couldn't give it your full attention [≈ you were scatterbrained ≈ you were unable to concentrate]. What might happen here? You might not finish the homework on time, and it might be loaded with mistakes. Alas, you would have to make another time to work on it.

Don't argue with me that you're living in a world of distractions [≈ in the age of distractions] that affect your ability to sustain attention. Just simply cut out the noise – cut out the distractions and interruptions. Start by finding a quiet place. Set up a 'do not disturb' room. Unplug from everything. Clear your desk. Get your head down and engross yourself in what you're doing. Find your sweet spot and get into the flow.

< If you hit the ball with the *sweet spot* of a golf club or a tennis racket, the ball will travel more powerful. The sweet spot in today's context refers to reaching to an optimal level on an activity that you're doing. >

# DAY 40
# ELECTRONIC-FREE TIME

While I was studying, I remembered that I needed to check an important email. The second I took out the phone, the ASOS app sent me a notification for clothes on sale. I clicked into the app and started to browse all the sales items. Then – oh, I'd always wanted to check out how to make that heart-shaped cake. Once the YouTube video played through, another video popped up: Ultimate Tiramisu Cake Recipe. That was tempting. Now, let me have a look…

Before I knew it, an hour had gone by. I realised I hadn't read that important email… My study mood had gone. I felt guilty and this made it even harder to refocus. Have you had a similar experience from time to time [≈ every now and then]?

As you can see, electronic products and the internet can fragment your attention span [≈ make your attention span shrink ≈ affect your concentration]. To increase your attention span, you have to create technology-free time [≈ device-free time].

< '-free' means without, so technology-free means without using technology [≈ disconnecting from tech]. Take a guess at the meaning of below '-free' related words.

| Hassle-free | Stress-free | Trouble-free | Alcohol-free | Nut-free | Option-free |
|---|---|---|---|---|---|
| Guilt-free | Sugar-free | Mistake-free | Fat-free | Pain-free | Duty-free [≈ Tax-free] |

What is duty-free? In Australia, customers pay a 10% goods and services tax (GST) on most products and services. Duty-free means that goods that you buy are exempt from paying GST. There are duty-free stores at the airport where you can buy products such as liquor, fragrance, food, souvenirs and tech at a cheaper price without GST applied. If you spend over AUD $300 at a store within 60 days of departure of the country, you can claim GST back at the airport. >

Did you just lose focus on today's topic after reading the contents of the angle brackets? I'm testing how quickly you can come back and refocus.

Set yourself up so that you won't be interrupted: Get off your phone. Put it on silent mode [≈ on mute]. If you keep mindlessly picking it up, put it out of sight [≈ put it away]. Or turn it off until you finish what you're doing. If you need to work on a computer, turn off [≈ remove] the internet, if possible. Without getting sidetracked [≈ getting derailed ≈ getting interrupted], you will find your flow [≈ enter a state of flow].

# DAY 41
# BREAKING DIGITAL ADDICTION

From the moment I wake up in the morning, I start to scroll through news, weather, Facebook posts, Twitter, Instagram, WeChat [≈ weixin (微信)], and the Twitter-like Weibo (微博). Before bed, I'll repeat my morning routine. In-between, I'll fiddle with the computer, glue my eyes onto the TV screen, and play electronic games…

I won't call it a day until I break through the level of the mobile phone game I'm playing. Once I've reached the next level, let me just play one more level… I sometimes keep watching TV dramas after midnight, one episode after the other. What 'stick-to-the-end' spirit! I've never done something consistently like this.

Is this you too? Are you attached to digital gadgets?

You are centred on these platforms from sun up to sun down [≈ from dawn to dusk ≈ all day long]. You know they're time filler tools [≈ big-time killers ≈ time suckers] and they eat up most of your valuable time, but you just can't stop.

Don't feel guilty. It's not your fault at all. These electric devices and programs are designed to be attractive to its users [≈ to be like a honeypot]. So blame the inventors! But I'll help you to cure this addiction.

Highlight the words or phrases below that are alternative expressions to 'addiction':

- If you're obsessed with social media platforms, delete or inactivate your profile for a while.
- If you're addicted to computer games, put them away, out of sight.
- If you binge watch Netflix, then cancel Netflix.
- If you're a smartphone addict, leave your phone in the other room. Do housework or sports instead or develop a new hobby to keep yourself engaged.
- If you can't help playing mobile games (such as *Candy Crush*, *Pokémon GO*, *Plants vs Zombies* or *2048*) most of the day for a long period of time, simply remove these unimportant programs.
- If you can't stop yourself from surfing websites, just log out and turn off the computer [≈ go offline].

By stepping away from these attractive technology and software, you can reclaim your life and give yourself more time.

# DAY 42
## BE BRAVE AND SAY NO

Harvey Mackay says, 'Don't water your weeds.' This is true. You are wasting time watering weeds, so please instead water the apples trees, tomatoes and Chinese roses in your garden. Similarly, don't invest your time in things or people that don't deserve your time. Whatever things that you don't really want to do, don't do them! You'll save yourself some time!

This means you need to know when to say no to invitations or requests (as long as you don't feel like it, that is). Ask yourself: Should I? Must I? Will I? If your response is no to any one of these, please just say the bloody word 'No'! How hard can it be?

< The words 'should', 'must' and 'will' are modal verbs that express possibilities of an action. >

It is your duty and your right to choose where to give your time and energy. The principle here is that it is all about you. Your time is yours to do with what you like. You're the one who controls and arranges it. Don't feel sorry or upset by saying no. You don't have to be a yes-man who tries to please or impress others [≈ becomes a people pleaser ≈ tries to be likeable to others ≈ caters to others ≈ is accommodating to others ≈ keeps others happy ≈ submits to the agenda of others]. Rejecting others in this way does not make you lose face. It doesn't mean that you're a bad-arse or that you're rude. It's a matter of you choosing what to do with your valuable time.

Say your friend wants to try out a fancy restaurant where the two of you have to wait outside for half an hour to get in. You say, 'No, I'm not doing that today.'

Say your boss assigns you extra work that you're unwilling to take on. You say, 'No, I don't have the time right now.'

Say your partner likes late afternoon grocery shopping. Tell them, 'No. Let's get out of bed early and go there as soon as the shop opens.'

< Being an early bird is another great way to save time! If you go shopping early in the morning, you won't have trouble securing a car park spot. The traffic is good too. You don't have to wait to go into fitting room or in a long queue to make a payment. It's so quiet! >

So, to earn yourself time, you have to get used to saying the bloody hard word 'No'! Disregard [≈ Abandon] any activities that don't add value to your life or that waste your time.

# DAY 43
## WAYS TO SAY NO

As today's title suggests, we're not going to talk about how to create time. Would you still like to go through the activity?

Are you going to respond 'No, thank you'? Bingo! That is the perfect way to refuse me. It saves you valuable time on something that doesn't add value. But I strongly recommend for you to spend 5 minutes scanning through because I'm going to show you two methods to say 'No'.

**Method 1:** Turn others away by being assertive. Just be straight with them. When asked for help, and you can't help, get back to them straight away: 'I have to say no.' or 'That's a no from me.' or 'I'm afraid I can't help you on this matter.' or 'The answer would be no.'

When you can't disclose confidential information being requested, just simply say, 'I refuse to answer.' or 'I can't give you that information.' It's that simple.

**Method 2:** Refuse to answer questions in a non-straightforward way, but do so in a polite way. Check out the scenarios below. Do you have any other sparkling ideas on how to politely turn away others?

| Their question | How to say no not straightforwardly | Purpose |
|---|---|---|
| Why did we break up? | You tell me! | Throw the question back to them. You don't have to answer the question anymore. |
| Can you please pick the phone up for me? | I'm sorry. I can't help you. My hands are tied. | State the reason why you can't help right now. |
| Can we please go through the system process now? | Let's talk about it next week. Or: Let's get to that at a different time. | Delay or propose a new time. |
| A marketing phone call or scam call [≈ spam call]: 'Am I speaking with Ms Gao? I'm calling from the Australian Energy Company…' | Is this a marketing call? Where did you get my number? | Throw one or two questions back to the caller. Then hang up. |
| | I don't need your service. Please put me on your do-not-call list. | Tell the telemarketer to stop calling you in the future. |
| | Let the phone ring. If the call is important, the caller will leave a voice message. | A silent rejection. |

# DAY 44
# DON'T COMPLAIN

Lots of people like grumbling about their boring, underpaid job, grousing about their terrible boss, complaining about poor public services, and so on. They are pouty and angry. They spew out their dissatisfaction [≈ get their dissatisfaction off their chest]. These people have a common name: a whiner. Some even consistently complain about the same thing to different people over and over.

Dwelling on situations that already exist robs you of precious time. It's no use crying over spilt milk.

< The proverb 'no use crying over spilt milk' is self-explanatory. The milk has already been spilled, and getting upset about it is useless. So don't spend your time worrying about something that you can't change. >

Rather than waste your energy questioning why things have not gone your way, you can change your way of thinking [≈ reframe your thoughts] instead. Treat it as an experience to make you grow. Try to understand why the situation happened. Use your time to figure out how to improve the current situation in the future.

Use the table below as guidance to help you stop complaining, giving you some more time.

| Useless complaint | Shift your perspective |
| --- | --- |
| This job is just so boring! | At least, I know what a boring job looks like, which gives me the determination to find a new job that I enjoy. |
| The bus is delayed again! | No worries. I can use the waiting time to mediate and relax. |
| The salesperson is unfriendly and abhorrent! | We all have bad times now and again. That person might have had a fight with her husband or have been blamed by her boss this morning. She isn't personally against me. |
| Why did the government make this new policy? | I am affected by the policy. But in the long run, the policy is good for the environment and for future generations. |
| I can't put up with her anymore! | She has taught me how to put up with a person. Not too bad. |
| I was given short notice by the landlord. I have to move out in 5 days! | It's the time for a change. A new place to live will turn out even better! |
| Why do all the shitty things happen to me! Why can't I catch a break? | I'm just being tested by God. I'm a resilient and capable person. I fight through. God has offered me the chance at the best life ever! |

# DAY 45
# ENJOY ALONE-TIME

In your life journey, there are times when no-one is around [≈ when you are by yourself ≈ when you have no company].

You shouldn't feel lonely or bored. You should feel like 'Wow, I finally get to have a little time for myself!' No time is supposed to be wasted. So, how can you best spend your time [≈ make best use of your time]?

Turn this time into a treat for yourself. There are heaps of things you can do:

- Have a sleep-in. Just sleep in a quiet and comfortable environment.
- Snuggle up [≈ Nestle down] on the sofa with a cosy blanket.
- Put the TV on. Watch your favourite TV show without interruption.
- Put on music. [≈ Play songs.]
- Read a popular book.
- Pour yourself a glass of wine.
- Head out for a drink. You might meet new friends.
- Sit in a fancy restaurant and enjoy a leisurely meal.
- Cook a delicious meal just for yourself.
- Go to the gym and work out.
- Take a bath.
- Go for a spa and massage to relieve tense muscles [≈ sore muscles].
- Go shopping for that expensive item that you've been craving for a long time.
- Go to an exhibition.
- Bask in the sun on the beach.
- Arrange a short trip for yourself, even if it's just going to the park nearby.
- Take a walk in [≈ Stroll through] the botanic gardens.
- Acquire a new hobby or skill.
- Think deeply and reflect.

If you prefer to do nothing, sit there quietly and listen to the clock ticking. Here, you are physically present with just yourself. You know who you are mentally and where you're at. Spiritually, you live in that particular moment. Feel your soul. Embrace solitude.

# DAY 46
# THE WORD – AWAY

Let's **steer** our conversation **away** today from alone-time. [≈ Let's drop where we were yesterday.] Don't **go away**. Sit back, relax, and let's read a story laden with the word 'away'.

Ten years ago, an airplane **took** me **away** from home. It was my first time **away** from my home country. I would be all on my own. But I wasn't **scared away**, and I **wiped away** my tears, knowing I was a grown-up and could be on my own.

I **tucked away** all my important documents: university certificate, birth certificate and copies of my passport. The beautiful city of Melbourne stirred my excitement. But living here wasn't like **getting away** for a holiday. The high rental prices and tuition started to **nibble away** at my parents' savings. I tried to apply for a part-time waitress job at Asian restaurants, but I was **turned away** by many because they required proficiency in Cantonese, which I didn't speak. One day on the tram, three teenagers stood too close to me and spat on me. I was scared! I didn't know how to respond and if I should respond at all. All I did was to **back away** and run off the tram quickly.

The wisdom that I **took away** from that experience was to not let such an experience **gnaw away** at your confidence. Give it a time.

My mentor also told me:

- Don't **run away** from your problems. The problems won't **go away** if you do not resolve them. Keep **chipping away** at your problems.
- Don't **throw** opportunities **away** since they do not often appear.

Here is advice from my university professors:

- Don't cheat in the exams. Never! You can't **get away** with it. [≈ You will be caught.]
- **Take away** electronic distractions while you are studying.
- Spend time reading. You will not be **pulling away** from your peers.

I learnt some of the following from my local friends:

- The Melbourne Show public holiday was **taken away** by the government.
- If your headache or toothache does not **go away** [≈ disappear], take some Panadol [≈ paracetamol].
- If a random drunk guy talks to you on the street, just **step away** [≈ stay out of the way].

Anyway, everything I've experienced and achieved all these years really **blows** me **away**!

What have you **taken away** from today's topic? I hope you **walk away** wiser. Don't **put away** your dreams. Continue to work very hard at them [≈ **beaver away** at them].

# DAY 47
## USE YOUR NOODLE

Muscles atrophy if they're not used for a period of time. The same goes for your brain. [≈ Your brain is no exception.]

Are there any other ways to express two things that are the same or have a similar nature? Use your noodle to think of three examples.

- ................................................................
- ................................................................
- ................................................................

< 'Noodle' is a slang here for 'head'. It is said that 'noddle' was the word, referring to the back of the head in the 15th century. The spelling has alliteration with the pronunciation of 'noodle' and looks similar. So 'noodle' has gradually become a more commonly used word (Greenwald, 2004). Do you believe in this origin? >

Cool. You just used your head [≈ fed your mind ≈ used your own intelligence ≈ got your mind working]! Here is what I have:

- USBs are not dissimilar to [≈ are similar to] portable hard disks.
- Sydney recently saw a drop in property price, and the same thing has started happening in Melbourne.
- Pumpkin puree is a good substitute [≈ alternative] for butter when baking.
- Travel agencies suffered during pandemic, and so did retailers.
- Learning mathematics develops your reasoning skills, which makes you smarter. Likewise [≈ Similarly ≈ Equally ≈ By the same token], learning a second language helps to sharpen your mind.

Let's give your brain a break [≈ a vacation]. Which line is shorter in the below picture?

Answer: They are at exactly the same length. This is the Muller–Lyer illusion. The top line appears to be shorter than the bottom. Was your brain tricked by the illusion?

# DAY 48
## READ VORACIOUSLY

Reading is a process that strengthens your brain. It makes you smarter [≈ boosts your intelligence]. By reading, you'll become a live Wikipedia [≈ a walking encyclopedia ≈ a renaissance man or woman]. You will be able to live and breathe any subject.

< 'Renaissance' is a French word, meaning rebirth. The Renaissance is the period between the 14th and 17th centuries when European arts, sciences and architecture developed. Leonardo da Vinci (1452–1519) was a true Renaissance man because of his talent in painting, mechanics, anatomy and architecture (Heventhal, 2021). >

Educate yourself on a range of things and you'll be able to talk about odd facts: Humans blink about [≈ roughly ≈ approximately ≈ around ≈ plus or minus] 17,000 times a day. The average woman spends almost [≈ nearly] 1 year of her life trying to figure out what to wear.

You'll get to know world history: the Industrial Revolution, the French Revolution, the Holocaust, the Korean War, the Vietnam War, the Persian Gulf War…

You'll have the knowledge on how psychology works: our brain processes that $999.99 is cheaper than $1000 (and though it's indeed cheaper, it's only by 1 cent!). That's why retailers reduce the price by 1 cent, to trick you.

You'll learn ways to create happiness, become rich, win over friends and influence people, keep fit, get a good night's sleep, keep a healthy relationship, plan your next trip, etc. How cool is that?

Now crack open a book, and dive into it. Do you like reading best-sellers [≈ best-selling books]? What is your favourite genre?

Below is a list of some genres:

| Romance | Cookbooks [≈ Cooking] | Horror | Military | Languages |
|---|---|---|---|---|
| Fantasy | Memoir and autobiography | Fiction | Sports | Poetry |
| Biography | Detective and mystery | Travel | Business | Paranormal romance |
| Self-help | Science fiction [≈ Sci-fi] | History | Gardening | Anthology |
| Spirituality | Young adult fiction | Thriller | Psychology | Comic book |

By the way, please read physical books [≈ real paper books] instead of reading ebooks [≈ reading electronically]. There's research that shows readers can remember more content when flipping the physical page (Wise, 2019).

# DAY 49
## KEEP YOUR MEMORY SHARP

Shoot! I couldn't remember if I locked the front door and turned off the gas. Where did I leave my mobile phone?

As I age, I can't recall things as well as I used to. Like my yesterday's lunch, which now seems really far away [≈ doesn't ring a bell ≈ seems like a distant memory]. Sometimes, the name of people that I've just met fall out of my mind instantly. The name of that product is just on the tip of my tongue. I've racked my brain and I can't get it out.

Oops, my brain went blank [≈ my mind was a complete blank ≈ my brain wasn't functioning ≈ I had a brain fart ≈ I had a mind-blank ≈ I had a mental block ≈ I suffered brain fog].

Oh, good. I was just holding the phone in my hand… Sigh, I really don't like having a memory like a sieve [≈ like a goldfish]. I'd love to have a memory more like an elephant.

< It's said that an elephant never forgets. An elephant's brain can weigh up to 5 kilograms. This makes it easier for them to remember places where food and water had been found in the past (Do Elephants Ever Forget?, n.d.). Their amazing memories also help recognise unfamiliar elephants from outside of the herd (Hutchinson, 2013). In contrast, a goldfish is commonly believed to have a memory span of only 3 seconds, although researchers have found it could be as much as several months (Baker, 2021). >

Keeping your mind sharp can help to avoid memory loss and prevent dementia. So let's do three exercises to strengthen your memory:

- Close your eyes, and attempt to remember all the objects around you.
- Learn the digits of pi (π) off by heart. Pi (pronounced 'pie') is the ratio of the circumference of a circle to its diameter. The digits of this irrational number never end. So you could memorise its first 100 digits after the decimal. Here you go:
3.14 159 265 358 979 323 846 264 338 327 950 288 419 716 939 937 510 582 097 494 459 230 781 640 628 620 899 862 803 482 534 211 706 79…
- Revisit past experiences. What did you have for breakfast yesterday, and the day before? What did we talk about between Day 20 and Day 30 of this book? Think about important events like your anniversary, big wedding day, school reunion – can you still recall those happy moments?

# DAY 50
# LEVEL UP YOUR BRAINPOWER

Scratch your head and try out an easy brainteaser. Which is heavier? A pound of **feathers** or a pound of **rocks**? Answer: Neither. Both weigh a pound! Did you fall for it? [≈ Were you fooled?]

Now let's level up games and keep your brain challenged!

First, solve the below Sudoku puzzle. The aim is to fill in the numbers 1 to 9 once in each column, each row, and each 3×3 square and not repeat a number.

| 8 | 7 | 6 | 9 |   |   |   |   |   |
|---|---|---|---|---|---|---|---|---|
|   | 1 |   |   |   | 6 |   |   |   |
|   | 4 |   | 3 |   | 5 | 8 |   |   |
| 4 |   |   |   |   |   | 2 | 1 |   |
|   | 9 |   | 5 |   |   |   |   |   |
|   | 5 |   |   | 4 |   | 3 |   | 6 |
|   | 2 | 9 |   |   |   |   |   | 8 |
|   | 4 | 6 | 9 |   | 1 | 7 | 3 |   |
|   |   |   |   |   | 1 |   |   | 4 |

Now, get a partner to play Chinese chess [≈ xiangqi (象棋)] with. The goal: checkmate or stalemate your opponent's king or general to win the game! The word 'checkmate' originates from Persian phrase 'shah mat', meaning 'the king is helpless!' (Patrick, 2016). The pieces: there are 16 pieces for each player. See their English names in below table.

| You (red) | 1 general | 2 advisers | 2 bishops | 2 horses | 2 chariots | 2 cannons | 5 soldiers |
|---|---|---|---|---|---|---|---|
| Your opponent (black) | 1 king | 2 guards | 2 elephants | 2 knights | 2 rooks | 2 cannons | 5 pawns |

Of course, each of the above pieces on the chess board are written in Chinese (illustrated in the table below). Now continue to strengthen your brain by turning into a Chinese language mode.

| You | 帥 | 士 | 相 | 馬 | 車 | 炮 | 兵 |
|---|---|---|---|---|---|---|---|
| Your opponent | 將 | 仕 | 象 | 馬 | 車 | 砲 | 卒 |

The rules? Elephants can't cross the river. They move diagonally two spaces. Rooks can only move in straight lines but in any number of spaces... Learn more yourself!

Seek out other healthy brain games like jigsaw puzzles, crossword puzzles, word searches, Wordle or Quardle games, murder mysteries nights, mahjong [≈ mah-jongg ≈ majiang (麻将)], Chinese checkers, UNO, Monopoly, Gobang, chess, Go or tic-tac-toe. Share some more fun games with me here:

..........................................................................................................
..........................................................................................................

Anyway, be a brainiac and improve your thinking and reasoning abilities!

# DAY 51
# ENTERTAINING WAYS TO LEARN ENGLISH

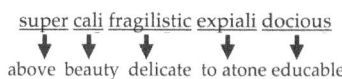

Learning a second language boosts your brainpower. From time to time you might feel stuck when you're learning another language. You feel that your hard work doesn't seem to get you anywhere. Or you feel jaded about learning it? Oh no! We all have that moment. Just sit back and relax. Train your brain into a new way of learning English. Refresh your mind.

Here's a game idea for a group of people: name a fruit, vegetable or protein for each letter of the alphabet (A to Z) one by one. Whoever runs out of names is out of the game. Here's an example:

> asparagus, brussels sprouts, cabbage, daikon, eggplant, fennel, guava, horseradish, iceberg lettuce, jicama, kale, longan, macadamia, nectarine, okra, parsnip, quail, rhubarb, shallot, turnip, ugli fruit, veal, water chestnut, xigua (西瓜), yams, zucchini

Or here's another game: think of a noun. What could you do to that noun by adding different verbs in front? For example, we live in an era of big data. What else could you do with the word 'data'? Some examples, in no particular order, include:

> store data, collect data [≈ gather data], scrounge up data, overwrite data, clean data, extract data, reset data, update data, derive data, strip out data [≈ eliminate data], populate data, validate data, summarise data, consolidate data, true up data, delete data, disclose data

What about collecting interesting words or phrases? That's not a bad idea.

**Jawbreakers** (sounds like something that could break your jaw! They are, in fact, a large round hard candy). **Xenophobia** (a fear of foreigners). **Supercalifragilisticexpialidocious** (unusual long word, meaning super good). Wednesday is often called **hump day**…

You could also watch the *Family Feud* TV program, which is a competition between two families aiming to win a car and $10,000. What do participants do?

The host Grant Denyer asks interesting questions, such as 'Name something that rhymes with tree', or 'Name something that people have to run to catch'. The program officers will have surveyed 100 people beforehand for these questions, and the top answers will be used. Contestants need to guess the best possible answers. What are your answers?

The possible answers to the first question could be 'free', 'bee', 'three', 'me', 'knee', 'see'. The answer to the second question could be 'bus' or 'pet'. What else can you think of?

# DAY 52
## PRACTISE ALTERNATIVE EXPRESSIONS

Another activity to spice up [≈ add excitement to] your language learning experience is to think of alternative expressions for different sentences. This also stimulates your brain!

To find similar expressions, you can start by looking for synonyms [≈ words that mean nearly the same thing] and antonyms [≈ words with the opposite meaning].

Let's work on the example sentence of 'In big cities, peak hour traffic is heavy.'

What is almost the same word for 'heavy'? Put your thinking cap on! Bingo! Some example words here: 'thick', 'bad', 'terrible', 'horrible', 'insane'… What would the opposite word be? 'Light'. So we can say 'In big cities, peak hour traffic is not light.' A little awkward, but it works!

Don't just limit your thinking to similar words. There are always plenty of ways to describe things. For 'heavy traffic', when cars are moving slowly or have stopped moving, you call it 'traffic congestion [≈ a traffic jam ≈ traffic gridlock]'. Now unleash your imagination and write down three alternative expressions of 'the traffic is jammed', either with a phrase or in a sentence.

..................................................................................................................................

..................................................................................................................................

..................................................................................................................................

Let's hop into a few alternative expressions. All together now!

< Don't confuse the phrase 'all together' and the single word 'altogether'. 'All together' means everyone and everything in a group together. 'Altogether' means 'completely', 'a total amount' or 'on the whole'. You've gone through 52 days altogether. Altogether, you're doing a great job! Nicely done! >

One way to exercise your brain is to think about objects and their surroundings and how they're related. When it's bumper-to-bumper traffic, think about what is happening to the street and cars? The street is experiencing a traffic headache and cars are not moving. So we might say the following:

The street is wedged tight. [≈ The street is clogged with cars. ≈ The street is heavy with traffic.] Cars are trundling by slowly. The traffic starts to back up. The traffic grinds to a halt [≈ stops ≈ is at a standstill]. There's a long line of vehicles that can't move. [≈ Vehicles have queued for kilometres.] It is massively backed-up.

Anyway, do you have any other great ideas to practise English or any other foreign language in a fun way? Share them with us.

# DAY 53
## TAKE A QUIZ

It's quiz time! Let's continue on with keeping your brain active. You have 30 seconds to answer each of the following five questions:

1. Who was the first man to land on the moon?
   **A.** Neil Armstrong  **B.** Buzz Aldrin  **C.** Michael Collins  **D.** Gene Cernan
2. What is the Arabic number for Roman numeral *XXIV*?
3. Using with the letter M, name a country, an occupation, a kitchen utensil, an actor, a school subject and a movie.
4. What are some English idioms or sayings that use the numbers one to nine in them? (For example, one-horse town, two left feet.)
5. How many triangles do you see in the image below?

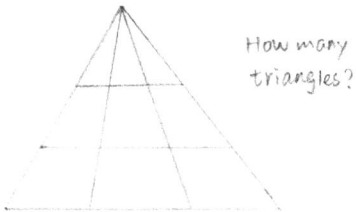

Below are my answers to these questions (and some explanations):

1. Neil Armstrong was the first person to step on the moon. In 1969, he and the two other American astronauts Buzz Aldrin and Michael Collins were on *Apollo 11*. They left a plaque on the moon: 'Here men from the planet Earth first set foot upon the moon. July 1969 A.D. We came in peace for all mankind.' Multiple-choice questions like this could appear in shows like *Millionaire Hot Seat*, an Australian TV quiz show. In the first round – Fastest Finger First – six contestants each have 10 seconds to answer 15 questions. The winner of the first round is given one grand [≈ a thousand bucks]. During the show, every contestant has the chance to win 1 million dollars by taking turns to answer the quizzes. Each contestant can use a lifeline (Pass, 50-50, Switch, Ask a Friend, or Ask the Host) once. The top prize is one million dollars! There are also other quiz shows such as *Pointless, Think Tank, The Chase Australia*.
2. It's 24. In Roman numeral symbols I, V, X, L, C, D and M stand for 1, 5, 10, 50, 100, 500, and 1000 respectively. These are the symbols from Arabic 1 to 10: I=1, II=2, III=3, IV=4, V=5, VI=6, VII=7, VIII=8, IX=9, X=10. Now you'll be able to see the patten and get to know how XXIV is equal to 24.
3. Malta, massage therapist, meat grinder, Mark Hamill, mathematics, *Minions*. You might be playing *Alpha Bucks* on 109 Fox Radio with Fifi, Fev & Byron if you heard questions like this. If you answer 10 questions in similar format given by the host in 30 seconds all correctly, you can win ten thousand bucks!
4. One for the road; two's company, three's a crowd; three squares a day; four corners of the Earth; five o'clock shadow; six ways to Sunday; seven-year itch; pieces of eight; nine day wonder; perfect ten. Your answers could be completely different from me for this question and question three. The more the merrier!
5. The answer is 19. Apart from all of the 18 triangles that you can count, there's the word 'triangle' included in the image itself!

Has your brainpower increased? Now design five quiz questions of your own and get someone else to answer them!

# DAY 54
# STUDY HARD

Hey English Builders, do you like money? If you do, stay tuned for this chapter. We'll be learning how to make money!

The first secret to making money is to study hard. Time at school is a golden time [≈ prime time] to learn. So please devote yourself to your studies. Your study attitude will turn into a lifelong attitude. What you learn and how you learn will all convert into your ability to earning money in the future.

Steve Jobs didn't finish school. Ralph Lauren flunked college. Bill Gates dropped out of Harvard. It sounds like that to become a billionaire, a CEO or a celebrity, you don't have to be academically gifted. In some cases, you could even drop out of school [≈ never complete the school ≈ be a school dropout]. Didn't you hear that *A* students work for *B* students and *C* students, and the top performers at school are not the wealthy ones?

< *A* students are those who get high distinctions (H1 or HD) in exams, which is a grade between 80–100%. A distinction (D or H2A and H2B) is given when you achieve 70–79% on your exam paper. *C* is for a credit (60–69%). P means a pass (50–59%). *N* is a fail (0–49%). This is how universities in Australia assess students. In China, 60% is normally considered the minimum pass mark. >

It is true that a decent score doesn't guarantee a rewarding job or an amazing life. A qualification is just a small part of your life. It does not define who you are. But you only hear half the story. Steve Jobs took a calligraphy class at college, which contributed to the beautiful typography in the design of the Mac computer. Ralph Lauren had a flair for [≈ had a talent in] fashion at a young age, and he studied business science for 2 years. Bill Gates actually did well academically while he studied at Harvard (Mejia, 2018).

At the end of the day, being an *A*, *B* or *C* student really doesn't matter. What really matters is how you spend each day at school growing knowledge and being in that social environment. This lays the groundwork for your future career and a healthy, comfortable lifestyle with sufficient income. This is why you should study, and study hard and smart! The more you learn, the more you can earn!

# DAY 55
# STUDYING CHANGES YOUR LIFE

You might not be particularly good at a particular subject at school, but you would be foolish [≈ babyish ≈ silly billy ≈ a silly duffer ≈ a dummy ≈ an idiot] if you don't at least give it your best shot. Why?

Let's consider how lucky we are that we can afford books. Impoverished children might never dream of the life we live. They may not be able to see and experience the world as we do for their whole life. Education plays a key in changing these kinds of circumstances. Because I truly believe this, every $1 earned from each sale of this book will go towards charities that help poor kids.

Each year around the Christmas, I receive a letter from the Smith Family asking for a donation. The Smith Family is an Australian non-profit charity with the goal of helping disadvantaged children through education in order to break the cycle of poverty.

Here's a recreation of one of these letters. It's written by Elena's mum who left school early many years ago. She encouraged her daughter to finish school in the hope that Elena would have a better future.

*To my dear daughter,*
*When you told mummy that you didn't want to continue school, I was shocked and heartbroken. Mum wants to tell you studying is so important. I didn't finish school and I couldn't give you a wealthy life. Mum doesn't want you to go through what I've gone through. My sweetie, don't give up school. It'll give you the chance to get a great job and stay away from living poor.*
*Elena, you're such a special and amazing girl. Mum is very proud of you. Love you.*

*Mum XOXOXO*

< What does 'XOXOXO' mean? 'X' here means a kiss and 'O' represents a hug. >

Even Elena's mum knows that completing school is the passport [≈ the gateway] to a good job to earn money to live a better life.

While you are at school, increase your academic and non-academic reading, learn methodology, practise listening and speaking, cultivate logical thinking abilities. Use all the resources available to you, my dear potential capable money-makers.

You never know when your study and your knowledge could make you rich. Like the the *Millionaire Hot Seat* TV show that we introduced in **Day 53 Take a Quiz**, you could take home 1 million dollars by just answering a couple of questions correctly! It can only happen when you receive the education to enhance your knowledge!

# DAY 56
# WHERE DOES MONEY COME FROM?

Money doesn't grow on trees. It requires effort to earn money, so you shouldn't spend it carelessly [≈ in a careless manner]. In what possible ways can you make money?

< Let's have some money-talk here. Think of idioms related to money, as many as you can. I'll go first: money talks; pick up the tab; burn a hole in your pocket; daylight robbery; a dime a dozen; foot the bill. Note down your answers here:

............................................................................................................................................... >

< By the way, money doesn't grow on trees. This is true in Australia. Paper money here does not come from trees anymore. Banknotes are made of a polymer, a type of plastic, making it waterproof and hard to counterfeit (Saiidi, 2018). >

The majority of people in Australia earn wages with their knowledge, experience and expertise to produce stable income in exchange of 8 hours of work per day. Doing a second job [≈ Doing a side job ≈ Having a side hustle] helps boost your income too. These are all active income.

You can also sell old items [≈ old stuff] on eBay for a bit of pocket money, or you could hold a garage sale [≈ a yard sale]. A smarter way though is to let your money work for you. Here are some ideas:

- Purchase shares in a clearing house and reinvest dividends into shares.
- Invest in property.
- Become a business owner by buying a franchise, a grocery shop or a café shop.
- Trade in antiques or gold.

In short [≈ To put it shortly ≈ In a nutshell], don't leave all your savings in bank accounts to just earn interest. This equates to just putting money in your piggy bank or hoarding money under your mattress.

Another way to earn money could be from gambling. But I suggest you do it just for a bit of fun. The chance of losing your hard-earned money is high, so think before you leap.

What about a lottery windfall? Well, if you're lucky enough, you could be the lottery winner, taking out $1 million or more from a Powerball draw. Though saying this, the chances of winning the lottery by picking six numbers from a pool of 49 numbers are 1 in almost 14 million (Lottery Mathematics, 2021). The odds of winning the jackpot [≈ hitting the jackpot] are 1 in 134.4 million (Australia Powerball Prizes, n.d.). You do the math.

At last, don't ever think about any kind of illegal deal! Any unethical, unearned and illegal income is a big no-no. Be it stealing [≈ being sticky-fingered], conning money from people, setting up a phoenix business, dealing in ice (or meth and cannabis), or trafficking or growing opium poppies. If you do any of this, you're going to ruin your life!

# DAY 57
## WHAT IS YOUR CURRENT FINANCIAL STATUS?

To learn how to manage money better, let's have a look at where you are financially. Complete the below survey honestly.

1. How many years have you been working?
   - ☐ 0   ☐ 1–5 years   ☐ more than 5 years
2. How much have you earned after tax deduction in Australian dollars (AUD)?
   - ☐ $0   ☐ $1–$250,000   ☐ more than $250,000
3. How much have you saved in that time?
   - ☐ $0   ☐ $1–$100,000   ☐ more than $100,000
4. Have you noticed that your hard-earned money doesn't increase with the CPI (consumer price index)?
   - ☐ Yes   ☐ No
5. What is your current financial status?
   - ☐ I live beyond my means.
   - ☐ I just have enough money to live. [≈ I scrape by. ≈ I get by.]
   - ☐ I have both active and passive income.
   - ☐ I'm a millionaire, a multi-millionaire or even a billionaire. I'm wealthy.

< For question 2 and 3, if AUD isn't your local currency, do the survey by converting your earnings and savings into AUD using the RBA (Reserve Bank of Australia) exchange rate (as of today). The below table is a list of symbols and ISO codes of some other currencies. Do you know in which countries each of the below currencies belong to? Do you know how to pronounce each of them?

| $ USD | $ CAD | $ LRD | ₽ RUB | lei RON | £ GBP | ₫ VND |
|---|---|---|---|---|---|---|
| € EUR | ₹ NPR | S/. PEN | kr NOK | ₩ KRW | R ZAR | zł PLN |
| RM MYR | د.إ AED | $ ARS | R$ BRL | $ MXN | ₺ TRY | ل.ل LBP |

>

If you've ticked the very last box above in the survey, or you're living without the worry of money, or you can retire early, you can skip to the next chapter. If you're not satisfied where you are right now, instead of complaining that your wages lag behind [≈ stall] while the cost of living accelerates year by year [≈ your wages are not keeping up with living expenses], you could read some money-management books such as *Rich Dad Poor Dad* by Robert T Kiyosaki, *The Barefoot Investor* by Scott Pape, *Why Didn't They Teach Me This in School?* by Cary Siegel or any other popular books on money. Read these sorts of books to develop your financial literacy, and start practising your money-management skills.

You will no longer be broke [≈ be skint ≈ be behind on rent ≈ be short on cash ≈ be strapped for cash ≈ be pressed for money ≈ run out of money ≈ have no money to spare]. Instead, you could become quite well-off [≈ stinking rich ≈ filthy rich ≈ loaded ≈ a moneybag ≈ a high-roller].

# DAY 58
# GROW YOUR SAVINGS

We learnt a few ways to increase your income a few days ago. But this is far from achieving financial freedom. One way to achieve financial freedom is through the following wealth-boosting formula:

Savings = Income − Debt repayments − Spending

For the majority of people, their main income source is a monthly salary. Based on [≈ As per] the formula above, the more savings, the better, right? The secret here is to master the skill to maximise your income. All you need to do is to devote your time and effort in becoming an expert [≈ a pro ≈ a wizard ≈ the very best] in your field.

Of course, you don't have to be a talented sports player or a piano player without equal [≈ who has no equal]. If you are already though, I congratulate you! You're probably super-rich already. I'm also not against becoming a dabbler in many areas: a jack-of-all-trades. But you really need to master a profession to guarantee financial income.

< A 'jack-of-all-trades' is a compliment for a versatile person who is able to do many things. The additional phrase 'master of none' was added after 'jack-of-all-trades' later on, meaning the person dabbles in too many areas, but they're not an expert in anything (Wasserman, 2019). >

The second item in the formula above is debt repayments. What will happen when all of your debts are cleared up? You can potentially save more money. The earlier you pay off your debts, the better.

Now, let's turn the formula around:

Spending = Income − Debt repayments − Savings

Keep this formula in mind. You should set up a target for saving money each month, *before* any spending. Only when you have extra money, can you start to invest and let your money work for you!

Focus on the amount of outgoing money in your daily life! The less you spend, the more savings you'll have and the more investments you can make!

# DAY 59
## TRACK SPENDING PATTERNS

To reduce your spending, you first need know where you're spending every dollar. Broadly speaking, your expenses can be categorised into *fixed expenses* and *variable expenses*. You don't have too much control over fixed items, such as your rent and utility bills. You have to pay them regularly. Variable expenses, however, are able to be controlled by you, the master of your money. Use the table below as a guide to help summarise where your money goes. List all of the last month's expenses in your notebook then complete the table for yourself.

| Category | Nature | Monthly spending item | Spending | % of total spending |
|---|---|---|---|---|
| Fixed expenses | Unavoidable | Mortgage or rent | $1650 | 55% |
| | Reducible | Utility and internet bills | $200 | 7% |
| | Reducible | Insurance | $300 | 10% |
| Variable expenses | Reducible | Eating and food | $400 | 13% |
| | Reducible | Clothes and shoes | $300 | 10% |
| | Uncontrollable | Emergency or unexpected expenses | $150 | 5% |

Insurance can seem a bit expensive. In Australia, it's best to purchase private health insurance before the age of 31. Otherwise, you'll be levied with higher tax. Owning a property means that you need home and contents insurance to protect you in case of damage or the loss of your property due to fire, flood or theft, etc. Purchasing life insurance, total and permanent disability insurance or income protection insurance makes you entitled to a payment if you're unable to work due to illness or injury. There's also trauma insurance, phone insurance, pet insurance, furniture insurance or even funeral insurance.

For unexpected things, if it happens, it happens. You can't really control it. If you accidentally lock yourself out of your home, it could cost you 150 bucks! But there's a saying in China: You lose money for something unexpected to avoid misfortune (破财消灾). So don't be too sad if you don't seem to be lucky!

I hope you've got a clear view for where your money goes. Feel free to turn the table above into a bar chart. You can even use a line chart or a clustered stacked column chart to keep track of your spending for a couple of months. This could help you reduce bad spending habits and avoid blowing money [≈ overspending ≈ splurging ≈ lashing out ≈ splashing out ≈ shelling out ≈ forking out] on unnecessary items. Keep an eye on any expenses you can reduce. Can you do something about it? You could start by having one day per month where you don't spend any money.

# DAY 60
## A PENNY SAVED IS A PENNY EARNED

A savvy way to increase your bank account balance is to behave frugally [≈ to be frugal]. Don't live month to month [≈ Don't live pay cheque to pay cheque], and don't leave yourself without a financial buffer. You can save up for a rainy day and squirrel away the money for the big-ticket items (such as houses and cars), or put some of your income away for the kids' education.

Please save money whenever possible. Here's how:

First (and foremost), when you're not economically abundant [≈ affluent], possessing luxurious [≈ high-end ≈ lavish] items is just unnecessary.

< Luxury brands include Prada, Louis Vuitton, Gucci, Cartier, Hermes, Saint Laurent, Omega, Porsche, Miu Miu, Fendi, Rolls-Royce, Givenchy, Valentino, Dolce & Gabbana, Versace, Dior, Burberry, Lamborghini and such. >

Second, don't use credit cards [≈ say goodbye to credit cards ≈ say bye-bye to credit card debt] if you can't control your overspending habits.

Third, call up your utility vendors to negotiate a better contract for a lower bill. Ask for discounts from the sales representative. This also applies to when signing up the home internet contract. Just ask!

Fourth, consider if you really need all those streaming services such as Netflix, Stan or Foxtel. Subscription fees could vary from basic $10/month to an ultimate package of $99/month. How often do you watch such paid TV?

Also, instead of buying something brand new, how about looking for a second-hand item instead? (For example, a coffee machine on eBay, a homeware from antique market, a travel suit from workmate.)

Attention, please: I'm not asking you to cut out all of your spending [≈ be overly thrifty ≈ be frugal ≈ be stingy] like a cheapskate [≈ a scrooge ≈ a penny pincher]. You *could* scrimp on food and never go out to restaurants, wear the same clothes every day, squeeze out savings and never buy gifts for friends. OMG! But you're probably not enjoying life if you're scrimping too much. It can't hurt to live a little. But be mindful. Tomorrow let's do some savvy shopping together!

# DAY 61
## SHOP SMART

I've got some strategies for shopping smart. All you need to do is stick to some of these strategies before tapping your card on the EFTPOS (electronic funds transfer at point of sale) machine.

**Wait for a while.** When you're tempted to buy [≈ have the burning desire to get] something that has just come out, like a newly released iPhone, wait for a few days (or longer) before making the final decision to buy it. Challenge yourself. Ask: do I really need it? This is to avoid spending money on unnecessary items on impulse.

**Think three times: is it worth my money?** For example, you pay $10 for a plain white T-shirt, which only lasts two or three washes. You might only wear it once and then it might stay in your closet forever. Is it worth buying in the first place? Buying clothes just because they're cheap or on sale is not the most budget-friendly way [≈ cost-effective way ≈ economical way] to be. Instead, focus on quality rather than quantity.

**Wait for holiday season sales.** Shops will eventually slash prices [≈ offer discounts] on goods [≈ Everything will eventually be on sales] around particular times of the year, such as the end of the financial year (30 June each year in Australia) or on Black Friday, Christmas or New Year's Day.

< Black Friday is the Friday following Thanksgiving. It's 'black' because the colour black is used to indicate profit, whereas red means a loss in accounting. Black Friday is a profitable day for retailers. The Monday following is called Cyber Monday, where tech products often have big sales. >

**Make a bargain.** [≈ **Haggle with vendors.**] When buying a car, a fridge or other big-ticket items, always bargain with the sales consultant [≈ sales personnel ≈ sales representative ≈ sales rep ≈ salespeople]. Say things like 'It's over my budget. [≈ It's out of budget. ≈ It's out of my price range.] What can you do for me?'

**Use coupons or promotion codes.** If you look around long enough, you might find some sort of discount coupon or promotion code for a product you're after. This gives you some bang for your buck. But spend only when you have to.

Handy tip: keep an eye on your receipts after you buy something to make sure items have been scanned correctly and you've been charged for the right amount.

Remember: a penny saved is a penny earned. So shop smart.

# DAY 62
# DEFINITION OF A RELATIONSHIP

What is a relationship? A relationship is any connection between people. Over the course of your life, you might meet [≈ encounter ≈ come across] up to 80,000 different people (Vital, 2013).

I would classify these 80,000 people into three tiers of relationships:

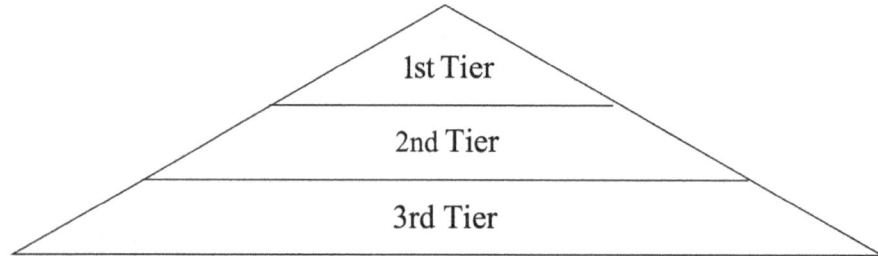

The bottom tier is superficial relationships. This includes strangers that you mingle with on the street, on public transport, at bars or clubs, while travelling overseas, in a social gathering, on an online forum… You might have exchanged [≈ swapped] contact details, but you might only meet up with them once or twice in your life.

On the second tier, you're moving into the deeper connections where you interact with people (your close friends, neighbours, co-workers, boss, etc.) on a regular basis.

Your partner, parents, grandparents, kids, grandchildren, acquaintances, and extended family members come into the first tier of the pyramid graph.

Be mindful that this pyramid is not static. Depending on the strength of your connections, and changing situations, people could move up, down, out or into the relationship pyramid. A friend could be closer to you than a brother. Your stepfather could treat you much better than your biological dad. You could lose touch with one of these people in the second tier and form a new deeper relationship with someone from the bottom tier.

In the pyramid above (or around it), write in some of the people in your life and where on the pyramid they might sit.

Esther Perel says, the quality of your life ultimately depends on the quality of your relationships. And it's the quality of your relationships, not the quantity, that matters.

< Esther Perel is a Belgian psychotherapist, New York Times bestselling author, the host of podcasts *Where Should We Begin?* and *How's Work?*. She specialises in modern relationships. She's also fluent in nine languages! >

It's true that you won't date, marry and live with even a hundred of those 80,000 people. So, in this chapter, let's explore friendships and focus on building up your closest relationships: your significant other, and your family members.

# DAY 63
# FORGE GENUINE FRIENDSHIPS

It sounds cliché: friendships are all about 'give-and-take', where you scratch their back and they'll scratch yours. But it is sometimes true.

Think about this: How many friends do you have now? How many of your friendships have drifted apart [≈ grown apart ≈ gone south ≈ gone cold ≈ gone sour]?

< 'Gone south'? Why not 'gone southeast or gone north'? One of the explanations for this phrase is that on a compass, north is *up* while south is *down*. So 'go south' means to fall, disappear or quit (Kyff, 2006). Ahh! >

When a friendship fizzles out, is it mainly because one party (or both) stopped nurturing the friendship. Or is it because they were friends you couldn't rely on in difficult times or they were only superficial or shallow friends?

That's fine. You don't have to deepen connections with everybody. You only need a couple of besties [≈ close personal friends ≈ trusted good buddies] and soulmates with whom you feel comfortable.

To nourish a deep and rewarding friendship, you need to care genuinely about them, have their best interest at heart, make progress [≈ make headway ≈ forge ahead] together, feel happy for their achievements, and just *get* them [≈ understand them].

Your firm friends will do the same for you, encourage you, bring out the best in you, share their emotions with you, and stay with you when you're in trouble, even if you've been out of touch for a while.

So, please cherish these amazing friends because they're hard to find [≈ they're true treasures]. One last reminder: if your friend gives you an apple (Fiji, Modi, Pink Lady, Golden Delicious, Jazz, Granny Smith), appreciate it. Don't question why they gave someone else two apples, or a rockmelon, dragon fruit, nashi pear, unseeded grape, nectarine, apricot or loquat. Instead, ask what you've given back to the friendship to make it closer and stronger.

# DAY 64
# MY FAMILY MEANS THE WORLD TO ME

Hi there, relationship nurturer. What does your family mean to you? Have you ever thought how much love you've got from them? Can you imagine a life without your family?

American musician and composer Peter Buffett says, 'It didn't matter how big our house was; it mattered that there was love in it.' A quote from Canadian-American actor Michael J Fox is 'Family is not an important thing. It's everything.' Novelist Sir Walter Scott also quoted 'Blood is thicker than water.'

< The idiom 'blood is thicker than water' means to hold a family bond close over everyone else [≈ means that family relationships take precedence over others ≈ means that family bonds are important]. But the original saying is 'blood of the covenant is thicker than water of the womb'. The water of womb protects a foetus when a woman is pregnant. So it actually indicates that the blood on a battlefield is stronger than family ties. We use it in a completely opposite way today (Ross, 2016). >

Do you agree with the quotes above? I do. Your family should be everything for you [≈ should be your number one ≈ should always come first]. Think about them:

- Are your mum and dad [≈ your folks] protective of you? Do they have your best interests at heart all the time? Are they willing to sacrifice everything for you?

- Has your significant other given unwavering [≈ unflagging ≈ unyielding] support no matter what?

- Are your close loved ones (parents, partner, in-laws and relatives [≈ your next of kin ≈ your nearest and dearest ≈ your immediate family members]) always there at the drop of a hat, standing by your side through thick and thin?

You won't get this sort of love from anyone else. So, become a family-oriented person! Pour your heart out for family.

< Many westerners are interested in my thoughts on the Chinese one-child policy introduced in 1979 and gradually phased out [≈ abandoned ≈ scrapped] in 2015.

I'm the only child in my family. [≈ I'm a single child.] I didn't have any siblings to play with when growing up. I did get unconditional love and attention from my parents. With the one-child policy, families who had only one child were rewarded with a certificate. But if the family gave birth to a second child, the parents would often be laid off work, which meant family income would be cut off. The policy did, however, moderate the population and lift up the poverty level. But it did cause a lot of abortions too. Is this humane or ethical? What is your opinion on this? >

# DAY 65
# FALLING IN LOVE

Have you ever fallen in love [≈ become madly in love ≈ fallen head over heels] with someone?

< 'Head over heels' is like doing a cartwheel when you're upside down. It evolved into the meaning of 'falling in love' during the 18th century (Head Over Heels, n.d.). >

How does it feel to be in love? Do you tick any of the below signs of falling in love?

| You can't get them out of your head. | Just the thought of them makes you smile. | You two hit if off [≈ clicked] straight away. |
|---|---|---|
| You can't stop staring at them. | You get fluttery feelings when you see them. | You know their favourite food. |
| You picture your future life with them. | You talk about them all the time. | You feel your life is wonderful and perfect. |
| They take your breath away. | You can't wait to introduce them to friends and family. | Their annoying quirks are attractive. |

Does that person pop into your head right now? Alright, take out your phone and let your Prince Charming or Princess Charming know that you're missing them:

'Sweet pea, I miss you. [≈ Darling, I've been thinking about you. ≈ Honey, you're on my mind all day long. ≈ Babe, I can't wait to see you again. ≈ Baby, I wish you were around now. ≈ My dear, I can't stop thinking about you.]'

< *The Bachelor* and *The Bachelorette* are reality TV shows where you can look for romantic expressions. For *The Bachelor Australia*, the host Osher helps one man to find love from over 20 candidates in a big mansion. Girls get the chance to go on a date with the Bachelor, either individually or in the group. At the end of each episode the bachelor decides who receive his roses. Candidates are eliminated one by one until there is one last candidate standing, who wins the Bachelor's heart. *The Bachelorette Australia* is the opposite, with a bachelorette picking her 'prince' from the candidates.

There's a lot of gossip and romance in the show. Most new couples break up after the show finishes filming, though. So don't take the show too seriously. But please take your romantic relationship seriously. Say those three big words out loud if you fall for someone ('I love you.'). I really hope your relationship lasts forever. >

# DAY 66
# TRUE LOVE

What does true love look like? Draw a love symbol (♥) in the checkbox down below if you agree the situation demonstrates true love.

- ☐ You love your significant other, warts and all.
- ☐ Both of you stick together, no matter what.
- ☐ You slam the door shut after an argument with them. An hour later, you're back home with their favourite snacks.
- ☐ Your significant other still gives you butterflies and makes your heart skip a beat after being married for a decade.
- ☐ When your partner sits on the toilet, and you're nearby, you don't feel disgusted.
- ☐ You do not feel embarrassed by farting [≈ breaking wind ≈ making air come out of your bowels] in front of them.

< They say love is like a fart: if you have to force it, it will become a shit at the end. Obviously, forced love is not true love. >

What can you do to maintain long-lasting love [≈ keep your romantic love story alive ≈ sustain a healthy relationship ≈ nurture a long-term relationship]?

Surprises don't need to happen just on Valentine's Day. You could:

- Book an unexpected spa for your love, or a short trip, or a fancy dinner.
- Leave her a warm note on the dining table out of the blue [≈ unexpectedly].
- Prepare a surprise gift, deep from the heart, for him.
- Drop into his lap and kiss him.

Companionship should be an everyday thing. You could:

- Cook a delicious meal together: be a head chef and a sous chef together.
- Sign up for a pottery course or a class in what interests both of you.
- Cuddle. [≈ Sit or lie down on the couch hand in hand.]
- Give each other space – this is paramount.

Commit wholeheartedly. You could:

- Be good partners who bring out the best in each other.
- Be honest with your partner. [≈ Nothing is hidden.] No cheating.
- Offer steadfast [≈ faithful] love to each other.

# DAY 67
# GETTING MARRIED

Getting married is one of the defining moments in life. In western culture, often when the girl gets married, she changes her surname into her husband's surname. We don't do this in China. Normally, in China we follow father's last name, and we could share the same surname with other people not from the family. Sometimes, when westerners notice two Chinese people have the same last name, they ask, 'Are you two from the same family?' This isn't a correct assumption. In Australia, you might have an idea about someone's marriage status by their title, as seen in the table below:

| Title | Example | Indicates |
|---|---|---|
| Master | Master Josh | A young man under the age of 18. |
| Mr | Mr Chris | An adult man. Men always uses 'Mr', no matter their marriage status. A man never needs to worry about their title. |
| Mrs | Mrs Oliver | A married woman. |
| Ms | Ms Monica | A woman who doesn't want to state whether they are married or not. |
| Miss | Miss Lily | A woman who is unmarried. Normally used for a girl in her 20s. |

< Do you have any of these kinds of people around you? Mr Forgetful, Mr Messy, Mr Sarcasm, Mrs Efficient, Mrs Nosy, Mrs Tidy, Miss Italy, Miss World, Miss Ohio. By the way, 'Mr' is short for 'Mister', 'Mrs' and 'Miss' for 'Mistress'. What about the title 'Ms'? Is it an abbreviation of 'Mistress' or nothing (a made-up word)? >

From the moment you get engaged, you'll have different roles to play (the bold words in the paragraphs below).

I'm engaged! With my man down on one knee [≈ with one knee on the ground], he put the sparkling ring on my finger and asked me, 'Will you marry me?' I said, 'YES!'

If you're getting married, plan the wedding ceremony well ahead of time because many wedding venues get booked out months or years ahead of time.

Finally, the big day has come. During the wedding ceremony, as the **bride** and **groom**, you hold hands, tie the knot, and say your vows ('till death do us part').

< In China, the tradition for guests to bring in small gifts has changed into giving money to the family. In Australia, you can use a wedding gift registry service to communicate gift preferences as a guide for your guests. >

Congratulations! You've entered the 'marriage gate'. [≈ You got hitched.] You're a **married couple**! As **newlyweds**, you'll be off honeymooning [≈ be on a honeymoon].

Later on, she is pregnant [≈ is expecting ≈ has a bun in the oven ≈ is having a baby].

Soon, you're expecting a baby. You're a **mama-to-be** and a **dada-to-be**. When your partner delivers [≈ gives the birth to] the bouncing baby, the two of you become a **mum** and **dad**.

Enjoy the love journey!

# DAY 68
## MANAGING A MARRIED LIFE

Marriage is a big commitment. It is not just about two people living under the same roof, owning a joint bank account, possessing joint property or sharing possessions like cars, furniture and appliances. (You can even share bills! Don't be surprised if you see a married couple share their bills in Australia. It's not quite a thing in China.)

It's about sharing and contributing with each other. Each party is obligated to:

- Share domestic tasks. [≈ Do their share of the household chores. ≈ Offer a hand for household duties.]

- Take care of errands [≈ Run errands]: go to the supermarket, bank or cleaner; take mail to or fetch parcels from the post office; fill the car with petrol, etc.

- Take part in childcare (feed the baby, groom them, bathe them, put them to bed, get nappies for them, button clothes for them, etc.)

- Drop your kids off at school and pick them up.

- Participate in any aged care for elderly family members.

< In Australia, if the mail is delivered to the right address, but it's not addressed to you, all you need to do is to mark 'RTS' on the envelop, and throw it back into the red Australia Post mailbox or return it to the post office. RTS stands for 'return to sender'. >

< In Australia, at fuel stations (such as Ampol, BP, Caltex, Shell, United Petroleum, etc.), you need to pump petrol yourself. In China, there's normally a service guy who works at the station and who will fuel up the car for you. >

If you are the only breadwinner at home, don't take for granted what your partner does around the house. A housewife's job, or a househusband's job, might be more 'boring' than a full-time job, but it's still a lot of work. For a stay-at-home parent, understand that your husband or wife works hard to support the family. This is not an easy job. Make sure you don't keep yourself isolated from the society. Dress yourself up [≈ Doll yourself up] and go out whenever you can.

Supporting your spouse and encouraging them is important. Appreciate your spouse's efforts for the family.

Now, say something nice to your spouse as if you are married. Write it down here:

..................................................................................................................................

..................................................................................................................................

Who doesn't want to be in a state of nuptial bliss? There is a principle: when you're happy, I'm happy!

# DAY 69
# PARENTING

What type of kids do you want to raise? A black sheep of the family, a selfish kid, a rebellious kid, a sassy [≈ disrespectful] kid, an amenable kid, a happy kid or a kid with other qualities? The truth is that no-one gets a second chance to raise a child.

How will you express your love to your kids? Should you be the 'bad cop' or the 'good cop'? Cross each of the boxes below if you agree.

Pay attention to the phrases in bold here about how to express 'in terms of...' in five different ways.

**In terms of interactions,** you impose your view on the kids [≈ brainwash your ideas onto the kids] ☐ or you listen to your kid's needs and thoughts ☐.

**In reference to your company,** you share a bond with the kids ☐ or you spend time with the kids, building blocks with them or reading books or running on the grass with them ☐. Or you sit there, playing with your mobile phone instead of with the kids ☐.

**Concerning discipline,** you disregard your kids' misbehaviour [≈ unlovable behaviour] ☐. Or you set the ground rules. They will cop it [≈ face the music] if they're in the wrong ☐.

**In regards to love,** your children are raised entirely by their grandparents because you're too busy ☐ or you spoil and coddle them, giving them whatever they want ☐. Or you're a caregiver and dote on [≈ love] them and become a role model ☐.

**Regarding expectations,** your kids have to measure up [≈ live up to ≈ meet up] to your high expectations. Jenny this, and Jenny that. Your kids are never good enough ☐ or you praise your kids for their efforts quite often – your kids are the best and you're proud of them ☐.

**When it comes to freedom,** you keep your kids in the nest [≈ swaddle your kids] ☐ or you let your kids experience everything, ups and downs – you give them more leeway to make decisions ☐.

If you disagree with any of the above modes of parenting or have your own way of bringing up your kids, please share with us any of your upbringing [≈ child rearing] skills below.

..................................................................................................................................
..................................................................................................................................
..................................................................................................................................
..................................................................................................................................

# DAY 70
## CELEBRATE LIFE WITH THE FAMILY

Today, let's brainstorm [≈ have a brain dump on] fun activities to celebrate life with your lovely family. Basically, it's spending time together, laughing with each other, telling stories, and creating happy moments.

I'll go first:

- Take photos of your life together; take road trips; take dancing lessons.
- Make videos together; make origami boats, paper planes or a thousand paper cranes; make cardboard spinners; make cookies and cupcakes.
- Play card games together; play board games; play charades; play rock, paper, scissors; play hide-and-seek; play an escape room.
- Go go-karting together; go laser-tag; go bowling; go camping; go skiing; go ice-skating; go ice curling; go paintballing; go shopping.
- Visit a farm together; visit a park; visit a museum; visit an aquarium; visit a historical site [≈ a historic interest area]; visit a zoo.
- Do exercise together; do gardening [≈ do yard work]; do magic tricks.
- Have a picnic together; have a BBQ; have a fancy dinner; have a scavenger hunt.

< *Charades* is a classic guessing game where a person acts out a word or a phrase within a selected category (movies, books, songs, food) and the rest of the group have to try to guess what it is. >

< A scavenger hunt is a game where the players hunt for things based on given clues. This might be something like 'find something squishy' or 'find something light'. >

Of course, you don't have to always use the above verbs (take, make, play, go, visit, do, have) for an activity. You can also watch movies, sing karaoke, collect leaves, feed the pelicans, bounce on a trampoline, or even brainstorm with your family what they love to do. The whole family can do this together.

Now it's your time to share your brilliant ideas with us in the blank lines below, and share your greatest joys with your family.

# DAY 71
## LET IT GO

Conflicts and fights in relationships are normal. Are the arguments and quarrelling mainly due to a miscommunication?

< 'Mis' is a prefix, modifying a word with a negative meaning. Prefixes are a group of letters that are placed in front of a word [≈ added to the beginning of a word] to change the meaning. Highlight words with the prefix 'un' on today's activity. In these cases, does it give the opposite or negative meaning for the word? >

Remove 'mis' from the boxes below. Start to communicate, understand and hear what your partner is saying.

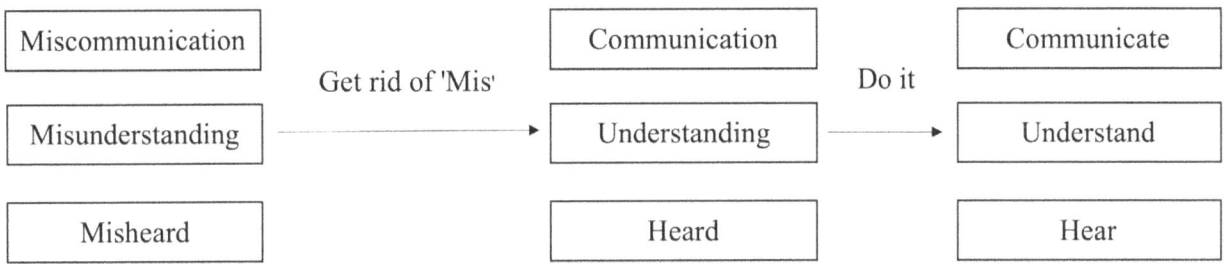

What if the two of you find that you can't make the relationship work [≈ keep it going]? Your partner is unhelpful in your life goals. Their untidy lifestyle becomes unbearable to you. Both of you just become unhappy. Unfortunately, breaking up seems the best option, though it could be the unwanted ending for the relationship. Time heals all wounds. Don't be afraid.

A while ago, my long-distance relationship didn't work out. In the end, the handsome and talented Chinese guy who I was in a relationship with changed his mind about starting a life with me in Australia. We broke up [≈ We split up ≈ Our relationship ended ≈ Our relationship was over], just like that.

It was not fine. It hurt badly. [≈ It was painful experience. ≈ It hurt like hell.] I struggled emotionally. It was heartbreaking. [≈ It was heart-wrenching. ≈ My heart sunk.]

Eventually, I moved on. I wouldn't have had so much free time to work on this book and doing other fun things if we'd stayed together. Who knows what will happen after a break-up? They say some people come into your life, teach you something and then you have to let them go. So, let go. It can be liberating.

# DAY 72
# GIVING UP ON AN UNWORTHY RELATIONSHIP

Today, I want to talk to the girls who are suffering in a relationship: chasing the guy too hard, almost like chasing after a celebrity. The guy is just not that into you.

Here are some red flags to look out for:

He never contacts you first. Whenever you text him, he can't be bothered to text you back, or it always takes him forever to get back to you. Come on. We live in the 21st century – everyone wakes up and checks their phone (across the day and before bedtime). He may say he's too busy. Hell yeah, he's too busy for you! You're never his priority. He also blows hot and cold like a flick of the switch, or he tries to change you, or he sees you only for sex. You're not in his future plans for settling down. Also, look out for [≈ be cautious about] pickup artists (abbreviated PUA) – these 'artists' (narcissists, sociopaths, manipulators) give you the impression that they're the prefect guy on the first few dates. They're actually just using various tactics to seduce you. (Tactics such as the 7-hour rule – where they spend about 7 hours with you to get you comfortable around them. They post amazing photos and videos on social media to show their interesting and charming life. They 'peacock' – where they dress in a particular fashion or manner, or adapt their behaviour to make them stand out to you and attract you to them!) They're not in a genuine sense. They flirt with other girls while in the relationship with you, or even date them. What a jackass [≈ an arsehole ≈ a bastard ≈ a scumbag ≈ a trash ≈ a garbage human ≈ a son of a bitch]! They cheat and they lie a lot. Guys, if you're not planning to form a genuine relationship with a girl, can you please not send her mixed signals?

If a guy really likes you, he'll see the beauty in you. He'll take you out for fun activities. He'll introduce you to his friends and family. He won't leave you wondering if he's into you. Stop wasting your valuable time on these guys. Trust me. He'll leave you the moment he finds someone else. Stop texting him. Refuse to pick up his call. (He probably won't initiate it, anyway.) Or just block his number. Say bye-bye to him! It's not your fault at all. It's his loss. You just haven't met the One yet. Don't be a stage five clinger!

< A 'stage five clinger' is someone who's overly attached and doesn't give up on others even though there are clear signs that they have no interest in you. >

Move on. There are plenty of fish in the sea. [≈ There are plenty more fish in the sea.]

There is someone out there who deserves you. You'll find someone who:
- Trusts you.
- Accepts and appreciates who you are.
- Treats you like a princess.
- Makes you laugh, and laughs with you.
- Shares a wonderful life with you.

There are also green flags that you can spot in a healthy relationship. What green flags should you look out for? Write some down in your notebook.

# DAY 73
# THE LEFTOVERS

☐ 3 ☐ 0 ☐ +

Hello ladies and gentlemen, please answer the below yes-or-no questions to see if you fit into today's topic.

Tick the boxes below if you answer *yes* or cross the boxes if you answer *no*:

- ☐ Are you still single at the age of 30?
- ☐ Are you a bachelor or a bachelorette?
- ☐ Are you too picky with your relationships?
- ☐ Are you being pressured to lower your standards in a partner?
- ☐ Are you wondering how to stop having the 'solo status'?
- ☐ Are you feeling it's so damn hard to find your soulmate?
- ☐ Do you find the people that you've been dating are not good enough to spend the rest of your lives with?

If most of your answers are yes to these, it doesn't mean that you have problems. There is nothing to worry about since you are not alone [≈ you are in good company]. There is nothing to be ashamed of in being single. You are not 'the leftovers'.

I didn't find my right match in my 20s. When I went back home to China, each time my relatives and friends were insistent with me: 'Next time when you come home, bring back a boyfriend.' or 'I'm so worried about you. You're not young anymore.' or 'Don't be too picky. Just any okay man will do.'

Of course, I want to settle down with the right guy. But I'm happy no matter what – no matter if I'm single, or I have the right partner. Being single gives me plenty of free time that I can use to do the things I'm passionate about. If I had my Mr Right, we could share our lives and do so many interesting things together!

Get married only when you are ready. Get married according to your own clock. To settle down with the wrong guy is worse than being single. So don't rush into a marriage or hook up with someone just because you're turning 30 and freaking out.

In western culture, 30 years old is still young. So believe in love! You'll find your one in a million [≈ one in a billion] eventually! It's worth the wait.

< One divided by a million equals to 0.000001. So one in a million means the person or the thing is rare and special. >

# DAY 74
# THE WORD - AT

Question: Where do you normally see the 'at sign' or 'commercial at', the @? I'll show you my observations **at** the end of the day. What are we going to do in-between? Let's look **at** the preposition 'at' in six bullet points:

- In Australia, wave **at** the bus when it approaches. The driver might not stop **at** the bus stop if you don't.

- I'll meet you **at** Flinders Station **at** 10 am tomorrow morning. Get back to me **at** about 5 pm tonight if the time suits you. What do 'am' and 'pm' stand for? 'Am' stands for the Latin *ante meridiem* (before midday) and 'pm' is the abbreviation of the Latin *post meridiem* (after midday) (Hiskey, 2010).

- Where are you **at** with your English studies? Don't say 'My English is poor.' Why? You'll never be good **at** English if you keep saying that. Stop apologising for your limited English, okay? No-one will even notice your 'poor' English.

- Driving **at** night-time [≈ Night driving] is dangerous. Watch out for [≈ Be cautious of] pedestrians and bicycles. Don't stare directly **at** the oncoming vehicle.

- We frown **at** office romance. [≈ Workplace romance is frowned upon. ≈ Office relationships are a taboo subject. ≈ Don't hook up with your workmates.]

- **At** Halloween, kids dress up in spooky costumes and knock one door **at** a time in the neighbourhood to 'trick-or-treat' and ask for lollies or candy! It's said that Halloween started with Samhain, an ancient Celtic festival to mark the beginning of winter. People **at** those times lit the bonfires to ward off ghosts and evil spirits.

**At** this stage, let me tell you where I see the @ sign. The @ is a symbol on my computer keyboard. Most of the time, I see it in email addresses (for example, theEnglishBuilder365@gmail.com). It's also used quite often on social media platforms to tag or call out a specific user (for example, @Jessie). Some people might still use the @ symbol for the rate of something (for example, I read books @ 1 page/day). Keep **at** this speed, please, @EnglishBuilder!

# DAY 75
# FLAT OUT LIKE A LIZARD DRINKING

In today's constantly connected world, everyone is hustling [≈ everyone seems to be on the run all the time]. Our days are jam-packed. [≈ We all have jam-packed schedules.]

Work can be full on. [≈ You are swamped with work. ≈ You are on the go for the whole day.] Emails pile up. [≈ You are inundated with emails.] Mobile phones ring constantly. [≈ The phone never stops ringing.] Your boss is demanding [≈ pushy] and bossy [≈ overbearing], giving you a mountain of work [≈ a shitload of work].

Phew! I have so much to do! [≈ There's too much to take on! ≈ I have a lot on my plate! ≈ I'm biting off more than I can chew! ≈ I have too many irons in the fire!]

< The idiom 'bite off more than you can chew' originated in America. In the 1800s, people chewed tobacco. Eventually someone might take a bigger bite than they could chew. Nowadays, it refers to someone taking on more tasks than they can handle (To Bite Off More Than You Can Chew (Origin), n.d.). >

You bury your head in work. You can't breathe and feel that you're drowning. You're snowed under at the office.

< To be 'snowed under' means that you are overwhelmed, and you have lots of things to do. You can also use the expression 'I'm as busy as a bee.' or 'I'm as busy as a beaver.' or 'I'm as busy as popcorn on a skillet.' or even to show off Australian slang: 'I've been flat out like a lizard drinking!' >

Back home, you have to cook for the family, take care of the kids, do the laundry, iron your shirts... all day long, every day. These tasks seem to be never-ending. [≈ The tasks seem to have no end. ≈ The tasks appear to be unending [≈ endless].] At the end of the day, you feel like you just finished a marathon.

# DAY 76
# FEEL YOUR OATS

One day, you just burn out. You are tired [≈ exhausted ≈ spent ≈ depleted ≈ drained out ≈ wiped out ≈ whacked ≈ frazzled ≈ buggered ≈ shagged ≈ bushed]. You are knackered! [≈ You are a complete wreck!] You drag your feet home. [≈ You're on your last legs.] You lay down [≈ crash out ≈ collapse] on the bed when you get home, feeling overwhelmed, fatigued, powerless, empty, groggy, defeated, and hopeless…

You start to wonder: how come some people are always full of energy [≈ energetic and refreshed ≈ in a great form ≈ a ball of fire ≈ a powerhouse]? Let's debunk the myth [≈ strip away the myth].

< A 'ball of fire' describes an active and dynamic person with lots of energy and enthusiasm. In the early 1900s, the phrase was used to refer to 'a glass of brandy' (Ball of Fire, n.d.). 'Great balls of fire!' is used to show surprise, similar to the use of 'Wow!' >

Here's a quick solution for the afternoon energy slump [≈ energy drain]:

- Have lunch that includes protein and carbohydrates.
- Drink plenty of water or pour yourself a cup of Joe [≈ a cup of java ≈ a cup of coffee]. Tea can also be used for a pick-me-up. But do not consume too much caffeine [≈ do not overdo the caffeine]!
- Switch off your phone and have a nap.
- Go for a 10–15 minute walk outside.

< Why does a 'cup of Joe' mean a cup of coffee? One of the theories suggests that the term originated from World War I when the secretary of the navy Josephus Daniels imposed a ban on alcohol on US navy ships. This made black coffee the strongest drink that sailors could get on the ship (Why Is Coffee Called "A Cup of Joe"?, n.d.). >

When you are stressed out, talk to the people who you trust. Also, keep company with positive people, not those who talk negatively all the time. These tips can prevent you from reaching burnout point.

Are you curious about a long-term solution to 'feeling your oats' [≈ supercharging your energy ≈ rejuvenating yourself ≈ revitalising your life]? Use your energy to work through this chapter, please. Great balls of fire!

< 'Oats' are an edible cereal. When a horse is fed oats, they become energetic and high-spirited! >

# DAY 77
# CHILL OUT

We are biological and emotional beings, not mechanical robots. We work hard and we should wind down [≈ relax] even harder!

There are heaps of ways to relax and enjoy your life.

In the bullet points below, circle any phrases that mean 'relax your body and mind':

- Go home and kick your feet up and relax.
- Sprawl out on the sofa and watch something on Netflix, Stan or other TV streaming services.
- Let loose and simply take an afternoon nap [≈ take a siesta].
- Go out jogging or play some sport to let off some steam [≈ blow off some steam].
- Take a break and travel to new places. Let your hair down. It will be a welcome respite from the pressures of life.
- Travel to a tropical island and take a laid-back holiday.
- Head to a hot spring to relieve your burnout.
- Spend money on some experiences, not possessions. But, of course, if you've been wanting to get a pricey item, say a Louis Vuitton bag, as long as it will satisfy you and you can afford it, do it. You deserve it.
- Switch off the TV. Turn off the computer. Put down your phone. [≈ Step away from technology.] Switch off for a while.
- Spend quality time with your kids and partner – mellow out [≈ relax].
- Invite friends or neighbours over for an afternoon tea to unwind [≈ turn off your mind ≈ clear your head ≈ reset your mind ≈ shut down your mind ≈ take your mind off it].
- Play video games for entertainment. It can be relaxing and stress-free.
- Lose yourself in a movie or a book. You'll be entertained and amused.
- Have some quality alone-time [≈ me-time]. This can be a great relief.

I'm not asking you to indulge yourself all the time. You need to know when to slow your life down a bit and have some fun!

Here is a proverb: 'All work and no play makes Jack a dull boy.'

< The proverb means that working without a rest [≈ without time off] is no good for a person's wellbeing. The proverb actually has the second part: 'All play and no work makes Jack a mere toy.' Does it? And why is it specifically Jack? Can I substitute any name into the person I'm addressing? >

# DAY 78
# ZEN OUT

Hush! Be quiet...

Sit in a quiet place, on a mat, or in a chair, with your back straight. Close your eyes. Breathe. [≈ Inhale and exhale. ≈ Breathe in and breathe out.] Let your breaths come and go. Do not regulate it.

Start with a body scan: feel your arms, your upper body, your legs and your feet. Ease the tension in your muscles and relax.

Now touch your soul.

- Think of nothing. When your thoughts go astray, concentrate on your breathing.

- Picture this: You are lying on the beach on a sunny day. The waves are producing beautiful music. It's just the sky, the sand, and you. Are you feeling the serenity that nature brings?

- Use your imagination. You've stepped into a secluded park or a nature trail. It's as quiet as a convent. Enjoy the tranquillity. This is an oasis of peace.

- Reflect on your day or the previous day or the past week. What happened? What was impressive? What did you learn? How did you progress?

Wait for a second. What are we doing? We are meditating.

There are numerous kinds of meditation, like Taoist emptiness, loving-kindness, qigong (气功), mindfulness, and so on. Pick a type of meditation to calm you. Free up some time to mediate on a daily basis. [≈ Allocate time daily for meditation. ≈ Squeeze out time to meditate daily. ≈ Carve out some time to meditate daily. ≈ Make time to practise meditation.] Make meditation into everyday routine.

Choose any 5-minute period in your day to do this. It could be while you're waiting for public transport, cooking, washing clothes, or even while on the toilet. Any posture will do (sitting, standing, lying, leaning, kneeling, squatting, crouching).

The whole purpose is to unwind and reboot your brain [≈ clear your mental clutter ≈ clear your mind ≈ get yourself a smiling mind].

# DAY 79
## GET UP TO EXERCISE

Let's stand up, stretch and exercise together. Here are a few things we can do:

**Planks.** Place your forearms on the ground. Position your elbows directly underneath your shoulders. Keep your feet together with only toes touching the floor. Look down at the floor. Make sure your body forms a straight line. Hold for the maximum possible time. Have a competition with your family members to see who can plank [≈ hold the plank] the longest.

**Sit-ups.** Lie on a yoga mat with your knees bent in front of you. Keep your feet flat, and place your arms by your sides. Let your partner hold your feet down. Curl slowly forward to bring your elbows to the knees and curl back down to the start position. Repeat this 30 times or more.

**Push-ups.** Find some space. Start with a plank position with your arms outstretched and your back straight. Lower yourself by bending your elbows. Keep your back straight and your core engaged. Use your hands to push back up to the starting position. Repeat as much as you can at your level of fitness.

**Chest to ground burpees.** Start in a standing position then drop to do a push-up. Stand up and jump in the air! Repeat 10 times.

**Squats.** The squat is a lower body exercise. Take a wide feet stance, a bit wider than shoulder-width apart. Put your arms in front of you [≈ Put your arms forward] for balance. Keep your chest straight. Your heads should also be up, and look straight ahead. Sit downwards as if you are about to sit in a chair. Your knees should not be more forward than your toes. Down. Up. Down. Up. Do 20 repetitions. Do three sets of these.

< The word 'squat' makes me think of 'squat toilet'. These are the most seen public toilets [≈ communal toilets] in China. Australia has mostly sitting toilets. It's funny to see that on the back of the toilet door in Australia, there are often instructions with pictures of dos and don'ts on the use of the toilet: instructions such as 'sit on the toilet during use', 'do not stand on the toilet' or 'do not squat on the toilet seat'. >

Take a break and cool down now.

There are many other exercises you can try out, such as Russian twist, flutter kicks, lunge, dead bugs, box sit ups, mountain climbers, seated knee tuck, jumping jacks, and so on.

All the above exercises each have a Guinness World Record. But you do not have to exercise to break a world record [≈ smash the world record ≈ set the world record ≈ claim a new record]. Exercise for your own benefit: keep your energy levels high [≈ keep your energy boosted]!

# DAY 80
# EAT HEALTHY

A healthy diet gives you a happy tummy, gives you fuel, and boosts your energy. So what should you eat?

Eat a rainbow! Red, orange, yellow, green, blue, indigo and violet are the colours of a rainbow. When you eat the rainbow, you eat fruits and vegetables with a spectrum of colours that are good sources of vitamins (vitamins A, B, C, D, E and K), minerals (calcium, copper, iron, potassium, sulfur, sodium, zinc, and so on) and carbohydrates, all helping to promote your energy. List three foods for each food colour in the column 'Your nominated food'.

| Food colour | My nominated food | Your nominated food |
| --- | --- | --- |
| Red | Watermelon, radish, pomegranate | |
| Orange | Pumpkin, papaya, Dutch carrot | |
| Yellow | Mango, pineapple, yellow pepper | |
| Green | Spinach, okra, snow pea | |
| Blue, purple and black | Blueberry, eggplant, plum | |
| White, tan and brown | Cauliflower, garlic, potato | |

If you are not allergic to nuts [≈ not intolerant of nuts], include a wide range of nuts in your eating plan too. Eat walnuts, pistachios, pine nuts, pecans, peanuts, macadamias, hazelnuts, chestnuts, cashews and almonds. They're nutritious and give your body energy!

Don't forget an array of [≈ an assortment of] edible seeds: chia seeds, flaxseeds, sesame seeds, hemp seeds, sunflower seeds, pumpkin seeds, poppy seeds, pomegranate seeds, psyllium husks. They are packed with nutrients and increase your energy levels!

Don't miss out on protein either: eggs, seafood and fish, poultry (turkey, chicken, duck, quail), red meat (kangaroo, veal, pork, venison, lamb, mutton, goat, beef), dairy products, and legumes (chickpeas, lentils, beans), etc.

I hope you are not a picky eater [≈ you are not particular with any food]. Eat healthy, nutritious, light or mild meals during the day to boost your energy [≈ replenish your energy]! Don't eat too much [≈ Don't stuff yourself ≈ Don't overeat ≈ Don't be too full ≈ Don't become stuffed full ≈ Don't be replete] though – this can drain your energy. It would be counterproductive!

# DAY 81
# KEEP OFF JUNK FOOD

What is junk food? Give me a definition or your understanding of the term 'junk food' below.

.................................................................................................................................

.................................................................................................................................

.................................................................................................................................

To me, junk food is any unhealthy food that contains high sugar, salt, calories or saturated fat, but is low in nutrients. Fried food, chocolates, candy bars, salty snacks, desserts, pizza, and sugary drinks are popular junk foods.

Are you eating a bag of potato chips right now? Or have some stored somewhere in your cupboard? Oops, not good. Eating junk food frequently increases the risk of obesity and chronic diseases. It also drains your energy levels [≈ zaps your energy].

Why? Let's have a look at the nutrition information from the package of Red Rock Deli® Bourbon Glazed Sticky Ribs chips. An average quantity per 100 g contains: 2050 kJ energy; 7.6 g protein; 23.7 g fat; 59.7 g carbohydrate; 5.2 g sugars; 472 mg sodium and 1540 mg potassium.

Such high amount of fat – and no fibre – slows down your digestion, which displaces energy-boosting nutrients in your body. The added sugar increases your insulin level, leading to a quick drop in blood sugar and energy. Even worse, such food or beverages make you sluggish, tired, sleepy and craving [≈ hankering] more (Clear, n.d.)!

The tricky thing is that the manufacturers have researched on the best portion of each ingredient to put into the junk food to make people salivate and want more. So the bad news is that they can be addictive, while the good news is that it's not your fault.

When you're tired and feeling like sweet treats, go for it. But don't scoff them down! Eat slowly, and only a small portion.

Of course, your best option is to steer clear of [≈ stay away from] any junk food, and use some of the methods that I've shown you (eating proteins and nutrient-packed meals, exercising or whatever way best suits you) to get your energy back. When craving unhealthy food, eat fruit instead – it can be a great snack and help to keep your energy level high!

# DAY 82
## SLEEP LIKE A BABY

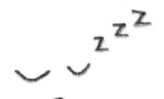

It's ten o'clock in the morning and you're yawning and drowsy [≈ sleepy]. Your eyelids are drooping. You drift off [≈ doze off ≈ fall asleep] in the meeting or in class. After a lunch break, your energy drops [≈ slumps ≈ is sapped] again. For the whole day, you are as flat as a tack [≈ you are lethargic ≈ you are listless].

< A 'tack' is a short sharp-pointed nail with a wide flat head. It's hammered in and doesn't come out above the surface. You are unenergetic when you're 'as flat as a tack' (Flat as a Tack, n.d.). >

At night, you can't sleep [≈ won't fall asleep ≈ barely sleep ≈ toss and turn ≈ are sleepless ≈ are up all night ≈ are wide awake]. Even counting sheep, or 'one Mississippi, two Mississippi, three Mississippi…' doesn't put you to sleep.

You suffer from insomnia. [≈ You are sleep-deprived.] The next day, it's a vicious cycle again. If you don't have quality sleep, how can you keep your energy high [≈ recharge your batteries ≈ keep bright-eyed and bushy-tailed] the next day? Below are two dos and four don'ts to help you with a good sleep:

- Reduce your caffeine intake. [≈ Limit your caffeine.]
- Increase your physical activity.
- Don't take your mobile phone with you to bed.
- Don't play video games after 10 pm at night.
- Don't study or check emails into the wee hours.
- Don't go to bed too late at night.

It's time to hit the sack [≈ hit the hay]. [≈ It's bedtime. ≈ Tuck into the bed.] Nighty-night! [≈ Have a good night's sleep!] I hope you sleep like a baby [≈ sleep like a log ≈ sleep like a top ≈ sleep soundly].

< Back in early 1900s, mattresses were made of a sack stuffed with hay. This is where the 'hit the sack' or 'hit the hay' idioms come from – meaning to go to bed (Smissen, 2016). >

< What about the idiom 'sleep like a log'? A 'log' is a part of trunk from a tree that has been cut down. Imagine a log on your bed, which hardly moves and stays in the same position. What about 'sleep like a top'? The use of 'top' here refers to a spinning top, which spins for a time but eventually becomes immobile. Both idioms describe a sound, restful sleep (Sleep Like a Log, n.d.). >

# DAY 83
## LIFE IS A COCKTAIL

Life is a cocktail: of romance – sweetness (when we fall in love or go out on a hot date), of excitement – fruitiness (when we graduate, get a job, get married, or have babies), of sadness – sourness (when we get laid off work or have a financial crisis), of painfulness – bitterness (when we fall ill or our loved ones leave us).

Life isn't always about the pleasant and happy stuff. [≈ Life isn't always a bed of roses. ≈ Life isn't always a bowl of cherries. ≈ Life isn't always sunshine and rainbows.]

< The idiom 'life is just a bowl of cherries' originates from the title of a song from 1931. It means that everything is just great. However, it's now used somewhat ironically (Life Is (Just) a Bowl of Cherries, n.d.). I didn't get the job, and I lost my wallet today. Life is just a bowl of cherries, right? >

Life is like a roller-coaster. [≈ Life is a roller-coaster ride. ≈ Life is full of ups and downs. ≈ Everyone has highs and lows. ≈ There are twists and turns in life. ≈ There are good times and bad times. ≈ We all experience ebbs and flows in our life.]

< When riding a roller-coaster at the amusement park, why don't you fall out when you are upside down? Physics can explain. In short, it is the inertia that keeps you from falling off at the top of the loop. The pushing force is stronger than gravity that pulls you towards the earth. Well, physics and the safety bars. >

In this chapter, I'll show you how to become mentally strong [≈ become mentally tough ≈ be strong-minded ≈ build mental toughness] so you can power through when life gets your down [≈ knocks you around] in three situations: Situation A (when you're having a hard time); Situation B (when you get turned down again and again); Situation C (when you're struggling with something going on in your life).

In the graph (right), the x-axis represents your lifetime. The y-axis symbolises your ups and downs. The wave line indicates your life experiences. Now mark the situations A, B and C for the abovementioned situations on the line: where would you be? Also, think of three events or scenarios where you feel up in the world, or feel on top of the world. Mark these as D, E and F on the graph accordingly.

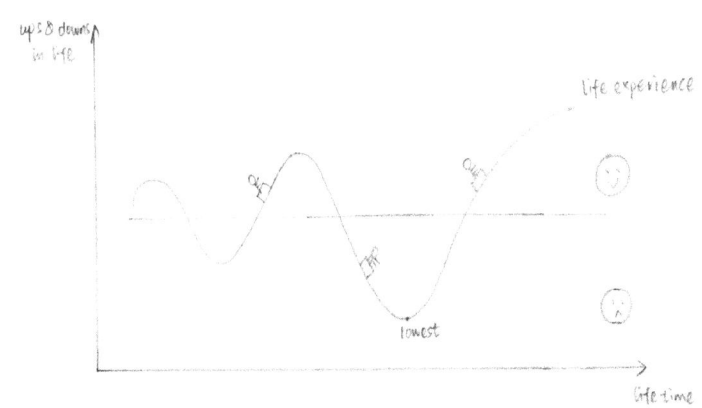

Before you go, have a think on other metaphors about life. I would say life is like a box of chocolates; life is like a cup of coffee; life is like a camera; life is like the ocean; life is like riding a bicycle. Can you imagine why?

# DAY 84
# IN YOUR DOWNTIME

Like we said yesterday, life sometimes throws us a curve ball. It's harsh sometimes. Everyone at some stage will hit rock bottom. This is the Situation A that you marked yesterday.

Have you ever experienced a dark time [≈ a tough time] in your life? Such a period of time is where everything in your life seems to be falling apart: a setback in your studies, a career failure, a broken marriage – you just felt like you lost everything. Reality bites. [≈ Reality slaps. ≈ Reality is harsh. ≈ Adversity strikes. ≈ This is what life has thrown at you.] Your life 'punches' you in the mouth. It hits so damn hard. You feel hopeless, questioning why all this has happened? Your universe collapses inwards, and you just want to hide from the world…

I hear you.

We all have those times. And if it hasn't yet, one day it will.

But here's what you shouldn't do when you're at an all-time low:

- Don't hide. Come on. It's not the end of the world. Even if it is, you get to see what it looks like. Maybe a new world can be created out of this.
- Don't feel depressed. This is already the lowest point. You won't be worse off.

What should you do then?

- Take the frown off your face. All difficulties, hurdles, obstacles, and roadblocks that life throws at you are temporary [≈ short-lived ≈ not permanent]. They do not last. [≈ They will pass.]
- Put your head up. Roll up your sleeves. Do whatever you can do to improve the situation. Move forward and upward.

Believe me, you will survive. You will get through. [≈ It will pass.] A better life is waiting for you. [≈ A better life is on the way.] Your life will fall into place. The sun will come up tomorrow.

Tomorrow, I'll show you how to stay positive [≈ have a positive frame of mind] and adopt a forward-looking approach.

# DAY 85
# STAY POSITIVE

Dear life-troopers, what do you see in picture below?

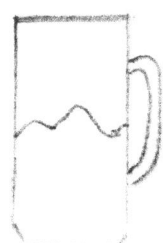

Do you see the glass half empty? Are you the glass half-empty kind of person? Why is the glass not full? Hey, don't be gloomy and pessimistic. Remove those negative thoughts. [≈ Shake off the negativities.]

Or do you see the glass half full? Are you the glass half-full kind of person? Hey, I have half a glass of water and half a glass of air! How cool is that? It's better than nothing!

Or is it orange juice to improve your vitamin C level, full-cream milk for your bone health, a cocktail for your romantic date, or iced coffee to quench your thirsty?

You can think ahead with the big picture in mind: I'm confident that I'll fill the glass one day. What if I change it into a bigger glass, and fill it with whatever drinks I love? I could change the glass into a wine glass, a goblet, a Pilsner, a Weizen, a snifter, a tumbler, or a mug, a teacup, a plastic water bottle, a stainless-steel flask – and not just one glass. I'll make it two, three or more – there are so many possibilities!

Good on ya! See, there are unlimited possibilities, depending on how you'd like to see that 'glass' of 'water'. Tunnel vision will only give you half a glass of water. Take a holistic and long-term view. Apply a positive attitude to your life.

If you stumble on the negatives: I failed exam. I was laid off. I'm dirt poor… Remember, it's all just temporary. Look ahead, move onwards and upwards. When life gives you lemons, a real trooper makes them into lemonade, lemon tart, lemon cake, lemon chicken chow mein…

< The phrase 'when life gives you lemons, make lemonade' is used to encourage optimism. Grace Helbig says, 'When life gives you lemons, take them, cause hey, free lemons!' Davin Turney says, 'When life gives you lemons, sell them and buy a pineapple.' What do you want to do with these free lemons? >

# DAY 86
# KEEP KNOCKING

If you knock on a door, you might have the door slammed in your face. SAD. No-one wants to be rejected. It's indeed upsetting and uncomfortable. What would you do in Situation B in the Day 83's graph, my dear life-trooper?

SMILE. Say, 'Thank you, next!'

You knock on the door again. Even worse. No-one will listen to you. No-one is interested in what you're selling. They even yell at you! It hurts. You are crying! Remember: not all customers need your product and service.

SMILE. Say 'I'm sorry. It's your loss. Bye!'

Keep knocking. Keep going. You finally make your first deal! BIG SMILE. Yay!

Your potential clients might turn their nose up at the product you're pitching. You might get turned down by a job interview or turned down by a girl after a proposal. Don't take it to heart. [≈ Be light-hearted. ≈ Be carefree.]

Do not despair [≈ Do not give up hope] after a knock-back [≈ rejection]. Find out why and move forward. Sometimes it's not because you're not good enough. Sometimes it might be one of the following:

- Your potential client was having cashflow issues.
- The company was shrinking anyway and there were no job opportunities at all. The job position wasn't real, and the company conducted interviews only for branding and advertising purposes. No wonder you didn't get that job offer.
- The girl wasn't ready to get married and have kids just yet.

So don't blame yourself or feel unvalued. Appreciate that such experiences help you to become thick-skinned. With your resilient nature, you will bounce back stronger, ending up with something even better. SMILE.

< The use of 'thick skin' originally referred to thick rinds of fruits and vegetables. A 'thick-skinned person' developed initially into a stupid person before referring to someone who's not easily hurt by the comments of others, or by criticism. The opposite idiom is a 'thin-skinned person' (Kelly, 2016). >

# DAY 87
# HANG IN THERE

Life continues. You find yourself moving to Situation C on the graph from Day 83. Now you're struggling, being diagnosed with diabetes, experiencing parents' divorce, struggling to make ends meet, or getting stuck in your English studies. Maybe it's all of this at once.

You get stressed out. [≈ You become overly stressed. ≈ You're under huge pressure. ≈ You're under a truckload [≈ boatload] of pressure.] Now you're just exhausted.

Whatever the case, don't play the victim card 'Why me?' It doesn't help at all. I understand it's so damn hard when you're in a jam [≈ in a pickle ≈ in a difficult situation], and no-one can possibly understand the pain that you're going through.

But promise me this: hold up your head. Hang in there [≈ Hold on], okay? Hanging in there doesn't mean literally hanging there and taking no action. Hanging in there means to not stop or not to go backwards.

Take a breath. Take it easy. Take a rest.

< Hey, if you just can't breathe under the suffocating pressure, I suggest you go to a smash room or stress release break room where you can break stuff to relieve pressure! Such places exist! Or do something gentle, such as colouring, doodling, squeezing a squishy ball or fidgeting with a fidget cube or fidget spinner. >

Don't quit yet. Face it. You can cope with it [≈ deal with it]. Believe every cloud has a silver lining [≈ there is a light at the end of the tunnel ≈ there will be a glimmer of hope and an end to the suffering]. Be mentally strong. [≈ Be mentally tough. ≈ Make yourself strong.]

Use your struggles as fuel. Convert skyrocketing pressure into motivation. Push yourself to your limit. [≈ Push shit uphill.] Henry Kissinger said, 'A diamond is a chunk of coal that did well under pressure.' You're unbeatable. You're unbreakable.

Before you go today, please write down three similar expressions to 'Make yourself strong' on the lines provided. Refer back to **Day 83 Life Is a Cocktail** and find answers if you're stuck.

≈ ...........................................................
≈ ...........................................................
≈ ...........................................................

# DAY 88
## DON'T INDULGE VICES

Whatever you're struggling with right now, don't try to alleviate it or release your pain by drinking excessive alcohol [≈ drinking like a fish], smoking heavily or binge eating. I'll explain why.

< The phrase 'drinking like a fish' means that a person has consumed too much alcohol. Does a fish technically drink water? >

When you're drunk [≈ smashed ≈ blitzed ≈ tipsy ≈ hammered ≈ wiped out ≈ sozzled ≈ intoxicated ≈ in a stupor], your speech is slurred; your head is spinning; you can't walk straight; you can barely stand up. In time, it's possible that you end up in a coma or you could even die because of heavy drinking [≈ boozing].

Sober up! [≈ Wake up!] If you become an alcoholic [≈ a boozer ≈ a boozy person], you'll have to visit a detox treatment centre [≈ rehab], and you have to become mentally strong to quit the bad drinking habit.

Smoking or vaping for some people is stress-relieving. Unfortunately, it is just short-term relief. In fact, nicotine in cigarettes increases your heart rate and blood pressure. It causes more stress and anxiety, and even mental health problems in the long term. In Australia, one packet of 20 cigarettes could cost you $40. How expensive! Once you've become addictive, it could cost you a fortune a year! Do the math.

Do you also tend to crave eating more when you're stressed? Emotional eaters or eating too much can lead to weight gain, obesity and increased risk of heart disease and even diabetes. Do you really want all these harmful impacts? Probably not!

So is it worth drinking, smoking or overeating to escape from reality? They won't resolve any of your problems in the end. They could even worsen your health and cost you money!

At the end of the day, you have to build up your mental strength and resilience, brace yourself for the storm, and move on from there. I'll show you how tomorrow!

# DAY 89
## THINK LIKE A MARATHON ATHLETE

Have you ever run a long-distance race like a half marathon, a marathon or an ultramarathon? Did you finish the race? Did you have a moment that you really wanted to give up? How did you overcome the difficulties?

< The length of a full marathon is 42.195 kilometres (26.2 miles). An ultramarathon is any run that exceeds the full marathon distance. It could be 80–160 kilometres (50–100 miles) long, or even longer. >

You could consider that life is actually a marathon that you run against, but for yourself only. It's not a 50-metre sprint.

Here are a few tips to give yourself a marathon athlete's mindset:

- Completing a 42-kilometre run or more in one go would be terrifying. Break down the race kilometre by kilometre.
- Stick with raw [≈ steely ≈ ferocious ≈ unblinking ≈ obstinate] determination [≈ grit]. Stick it out till the end.
- Think three words: endurance, persistence, and perseverance [≈ stick-to-itiveness].

Just hang in there when things are tough. You might need an indomitable spirit [≈ an iron will ≈ perseverance ≈ tenacity ≈ fortitude ≈ stamina] to smile and appreciate all the tough experiences. The below picture shows why you should continue on in your life marathon.

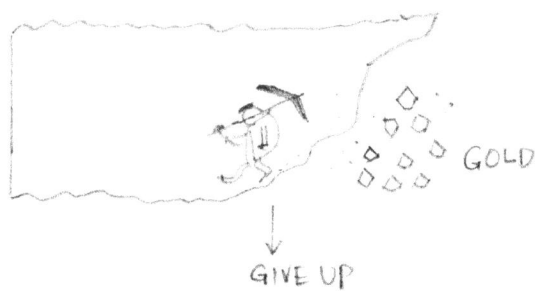

My conclusion is that you should finish the race. Don't leave things unfinished. [≈ Don't leave things half-done or undone. ≈ Don't leave things halfway. ≈ Don't go unfinished. ≈ Don't do things by halves. ≈ Don't give up the ship.] If you recall the graph from Day 83, the x-axis represents your lifetime. You can only go forward. So look forward. Go forward. Prove to me that you're an amazing and uncompromising trouper!

< A 'trouper' (sometimes 'trooper') is someone who works hard and keeps trying, even when the situation is difficult. They're as tough as nails! >

CHAPTER 11 - A Happy Person

# DAY 90
# KEEP YOUR SOUL HAPPY

Smile and laugh each and every day. Each day passes you by regardless of your mood. So why not live with happiness on a daily basis?

How would you express yourself when you are in a happy mood?

I'm happy. [≈ I'm super happy. ≈ I'm blissfully happy. ≈ I'm extremely happy. ≈ I just couldn't be happier. ≈ I'm very pleased. ≈ I'm delighted. ≈ I'm stoked. ≈ I'm rapt. ≈ I'm elated. ≈ I'm thrilled. ≈ I'm excited. ≈ I'm pumped. ≈ I'm gratified. ≈ I'm ecstatic. ≈ I'm hyped. ≈ I'm chuffed.]

In addition, there are expressions like 'I'm as happy as Larry.' or 'I'm as happy as a clam.' or 'I'm as happy as a lark.'

< Psst! Who was 'Larry'? One of the suggested origins of this phrase could be Larry Foley, an Australian boxer in the 1890s. He was undefeated and won $150,000 in a big fight. A New Zealand newspaper reported 'Happy as Larry' as the headline of the article. Larry's story became well known, and soon people started to use the phrase when they were overjoyed (Payton, 2015). >

< Why are clams happy? The full version is 'I'm as happy as a clam at high tide.' Why is that? Hmm. Clams are easily seen at low tide. When the water is high, they are supposedly happy because they are less likely to be caught and eaten (Hersh, 2012). >

< How happy is a lark? A lark is a type of brown bird. If you listen to their song, it is pleasant and melodious. >

You can also say, 'I'm walking on the moon. [≈ I'm over the moon. ≈ I'm on cloud nine. ≈ I'm in seventh heaven. ≈ I'm over the rainbow. ≈ I'm on top of the world.]'

Wow, happy days! I simply can't wipe [≈ take] the smile off my face. That's terrific! Keep that gorgeous smile on your face. In this chapter, I'll give you eight 'magic wands' to help you gain true happiness.

# DAY 91
# PRACTISE GRATITUDE

Be happier Magic Wand #1: be genuinely grateful each day. This can increase your wellbeing and self-satisfaction.

Now let's take stock of what you've got. What are you happy about in your life? Using the blank lines below, write down two things that make you happy. Some examples are:

- I'm alive.
- I'm fit and healthy. [≈ I'm in near perfect health.]
- I have a roof over my head. [≈ I have somewhere to live.]
- I have food and water.
- I have a happy family.
- I have two lovely kids and a husband who loves me.
- I have a decent job. I have money in the bank.
- I'm confident and attractive.
- My business is successful.
- 
- 

Dear readers, have you noticed the above sentences all start with subject 'I' or 'My'? Are there any other sentence starters that we can use? Write any down you can think of in the lines below. Here are some examples:

- A fancy car, a nice house and a beautiful girl are what I have now.
- What I really appreciate is that my work is close to home.
- Living in a peaceful world, without war or pandemics, is the best thing.
- 
- 

Live your life with gratitude, meaning be grateful for whatever you've got. Learn to appreciate everything on a daily basis. Appreciate [≈ Be appreciative of] what you have right now, be it money, health, family or career. Check out what you have, not things that others possess but you haven't got. If something is meant to be yours, you'll get it sooner or later. Accept everything that life has to offer.

Say it loud out: I'm grateful for what I have. [≈ I'm thankful for what I have.] How are you feeling right now?

CHAPTER 11 - A Happy Person

# DAY 92
# SAY THANK YOU

*Thank you ♡*

Becoming a happy person Magic Wand #2: show your appreciation for others **often**. I'm not asking you to give your thanks **every second**, **once a minute** or **hourly**.

Here are my suggestions:

Share your thanks with whoever helps you – do this **daily**. Say 'Thanks for your help. [≈ Thanks a bunch. ≈ Thanks heaps. ≈ Thanks a ton. ≈ I can't thank you enough. ≈ Thank you for your kindness. ≈ Thank you so much. ≈ I truly appreciate your help. ≈ Much appreciated.]'

Say 'I owe you one. [≈ I owe you a big one. ≈ I owe you big time. ≈ I am in your debt.]' Return the favour in the future when you can.

If you received a present from your friend or workmate, let them know that you are really happy, by saying, 'Thanks for your gift. It's a nice gesture. I love it! You've made my day!' or 'Wow, thank you! That's beautiful. How kind of you! [≈ You are very kind! ≈ That's very kind of you!] You shouldn't have! [≈ You didn't have to!]'

Leave a note for your partner on your dining table **weekly**. Be specific on what you appreciate them for: 'My darling, thank you for cooking for me and doing dishes for the whole week. A hearty thank you.'

Write a thank you card to your parents **monthly**: 'Mum and Dad, everything I've got is from you, including my life. Thank you for raising me. I can't repay the debt. [≈ I am deeply indebted to you.] It's beyond measure. I love you, Mum and Dad.'

You might have noticed some bold words in today's activity are adverbs that express definite frequency. You don't have to say thank you to the people around you **fortnightly**, **quarterly** or **yearly** [≈ **annually** ≈ **once a year**]. The frequency of sharing your *thank you* should be indefinite: **always**, **frequently** or **regularly**, but not **occasionally**, **rarely** [≈ **once in a blue moon**], **infrequently**, or **never**.

Hey, if the book has inspired you, you can simply thank me later!

# DAY 93
## SPREAD YOUR KINDNESS TO THE PLANET

Living a happier life Magic Wand #3: appreciate the little things that the environment provides for you. This could be the heat and light from the sun, the air we breathe, the water we drink, the food we eat, the medicine we use, the materials for our homes, the fuels for our transportation… Don't take it for granted. Give back to the planet.

Let us brainstorm little but inspiring ways that we can do to make our Mother Earth great. Put down your acts of kindness on the blank lines in the table below.

| Purpose | Kind action |
|---|---|
| Protect forests | <ul><li>Print double-sided pages, or even go paperless.</li><li>Buy second-hand books.</li><li>Stop junk mail or cancel unnecessary mail posted to your home.</li><li>..........</li></ul> |
| Save water | <ul><li>Use a washing machine and dishwashing machine.</li><li>Water plants using washed rice water.</li><li>Turn off [≈ Shut off] the running tap after use.</li><li>..........</li></ul> |
| Help animals | <ul><li>Find a home for a street dog [≈ a stray dog].</li><li>Go vegetarian or vegan. [≈ Go meatless. ≈ Eat plant-based food.]</li><li>Do not wear fur or leather.</li><li>..........</li></ul> |
| Reduce environmental pollution | <ul><li>Abandon plastic bags. Use reusable/cloth bags.</li><li>Use public transport [≈ Drive less] if possible.</li><li>Pick up pieces of trash on street and toss them in the bin.</li><li>..........</li></ul> |
| Conserve energy | <ul><li>Install solar panels.</li><li>Use LED down-lights (10 watt ≈ 830 Lumens) and ditch halogen bulbs (53 watt ≈ 800 Lumens). (The wattage to lumens conversion is a rough estimate and it varies by manufacturer.)</li><li>Turn the lights off [≈ Flick off the lights] if you don't need them.</li><li>..........</li></ul> |
| Avoid food waste | <ul><li>Cook just the right amount for each meal. Avoid leftovers.</li><li>Take any unfinished food from the restaurant back home.</li><li>Turn rotten bananas into banana cakes or smoothies.</li><li>..........</li></ul> |

Your gesture of kindness will make a huge difference [≈ a stark difference ≈ a noticeable difference] to the natural world. In return, we feel happiness from doing good. What else would you like to do to change the world?

# DAY 94
# HAVE A HEART OF GOLD

Making your life happier Magic Wand #4: become a good-hearted, thoughtful, kind, amicable person. Be selfless and generous. Have a big heart. [≈ Have a warm heart. ≈ Have a kind heart.]

How do you achieve this? Here are a few things:

- Share love with your family, friends, workmates and the people around you.
- Share with others your wisdom, knowledge and experience in a genuine sense.
- Give away your money. Be philanthropic.
- Donate [≈ Hand out ≈ Give away] your clothes, books, toys and other unwanted stuff to those who are in need. Give these items a second life.
- Do something charitable or volunteer.
- Buy breakfast for someone who is homeless [≈ rough sleepers ≈ people sleeping rough].
- Say thank you to the driver when you get off the bus. Most bus riders in Australia do this.
- Keep a big smile on your face. The people around you will throw back a smile your way! Smiles are contagious.
- Give someone a sincere compliment to brighten their day.
- If you hold a grudge against somebody or have a chip on your shoulders, learn to forgive. Bury the hatchet.

< In Melbourne, there are lots of ways to donate. Clothes donation bins are dotted around train stations and shopping centres. You can also drop off your pre-loved goods over the counter at the Salvation Army Stores [≈ Salvos Store], Red Cross shops or other donating stations. You can even book online and arrange a pickup at your address. >

< In recent years in China, no-one has been willing to help the elderly when they fall over in the middle of the road. How weird? Do bystanders turn a blind eye? Are they heartless? Maybe not. There have been cases where a passer-by lent a hand and then later on was framed by the elderly person and their family. Some people even pretended to fall on the floor to get compensation from whoever helped them up! How tricky! What would you do if you were just passing by a situation like this in China? In Australia, based on my observation, if you don't offer a helping hand, it would be un-Australian of you. >

Give willingly. By giving away in an authentic and genuine manner, this will make others happy and warm. It will increase your happiness levels too.

# DAY 95
## STOP COMPARING YOURSELF TO OTHERS

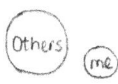

To be incredibly happy Magic Wand #5: don't compare yourself with others.

As human beings, we tend to compare ourselves a lot. Have you ever had feelings of sadness or jealousy after checking your social media posts? You might think something like:

- Dahlia's got everything I could want in her life. I envy what she's got.
- I am envious of Katie's career achievements.
- I am green with envy that Johanna travels around the world all the time.
- I get a jitter of jealousy when I see how much Kyra enjoys her life.
- Gosh, Jaylene is gorgeous! I'm so jealous!

Sometimes these people with their shiny lives – their Facebook posts or Instagram feeds – make you feel inferior, inadequate, and less confident about your life. This comparison with others steals your joy [≈ steals your happiness ≈ leads to unhappiness ≈ is the thief of joy].

You shouldn't compare yourself unfavourably to others at all! Why? People use social media to flaunt the best side of their life, showing off their artwork, their wealth or their relationships. You are comparing their strengths with your weaknesses. We are all unique in our own way. Our genes are unique. The environment we were raised in, and our experiences growing up, all differ. Everyone has their own problem [≈ conundrum]. You are not worse off than anyone else.

Another thought: change your mindset. Instead of being unhappy for the success of others, ask yourself: what can I do to achieve the same result?

What you didn't see is that Katie has spent an hour each night working on her qualification over the last 2 years while you spent that time watching TV dramas or flicking through TikTok videos. Jaylene looks attractive because she has a passion in fashion. She's been working hard in this field since she was young. The point is not to ask why you can't have this or that. Question whether you can better yourself.

If you just can't stop comparing yourself to others, delete your social media profile. You can live without it.

CHAPTER 11 - A Happy Person

# DAY 96
## STOP COMPARING

To be incredibly happy Magic Wand #6: end comparisons with others right now.

You might argue that comparing yourself with those who are 'inferior' to you actually gives you a weird happy feeling.

Do you think something like any of the following?

- I'm doing better than Charlie in every aspect of life.
- Joseph's not as good a swimmer as I am. He's not even close.
- My CV puts Melody's CV in the shade.
- My exam results were far better than Ross's results.

< Here is another tricky way to express that something is better, taller, shorter… Ryan outjumped a kangaroo. Women often outlive their husbands. Overseas sales outstrip the domestic market. In Australia, sheep outnumber people. Do you find a pattern in these sentences here? >

This comparison seems to boost your self-esteem, making you feel better about yourself. Again, it's an unfair comparison. You are comparing apples and bananas [≈ comparing apples and oranges ≈ comparing apples and pears ≈ comparing chalk and cheese]. Remember, everybody is different. It makes no sense [≈ It is pointless] to compare your 'strength' against the 'weakness' of others.

< What is the difference between apples and oranges? Well, apples could be red, yellow, pink or green in skin with white or red flesh while oranges are orange inside and outside. Apples tend to be crisp, but oranges are juicer. So when comparing apples to oranges, you are comparing two different things (or people) that are incomparable. >

Really, just who do you think you are? Such happiness from comparison to others is just short-term. Sooner or later you'll start comparing who is performing better than you. You'll even realise that a robot can outsmart you when playing chess. This will deprive your joy.

I suggest you compare apples to apples only – yesterday's self to today's self. Start to appreciate the beauty of the differences between yourself and others. You will end up happier.

# DAY 97
# LEAVE TOXIC FRIENDS BEHIND

To become a happier person Magic Wand #7: distance [≈ free ≈ disconnect] yourself from toxic friends. You don't need such negative people in your life.

What exactly is a toxic friend, you ask? They might be someone like the below:

- They are naysayers or joy-killers who affect your enthusiasm.
- They are pessimists who project their negative mood onto you and bring down your mood.
- They are control freaks or manipulators who pressure you to change or do what they want you to do while acting as though [≈ as if] they are always right and superior.
- They are slanderers who badmouth you when your back is turned [≈ talk behind your back]! Their words are hurtful. They backstab you [≈ stab you in the back] and even rat you out.

If you stay friends with these rubbish people, you'll start to doubt yourself and your capabilities, and you end up being unhappy and not confident about yourself at all.

The first thing to do to bring back your happiness: identify these bad, fake [≈ unreal], destructive friends. Don't be overwhelmed by how negative they are and their snide [≈ unkind] comments. [≈ Don't let their opinions hold you back. ≈ Don't let yourself get dragged into their comments. ≈ Don't care what other people think about you.]

Stop worrying about what they think. Ignore them. What they think of you doesn't matter. You don't need to live up to their expectations. Likewise, don't be judgemental [≈ judgey] and censorious to others. Don't deny others their own enthusiasm.

The second thing to do is this: don't let the nasty people win. Ditch them. [≈ Lose them. ≈ Cut them loose. ≈ Cut ties with them. ≈ Discontinue your relationship with them.] No-one has the right to put you down [≈ bring you down ≈ drag you down ≈ dull your sparkle]. Keep them away. [≈ Keep them at your arm's length.]

It's thought that you are the average of the five people you spend the most time with. So surround yourself with friends who make you truly happy.

# DAY 98
## LOWER EXPECTATIONS

The last but not least Magic Wand #8 for happiness that I'd like to share with you is to expect less from yourself and others.

Think about this. You dreamed of studying at Harvard University and worked extremely hard to get the admission offer. Or you assumed the job promotion should be given to you since all the signs were pointing to it being yours. You were planning the big wedding date with the most beautiful woman in the world (in your eyes). Or you thought the handsome and mature man was your forever love.

In the end, Harvard did not accept you; the promotion went to your workmate who was less experienced; your partner left you out of nowhere. Would you be disappointed and anxious, and left questioning why you couldn't get what you wanted through all that effort? The problem here is that your high expectations led to [≈ were a recipe for] disappointment and anxiety, robbing you of happiness. So, what should you do to be a happy little elf?

Set yourself high expectations. [≈ Set yourself gold standards.] Exhibit the best of yourself in whatever you do. At the same time [≈ In the same breath ≈ Concurrently], sometimes you can lower your expectations on outcomes. Or don't set the bar for the final result at all. As long as you've worked your utmost, whatever the end results are, you will be happy. When God closes one door, he opens a window. So simply enjoy the journey along the way.

Don't expect too much from others. For example, don't expect your partner to be 100% perfect all the time. They might not be able to be career-driven *and* have plenty of time with you *and* do all housework chores all at the same time. So if your husband does the gardening, you should be happy and appreciate the effort. If you start to complain: 'Why can't you help out washing, cooking and other housework chores?' he will probably never live up to your high expectations. Your endless complaints to your husband might result in a fight, which makes you even more disappointed with him arguing about doing housework chores.

Keep in mind: All eight magic wands won't function if you don't choose to be happy or let the behaviours of others control your happiness. You are responsible for your own happiness – no-one else is. Relax. Keep your soul happy!

# DAY 99
# THE WORD - OUT

**Hear** me **out**! We're going to **check out** two things today, using lots of 'out' words.

First, **check out** the below statements. These are 'do' or 'don't' instructions. **Cross out** or **strike out** any checkbox if it's something that you shouldn't do.

- ☐ Don't commit crime. You can't **break out of** prison like in the movies. You'll have a difficult life after you **get out of** jail.
- ☐ Give your stomach a break and **flush out** the toxins from your body.
- ☐ Go home and **clear out** your closet. You'll feel delighted afterwards.
- ☐ If you behave yourself, you will **stay out of** trouble.
- ☐ **Keep out of** any area where you spot a No Trespassing **Keep Out** Sign. It's normally the private property that you're not allowed to enter.
- ☐ **Wait out** the difficulties. Things will always **balance out** in the end.
- ☐ **Map out** [≈ **Chart out**] your future. Act on this plan. You will eventually **live out** your dreams.

Secondly, **check out** what happened to me in just one day:

- I **jumped out of** bed. [≈ I **sprung out of** bed. ≈ I **got out of** bed.] The house was **out of power**. [≈ The house was bathed in darkness. ≈ The house was pitch black. ≈ There was a blackout.] There was a power outage.

- While I was **heading out** [≈ **going out**], I found I had **worn out** my shirt. I **whipped out** the wallet, and I couldn't find my credit card to pay for my coffee. I then **locked** myself **out of** the car!

- I **sent out** an email to my friends. A few of the email addresses were **out of date** [≈ no longer valid].

- My boss promised me a salary rise, but he eventually **chickened out** [≈ didn't do what he had promised].

- I **ran out of** toilet paper. The supermarket had also **run out of** stock!

- I had an important call to make but my phone was dead [≈ the battery was **out** ≈ the battery was flat ≈ the battery had **gone out**]. I accidentally stomped on it and it was **out of shape**!

- The Christmas party that I hosted **got out of the hand** [≈ got out of control].

How can I **get out of** these situations? **Pour out** your thoughts here, and **help** me **out** [≈ **figure** it **out** for me ≈ **sort** it **out** for me ≈ **work** it **out** for me], please.

Anyway, see you tomorrow! Don't **miss out** on the rest of the book.

# DAY 100
# IDIOMS ABOUT BODY PARTS

English Builders, I'm happy to see that you're still in business. Are your ears burning? We were just talking about you. Please pay heed [≈ pay attention] to some fun idioms from head to toe today because knowing these phrases might give you a head start [≈ give you an advantage].

I want to tell you a story about two girls, Trina and me. We grew up together. We shared our tooth fairy stories. Both of us loved snapping our fingers, knowing it was not elegant for girls.

< The 'tooth fairy' is an urban myth told to children. When a child's baby teeth fall out, the tooth fairy is said to leave a gift under the child's pillow in exchange for the tooth. >

Our school held a public speaking competition at my dad's office building where it had ample elbow room [≈ a room that's not too crowded]. It was in our neck of the woods [≈ close to where we lived]. I didn't know how my audience would respond to my prepared speaking notes, so I played it by ear [≈ did it off the cuff ≈ improvised] while making my speech. There wasn't a dry eye [≈ People were emotional and crying] in the room during my speech. Trina and myself were toe-to-toe [≈ competing against each other], but I won in the end.

Ever since then, Trina stopped talking to me. She was good at studying at almost everything, but she started to look down her nose at me [≈ think she's better than me]. She put her foot in her mouth [≈ said things that were embarrassing] and shot her mouth off [≈ boasted too much].

She had changed. She didn't even bother to say sorry when she stepped on my toes. She gave me the cold shoulder, and this made my blood boil. I gritted my teeth. [≈ I was angry.] I didn't like her much anymore. I kept on my toes [≈ I was alert] about how she would act against me. Trina moved out of the city with her family that year. Looking back, how silly we were! I haven't seen her decades. I hope she's alright.

When we caught up earlier this year, we apologised to each other and laughed at our childish behaviour! She was a sight for sore eyes. [≈ I was very pleased to see her again.]

Fantastic! We've completed the first 100 days of English (house) building. What is your rating for the book so far? Is it a treasure or just rubbish? I'm all ears. [≈ I'm listening fully.] Hopefully it's helping with your English.

# DAY 101
## CHECK YOUR EMOTIONAL TEMPERATURE

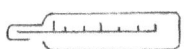

What are you feeling right now? Broadly speaking, anger, disgust, fear, sadness and happiness are considered the main five emotion categories. Let's test your emotional temperature today. Ready?

Let's assume your normal emotional temperature averages around 37°C (98.6°F), the same with your body temperature.

< 'C' stands for Celsius and 'F' stands for Fahrenheit. To convert temperatures from Celsius to Fahrenheit quickly, multiply °C by 1.8 and add 32. The freezing point of water is 0°C (32°F) and the boiling point of water is 100°C (212°F). >

Now, pick a feeling from the below thermometer artwork for each of the situations below. If your exact emotion isn't listed here, write it down somewhere within the thermometer. Then average out your temperature across all the situations.

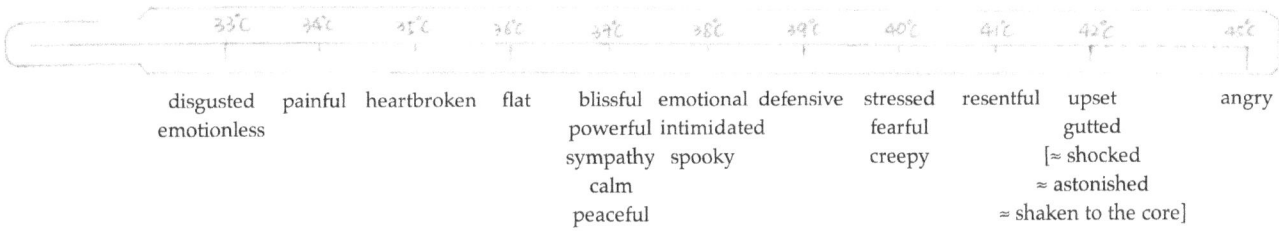

- I'm in love.
- I just watched some news about a horrible murder.
- A magnitude-6 earthquake just happened! My house was shaking for a couple of minutes! Luckily, no-one was injured.
- I smelled something stinky [≈ unpleasant]! It's awful!
- I walked on the beach on a sunny day, felt the warm sand, listened to the sea waves crashing, and smelled the salty air.
- Rebecca was pointing to me and yelling at me!

What's your average temperature?

Please feel free to design a thermometer with a different temperature range (for example, from 0°C to 100°C, or −30°C to 30°C) and add a series of emotions down below.

Emotions are a part of everyone's life. You shouldn't hide [≈ shouldn't bottle up] your emotions. You can always bring your temperature back to normal by controlling your reactions. We'll explore this over the next couple of days.

# DAY 102
## I'M SO SAD

There are days when you're feeling out of sorts [≈ you're feeling blue ≈ you're downhearted ≈ you're downbeat ≈ you're downcast ≈ you're down].

< It's said the expression of 'out of sorts' is from the printing world, which was a manual and laborious process many years ago. The letters that made up words were called sorts, which had to be picked up by typesetters. Sometimes, they ran out of sorts (letters) when composing a page. This would make them frustrated (Out of Sorts, n.d.). >

There are things that can make you sad: being diagnosed with an illness, having a fight with a family member, moving house, experiencing a tough and awful day at work, saying goodbye to a great friend, losing a loved one. Sometimes, you could even just feel sad out of nowhere.

Your emotional temperature here is 32°C.

It's okay, baby. Everyone has this kind of day. Don't get too harsh on yourself. You don't have to say anything. Come here, I'll give you a hug. Are you feeling any better?

Cry it out if you want to. Hug someone. Hug your pillow or teddy bear if that would help. You don't have to hide your sadness. Below are some things that might help ease your sadness:

- Write your feelings down in a journal. [≈ Put your feelings down in a diary.]
- Spend time with your pets – spend time patting them. They'll touch your heart [≈ touch a soft spot].
- Dry your clothes or bedsheet under the sun. Give them a nice, fresh sunshine smell.
- Take a bubble bath, then fall asleep in bed.
- Engage in a 'guilty pleasure' whatever that may be (shopping for an expensive item, going to a fine-dining restaurant, watching a particular TV series).

Do some of these, and your sadness won't stay around forever. Your emotional temperature will gradually come back to 37°C or so.

# DAY 103
## CRY IT OUT

Your tears are an outlet for feeling joy, sadness and pain. If you wanna cry, then cry it out – sobbing, weeping, wailing, whimpering, bawling, blubbering, scream-crying, or curling up into a ball, hiding under the quilt, hugging someone. It's an emotional release.

The loss of a beloved family member or a friend can be a difficult time. You can be left heartbroken and need to cry your heart out. I know how this feels.

In 2010, my grandma fell seriously ill just before I left for Australia. Saying goodbye to her was really tough. I sensed it could be the last time that I held her and hugged her. And it was. I was trying hard to hold back my tears [≈ gulp back my tears] as she smiled at me. Grandma taught me so many things, including how to be strong and positive in life no matter what. She was born poor during the wartime. She never went to school. [≈ She received no education.]

But Grandma had amazing cooking skills. She cooked for me every time I visited her: she made steamed buns, steamed bread, dumplings, noodles, a variety of pancakes, and so many other yummy dishes! It was my grandma who ignited my love of cooking when I was young.

Grandma lived in a house with a big yard where I played rubber band jumping and rope skipping, kicked a shuttlecock about, and hula-hooped every day after school. A lot of my childhood wonder and happiness happened there.

Grandma left us [≈ passed away] a few months after I saw her in 2010. I couldn't make my way back home. I wept bitterly. [≈ I wailed. ≈ I cried out loud.] I felt helpless in Australia. I didn't even get the chance to tend to her in her last days. It was heart-wrenching. [≈ It was disheartening.] I miss you, Grandma.

As I wrote this, tears came out [≈ my eyes filled with tears ≈ I was flooded with tears ≈ I was crying ≈ I was welling up ≈ I was tearing up ≈ I was teary ≈ my tears flowed ≈ I had tears streaming down my eyes]. I was choked with emotion.

< In March 2022, unexpectedly and suddenly, Blaise, one of the owners of Busybird, who helped me to self-publish this book, passed away, just before my manuscript was ready for the layout. I cried when I received this devastating news.

Blaise was such a warm and lovely soul. She guided me through almost all of my publishing journey, and she regularly shared her knowledge and experience with me. I just can't thank her enough. I'm sad that she didn't get the chance to see my book come together in the end. I didn't get the chance to teach her Chinese – she was keen on learning it. My heart is with her and her family. >

## DAY 104
## I'M DESPERATE

Life's not always sugar sweet. You'll be pushed into a state of hopelessness, anxiety, confusion or uncertainty at some stage in your life.

Let me share my job-searching experience many years ago. After sending over 200 resumes and sitting through 20 interviews, I didn't get any job offers. I was turned down time and time again. I felt stuck! I felt hopeless [≈ lost all hope].

I felt unwanted, frustrated [≈ disappointed ≈ depressed ≈ dejected] and desperate. I felt my life was a failure and I had nothing. I broke down, sat in the corner of a dark quiet street on a cold winter night and cried my heart out [≈ cried my eyes out].

Do you agree that things like this can bring down your emotional temperature to 30°C or below? Does it feel like it could last for a while?

Dear English Builder, come on over, I'll give you a warm hug and lend you a shoulder to cry on. It's okay. You're not alone. I have these days. We all have these days.

First and foremost, acknowledge your emotions. Accept them. It means that you care about yourself and your life. Hold onto the belief that it'll get better eventually.

In fact, think about what worries and struggles you're suffering from right now. Are you in pain [≈ in agony]? Has something made you pensive, or upset you [≈ made you feel uneasy]? Maybe write down some of your feelings below.

.................................................................................................................

.................................................................................................................

.................................................................................................................

.................................................................................................................

.................................................................................................................

If you really can't cope with these things yourself, then family, friends, workmates, psychologists, police officers or even neighbours are all there to help. Talk to them.

Don't lock yourself at home thinking about what's going on in your life. Work on whatever you need to work on. Search for meaningful and fun activities – maybe through Meetup, Eventbrite, or local council noticeboards. Fill your day with activities. You'll look back many years later and find ways to appreciate these hard times.

# DAY 105
# I'M PISSED OFF

Things don't always go your way. What situations could trigger your anger [≈ cause an angry response]? Would you be fuming if the following situations, or similar, occurred to you? Highlight any words or phrases meaning or showing 'angry' in each of the bullet points.

- Oscar ruffled my feathers because he was one hour late for my birthday party without any valid reason!
- When Martin started to yell at me, it raised my hackles!
- Tony lied to me again – this got me so riled up.
- Edward popped my personal space bubble [≈ pushed my boundaries]! I'm pissed off! [≈ I'm fuming! ≈ I'm vexed! ≈ I'm miffed! ≈ I'm peeved! ≈ I'm in a huffy mood!]
- I flipped my lid [≈ was angry suddenly] the moment I found out my boss gave the bonus to everyone in the team except me!
- I'm getting worried about Karen. Since last month, she's been refusing to pick up the phone! She sent me aggressive emails after I tried to call her. What's the matter with her?
- My kids' naughty behaviours irk me a lot lately. I'm not happy [≈ I'm not pleased ≈ I'm unhappy ≈ I'm grouchy] with them.
- I hit the ceiling when one of my staff was caught embezzling company money [≈ transferring company funds into his personal accounts]!

< For the second last bullet point above, no matter what, never ever mete out corporal punishment to your kids. Time-out, caning, flogging – none of these are okay! >

< For the last bullet point, when you 'hit the ceiling' or 'hit the roof', you become very angry. But if you 'hit the wall', you've reached a point where you can't make further process. >

When you are angry [≈ When you are pushed to a breaking point ≈ While in a rage ≈ While in a fury], what possible reactions do you have? Your heart rate increases, your blood pressure rises, your body shakes and you're out of control. You rant [≈ yell ≈ raise your voice] to others, throw things, slam the door and storm out of the room...

Grrr!

# DAY 106
## MANAGE YOUR ANGER

Hold on, before you completely lose your temper [≈ fly off the handle ≈ go postal ≈ go ballistic ≈ go berserk ≈ flare up ≈ blow your top ≈ blow your lid ≈ blow your stack ≈ boil over ≈ reach boiling point], pause for a moment. Take a deep breath. Wait 20 seconds or count from 1 to 20 slowly.

< How does 'fly off the handle' relate to losing control of yourself [≈ losing your composure]? Think of an axe-head becoming loose. It could fly off the handle, possibly striking anyone or anything close by (Fly Off the Handle, n.d.). >

During this short time, ask yourself if the trivial things that triggered your anger still matter. Do they matter after a couple of days, or a year later? Probably not.

If you still can't cool down [≈ can't soothe your nerves ≈ can't calm down your nerve], go for a walk, put on headphones and listen to music.

Don't categorise yourself into 'I'm cranky. [≈ I'm grumpy. ≈ I'm cantankerous. ≈ I'm fractious. ≈ I'm irritable. ≈ I'm moody. ≈ I'm short-tempered. ≈ I'm hot-tempered. ≈ I'm foul-tempered. ≈ I'm ill-tempered.]' or 'I have quite the temper. [≈ I have a fiery temper. ≈ I have a nasty temper. ≈ I have a peppery temper.]'

You'll become what you say, remember?

Anger is an emotion that we all experience but it can be managed [≈ controlled ≈ regulated ≈ harnessed ≈ kept in check].

Understand that your anger is never the solution to a problem. Don't forget yourself. Keep your temper and keep your cool. Never curse or hit out at others in anger (you'll regret this later because you couldn't think clearly at that point of time). Once you're in a calm state, communicate with others and get the problems fixed. Done!

# DAY 107
## LAUGH OUT LOUD

Laughter is the best medicine. When you laugh, you release endorphins and happy hormones, which gives you a fantastic emotional temperature.

Smiling, chuckling, chortling, giggling, tittering, smirking, snickering and grinning ear to ear, belly laughing, rolling on the floor laughing, falling off the chair laughing, laughing in hysterics, laughing awkwardly… I don't mind how you smile or laugh. Please make yourself comfortable and laugh with me now.

Q: Did you have a haircut?

A: No, I got them all cut.

Q: What do you call someone with no body and no nose?

A: Nobody knows.

Do these dad jokes crack you up?

Watch TV shows that you think are funny such as *Friends*, *The Big Bang Theory*, *How I Met Your Mother*, *Young Sheldon*, *Mom*, *Silicon Valley*, *The IT Crowd*, *The Office*, *Modern Family*… if these sitcoms don't make you laugh hard, you can watch the bloopers from these shows.

Have you heard of laughter yoga? This is where a group of people gather together to just laugh out loud. Laugh like you're a young child, a young person, or an elderly person. It looks hilarious! Just by watching laughter yoga, you probably can't stop laughing now.

Hmm, let's turn to a stand-up comedy show now. Gabriel Iglesias was telling a story. When he was hanging out with his two Aussie friends, he joked about Bundaberg, a rum brand. The bottle looked similar to a Coca-Cola bottle, but with a polar bear on it. When you drank it, you would certainly realise it wasn't Coke! (Audience laughs out loud.) If you don't know Bundaberg rum, it's not that funny. Even if you know the Bundaberg rum, it doesn't sound funny to you. Nah, you won't even understand what the laughing is all about. LOL! It's culture difference then <shrug shoulders>.

< 'LOL' or 'lol' is an abbreviation for laugh out loud, often used in text messages. There are many other texting abbreviations and acronyms: DIY (do it yourself), GOAT (greatest of all time), IDK (I don't know), FAQ (frequently asked questions), IMO (in my opinion), JK (just kidding), TGIF (thank God it's Friday), TLDR (too long; didn't read), YOLO (you only live once), etc. >

Tell me what never fails to make you laugh?

# DAY 108
## BREAK OUT OF EVERYDAY BOREDOM

I'm bored with the daily grind. I'm fed up with the humdrum routine. It's exactly the same every day: wake, eat, work (repetitive, mind-numbing, monotonous [≈ boring ≈ mundane ≈ lame]), eat, home (repetitive, cooking, washing, watching TV, internet surfing), eat, sleep, repeat. Jeez, your life looks like it's plain vanilla [≈ it's banal].

< Vanilla is common ice cream flavour. So if you say something is 'plain vanilla', you're referring to that thing being boring and plain. >

Come on! Spice up your life! Variety is the spice of life. How? Here is the antidote to boredom: do repetitive tasks in different ways and make them entertaining.

Maybe you can wake up in different ways: wake up with a smile; cover yourself under the quilt and stretch; open your eyes as slowly as you can; rub your eyes and yawn; half close one eye and swap your eyes a couple of times before getting up…

For your meals: try different combinations of vegetables and protein. Try different ways to cook. Try out new restaurants. Don't order the same food on the same menu every time. By the way, you can eat with spoons, chopsticks, knives, forks, or even with your hands…

You're not a robot. Even if laborious data entry is what you do each day [≈ all day every day ≈ each and every day] for a job, think of your keyboard as a piano. Make different rhythms – you can play beautiful songs.

Do you get my point? I'll leave it to you to explore how you can make sleep fun. Maybe wear different pyjamas, sleep naked, sleep in different positions, sleep with a YouTube video playing soothing rain or ASMR (autonomous sensory meridian response) sound on. Surprise me.

Make every day an adventure. Do something new. Every. Single. Day. Stay tuned. We'll be learning how to keep your soul alive and participate in fun things in this chapter.

# DAY 109
# FINDING YOUR PASSION

We talked about finding new ways to perform your daily routine [≈ the day-to-day grind] yesterday. In this way, you can go about your life like a treasure hunter. Search for things that you love passionately and 'dig' them up.

Let's play a game! Two truths and one lie. Make three statements, either about your passions, something that you'd like to put your heart and soul into, or about something that you hate doing. There must be one statement that is a lie but which sounds like a truth.

I'll go first:

- I'm fond of being creative.
- I'm mad for cricket.
- Lying would be the last thing I would like to do.

Guess which statement is a lie? Now it's your turn.

- ........................................................................................
- ........................................................................................
- ........................................................................................

Here's a collection of saying something with enthusiasm: I love doing sports. I'm passionate about helping others. Singing is my jam. Drawing is my cup of tea. I'm a history buff. I'm crazy for basketball. I'm obsessed with make-up. I'm a photography enthusiast. I'm an adventure junkie. I'm into music in a big way. I'm a total sucker for CDs. I'm keen on trying out all foods. I have a penchant for writing. I have a great affection for language. I revel in tennis. I'm drawn to travelling. Anything related to animals always piques my interest.

Here are ways to express something that you don't like a bit. Just add 'not' after 'I'm', or 'don't' before the verb 'do' in above examples. Or use these: High tech is not my shit. Boxing is not my sport. Smoking is not appealing me. I dread going to drawing classes. I have no taste for boardroom meetings. I am half-hearted in my job. The second I started reading the book, I lost interest.

I hope today's game has helped you find your spark and ignite your passion. Follow the bliss, and your life becomes interesting and full of energy.

# DAY 110
## ALWAYS BE A LEARNER

Another secret in making your life more exciting is to become a lifelong learner! Keep learning whenever, wherever and however you can.

Today, when I clicked onto Google's homepage, Stephen Hawking's 80th birthday popped up on Google Doodles. Take a guess on which date that I checked in? What are Hawking's theories? Why does Google's logo have four colours? Is it just four colours? Are there any other questions that you'd like to ask and have answered here?

My point here is to be curious about knowledge and new things. Don't live under a rock like this:

- When others talk about the US Capitol riot in 2021, you have no clue.
- When a group of people discuss the book of *Sapiens: A Brief History of Humankind*, you have no idea what they're on about.
- When it comes to internet terminology, you don't know what 'you are lurking', 'boot you out [≈ kick you out ≈ throw you out] from the group', 'don't feed the trolls' or 'catfishing' mean.
- When everyone at work is talking about cleaning their coffee machines, your response is 'I don't have the foggiest idea how to do it.'
- You're clueless about how to download apps onto your mobile phone.
- You don't know where to find fun activities in your local area.

Gees! [≈ Jesus! ≈ Gosh! ≈ Goddamn! ≈ Jeepers!] You don't know your arse from your elbow [≈ don't know anything about a subject]! Seriously, what do you know? Beats me. [≈ I don't know.]

Please keep a curious mind. Expose yourself to new ideas; equip yourself with a wealth of knowledge [≈ arm yourself with a body of knowledge ≈ become an expert]; experience new things. The more you learn and act, the more you'll realise that there are more adventures to explore. So read, listen, observe, think and experiment. Be a sponge. [≈ Chase knowledge. ≈ Acquire new knowledge.]

< A sponge is a substance that can absorb water or other liquid. If you're like a sponge, you are curious and able to absorb a lot of information. >

To coin a phrase [≈ As the proverb goes ≈ As the wise saying goes ≈ It is an old adage ≈ There is a saying that ≈ Conventional wisdom suggests that]: 'It's never too late to learn! It's better late than never.' Keep learning along the way, from the cradle to the grave. Become a lifelong student. Age is no barrier. [≈ Age can't hinder you.]

# DAY 111
# EMBRACE CHANGE

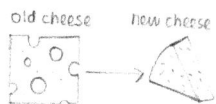

Hi everyone. From the first day of you reading this book up until now, have you been experiencing any changes? It could be subtle changes such as trying out a new hairstyle and making studying English part of your daily ritual. It could also be big, dramatic changes like moving to a new city, losing your job, or breaking up with your loved one.

Like it or not, change is a part of life [≈ change is inevitable ≈ change is always coming ≈ things are always changing ≈ the only constant is change]. The interesting thing is that many people try hard to avoid change [≈ are resistant to change ≈ averse to change ≈ are reluctant to get out of a stable situation].

Why not embrace change and treat it as a new adventure? Give me some verbs on what you can do with change? Refuse, anticipate, sniff out, accept, monitor, enjoy? Put down your answers here:

.................................................................................................................

The popular book *Who Moved My Cheese?* written by Dr Spencer Johnson, talks about two mice (Sniff and Scurry) and two little men (Hem and Haw) living in a maze with an abundance of cheese that they all love. However, when the cheese starts disappearing [≈ dwindling] day by day, the four characters react differently. Sniff and Scurry notice the change and they scurry off [≈ move quickly] to look for new cheese. Hem and Haw refuse to accept the fact that the cheese has gone. They stay where they are, only hoping the old cheese will be coming back. In the end, the two people realise that they have to make the move to get the new cheese.

< The names Hem and Haw come from the phrase of '*hem and haw*', which means to speak hesitantly or act indecisively. Hem mimics the sound of clearing your throat. Haw is also a sound of hesitation to avoid answering question directly (What Does Hem and Haw Mean?, n.d.). >

Cheese cannot last forever. It has to be consumed sooner or later. You have to make the move. The quicker you let go of old cheese and start moving, the sooner you'll find new cheese. It's safer to search in the maze for the cheese rather than remain in a cheeseless situation.

Your old place, old job or ex-partner are like old cheese. Losing them sounds scary and unacceptable. If you hold onto them too long, they start to smell like spoilt milk and grow mould. So move on. Stay positive and active. Discover the new cheese that life offers! Give it time. You'll find yourself truly enjoying new cheese (the new house is vibrant; the new job pays me surprisingly well; I met my lifelong partner). Such life-altering [≈ life-changing ≈ life-transforming] experience (new cheese) becomes your personal story of which you're proud to share.

Most importantly, the new 'cheese' could taste even better: fresh, meaty, creamy, salty, tangy, buttery, nutty, fruity… Wow!

# DAY 112
# SEIZE NEW OPPORTUNITIES

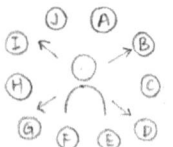

There are always opportunities out there. Make sure you're always on the lookout for new opportunities.

If you don't seek them out, they will never come to you. Lying in bed, doing nothing or playing with your phone, doesn't make a new opportunity. You also don't generate opportunities by sitting there watching movies [≈ becoming a couch potato], no matter what types of movies you are watching.

You need to put yourself out there. Here are three kinds of actions that you can take and why you should take then:

- Ask for what you want. (Opportunities don't knock by themselves.)
- Prime yourself for the opportunity. (If you don't prepare yourself for when an opportunity knocks on the door, you won't have the strength to even open the door.)
- Keep asking for what you want and keep preparing yourself for a golden opportunity. (Opportunities finally come, and now you can kick down the door quickly!)

This sounds easy, right? But lots of 'adventurers' didn't start with their first step. If you're thinking – it's too scary to convince someone to give me a chance, to negotiate for a pay-rise, to ask for investment fund to start a business – by not asking, you won't ever get the chance. What will you lose by asking? Nothing! It would be a shame if you don't ask at all. So I implore you: overcome your inner fears. Simply go out and ask!

Once an opportunity comes your way, don't let it slip away [≈ don't let it pass you by ≈ don't flush it down the toilet ≈ don't waste your shot ≈ don't miss the boat]. Seize the opportunity. [≈ Harness the opportunity. ≈ Grab the chance. ≈ Grasp the chance. ≈ Take the chance.] Opportunity never knocks twice at any man's door! Most of time, it's now or never [≈ it's once in a lifetime].

< If you've 'missed the boat', you've missed out on an opportunity. This idiom stems from back in 18th century, when if you arrived late for the scheduled boat, you wouldn't be able to catch it. You missed the boat! This idiom refers to chances in many situations, such as opportunities to become rich, to get promoted, to live a better life. >

Make good use of a golden opportunity. [≈ Give it your best shot. ≈ Do everything that you possibly could.] In all likelihood, it's well worth the effort [≈ worth trying]. It will add to your exciting life adventures ahead!

CHAPTER 13 - A Life Adventurer

# DAY 113

Let's solve a nine-dot puzzle. You need to connect all the dots with four straight lines without lifting the pen from the paper.

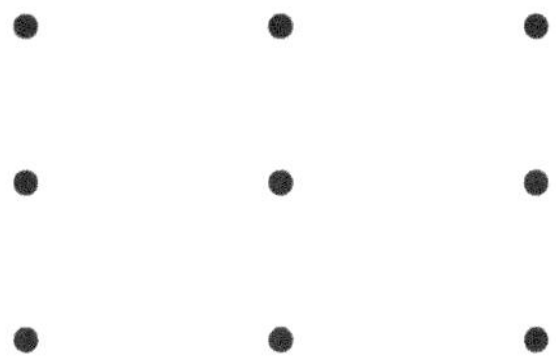

•   •   •

•   •   •

•   •   •

Eureka! The only way to do it is to think outside the ~~box~~ beach [≈ think outside the ~~square~~ squirrel.] Extend your lines outside of the 'box' in the picture above, you'll have the puzzle solved.

< The term 'eureka' is attributed to the ancient Greek scholar Archimedes. He stepped into a bathtub, noticed that the water level rose. The more he immersed himself in the water, the more water overflowed. He suddenly realised that the volume of water displaced depended on the volume of the part of his body he immersed [≈ submerged]. He jumped out of the tub, running naked in street, and shouted 'Eureka! Eureka! Eureka!' (Biello, 2006) This was the moment that he discovered the principle of buoyancy. So a 'eureka' moment is a light bulb moment [≈ an 'aha!' moment] for sudden inspiration. It means 'I have found it' in Greek. >

< The Eureka Tower is one of the Melbourne's most iconic buildings. The Tower is 297.3 m in height. It's named after a rebellion during the 1854 Victorian gold rush, called the 'Eureka Stockade'. >

Hey, are < > really just angled brackets? Could they be less-than and greater-than signs too? Or is it a broken diamond shape? What do you see? Unleash your creativity. [≈ Harness your creativity. ≈ Sharpen your creativity. ≈ Unlock your creativity. ≈ Stimulate your creativity.]

You may wonder: where is today's title and drawing? This is not an editing error. Use your imagination to add a title and a drawing after the Day 113 heading. If you can't think of something, try to think beyond the conventional and use some of the below strategies to help generate ideas:

- Draw as many wave lines, circles or squares as you can in 1 minute.
- Get yourself bored on purpose. Take a seat. Don't pick up your phone or turn on the TV or read a book (including the book you're reading right now).
- Take a long shower or a long bath.

What types of ideas did you end up having in each of these situations?

> sparking ideas, big ideas, bright ideas, fresh ideas, creative ideas, original ideas, crisp ideas, madcap ideas [≈ nutty ideas ≈ crazy ideas], wacky ideas, spiced-up ideas, half-baked ideas, rotten ideas, unconventional ideas, stillborn ideas

# DAY 114
# BREAK THE RULES

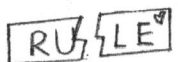

Do you rate yourself more of a conformist or a nonconformist? Conformists tend to think and behave like everyone else. They are obedient and conservative. They hew to the rules [≈ abide by the rules ≈ do things by the book].

By contrast, nonconformists are those who refuse to adhere to [≈ do not conform to] the rules or ideas that most people follow. They have unconventional ways of doing things.

In your opinion, which of the below social or moral rules are you allowed to break? Which rules are best to follow? Tick the checkboxes for rules that you must obey. Put a cross in those that you can disobey.

Here's a list:

- [ ] A dating rule: No kissing or sex on the first date.
- [ ] An office rule: Try hard to make conversation with workmates in the kitchen during a break.
- [ ] A driving rule: Fasten your seatbelt before you drive.
- [ ] An escalator riding rule: Stand on the left side of the escalator.
- [ ] A rule for boarding a train: Wait to the side to step onto the train while others are stepping out.
- [ ] An Australian Taxation Office (ATO) rule: Lodge individual tax returns by 31 October each year.
- [ ] A reading rule: Read a book silently, without voicing the words out loud.
- [ ] A cooking rule: Follow the recipe throughout.
- [ ] A dining table rule: A fork is held in the left hand and a knife with the right hand.
- [ ] An eating rule: You can't eat your food after you drop it on the floor. (If you grab and eat the food quickly after it hits the ground, this is called the 'five second rule'.)
- [ ] A COVID-19 rule: Wear facemasks when in public.

< In Australia, standing to the left on an escalator is the norm. The right side is used for those who are walking up and in a hurry. >

< In Australia, individuals are responsible for lodging their tax returns by 31 October each year. If 31 October falls on the weekend, the due date is extended to the next business day after 31 October. If you miss out on the deadline, you'll be fined unless you're registered with a tax agent by 31 October. >

There are no standard answers. Laws provide a framework of ethical dos and don'ts to follow. For everything else – your dreams or lifestyles – I encourage you to deviate from the norms [≈ step outside the norm] where possible. Take on the adventure!

# DAY 115
## TALK TO PEOPLE

Each person's particular life experience could be thought of as an adventure like no other. Use every opportunity to grab whatever comes into your life.

Would you talk to a stranger? Maybe you meet a commuter [≈ a fellow traveller] on the train, a person standing behind you in a line, or a passenger when you're getting into the elevator. Nod and make conversation with them. Don't keep away from people. [≈ Don't shun people.] People are not monsters. Most are happy to chat unless you bump into one of those rude strangers who wants a fight [≈ wants to pick a fight]. Agreed?

While riding Uber, Didi, Ola or a taxi, talk to your driver. You can find out something interesting about their life experiences from them. Maybe a sales manager who has chosen to be an Uber driver after retirement will open up about his luxury lifestyle. Maybe a Brisbane driver who worked in Perth during the mining boom days will talk about the crazy living costs in Perth back then! Maybe the taxi driver is someone from Somalia who came to Australia with his aunty and is excited about his upcoming trip back home since he hasn't been home for 20 years.

Are you scared to talk to C-Suite executives [≈ senior executives ≈ CEOs, CFOs, COOs and CIOs]? Then force yourself to! They are witty. [≈ They have a sharp wit.] And they are good at talking to people too!

Don't just hang out only with old friends all the time. Try out a different crowd. Maybe you can find new people while partying, travelling, going to music festivals, attending industry conferences and training courses, joining Laneway Learning classes, becoming a gym member. The list goes on and on. [≈ The list is endless.]

< Partying is a part of western culture. There are many types of parties that you can go to. Here are a few examples:

| A ball  | Welcome function | Christmas party | Prom party    | Wedding ceremony |
| ------- | ---------------- | --------------- | ------------- | ---------------- |
| Banquet | Baby shower      | Costume party   | Cocktail party | Birthday party  |
| Soiree  | Farewell dinner  | Housewarming    | Hens' night   | Bucks' party     |

A hens' night is a party only with girls celebrating a bride-to-be before a wedding, while a bucks' party is for a bridegroom about to get married. >

Mingle with others in these activities and find out more about your new friends!

# DAY 116
# START WITH A GREAT CONVERSATION

Wow, it's been a wild ride [≈ an exciting trip] in this chapter so far. Amazing! You should take on life adventures and become an interesting and funny person [≈ a comedian ≈ a person with a wicked sense of humour]. Let's start with some great conversation.

By the way, I like your dress. It's so pretty! [≈ That's lovely!] You are gorgeous!

What am I doing? Right, I'm giving you a compliment. This is a great way to start conversation and build up rapport. Of course, if you're not wearing a dress, I would compliment you on the other things you're wearing today, be it your watch, necklace, glasses, sweater, shoes, or T-shirt.

If someone compliments you, reply passionately, 'Thank you. I like it too! I got it from Bali last year.' A dull person would say, 'Hmm, it's just okay. It's an old dress. I don't like it anymore.' (Then why are they wearing it?)

Are these conversations boring?

'What did you do over the weekend?' 'Well, nothing much.'

'Have you watched any movies or read any books lately?' 'No.' 'Anything exciting?' 'Not really.'

If you really have nothing exciting to share, please be interested in what others have to say. At least, ask the same question back. You can also apply the 5 Ws (when, where, who, what, why) and 1 H (how) principle to show your interest in the stories or opinions of others. For example, 'When was that? Where is it? [≈ Whereabouts?] Who did you go with? What would you do if you were me? Why is that so? [≈ Is that right?] How do you feel? How big is too big? How does it work?'

Don't forget to give timely feedback while you're listening to someone: 'That's good to know.' [≈ 'That's great.' ≈ 'Yep.' ≈ 'Exactly.'] 'Well said.' [≈ 'Love your comments.']

# DAY 117
# GET YOUR FEET WET

Dear adventurers, do you dare to do something new?

When you do something different from past experiences [≈ you try something that you've never experienced before ≈ you explore uncharted territory ≈ you get into a new field ≈ you seek out new experiences ≈ you're a first-timer for an activity], you could struggle at the start, and the challenge could seem insurmountable.

But if you take up the challenge [≈ do not shy away from the challenge] and are stout-hearted [≈ brave and determined], you'll find a new side of yourselves and gain new skills. Have fun! If you fail, just have another go [≈ attempt it again ≈ try again]. It will be a massive learning curve.

If you still can't quite twig [≈ can't wrap your head around] the new thing after a couple of tries, don't get frustrated. Just keep going. In the end, you will thank yourself for trying something new. You'll be breaking the monotony of a routine life!

So get out of your comfort zone [≈ step out of your comfort zone ≈ say goodbye to your comfort zone]. Enter your stretch zone, growth zone or even panic zone. [≈ Branch out.] Keep putting yourself out there. Make trying something new into a daily habit. It's actually addictive!

Be bolder, even. Why not put your application in for *Australian Survivor*, an adventure game show where becoming the sole survivor could earn yourself half a million dollars in prizes? All you need to do is to pass through physical and mental challenges. Outwit, outplay and outlast the others when competing. It's not just about how to fight for your food on an isolated island. It's more about the subtle and strategic moves against your opponents and team members. You need to manipulate the game and your teammates to avoid being voted out by your tribe and to become the last man standing.

What activities are on your wish list? Don't hesitate and don't wait. Give it a go! [≈ Go for it! ≈ Go nuts! ≈ Go bananas!] Have a crack at something new. [≈ Give it a crack. ≈ Take a shot. ≈ Have a stab at it. ≈ Have a red hot go.] Go get your feet wet. [≈ Go dip your toe in the water.]

< 'Get your feet wet' means to do something for the first time. Imagine a swimmer who wants to go into the water. They put their feet into the water slowly (get their feet wet) to test the water before they jump in (Get Your Feet Wet, 2019). >

# DAY 118
# LOVE YOURSELF FIRST

So far we've explored ways to get you out of a rut, to start living an interesting and thrilling life daily – this is all fantastic. Another idea to take on more adventure is to face your fears and do something scary [≈ do something that scares you]. You might feel some discomfort initially, but you'll grow and be glad that you tried. These could be things like:

- Ask for constructive feedback from your boss and your family members.
- Find ways to establish a connection with a celebrity that you like.
- Try out entrepreneur Jia Jiang's 100 days of rejection experiment.

< Jia Jiang, the developer of Rejection Therapy, did a TED Talk 'What I learnt from 100 days of rejection'. He attempted a few different tasks: to borrow $100 from a random person; to request a burger refill at a restaurant; to request to play soccer in someone's backyard. Now go listen to the talk if you haven't already heard it. >

I'm not asking you to take silly risks to be adventurous here. The below two examples are downright silly actions that you shouldn't do at all!

**Example #1:** A promising Australian rugby player ate a garden slug as a dare when he was 19 years old. He suffered a rare infection 3 months later and became paralysed. Around-the-clock care was required for him for the rest of his life. He died 8 years later (Hanrahan, 2018).

**Example #2:** In recent years, a number of students have killed themselves [≈ committed suicide ≈ taken their own life ≈ ended their life] while studying abroad, often just because they couldn't do well in exams. Hey, it's seriously not a big deal if you fail a subject. You are allowed to fail! And failure is actually a key to success! (Jump onto **Day 128 Welcome Failure** for inspiration, if you like.)

No-one deserves an end to their life like this! How stupid, silly, thoughtless and irresponsible! Please promise me: be kind and gentle to yourself. Love yourself. This is the premise of all adventures. Let's wrap up this chapter by figuring out some fun adventurous things that you could do! Below are four ideas from me.

- Where's Wally? Go find Wally!
- Watch for shooting stars and make a wish!
- Go to the drive-in cinema, or go horse riding in Melbourne!
- Book a Melbourne Sunday market stall and sell your pre-loved items!

< Knock, knock. Who's there? Wally. Wally who? Wally is a man in red and white striped shirt and hat, distinctive from other people in the crowd. He shows up in a series of puzzle book called *Where's Wally?* where he travels to the beach, mountains, and a whole lot of other places with a walking stick, camera, belt and other items. Some countries call Wally different name (such as Waldo, Charlie, Walter, etc.). >

Now, write down your adventure ideas in your notebook. Write down as many as you can! Go wild! Then experience them one by one.

# DAY 119
## SUCCESS IS THAT SIMPLE

To the big achievers out there: what is success to you? Having lots of money? Becoming famous? Having a loving family? Having a fulfilling career? Or helping others find success?

Each of us defines success differently. One thing for sure is that you don't have to become a celebrity to be successful. An average person [≈ An average Joe or Jane ≈ Ordinary people] can achieve extraordinary things just with raw determination.

< Who's Joe? Joe is a common name. It's the nickname for Joseph. An average Joe or ordinary Joe refers to an average man. The average Jane is the female version of average Joe. >

As an English Builder who aims to improve their English consistently, you are already an excellent achiever [≈ a humdinger ≈ a belter]. This is the start of striving for excellence [≈ pursuing brilliance]. Once you become determined to be the best in what you do, then here's a secret formula from me:

$$\text{Success} = \frac{[30\%\text{Luck} + 70\%(\text{Admiration for Your Idol} + \text{Confidence} + \text{Good Habits} + \text{Failures})]^{\wedge(\text{Consistency} \times \text{Patience})}}{\text{Your Own Pace}}$$

Let me explain it:

**The numerator:** Seven elements in total. Below is the breakdown analysis.

- **The 30% part:** Your 30% luck seems to be uncontrollable, but the harder you work on the 70% part, the luckier you'll get!

- **The 70% part:** The more you work on each of these elements (admiration for your idol, confidence, good habits, failures), the better your chances of success!

- **The power:** Consistency × Patience. The more you stick to them, the easier it is to reach success!

**The denominator:** Only one element – Working at your own pace. There's no comparison to others – when the number is smaller, you'll succeed quicker!

You're now thinking I'm making sense, right? Please bring in your mathematical brain. Under what assumptions is the above formula valid and correct? I'll give you a hint here. I assume each of the elements on the numerator is a whole number (0, 1, 2, 3, 4…), while the denominator (your own pace) is the counting number (1, 2, 3, 4…), and the result in square brackets is greater than 1.

English Builders, use the formula. It's not that hard to do. You'll kick out fate and taste of victory in the end. If it confuses you, don't worry. We'll break down these elements in detail over the next 12 days.

# CHAPTER 14 - A Big Achiever

## DAY 120
## SHOULD I BELIEVE IN ASTROLOGY?

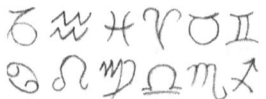

Destiny, or luck, controls 30% of your life. You have control over the other 70%. We will look at 30% today from astrology horoscope perspective. What is your zodiac sign? Fill in the sign based on your date of birth. I am a _____ or I am an _____ .

| Earth sign | Air sign | Water sign | Fire sign |
|---|---|---|---|
| Capricorn (22 Dec–19 Jan) | Aquarius (20 Jan–18 Feb) | Pisces (19 Feb–20 Mar) | Aries (21 Mar–19 Apr) |
| Taurus (20 Apr–20 May) | Gemini (21 May–20 Jun) | Cancer (21 Jun–22 Jul) | Leo (23 Jul–22 Aug) |
| Virgo (23 Aug–22 Sep) | Libra (23 Sep–22 Oct) | Scorpio (23 Oct–21 Nov) | Sagittarius (22 Nov–21 Dec) |

Reading your zodiac sign can be so much fun. When Saturn falls into your chart, you'll have great opportunities to succeed in all areas of your life: your wedding bells are ringing; you might get involved in buying or selling property; a major career transition could be underway. This is your year. Take the chance. It's your turn to shine!

< Saturn is not the only ruling planetary body. There are other rulers such as Mars, the sun, the moon, Mercury, Venus, Rahu, Ketu and Jupiter. Jupiter is one of the biggest and brightest planets in our solar system. It takes around 12 years to travel [≈ revolve] around the sun. Jupiter will stay in at each zodiac sign for about 12 months. Auspicious Jupiter also brings luck, abundance and optimism. >

Let's look at the eastern horoscope now. The table below is an example of your horoscope with the year that you were born. The year is defined by the Chinese lunar calendar, so you could be a Tiger if you're born in the early part of 1987 in the western calendar.

| Rat 1984 | Ox 1985 | Tiger 1986 | Rabbit 1987 | Dragon 1988 | Snake 1989 |
| Horse 1990 | Sheep 1991 | Monkey 1992 | Rooster 1993 | Dog 1994 | Pig 1995 |

So check out the calendar before writing down your Chinese zodiac sign [≈ animal sign]. My animal sign is _____ . [≈ I am a _____ or I am an _____ . ≈ I was born in the year of _____ .]

When it's your Ben Ming Nian (本命年) (the year of when you were born), it's believed to be ominous. You'll suffer from misfortune and adversity over the course of that year.

Hey, do you really believe in astrology? Do you think it's a hoax? Or maybe you're not an astrology believer but you just like reading your signs to analyse your personality and find out what could happen to you in the following month or year. Whether you believe in astrology or not, at the end of the day, you are the one who controls your fate [≈ your destiny is in your hands ≈ you are in charge of your fate]. You can achieve your dreams against all the odds.

# DAY 121
## TIDY UP YOUR LIVING AREA

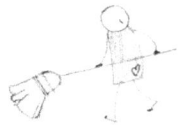

Imagine this: a scruffy backyard, a messy garage, an untidy bedroom, a jumble of old clothes in the wardrobe… The sink has a mess of dishes. The carpet is grimy. There's disarray everywhere. Chaos! Will you live in a place like this? I reckon not.

Hurry up! Get rid of the mess at home. [≈ Declutter your house.] Throw away unused items. Keep your en suite in top shape. Keep your living room tidy [≈ spruce and clean]. Keep your kitchen immaculate. Keep the table spotless [≈ spick and span].

Why? In Chinese geomancy [≈ feng shui (风水)], the cleanliness of your house keeps you refreshed and brings you luck. Wealth and success will follow.

So, go do your housework [≈ household chores]. Here are some chores to keep you busy:

- Make the bed.
- Wash the laundry. Hang out the laundry. Fold the laundry.
- Wash the dishes.
- Mop, sweep or vacuum the floor. [≈ Do the mopping, do the sweeping, do the vacuuming.]
- Dust the house.
- Scrub the toilet.
- Mow the yard. Weed the garden.
- Trim the trees. [≈ Prune the trees.]
- Take out the rubbish [≈ trash].

< Making your bed every morning isn't just for the tidiness. It can also make you more successful! William H McRaven mentioned in his book *Make Your Bed: Little Things That Can Change Your Life… and Maybe the World*, making the bed is an easy task and by doing so, you've accomplished the first task of the morning. This will encourage you to complete more and more tasks each day! >

< 'Rubbish' is British English, while 'trash' is American English. As you may aware, some vocabulary is different between British English and American English. For example, British 'chips' are American 'French fries'. British 'flats' are 'apartments' in American English. 'Rubbers' in British English become 'erasers' in American English.

Some spelling also differs between the two types of English. Colour, centre, enrol, licence is written in British English. The American English style would be color, center, enroll and license. The British brought English to America in the 16th century. Noah Webster, a lexicographer, made the American version of English just to show cultural independence (Differences Between British and American English, n.d.). >

# DAY 122
# ROLE MODELS AND IDOLS

Let's move to 70% part of the success formula. The very first one is to look for an admirable idol. The word 'idol' has three meanings: a statue that is worshipped; something that you like; someone who you admire [≈ adore].

< When looking up a word in a dictionary, take a moment to check out all of its explanations. This process helps you to better understand homonyms (words that have the same spelling but different meanings). >

An idol in the more modern context refers to someone who you look up to. This person could embody [≈ have ≈ possess] good qualities (knowledge, determination, a good heart, generosity, etc. [≈ and so on ≈ and more ≈ and stuff like that ≈ and a dozen others ≈ and all that jazz ≈ and other similar things ≈ and whatnot]) that you are pursuing or emulating in your life.

Your role model [≈ The target of your admiration] could be someone in your family. For example, my dad is my personal hero [≈ I idolise my father]. Dad has set good examples for me. He has had a big impact on my life [≈ He is significant to me] in many ways. Dad is my absolute rock.

You could also be motivated and inspired by a celebrity in any field. Melbourne-born actor Chris Hemsworth showcases being a great family man with a huge success in his acting career. American former basketball player Michael Jordan tries even harder every time he fails in something. Canadian-South African supermodel and dietitian Maye Musk has worked hard and successfully raised kids in spite of family struggles. At the age of 71, Maye even wrote her book, *A Woman Makes a Plan*.

No matter who you pick as an idol, copy what they do [≈ emulate them ≈ mimic them ≈ take a page out of their book].

< When 'taking a page' [≈ taking a leaf] out of someone's book, you are copying what that person has written, so the idiom means that you are imitating someone. >

Don't copy blindly [≈ mindlessly], though. Be inspired to get what needs to be done. This boosts your moral and increases your chances of success.

# DAY 123
# APPEARANCE MATTERS

Let's talk about the confidence element from our success formula over the next three days. Review **Day 36 Have Faith in Yourself** to continue building your inner confidence [≈ your confidence from within] – this is the foundation of success! In this chapter, let's build unbreakable outer confidence to accelerate success!

Wait! Some people say that beauty is only skin deep [≈ looks are superficial ≈ appearances aren't everything ≈ you can't judge a book by its cover ≈ a person's appearance doesn't tell anything about how kind they are].

Well, that's partially true, because your looks do matter. They increase your chances of success. Why?

Imagine this: You're interviewing two candidates. One wears nice, clean [≈ pristine] clothes, looking sharp and confident. The other one is sloppy [≈ lacking self-care], wearing wrinkled clothes and dirty shoes and has greasy hair. They have a coffee stain left at the corners of their mouth, and dirt in their nails. Who would you hire? I'm exaggerating here, but you get my point, right?

Who doesn't like a good-looking person [≈ a person with an attractive physical appearance ≈ a person who looks their best]?

When you notice a handsome guy [≈ a dashing man ≈ a natty man ≈ a guy who's easy on the eye ≈ a guy who's eye-catching] walking towards you, I bet you can't take your eyes off them. If a beautiful young lady [≈ a girl who looks radiant ≈ a bonny girl ≈ a pretty girl] passes by, you turn around as an instinctive reaction. Am I right?

See, looks can even increase your chances of finding the love of your life.

I'm not asking you to buy big brand and expensive clothes. But what you are wearing should suit your style and suit the occasion. Wear appropriately. Before leaving home, preen yourself. Wear perfume or aftershave. Shave your beard [≈ Get clean-shaven] if you're male. Wear subtle make-up if you're female.

Your disposition [≈ Behaving properly] is also important. Stand up and sit straight. No hunching! Walk and speak confidently.

Outward appearances are as important as inward beauty. Good looks are a plus. Make yourself feel good and attractive, and it will show on the outside. You'll attract success.

# DAY 124
## MAINTAIN A HEALTHY WEIGHT

One of the open secrets to looking more attractive is to stay fit [≈ stay in shape] by maintaining a healthy body weight. When you have a good figure, you'll look fit and attractive. Check out if you're in a healthy weight range for your height by using the below BMI (body mass index) calculator:

$$\text{BMI} = \frac{\text{kg}}{\text{m}^2}$$

What do you weigh? [≈ How much do you weigh?] How tall are you? [≈ What is your height?] Put your weight in kilograms to the first decimal place (e.g. 53.8 kg) with your height in metres (e.g. 1.65 m) squared.

< Don't confuse the two Latin expression 'e.g.' and 'i.e.' 'E.g.' stands for *exempli gratia*, meaning 'for example'. This is used to introduce an example. 'I.e.' is the abbreviation for *id est*, which translates to 'that is' and is used to rephrase or elaborate on something that has been stated. >

What is your BMI? The table below is an indicator of a healthy BMI or not:

| BMI score | Indicator |
| --- | --- |
| Less than 18.5 | You're underweight! |
| Between 18.5 and 24.9 | You're in a healthy rage! |
| 25 or over | You're possibly overweight! |

A person who is overweight [≈ out of the shape] might be considered not pretty enough by some. Do you agree with me?

< 'Not pretty' sounds better than 'ugly'. Speaking positive words sounds much better than using negative words. Similarly, if you wanted to express 'I'm stupid on this', use something like 'I'm not smart enough' instead. 'She is curvy' or 'He is full-bodied' sounds better than saying 'She/he is overweight'. Retailers often call oversized clothing 'plus size clothing' or the 'curve collection'. >

So keep the weight off. Become slim and lean. Join the fat farm if you really need to.

< In Australia, a 'fat farm' is a health spa specialising in health reduction for people who are overweight. *The Biggest Loser* is a TV show that helps those who are overweight to lose weight in a short period of time and establish confidence in themselves. However, research shows that many contestants gained weight back after the filming of the show, with contestants returning their old diet and sedentary lifestyle. See, you do need long-term consistency to achieve your goals. >

A person who is underweight [≈ too skinny ≈ too slender ≈ bony] is also not attractive.

But don't rely on the BMI number completely because the formula doesn't take account of your weight being due to more muscle or more fat. But healthy lifestyle habits – regular exercise (Day 79), nutritious food intake (Day 80 and Day 81), adequate sleep (Day 82) would definitely help you stay in shape and have the look of success.

# DAY 125
# THE RUN FOR 100 DAYS CHALLENGE

As I mentioned yesterday, one of the greatest ways to stay fit and keep in shape is to exercise regularly. I'll share my experience.

Over the first 3 years writing this book [≈ In the span of the first 3 years of writing ≈ In the middle of creating my book during the first 3 years ≈ Throughout the first 3 years of writing this book], I became more inactive than ever. I put on more than 7 kilos [≈ kilograms ≈ kgs]. My face was rounder and bigger. I even developed upper back pain. But then, I'd enough! So I started running for a 100 day challenge.

The first few days were extremely hard. I could only run up to 1 km, and I was out of breath [≈ gasping] quickly. My weight remained stable, but then I started to cut out the food that I love.

In the second month of the challenge, I could run up to 5 km consistently in 30 minutes. My belly was becoming flatter. [≈ I was getting a flat belly. ≈ I was getting rid of belly fat.] My stomach was smaller. I continued to watch my carbs and calories. My back pain gradually disappeared. My body felt lighter. I was energised again. I lost 4 kgs at the end of the second month.

For the third month of the challenge, I became comfortable with running 5 km and then even more. The back pain had gone, completely! Amazing. I lost another 4 kgs. As I approached publishing this book, I still jog almost every day. I even completed my first half marathon race at the Nike Melbourne Marathon Festival in 2021. I've dropped [≈ shed] over 10 kgs all up. It wasn't just the slimming down effect that made me feel good. I regained energy. I felt my lovely face shape come back. I could fit into smaller-sized clothing. I was so proud of myself!

If you'd like to test my challenge, get yourself a pair of comfortable running shoes, and go for a run! Take a few days' break in-between to rest your body. Or set up yourself 100-day challenges for any exercise other than running. Let me know what happens after 3 months. The proof is in the pudding.

< The original version of the idiom 'the proof is in the pudding' is 'the proof of the pudding is in the eating', which means that you can only judge something after you have tried it, just like the best test of a pudding is to simply eat it (The Origin of 'Proof Is in the Pudding', 2012). >

# CHAPTER 14 - A Big Achiever

# DAY 126
# BAD HABITS DO HARM

Dear big achievers: you are your habits [≈ your habits are who you are]. Habits are small actions that you perform every day without even thinking that you are doing them. Good habits help make a great life for yourself, and this can lead to success. Bad habits [≈ Vices] give you pleasure in the moment, but they could even gradually kill you [≈ take a toll on you ≈ drive your health into the ground], pushing you away from success. Why?

Take sleeping late as an example. Every night, you enjoy playing mobile phone games before going to bed [≈ before bedtime ≈ before bed]. More often than not, you end up going to sleep late [≈ being an evening type ≈ being a night owl ≈ burning the midnight oil].

This habit becomes detrimental [≈ harmful ≈ toxic] to your health. It can eventually lead to metabolic dysfunction, psychological and neurological disorders, and cardiovascular disease. Even worse, you have 10% higher risk of dying sooner than those who get to bed early (Haridy, 2018). Sounds horrible! You might be destroying your body [≈ You might be wreaking havoc on your body ≈ Your health might be deteriorating] bit by bit.

You are also aware that you have other bad habits, such as biting fingernails, picking your nose, smoking heavily, drinking too much alcohol, eating sweets or junk food uncontrollably, swearing, leaving clothes on the bed or watching soap operas continuously on the sofa. You might dream of body fitness but can't change your routine to put in exercise regularly.

The verb form '-ing' words above function as a noun, describing bad habits. These are called gerunds. Now convert some other words by using noun and adding 'ing' on the end: nail biting, nose picking, excessive smoking… You can fill in the rest yourself:

...........................................................................................................

...........................................................................................................

Then convert them into a bad habit addict, a noun form: a nail-biter, a nose picker, a heavy smoker… Complete the rest:

...........................................................................................................

...........................................................................................................

I'm sure you know the health consequences of these bad habits. But they seem extremely hard to stop [≈ quit ≈ break ≈ ditch ≈ move away ≈ give up ≈ weed out]. What can you do though? Just read on.

# DAY 127
## FORM GOOD HABITS

As we said, bad habits die hard [≈ are hard to drop]. So you don't have to quit them cold turkey [≈ go cold turkey], just wean yourself off [≈ taper yourself off] such addictive behaviour.

< I'm not talking turkey [≈ talking plainly] here. Well, I am. Roasted turkey is the centrepiece of a Thanksgiving meal in the United States and in Canada. To go 'cold turkey' means to cut down an additive action completely, not to gradually stop. Why? One theory suggests that a drug addict can become pale and clammy with goosebumps when they experience withdrawal, and this makes them look like a turkey carcass (Soniak, Why Is Abruptly Quitting Something Called "Going Cold Turkey"?, 2012). >

Whenever you feel like engaging with a bad habit, do something else immediately to help distract yourself. Something like:

- Do you have a fingernail biting behaviour? Just before putting your nails in your mouth, grab a stress ball or a pen to keep your hands busy.
- Craving a cigarette? Have some water instead.
- When you're feeling like an alcoholic drink, go for a walk instead.

If you repeat these habit distractors innumerable times, bad habits can be removed completely. And while you're doing this [≈ Concurrently], you can bring good habits into your life, such as exercising [≈ staying active ≈ having a workout routine] at least twice a week, eating and drinking healthily, reading whenever you can, and going to sleep on time. If adding these good habits all at once sounds overwhelming, just pick one to start with. Start with making the bed every morning when you get up, to keep the bedroom neat. Instead of saying 'I want to change' or 'I should change', reinforce 'I **must** change'. It's said that it only requires a consecutive 21 days of willpower to make a habit into a regular thing [≈ develop a newfound habit ≈ create a sticky habit]. For example, you **must** start making the bed straight after getting up. Try it out for 21 days! See what happens after 21 days!

< Why does it take 21 days to form a habit? Dr Maxwell Maltz came up this idea because he observed it took his patient about 21 days to adjust to the new change in their body either after a nose job or a leg amputation. No matter if it's exactly 21 days, or shorter or longer, each of habit (good or bad) can be learned or unlearned in that time. >

While adhering to [≈ sticking to] this new habit, practise [≈ cultivate] a new one: rise early [≈ get up early ≈ be an early riser ≈ be an early bird ≈ be up with the lark ≈ be a morning person]. Repeat until it becomes just another daily routine.

< The phrase 'early bird' refers to a person who is up early. It could also mean that those who act or arrive early will get an advantage. They're more successful [≈ have a better chance of success]. It comes from the proverb, 'the early bird catches [≈ gets] the worm'. But what does an early worm get? Does it get eaten? >

Living with good habits offers physical and psychological benefits, which gives you a huge advantage for a successful future. So make good habits stick, and keep them up.

# DAY 128
## WELCOME FAILURE

Welcome failure? Did I hear that wrong? Are you sure failure is an addition to your success formula, not a *subtraction*?

No, you didn't hear it wrong. Trust me: you are sure to stumble and fall on the road to obtaining your dreams. If you haven't, you are not trying hard enough. But I assure you, the more times – and deeper and earlier – that you fail, the higher your chances of success.

How you think of failure and deal with it is at the core of success.

Thomas Edison, the guy who invented light bulbs after 10,000 failures, said, 'I haven't failed. I've just found 10,000 ways that won't work.' See, failure is just one step forward [≈ a stepping stone]. So tune into Edison's mindset.

What did Edison do? He didn't dwell on setbacks. Instead, he learnt and moved on [≈ chalked it up to experience]. You can learn from Edison's actions.

I understand, no matter what I say and how Mr Edison showed you a great example for success, setbacks and failures still hurt. They suck. They gnaw at your self-esteem and self-confidence. But I bet that you won't fail 10,000 times to reach success. I bet you'll be luckier than Mr Edison. So, just keep trying again and again. You will fall forward, get back on your feet and stand up even stronger [≈ bounce back better than ever].

< Literally, 'get back on your feet' means that you stand up after a fall. This is how you learnt to walk as a young child. If you didn't get back up and keep trying each time you fell, you wouldn't be able to walk today. You possibly fell five times, but when standing up for the sixth time, you finally learnt to walk. You got back up on your feet when you were a little. Why can't you do it as a grown-up after you fall? >

In short, embrace failure. Keep your eyes on the prize. Just keep trying. Feel free to call them successful failures. Then once you've succeeded, you'll become a guru who can inspire others on why TUVWXYZ works and why ABCDEFG doesn't work. It's awesome, isn't it?

# DAY 129
## STORY SHARING - CHIN UP!

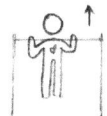

One of my personal goals was to pass IELTS exam with minimum scores in each band (reading, listening, writing and speaking) many years ago in order to secure permanent resident status (PR status) in Australia.

< 'Permanent residency' is the right to live in Australia permanently. It needs to be granted by the Australian Government. For skilled immigration, you need to meet certain criteria such as how long you've lived in Australia, your age range, your major at university, your English skills, etc. >

I sat in the first test. I failed the tests in all four bands. I tried a second time. I failed in reading, listening and speaking. In another test, I finally passed reading, listening, and speaking parts but that time I failed in writing! Sigh! In another test, I failed speaking. Again and again, I failed the tests [≈ I was unsuccessful ≈ I met with no success ≈ I did not manage to pass] in different ways.

I failed eight times like this! It was failure after failure time and again [≈ once again]. Honestly, I had a meltdown each time. But I kept telling myself, 'I do not have a fear of failure. I am unbeatable. [≈ I am invincible.] Snap out of it! It's not a big deal. At least I got closer each time. Brace yourself, Jessie! Walk tall. Chin up! Head up!'

**What I did** was continue to go all out on [≈ bear down on] my English study. Somehow, I managed to get my desired result on the ninth attempt! Imagine, if I didn't try that one last time, my dream of living in Australia would be crushed. **What I gained** from the experience was resilience. So don't lose hope, because if you do, your dream might fall in tatters [≈ your dream might be shattered ≈ your dream might fade away].

**What I'm trying to say is that** no-one likes the feelings of failure or hardship. **The point is that** positive attitude and continuous action will get you through the bad times. Otherwise, you will just have to stay still. **The question is**, are you brave enough to fight against odds? **All you need to do is** to keep going.

So **what I mean is that** whatever bad things you experience, just suck it up. **All I see is that** if you mean business [≈ you are serious and determined], you will succeed.

Do you see any pattern for the words in bold above? Now share any crushing failures you've had by applying similar grammar: 'The problem is...', 'What I do know is that...', 'The end result [≈ upshot] is...' Let me know your views on failure and how you deal with it.

# DAY 130
# CONSISTENCY AND PATIENCE WINS THE RACE

In the success formula, consistency and patience in the formula is very powerful – this speeds up success. Is this a contradiction? Being patient means to slow down. You can't rush things.

The formula isn't wrong. You are right as well. Success takes time, and it comes inch by inch. If it were quick and easy, everyone would be successful. Like it or hate it, success can come at a snail-like or tortoise-like pace.

You might have heard the well-known Aesop's fable 'The Tortoise and the Hare'. In this story, an arrogant hare ridicules [≈ makes fun of] a slow-moving tortoise. The tortoise challenges the hare in a race. The hare soon leaves the tortoise far behind. With confidence of winning the race, the hare stops and takes a nap midway. The tortoise just keeps going, slow but steady. When the hare awakes, the tortoise has just crawled past the finish line. This story tells us that slow, steady and consistency wins the race.

I know your race on the road to success is more difficult than the tortoise and the hare's race. Your race could take years to finish. Unfortunately, there are no shortcuts or cheat-code to win the race. You can't cut corners on this road.

Take small steps every day and do it consistently. Don't dream of overnight success. Don't tell me that you've mastered English by reading this book in one night. I wouldn't believe you! But if you read the book day by day, by now you would have done it for 130 days. Super-duper! Keep doing it! Small snippets of time each day will help you fly.

Also, please be patient [≈ have the patience of a saint ≈ don't lose patience ≈ don't let your patience wear thin ≈ don't run out of patience]. Don't rush. Give it a time. Your progress will grow like compound interest [≈ increase exponentially]. One day, you will reap what you have sowed. Time will tell! That's the power of consistency and patience. Missing either of these two elements, the success formula will lose its power because any number to the power of 0 is only 1.

As long as you always stand in a better position today than yesterday, even just a wee bit [≈ a little bit], you are on the right track!

# DAY 131
## AT YOUR OWN PACE

In today's fast-paced [≈ rushed ≈ hurried] world, people feel that success needs to come quickly – many people have achieved incredible success in their early 20s or 30s.

As we learnt yesterday, success does not happen [≈ come] overnight [≈ Rome wasn't built in a day]. I'm not asking you to build Rome, the Eiffel Tower, Notre Dame Cathedral, Arc de Triomphe, Stonehenge or Buckingham Palace.

I'm simply asking you to build your own house (much easier, huh?). Everyone will have a different style, a different budget and a different pace. Each of you will have a different construction process and take a different amount of time to complete the build.

To complete the last bit of our success formula, you need to work at your own speed. Let's review the formula once more.

$$\text{Success} = \frac{[30\%\text{Luck} + 70\%(\text{Admiration for Your Idol} + \text{Confidence} + \text{Good Habits} + \text{Failures})]^{(\text{Consistency} \times \text{Patience})}}{\text{Your Own Pace}}$$

Remember: it's your house, and it's your success. It is irrelevant to others [≈ It has no relation with others], so pursue it in your own timeline.

Stick to the formula. As for the rest, all you need to do is to take action (Chapter 3), hold faith and belief in your ambitions and yourself (Chapter 4), and make the best use of your time (Chapter 5). But you are not allowed to compare yourself with others (Chapter 11).

If I can't convince you myself, these big names could be an inspiration: Vera Wang designed her first dress at 40. Julia Child published her first [≈ debut] cookbook almost at the age of 50. John Pemberton didn't invent Coca-Cola until the age of 55. Nelson Mandela became president at the age of 76 after spending 27 years in jails…

We've said enough. Work on your dreams at your own pace. One day you'll make it.

# DAY 132
# DREAMS COME TRUE!

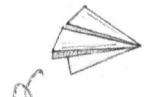

Back in April 2017, in a 4-hour general anaesthesia operation to take out [≈ extract] four wisdom teeth, I lost consciousness completely. This was a blank period of my life. The experience inspired me to do something more meaningful in life, so the idea of writing a book and sharing my overseas experience came about. Let's say it became one of my dreams.

Having a full-time job, and sometimes working overtime, meant that my time was constrained [≈ I didn't have plenty of time ≈ I didn't have much time ≈ I didn't have ample time ≈ I didn't have adequate time ≈ I didn't have abundant time ≈ I was time-poor ≈ I had a lack of time ≈ I was pressed with time ≈ my time was not sufficient ≈ time was not my friend ≈ time was my enemy ≈ time was not on my side ≈ time was a hurdle].

The only time that I had to type up these lovely English words on the screen during weekdays was early mornings, commuting between work and home, or an hour or so before bedtime. Over weekends, I went out to meet up with writers, joined free workshops for self-publishing and attended book launches. I gained knowledge, support and encouragement from so many like-minded people.

Although this book was written in fits and starts [≈ in bits and pieces ≈ intermittently ≈ sporadically], it was an enjoyable process. But I had bad days, days where I felt stuck and was short of [≈ ran out of ≈ lacked ≈ stuck for] ideas and the right vocabulary. I struggled with the slowness of the writing.

But 2 years on, I created over 170,000 words with my daily efforts. I started to feel the power of doing it consistently. I was heading towards my writing dream. I just simply couldn't believe I had made a 'book' by squeezing time through the cracks of my life!

Will Smith once said, 'You lay one brick as perfectly as a brick can be laid. You do that every single day. And soon you have a wall.'

English Builders, see, you've laid 132 bricks up to now. Good on you! You might not notice the difference every single day. But keep going [≈ continue on ≈ persevere] and you'll have a house in no time.

# DAY 133
# DREAMS COME TRUE?

While I was happy with my result writing the book, I reached out to a professional writer and editor, Ashley, who gave me this advice:

- Sell your book in one sentence. (Well, I'd never thought about that.)
- Your words need to be more exciting. (Well, I didn't know how.)
- What's your logic behind all 365 topics? (Well, I couldn't answer.)

Uh-oh! All I had done was the baby steps. [≈ It was still early days. ≈ There was still a long way to go.] I stared at the laptop screen, listening to the clock tick. I started to doubt myself. I thought:

- Why did I structure my book this way?
- Why were many topics that I wrote boring?
- Why was I ambitious writing a book this thick? I was mad. [≈ I was crazy. ≈ I was insane. ≈ I was deranged. ≈ I was unhinged.]
- What was I doing? Was writing the book even worth my time?
- When would my manuscript be ready to go out into the world?
- How would I even market the book after publishing it?
- Why had I worked so damn hard to write this book?

I was lost. I wondered what I had got myself into. I'd heard that many authors couldn't sell a single copy of their book after it was published! But there were only two options ahead of me:

- **Option #1:** Stop there. My artwork would never be completed, which meant my 2 years' writing time and effort would have been totally wasted.
- **Option #2:** Rework each page and each word to take it to a standard I would be satisfied with. (Writing is artwork – it will never be prefect.)

In the end, I selected the latter. Write – amend – rewrite – restructure – rewrite – amend – phew! – new ideas – start again – repeat. Writing became part of my life. I slept with it. I put down brilliant ideas the seconds they popped into my mind [≈ sprang to mind ≈ came up] in case they fizzled out [≈ slipped away ≈ disappeared]. Along the way, I kept reading, writing, listening and speaking.

A year on from this and the book was still in the works [≈ in the making]. I stopped asking when my dream would become true. (I really don't know when I stopped.) I stopped doubting. (I know it's a matter of time if I'm consistent.) So just hunt your dreams down doggedly.

# DAY 134
# DREAMS DO COME TRUE!

After such a long procedure that included consulting experienced writers, sourcing a trustworthy publisher, getting the best editor for my book, changing the structure again, rewriting almost every page and editing another thousands of times (such a gruelling and painful work!), the book was finally starting to come together.

OMG! I would finally reach my dream of becoming an author! By the end, it would be almost five years of consistent effort. I now smile about the book and shed happy tears.

What has this writing experience taught me?

- **Passion.** In many dictionaries, passion is defined as having a strong liking for something. My definition for the word is to behave like crazy. You do it no matter what and you also have fun whenever you do it.

- **Commitment.** In busy days of finishing work late, I only put down a few words each time. At this point, I doubted if my book would ever be completed, let alone to be packed up and sold to others. I doubted this millions of times. But I did it anyway. The longer I invested in the book, the stronger I felt my belief in it grew – the consistency of doing it – although it felt as if it were all as slow as a snail.

- **Financial.** To develop any interests or hobbies, you need to invest money. My accounting job gave me the financial backing to help develop the book. It helped to fund writing activities (and pay my home office mortgage, electricity bill, buy laptop and printer, etc.). So it's best to make sure that you have no financial worries while developing a hobby or doing something that you're passionate about.

- **Writing a book.** Don't dedicate your whole life to a 9-to-5 job. No-one will remember all that work you've done. Try something new. Do something more meaningful in your life. If I'd never tried writing a book, I would never have known how much time, effort, and energy it required. So I salute [≈ I take my hat off to ≈ I pay homage to] all writers, authors, and artists out there.

So dear readers, if you have been reading this book from Day 1 up until now, I believe you are standing in a better position than you did 4 months ago. Keep up the excellent work! Reap the reward when you finish reading. You've got greater things to conquer. Just do it! Dreams do come true with consistent (superhuman) effort!

# DAY 135
## LIVE OUT YOUR DREAM

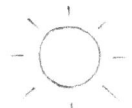

In **Day 17 Dream Big** or **Day 25 Your Final Decision**, you wrote down some dreams on a piece of paper (or possibly your notebook). It's time to take that out. Have you succeeded in any of your dreams yet? If you have, then congratulations! You're victorious! You've succeeded [≈ reached for the stars ≈ become accomplished]!

Celebrate your resounding success! I'm proud of you! You're living out your coveted life. See, dreams do come true when you put in tremendous effort [≈ exhausting effort ≈ excessive effort ≈ enormous effort ≈ vast effort ≈ strenuous effort], even if it's just a teeny bit each day. Are you pinching yourself? Are you crying for joy? Has your hard work paid dividends? How does it all feel? Write down your feelings below:

...........................................................................................................................

...........................................................................................................................

...........................................................................................................................

I'm happy for you! But please be humble [≈ remain unassuming ≈ stay modest]. Don't be complacent. [≈ Don't be smug. ≈ Don't gloat. ≈ Don't be conceited. ≈ Don't be cocky. ≈ Don't be bigheaded. ≈ Don't be arrogant. ≈ Don't be all over yourself. ≈ Don't get a swollen head.]

The more you grow, the more you will realise there is so much more that you don't know, so keep lifting yourself up. Become a better you! [≈ Become a better version of yourself! ≈ Bring out the best in yourself!] Self-improvement [≈ Self-enhancement] is worth doing. Continue to invest in personal growth for yourself. Nothing succeeds like success! [≈ Success breeds greater success in the future!]

You can unlock your full potential.

If you're still pursuing your dreams, close the book now, and endeavour to work on [≈ hammer away at] whatever you are dreaming of. Don't rush it. Success doesn't happen overnight, as we mentioned. It could be 1 year, 2 years, 3 years, 6 years, or even more. Again, the key is to be consistent in your effort, be determined and have faith in yourself. Eventually, I promise that you'll succeed and live out your dreams.

< To continue living my dream of being an author, I'm learning to build a website (**https://ilovemelbourne365.com**) – hopefully, it'll be ready by the time the book is released. (But if not, please just be patient with me). You can also check out or follow me on Instagram account **ilovemelbourne365** where I share some photos about life in Melbourne as a sort of supplement to this book. What about Facebook and Twitter? Managing multiple social media platforms would take away too much of my time, and I'm not a social media type of person. I even had no idea on how hashtags worked on Instagram when I created the account in April 2022! I also like the principle of 'less is more'. So let me start small and do it bits by pieces. But I'll make consistent effort! Cheers! >

# DAY 136
## THE WORD - UP

Let me **strike up** a conversation with you. Today, I will bring you a list of common verbs that are followed by the word '**up**'. Knowing this and using them in the proper context can be **the ace up your sleeve** [≈ give you an advantage ≈ be advantageous]. Alright, let's **roll up** our sleeves now and read a story full of the word 'up'.

All of a sudden, a storm **blew up** [≈ the weather turned stormy]. I was soaked. [≈ I got wet. ≈ I got soaked through. ≈ I was soaking wet. ≈ I was drenched. ≈ I was wet through.]

I was running late for the meeting when Zara **called** me **up**, 'Where are you?' she asked. I said, '**Coming up**! [≈ I'm coming!]'

When I stepped into our meeting room, I said, 'Sorry, I'm late. I was **caught up** by the rain. [≈ I was late because of the rain.]'

'No worries.' Zara **walked up to** me. 'As you know, we're going to **open up** a pop-up [≈ temporary] shop in Clayton. We're discussing the layout. FYI, Claire isn't in. She's been **throwing up** [≈ vomiting] the whole morning. But she'll **catch up** on her part tomorrow.'

Zara said, 'Chandler, please **fix up** the printer later on. Jade, can you please **check up** on a few things for me after the meeting? Emily, can you please **crank up** the volume on the speaker? We can't hear anything. Now I'm going to raise a question. How can we **beef up** [≈ strengthen] our internet security for all of our stores?'

Like

Okay, our time is **up**! Wow! You're now **up** to Day 136. If this book has **whipped up** your interest in English and blown your mind, give me a double **thumbs up,** or hit the Like button **right up over there. Keep it up**! **Look up** 'verbs' plus 'up' in the dictionary. You are **stepping up** your game! [≈ You will be getting better at this!] You are **going up** to the next level. **Up and up**.

Now **stand up**. **Loosen up** your body. Let's **catch up** tomorrow.

# PART 2 LOVE YOUR PROFESSION

To start building a house, you need sufficient money to buy the materials (bricks, wood, glass, blinds, curtains, ducted heating, solar panels, benchtops, etc.).

Where does the money for this come from? Your profession! Whether you're a 9-to-5 office worker, or a business owner, the more you earn, the better quality materials that you'll be able to afford for your house.

Let's get going!

# DAY 137
## CHOOSE YOUR OCCUPATION CAREFULLY

If you haven't entered the workforce, please do have a think on what you'd like to do for a career.

Often, we hear people say:

- If I could start again, I wouldn't be a taxi driver. I would study hard to get a law degree.
- If I had another chance, I imagine I would become a sportsperson. I would train hard and play hard to be the top ranking player in the world. I would be filthy rich [≈ extremely rich].
- If I were not a tour guide, I'd make my career in designing electronic games.
- If I were given a second chance, I would be a doctor, not working as a barista.

< A barista is a person who works at a café [≈ at a coffee bar ≈ at a coffeehouse ≈ at a coffee shop], serving and making espresso coffee. >

< All the above bullet points use the subjunctive mood to express a wish, which is not factual. The subjunctive mood can also be used to give a command or a suggestion, or to explore hypothetical situations. Can you spot them on the page? >

Of course, if you really want to reset [≈ start over] your career, you can do so at any time. And I encourage you to do so. Rather than sticking to something that does not motivate you and that makes you miserable, make the move. As you get older, it requires more energy and more determination to make it happen. No matter when, choose to do whatever makes you happy.

I'm not demanding that you listen to my advice. I propose that you take a moment. Your first few jobs are crucial. They add up to future experience. You might enjoy your profession and stay in the one profession for most of your life. Or you might even change your profession at some point in your life. Whichever happens, it all comes down to your personality and passion.

Now, brainstorm with me some occupation names. Write down your answers, including your dream career in the blank areas, and highlight your dream job. It is imperative that you know what you'd love to do.

---

magician, musician, counsellor, detective, priest, paramedic, therapist, dentist, nun, scientist, engineer, educator, chef, zookeeper, analyst, acupuncturist, courier, consultant, anaesthetist, auctioneer, copywriter, economist, trader, judge, astronaut, mathematician, archaeologist, veterinarian, architect, farmer, cartographer, painter, translator, blacksmith, handyman, technician, surveyor

..................................................................................................................................................

..................................................................................................................................................

# DAY 138
## WHAT IS YOUR PROFESSION?

If you're currently in the workforce, tell me what your occupation is [≈ what you do for a living]. Is it a job that's paid well? What is good about your job? What is bad?

I'm an accountant. Most people think accounting is boring [≈ dull]. But I find it fun. I'll explain. Our role has evolved from number-crunchers to storytellers. We are business partners and like business consultants. We ask questions like these: What are the risks and opportunities for business? What did we budget? What is the actual result? What is forecasted? Why are there variances between budget, actual result and forecast? What are the drivers? Should we shut down one unprofitable department or keep it? How do we run a plant more efficiently?

As a qualified accountant, we are able to work under huge pressure and still being well organised, and maintain high levels of accuracy. Attention to details is entrenched in our daily life.

However, one of the bad things is that we're treated like overhead costs because we don't seem to generate straightforward revenue like a salesperson, although we do add value. The salary at the start of a career in accounting is disappointing compared with the workload. Working prolonged hours [≈ extreme hours ≈ overtime ≈ for a long time] happens quite often. During the busy season, tax accountants and auditors could end up working 80–100 hours a week!

< How long are 80 hours? An Australian full-time employee normally works 38 hours per week (7.6 hours × 5 days). Lunch and break times are not included in this calculation. So, 80 hours is more than double a typical week of work! >

I'm still glad to be an accountant. The good qualities that I've developed during the years are incredible. As an accountant, you could end up in a CFO position, an author, or even a champion of *MasterChef*. Amazing!

In fact, every profession has its pros and cons. Computer programmers [≈ Coders] can design their own software products but they are often considered nerds by many and they have to keep up with the new technology that's changing constantly. Doctors are paid well but it takes them years of university study before becoming registered as a medical practitioner. And once they start work, they might have to be on call 24 hours. Being a freelancer sounds cool with freedom and flexibility, but chances are that you don't have a stable cashflow when starting out in the profession.

# DAY 139
## JOBS BY COLLAR COLOUR

From the very beginning [≈ From the get-go ≈ In the first place], have a think on what types of job that you'd like to be engaged in (a 9-to-5 office job, a trade or other service providing job).

My accounting profession is a desktop-based [≈ desk-based] job, which keeps me away from sunshine and rainy days. Such a white-collar job sounds like one of the safest jobs in the world and as regular as clockwork.

But hunching over a desk for a lengthy period [≈ prolonged sitting] without moving puts a strain on my body, leaving me sometimes with a stiff neck and back pain. Staring at the computer screen throughout the day damages my vision [≈ strains my eyes ≈ harms my eyesight]. It can also be mentally challenging with a lot of stress.

So, what about trade jobs? Plumbers, electricians, carpenters, plasterers, jointers, construction builders and other labour jobs fall into this category. In China, these blue-collar workers [≈ handymen ≈ tradespersons ≈ tradies] are looked down upon and the pay cheque is shitty [≈ pitiful]. By contrast, trade jobs are respected in the western world where the pay could be even higher than an office job. If you'd like to get your foot in this industry, be prepared to get your hands dirty!

You could also become a pink-collar worker working in service field. These sorts of positions include washroom attendants, nannies or babysitters, waiters or waitresses [≈ waitstaff ≈ caterers ≈ servers], nurses, retail clerks, etc. It's 'pink' because these jobs were predominately held by women back in the 1970s (Wood, 2020). Such jobs could be a physical challenge on the body, where you could stand for long periods of time and develop lower back pain, foot pain, bunions, varicose veins or swollen legs.

You could consider becoming a green-collar worker employed in the environmental sectors; a black-collar worker (miners or oil-drillers); a red-collar working in government. Or you could probably perform other collars jobs that you genuinely love.

Whatever colour collar you've chosen, be proud of what you do. You'll make a living all by yourself. [≈ You'll be financially independent. ≈ You'll support yourself financially. ≈ You can feed yourself.] Good on you!

# DAY 140
# BE A FISH IN A BIG POND OR A SMALL POND?

Are there any particular big companies that you'd love to work for? Have you built up any network or skills that could help you get through the job interview with this company and get your foot in the door? If you've nailed it, awesome! Please appreciate what you've got and get the most out of the work.

< When you get your foot in the door, you've succeeded with your very first step! The phrase alludes to salesman using their feet to block the door while doing door-to-door sales. This makes it hard for the owner of the house to close the door. >

Not everyone is lucky enough to get the golden opportunity to go into a massive multinational corporation [≈ a top Fortune 500 company ≈ a multibillion-dollar business] at the start of their career.

< Question: Who made the list on top Fortune 500 companies in the last few years? Are any of these companies in the list? Walmart, Amazon, JPMorgan Chase, Pfizer, Tyson Foods. >

You might work at a start-up business or a small-to-medium sized company, or even help out in a mum-and-dad business [≈ mom-and-pop business ≈ family enterprise].

Such business might not be able to provide you with extensive training, opportunities to grow, or provide employee benefits in the same way the big companies do. There's no need to feel ashamed by working there. More often than not, these small businesses are more friendly and like working with family. It's actually easier to get involved in all aspects of the business and develop into a professional all-rounder, whereas at a top-ranked company you might get stuck in a particular position, or your voice might be ignored, or your hard work might not be recognised at all.

The point here is that every company has its pluses and minuses. The company might be posting a profit [≈ making money] or operating at a loss. Or the company could be on the verge of collapse [≈ going bankrupt ≈ going bust] or go out of business [≈ enter voluntary administration ≈ be in receivership].

Wherever you are (in a big pond or a small pond), make the most of it. It doesn't matter whether you're a big fish or a small fish for now, as long as you're willing to swim the extra mile. No-one should stick to just one pond for life nowadays. It'll be just part of your beautiful career journey, for sure.

# DAY 141
# COMPANY, INDUSTRY, ECONOMY AND JOB SEARCHING

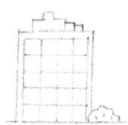

In today's highly [≈ fiercely ≈ intensely] competitive job market, companies are committed to sustainable development and actively being involved with social responsibility. For example, TOMS Shoes promise to give away a new pair of shoes to a kid in need for every pair of shoes that is purchased by the customer. Every bottle of Thankyou water helps fund water sanitation and hygiene programs in low-income countries. Nespresso has their recycling program send used coffee capsules [≈ coffee pods] to farmers, so the coffee grounds inside can be used as a compost. The material of the capsules (aluminium) is then recycled to make pens and other everyday products.

Working for a company that has values that align with your values is awesome!

When thinking about which industry you might want to find work in, just consider that some industries out there are reeling or disappearing – industries such as abacus manufacturing and match production, while new ones are emerging (Big Data and 3D-printing). Some industries struggle when the economy is tough, whereas some thrive during that same period of time. Consider whether COVID-19 impacted on any of the industries in the table below:

| Mining | Education | Food production | Property |
| --- | --- | --- | --- |
| Logistics | Restaurants | Financial Services | Construction |
| Airlines | Healthcare | Public transportation | Retail stores |

The economy has an immediate and firsthand impact upon job vacancy. When the economy goes gangbusters [≈ When economic performance is strong ≈ In a flourishing economy], there are more job opportunities expected in the market.

< Do you have a weird feeling for the phrase of 'go gangbusters'? The expression comes from an American radio program, *Gang Busters*, from mid-20th century. The program started with loud sound effects and excitements. Over years, the phrase has evolved to indicate that something goes well, not just the initial stages (Like Gangbusters, n.d.). >

In a frail [≈ crumbling ≈ sagging] economy, companies are pickier and expect employees to do more with less. They could even cut [≈ slim down ≈ fire ≈ sack ≈ axe ≈ lay off] staff. Think of what happened during the GFC (global financial crisis) in 2008. The stock market crashed [≈ plummeted]. Businesses collapsed [≈ shut down]. Millions of people lost their jobs, went broke and couldn't afford mortgage payments. Imagine: a job opening could receive hundreds of thousands of applications within a short period of time. It might take much longer to get a job in this sort of market.

But the boom and bust of the economy has little impact on how to seek a job. Follow your own rhythm. And be patient, as always.

# DAY 142
## GET YOURSELF READY

Since you've decided what types of job and industry you want to work in, it's time to consider your job expectations, which can help narrow down your selection. Ask yourself the following:

- What is the expected position and salary?
- Does company location matter?
- Are you looking for a full-time job, a part-time job or a casual job? Or are you looking for a permanent job, a fixed-term position, or a temporary role?

Below are some channels that you can use to start looking for a job:

- Apply online through Seek, LinkedIn, CareerOne, or a particular company's website.
- Contact an employment agency [≈ a recruitment agency] such as Hays, Hudson, Michael Page, Robert Half, Sharp & Carter, or other specialist agencies.
- Try cold calling a company or knocking on the door. The chances are slim [≈ It's a long shot ≈ It's unlikely], but it's worth trying. There might be a fighting chance. Who knows?

Keep in mind: Job hunting [≈ Beating the streets ≈ Pounding the pavements] is not hard. It's just a process.

In this chapter, I'm going to show you that you can get any job that you like in Australia. You don't need to have any relationship with anyone who's hiring in the company.

< If you're searching for a stable and well-paid job in China, you might need a parent who has valuable contacts who can offer you a job. This is called 'guanxi (关系)' in Chinese, which is similar to the word 'relationship' in English. But this is not exactly the same. To build up that 'guanxi', you might need to do something like give away your money or give an expensive gift to bond your relationship first. In Australia, you don't have to do this. If you like, a small gift like a bottle of wine or a notebook shows your appreciation to the person who helped get you the job. Under most circumstances, you can just get the job all by yourself. >

I don't suggest looking for the job in fits and starts. Just apply yourself consistently. Keep actively searching and stick to the process. Never give up the hope. You will find the best job for you at that time in your life. Are you ready mentally and physically for the work ahead? If so, let's start the process!

# DAY 143
# CRAFTING RESUMES AND COVER LETTERS

Okay, so it's time to draft your CV [≈ resume] and cover letter [≈ motivation letter]! There are numerous formats and templates for all occupations to be found online. Download one that you love and tailor it to suit your needs [≈ tweak it to meet your needs].

< 'CV' stands for *curriculum vitae*, which is a Latin term, meaning 'course of life'. There is no clear distinction between the use of CV and resume in Australia. [≈ Australians use the two terms interchangeably.] But some countries do distinguish them (What Is the Difference Between a Resume and a CV?, 2020). >

So, what do you need to put on your resume? Here are a few things:

- Include your name, residential address, mobile phone number and email address at the very top of the CV.
- Be clear about your career goals.
- List your education, key competencies and software skills.
- In work experience section, put down job titles and work periods for your current job and each of your past jobs. Work periods should be stated in reverse chronological order [≈ sequence]. Add a brief on the nature of the business and the size of the company. Responsibilities for each of your roles should be listed by bullet point.
- What are your key achievements in each role? It's worth mentioning them.
- Don't forget to showcase your ongoing professional development, if any.
- In the References section, putting down 'available upon request' would be sufficient. But you should have your referees' contact details ready because your potential employer will request a reference check normally after the second round interview.

Ideally, your CV should be one or two pages long, even if you have extensive work experience. When you don't have extensive work experience, preparing a candid cover letter is the key.

Use this chance to:

- State why you would work for the company by incorporating your research on the company's background, history or anything else that intrigues you about the company.
- Use concise examples to illustrate that you're capable of doing the job [≈ that you're the best candidate for the job].

Time spent crafting the CV and cover letter will pay off. A unique and wholehearted document for each job application will make you stand out from the crowd [≈ separate you from the herd ≈ set you apart from other candidates]. Once the application is ready, start circulating your CV with the cover letter as a PDF (Portable Document Format) online (as long as the file format for the job isn't specified). Good luck!

# DAY 144
# PREPARE INTERVIEW QUESTIONS

You've started to get your job applications out to the world, so it's time to practise commonly asked interview questions at home. Again, with the internet, you can find a whole lot of questions and example answers. Do your homework. Use the sample questions as a guide and make your own story. I'll only go through four must-prepare questions with you.

**1. Where do you see yourself in 5 years? [≈ What's your 5-year plan?]**

I set myself the goal of [≈ set my sights on ≈ envision myself ≈ visualise myself] becoming a qualified engineer in the next few years. Does that sound cliché? I really liked the idea that came from a popular career adviser YouTuber Deniz Sasal. Answer the question like this: 5 years are too long in this dynamic world. I can't guarantee where I'll be in 5 years' time. But what I can guarantee you is that if I'm selected for the role, I'll utilise my skills and do my best to work with you and the team to achieve the goal.

Of course, you can prepare your own brilliant answer!

< Can you list some of common cliché sayings? Put it down here:

.................................................................................................................

.................................................................................................................

.................................................................................................................

Here are mine: 'All that glitters is not gold.', 'What goes around comes around.', 'What doesn't kill you makes you stronger.', 'The apple doesn't fall far from the tree.' >

**2. What are your strengths?**

Singing is in my DNA. I have it in my blood. I was born for sports. [≈ I was born with sports-playing genetics.] I have a natural aptitude for painting. Hey, if you're not interviewing for the position of a singer, an athlete, a painter, these strengths are irrelevant. Dig deep to find your strengths that could contribute to the role. And provide examples.

**3. What is your greatest weakness?**

You can't say 'I'm terrible with numbers [≈ I'm not good at numbers]' if you're an accountant', nor 'talking has never been my thing' if you aim to work as a TV presenter. Figure out one or two weaknesses that won't cause damage to your interview, and state how you're taking action to improve the weakness/es.

**4. Why are you leaving your current job (or why have you left your job)?**

You're probably leaving for many reasons. It could be a high workload or too much office drama. Does your potential employer need to know these facts? Nope. Also, don't bad talk [≈ speak maliciously about] your former bosses and colleagues. Don't burn your bridges. It's a small world. Whatever valid reason you have, just simply say 'I'm looking to further my career growth. There are no career opportunities in my current company.'

# DAY 145
# MORE PREPARATION

Never walk into the interview empty-handed. [≈ Always attend the interview fully prepared. ≈ Don't come in for an interview blind.] There's still a lot of preparation to do.

Have you thought of examples to give for behavioural interview questions? Behavioural questions are questions based on an assumed situation to see how you reacted in past roles. Questions like 'Tell me a time when one of your team members was underperforming. What did you do?' or 'Give an example of when you solved a difficult problem. What do you wish you had done differently?'

CAR (context, action, result) or STAR (situation, target, action, result) methods help you answer the question and keep you on the track. Practise your answers until you can answer popular interview questions freely and comfortably.

Have a think about what questions you're interested in asking your potential employer: 'Is there any career support and training?' or 'How much staff do you have?' or 'What's the company culture like?' or 'What are your insights into this industry over the next 5 years?'

Get yourself a formal business suit and a pair of leather shoes if you're attending an office job interview. Don't wear business casual, or casual, or sporty. Runners, sandals, rubber thongs, flip-flops, shorts, three-quarter pants, cropped pants, gym gear, beach wear, sports training apparel – all these are a big no.

So, you seem to have prepared everything and you're confident and passionate about the jobs out there. You keep sending out applications [≈ circulating your resume and cover letter]. However, after submitting over 20 applications, you still haven't received a phone interview. It's time to challenge yourself. Think: Is what you've put on paper compatible with what the company is looking for? Does it stand out from the crowd? Review and rework the documents. If necessary, seek help from a professional.

Ah! Here is some more prep work. Set up your voice message on your phone (put down your name here on the blank dotted underline): 'Hello. This is ............... . [≈ You're calling ............... .] I'm currently not available. [≈ I can't pick up your phone at the moment.]. Please leave a message and I'll get back to you as possible as I can. [≈ Please leave your details after the tone. I'll call you back ASAP.]'

# DAY 146
# MEETING UP WITH RECRUITMENT AGENCIES

Your phone is ringing: it's a strange number. It could be a phone interview from an HR recruiter for a company or a recruitment agency. You get nervous.

Wait. You don't have to pick up the phone straight away. Let it ring out. Wait for the voice message to come in. Find out who called you. It's from a job agency! Ring them back in a quiet place when you're ready. They'll ask you some basic questions such as 'Tell me a bit about yourself.' and 'What do you do in your current role?', etc. When the conversation is about to finish, they normally schedule an interview time with you. Hooray!

Wait. Don't get over excited! An interview with a recruitment agency doesn't guarantee a job opportunity. But it's a great start. Treat it as a formal interview. Here are a few things to think about:

- First impressions are everything. For women, a little make-up will add some points for your first impression. Make sure spruce up, sharp, smart and corporate on the day. Look your best!

- Business formal [≈ Office attire ≈ Business attire ≈ Putting on a suit] is a must.

- Google the place. Work out how you're getting there. Don't run late.

Now you're armed to the teeth!

< When you're 'armed to the teeth', you carry many weapons. It's used figuratively here, meaning you're well-prepared or even over-prepared for the interview. >

Go in and have a chat with the job agency. You can tell them to keep your job search confidential so that your current employer doesn't know that you're looking for a job.

You will be asked questions similar to the questions in a normal interview with a potential employer. You might encounter questions like:

- What does your typical day look like in your current role?

- What's your current salary and what's your expected salary for your next role?

- Why are you leaving your current employer?

What a great practice opportunity! Show the best side of yourself and be honest. Recruitment agencies, of course, will present you to their clients if you leave a great impression and you're a perfect fit for the role. You never know.

# DAY 147
## TELEPHONE INTERVIEW

*Ring, ring, ring,* your phone is ringing again. You know what to do now.

This time around, the voice message says that the person is from HR from the company you've applied for a job with recently. Yeah! Awesome! Flick through your application to this employer. Review the company's background. Ring back when you're in a quiet place.

Some typical questions could be: 'Tell me about yourself.' or 'What is a typical workday like for you?' or 'What are your current job responsibilities?' or 'Why are you leaving?' or 'What made you apply for a job at our company?' Answer questions with confidence, and be concise. You'll get a sense if you're going to be selected before you hang up the phone.

If the caller says that they still need to phone other candidates or that it's just a screening process, they'll probably never call you back. They are not interested in what you say over the phone. If they're checking your availability for a face-to-face interview, they might say 'We have availability for you for an interview on Friday. What time will best suit you?' Great, you're successful. They like you! If you're currently working full-time, it's okay to negotiate an earlier interview time, such as before 8.30 am or 9.00 am.

The call could also come from the recruitment agency who you interviewed with. Great! They just referred you for an interview with their client!

It's not the time for a celebration or a reward yet. Move onto the next round of preparation. Check out the company's location and decide how to get there on the day for the interview. Do more research on the company's history, values, products, services, financial reports and any information available online. Get to know your potential boss's background through LinkedIn, if able. Go through interview questions again and think about the questions to ask your potential employers. After all, it's a two-way selection. Print out a couple of copies of your CV, cover letter and even your achievements at work. Take them with you on the day.

Don't run late on the day. Best of luck! [≈ Good luck! ≈ I wish you all the best! ≈ I wish you luck! ≈ Godsend! ≈ Godspeed! ≈ Touch wood! ≈ Break a leg! ≈ Fingers crossed!]

# DAY 148
## ACE YOUR FIRST ROUND INTERVIEW

Alright, the day has come. Dress up professionally. Arrive ahead of the scheduled time. Greet, and shake hands with your interviewer(s) firmly. Avoid a limp handshake [≈ a soft handshake] or a dead fish handshake [≈ a hard handshake].

You're now being ushered into the boardroom. Is this nerve-wracking? Relax, buddy. The interview is just a conversation with your potential employer. It's your time to shine – sit straight, smile confidently, and comfortably present yourself throughout. How? Let's see:

- **Answer professionally.** Keep it short and simple (the short name is KISS). Your answers should always be work related. Take your personal life or irrelevant interests off the table.

- **Show your passion.** You want the job so desperately [≈ so badly]! But don't say, 'I'm desperate for this job.' Instead, show it by explaining why you applied for the job and what you like about the position.

- **Demonstrate your competence.** You have a set of skills. [≈ Expertise is what you can bring in.] The job is right up your alley [≈ up your street ≈ very suitable for you]. You can show that you are confident that you'll fit the bill.

Use examples to prove that you have exactly the right qualities and personality that the company is looking for.

The interview goes smoothly. Phew! It's done! But it's still not time to celebrate just yet. Go home, draft a special thank you email and send it to the hiring manager or whoever interviewed you. Don't wait another day. This shows that you care (if you do care). Examples are everywhere online for these. But you should reaffirm that:

- You appreciate the chance for the interview.
- You learnt more about the company and the role, by which your interest in the role has grown even stronger.
- You're confident that you're a good fit [≈ you're well-fitted for the position ≈ you're the right person for the job ≈ you're right for the role], and you'll perform exceedingly well in the role.

Keep the email personalised [≈ Make the email special ≈ Customise the email] by mentioning some topics that you talked about during the interview.

# DAY 149
# NAIL YOUR SECOND ROUND INTERVIEW

After a day or two, your phone rings again! Now, you're invited for a second round interview. Oh yes! Your chances of getting the job are better now – 30% at least, if not more, I would say.

Come on! Get one last round of preparation in. Think about:

- Ask the interviewers' names if you can. Look for their LinkedIn profiles. What are their expertise and professional interests? Feel free to bring them up in the interview at the relevant time.

- Research the company again. Prepare some more in-depth questions. If you're applying for a finance-related role, you can ask questions like, 'By reviewing the annual report from the last year, I can see the parent company in America signed a 3-year contract with Chinese customers. What about our local office? Are there any competitive advantages in the Australian market?'

- More behavioural questions are expected in a second round interview. Think of examples like 'Describe a stressful work situation. How did you handle it?', 'Have you ever had conflict with your teammates?' Use the CAR or STAR technique mentioned on **Day 145 More Preparation**.

- Reflect on your first interview. Are there any questions that you could answer better or any skills that you haven't adequately addressed? Incorporate them into your second round interview.

Come to the interview and tell and sell your stories confidently and honestly. Write another follow-up thank you email right after the interview. Perhaps talk about an article or some news that you read online with your potential manager, and add any professional insight related to your potential role. Keep the email short and concise.

For instance, 'I recently read an article on CPA website about good data and bad decisions: the limits of accounting data. There are two interesting points from that I'd like to share with you:

- Accountants should not assume data entered by frontline staff members in system are correct and use it directly. Logic checking is necessary.

- Data quality and accuracy are vital. The interpretation of the data is equally crucial.

Phew! A long process! But it's still not the time to celebrate yet because you haven't been offered the job. Continue on with your job search. Don't slow down.

# DAY 150
# I GOT THE JOB!

One of the signs that you have been declined for a job is that you haven't heard anything from the employer for several days. In most cases, a human resources manager will send out a general email to everyone who is unsuccessful later on, indicating 'you are not what we're after' or equivalent. The excuse could even be 'you are overqualified'.

One of the good signs of getting the job is that your potential employer calls you up to request a reference check. Provide them with your referees' contact numbers, and leave the final decision to your potential employer! But please don't stop searching for job opportunities until you see the job offer [≈ employment contract] in paper!

Your phone starts ringing – *ring – ring – ring*.

You pick up (put down your name on the dotted underline here and below): 'Hi, this is ............................ speaking'.

They say, 'Hi ............................ . This is Steven from (write down your dream company here) ............................ . This is to inform you that you have been hired for the (note down your dream role here) ............................ position. Welcome on board…'

Oh dear god! I'm really lucky! [≈ Luck is on my side!] I got the job! It's too good to be true.

Whoo! Super-duper! [≈ Excellent!] Either you've just landed your first job, or upped your dream position. You have been selected! [≈ You are the last man standing! ≈ You have been picked out!] Congratulations! [≈ Congrats!] You deserve it! [≈ You earned it! ≈ You're a champion!] This is the fruit of your labour.

It does take time, effort and patience to land your dream job. Throughout all this, you were probably ambitious, frustrated, distressed, nervous, relaxed or excited. Or all of these things. It's quite normal, and each job hunter will go through many of these emotions. But by sticking to the methodology that I've shown you, you can get any job that you like! It's that simple!

Getting the job is just the start. Your past experience becomes irrelevant. Get yourself ready for the new position.

Be mindful though: No company is perfect, and no job is perfect. And you're so much more than a job.

# DAY 151
# WHEN IN ROME, DO AS THE ROMANS DO

Hey English Builders! Welcome to the Australian business world!

In the workplace, you can call me Jessie or Jess. Jess is short for Jessie. [≈ Jess is shortened version of Jessie.] I don't mind you calling me JG either (the initials of my first and second names). Or you can even give me a nickname. Likewise, you can call 'Sharon' 'Shaz' or 'Shaza', 'Frank' 'Frankie', 'Benjamin', 'Ben', 'Benny' or 'Bennie'. Do you see anything in common here?

If you were in China, you would end up calling me Ms Gao. 'Mr' or 'Ms' followed by a person's surname in business settings is often used to show respect. Well, when in Rome… please just use people's first name when interacting with everyone, including your boss.

< Hey, we are in Australia, not in Rome. The saying 'When in Rome, do as the Romans do' is attributed to Saint Augustine who found out that Saturdays were a fast day in Rome but not where he was living in Milan. Saint Ambrose offered him wisdom: 'I fast on Saturday when I go to Rome, but I don't when I'm here.' (When in Rome, Do As the Romans Do, 2021). Hence the proverb means that when you're in a foreign country or a new place, follow the local customs. >

There are also other courtesies [≈ politeness] in society that you need to follow. When someone opens the door for you or does you a favour, say 'Ta.' 'Ta' is an Australian slang for 'Thank you' or 'Thanks', both of which are used frequently in daily conversations. 'No worries. [≈ You are welcome. ≈ My pleasure. ≈ It's nothing.]' is a prefect reply. If you intrude or disturb other people's space, say 'Sorry' because everyone enjoys personal space in Australia. The other party will respond 'No worries. [≈ It's okay. ≈ That's all right.]' This is all a part of the culture of being polite.

Also bear in mind: hand gestures are not universal. For example, in emoji, the victory hand is also a peace sign. Chinese people use it as a victory gesture. But if you hold up two fingers the wrong way towards your workmates here in Australia, you will get in trouble. It's like sticking your middle finger up [≈ flipping someone the bird]. They may feel offended.

# CHAPTER 17 - An Aussie Culture Insider

## DAY 152
## WORK AUSSIE - LAID-BACK

'Achoo!' You just sneezed. 'Excuse me,' you say. Your workmates say, 'Bless you!'

< Why do people say 'Bless you' after someone sneezes? One of the theories dates back to the 6th century when Europe was experiencing the bubonic plague outbreak. Sneezing was one of the symptoms of the disease. It was Pope Gregory the Great who suggested people to say 'God bless you' following someone sneezing in the belief that it would protect them from death (Does Your Heart Stop When You Sneeze?, 2019). >

This is just a tiny part of what Australian working life can look. It's quite relaxed. You can have lots of fun here. If your workmates take public transport, they may walk into the office with sports shoes on and change into leather shoes later on. Each Friday, you can wear casual dress/clothes, but probably not shorts or Ugg boots.

< The name Ugg boots is said to be the shortened version of 'flying ugg boots [≈ fug]', which were worn by aviators in Australia during World War I (The Ugg Boot Story, n.d.). It could also come from the wife of the owner of the boot making company. She called the boots ugly (Sam, 2020). >

There are many interesting activities that you could do with workmates. Activities such as going out for coffee, lunch and after-work drinks, STEPtember, Movember, footy tipping, Melbourne Cup sweep, or even a company golf day. Enjoy!

< STEPtember is a fundraising event for people with cerebral palsy. You can donate money and sign up with workmates as a team with everyone taking 10,000 steps every day for the whole 30 days in September as a challenge.

Movember happens in November and is where men are encouraged to grow their moustaches and raise money for health-charities while they do so. This is to raise awareness of men's health.

Footy refers to Australian Rules Football. Many employees engage in footy tipping each year. Each participant contributes, say, 10 bucks, and the money goes into a prize pool. Everyone bets for the winner of each football game each round. The person who chooses the most winners (or sometimes the least) will share the money in the pool at the end of the season. Some super fans even participate in AFL SuperCoach, which is another level of online competition! It might take you a while to get a hang of this competition! Basically, you play a coach role. Working within a salary cap, you pick a team with 30 real AFL players (8 forwards, 11 midfielders, 8 defenders, and 3 rucks). Each week, you choose your starting 22 players before the round starts. These players' real performance will contribute to the scores of your team. The team with highest score each week will win $1000, and the top SuperCoach at the end of home-and-away season will be awarded $50,000!

The Melbourne Cup sweep is horse betting on the Melbourne Cup race. Each entrant draws a ticket with one of the horses participating in the race. Cash is collected and the prize pool is awarded to the person with the top three horses in the race.

These two popular Aussie sports (Aussie Rules football and horseracing) will be introduced in more detail in Chapter 38. >

# DAY 153
## WORK AUSSIE – EVERYONE'S EQUAL

Aussies call their friends 'mate'. Or sometimes they call co-workers 'mate', taxi drivers 'mate', strangers in the street 'mate'... Basically, you can call everyone 'mate'. The word 'mate' originated from the German word 'gemate', meaning to share a meal at the same table (Burin, 2015).

Mateship is thought to be stronger than friendship, and is part of Australian culture, promoting the idea that everyone is equal. This is often reflected at work too. You can sometimes treat your manager how you treat other colleagues – you don't need to be submissive. Speaking your mind freely is the western style. Say 'yes' if you agree, and say 'I disagree [≈ I don't agree]' if you're the opposite.

In addition, senior positions are not always a priority or advantageous. Why? Below are some examples of what my boss did:

- He gave me the last seat in a meeting. He stood up for the meeting instead.
- He held the door open for me.
- He did trivial jobs himself (such as booking airline tickets or filling out expense claim forms).
- He knelt down on the floor sometimes when teaching me something about work.

< In Australia, carpet flooring is often installed in office buildings and school classrooms. When you sit at your desk asking questions, your boss or your tutor could kneel or sit down to answer. >

However, if you work in China, the culture is different. Often, the way that respect is shown differs between the two countries. In China:

- It's better for you to give your seat to your boss when the number of seats is limited.
- You need to walk quickly to the entrance of a room to open the door for your boss.
- You might act as your boss's personal assistant from time to time: top up their mobile phone, make tea, clean their desk and office, or you might even cook for them!
- Your boss wouldn't kneel near you to chat since in Chinese culture touching your knees on the floor shows your utter respect to the other party. If you'd like to ask your boss questions, stand up while he's explaining to you. And when they criticise you, you'd better not talk back.

If you are a boss in China, then lucky you!

# DAY 154
# AUSSIE SLANG

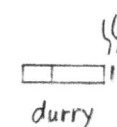
*durry*

Slang is any language used in an informal setting, and **Straya** [≈ Oz ≈ Australia] has a lot of interesting slang.

For instance, 'The bus is as slow as a wet week' means the bus is very slow. '**Garbo**' is a nickname for a garbage collector. Aussies also call tradespeople a '**tradie**', postman/postwoman '**postie**', truckdrivers '**truckie**', politicians '**polly**', and so on. The end part of the words often includes 'ie' or 'y'.

In the workplace, locals like to speak casually, and sometimes using slang. This is part of the work culture that you shouldn't miss out on. Use slang in an informal chat or your co-workers will give you a '**Crikey!**' look. Read on to learn more. The slang words below are all bold. Circle any phrases and explanations that you've never heard of.

My friend set me up with a date with an **Aussie** [≈ Australian] bloke, Ivan, yesterday. He looked so cool in his **sunnies** [≈ sunglasses]! We met in the early morning and ate at **Maccas** [≈ McDonalds]. While we were having egg and bacon for **brekki** [≈ breakfast], a **birdie** [≈ bird] flew over, watching us. Then we went to the **servo** [≈ service station ≈ petrol station] to fill his **ute** [≈ utility vehicle] up with petrol. His **rego number** [≈ car registration number] is 1AB2CD. We also bought some **chewie** [≈ chewing gum]. There's a **Bottle-O** [≈ bottle shop ≈ liquor shop] and a **dunny** [≈ toilet ≈ loo ≈ bathroom] close by. He told me he loved **dog's eye with dead horse** [≈ meat pie with tomato sauce], but he didn't like **durry** [≈ cigarette ≈ fag ≈ ciggy] at all. He's also not the guy who normally **spit the dummy** [≈ lose the temper].

< In Victoria, you can find some interesting slogans under the rego number on a vehicle number plate. The ones that I spot on the road are: 'Victoria – On the Move', 'Victoria – Garden State', 'Victoria – The Place To Be', 'Vic – Stay Alert Stay Alive' and 'Victoria – The Education State'. >

Heavy rainfall came that **arvo** [≈ afternoon]. Neither of us brought a **brolly** [≈ an umbrella]. Ivan invited me for a **cuppa and bikkie** [≈ a cup of tea or coffee and biscuits] at home. He said, 'Come over this Sunday. I'll throw a **barbie** [≈ barbecue ≈ BBQ]. How about we **throw a shrimp** [≈ **a snag** ≈ a sausage] on the barbie?' I said, 'Thank you. This sounds great! But you know cleaning the grill is a **hard yakka** [≈ hard work].' Ivan's a guy I could potentially fall in love with. I was definitely feeling some sparks there.

Is this story **easy as**? **Hilarious as**? Or **sweet as**? Aussies sometimes put the word 'as' after an adjective just to emphasise that adjective. **Bloody oath.** [≈ That is true.]

# DAY 155
# ENTITLED LEAVE

Let's warm up today's topic with some of the types of leave you're entitled to in the workplace in Australia. Shall we?

| Entitled leave | Explanation |
|---|---|
| Annual leave | A full-time worker is entitled to a minimum 20 days of annual leave per year. The number of days is pro-rata for part-time workers. Employees can also cash out annual leave. |
| Long service leave | Each state is different. In Victoria, you can take approximately 8.66 weeks of leave after 10 years of continuous service with one employer. After 7 years, you can take it on a pro-rata basis (Ashley, 2018). |
| Garden leave | This is an agreement where an employee is leaving a job but they stay away from the work for a notice period while remaining on the payroll. |
| Sick leave or carer leave | A full-time employee is eligible for 10 days of sick leave a year. Unlike annual leave, accumulated sick leave cannot be exchanged for money when you leave your job. |
| Public holidays | Public holidays are days that workers do not have to go to work but for which they still get paid. Some employees receive 1.5 times their ordinary salary or get double paid when working on these days. |

Bereavement leave, maternity or parental leave, and study leave are also often available in the workplace.

It is your right to use the leave available to you. When you're crook [≈ you're ill ≈ you fall ill ≈ you're sick ≈ you're feeling unwell ≈ you're under the weather ≈ you're not feeling well ≈ you're out of sorts ≈ you're feeling lousy], please call in to make use of your sick leave.

If you have a cold or the flu, your workmates don't want you to come into the office to spread germs. You can tell your manager 'I have a bit of a head cold and a running nose [≈ a runny nose].' Other common reasons to use sick leave might be:

- I've been struck down with gastro (diarrhoea).
- I have a migraine [≈ a very bad headache ≈ a splitting headache].
- I have my period. I've got stomach cramps. (For girls to use only.)

Some people miss a day at work just because they don't feel like going, so they pretend that they are sick. Such day is called a 'sickie'. Excuses to 'chuck a sickie' might include tooth pain, back pain, sunburn, vomit, stress, or mental health issues. Your boss might not be fully convinced. But it's your entitled leave.

# DAY 156
# PUBLIC HOLIDAYS

Public holidays are days off work for many professions. Yay! In Australia, the dates of the public holidays differ [≈ vary] for each state. Let's get to know some Victorian public holidays today.

**New Year's Day (1 January).** Festival-goers flock into the city at midnight the night before (31 December). They watch fireworks and count down to celebrate a new year. The day after New Year's Eve is a public holiday.

**Australia Day (26 January).** On this significant day, Aussies often fire up barbies at home, and new immigrants often make a pledge to become Australian citizens. However, some actually call it Invasion Day because it marks the day when the First Fleet landed at Sydney Cove and Captain Arthur Phillip raised the British flag, on 26 January 1788. This day is considered the start of a long colonisation of people and land that has severely impacted the First Nations people.

**Good Friday and Easter (March–April with dates varied each year).** Good Friday is the day that Jesus Christ died by crucifixion. Good Friday is held on the Friday before Easter Sunday. Many shops and businesses are closed on the Easter Friday. People often eat hot cross buns at Easter. Kids eat chocolate Easter bunnies and hunt for chocolate Easter eggs. Christ was resurrected and came back to life on Easter Sunday. Rabbits represent rebirth and new life. Easter ends with Easter Monday.

**Anzac Day (25 April).** ANZAC stands for Australian and New Zealand Army Corps. This day carries a lot of significance for Australians as they commemorate those who served and died in previous wars. Each community holds a dawn service early in the morning. Hot dogs or sausages are often provided. If 25 April falls on a weekend, there will be no extra public holiday on the Monday in Victoria.

< Remembrance Day (11 November) is not a public holiday, but it is a memorial day to remember [≈ recall] those soldiers who died since World War I. People often wear a red poppy and a minute's silence is observed at 11 am. >

**Queen's Birthday [≈ Monarch's Birthday] (the second Monday in June).** The current queen of the Commonwealth, Queen Elizabeth II's (Elizabeth Alexandra Mary's) actual birthday is on 21 April. Stores are open with restricted trading hours. People take advantage of a long weekend (Saturday, Sunday and Monday) to travel, socialise and relax. There is a parade in the city to celebrate the event.

< Sadly, the queen passed away on 8 September 2022. Australians were given a one-off public holiday on 22 September to mourn the death of Queen Elizabeth II. >

Victorians also enjoy another five public holidays a year: **Labour Day (the second Monday in March), Footy Grand Final (the Friday before the Saturday AFL Grand Final in September), Melbourne Cup (the first Tuesday in November), Christmas Day (25 December)** and **Boxing Day (26 December)**.

# DAY 157
# SANTA IS HERE!

Hooray! Christmas is drawing near [≈ approaching ≈ arriving ≈ on the horizon ≈ coming soon]! Santa Claus is coming to town. 'Jingle bells, jingle bells, jingle all the way. Oh, what fun it is to ride, in a one-horse open sleigh, hey!'

I wish you a very, very merry Christmas! [≈ Merry Christmas!]

Let's look at a few things associated with Christmas [≈ Xmas].

- **Santa Claus.** Santa is also called Saint Nicholas [≈ St Nick], Father Christmas and Kris Kringle. The old version of Santa did not wear red but green (Buddy the Elf, n.d.). At your workplace, you might exchange small gifts with workmates in a gift giving tradition called Kris Kringle.

- **Santa's reindeer and snowman.** Reindeer are large deer with long wide horns living in cold northern areas. In the Southern Hemisphere, Christmas is in summer, so you can enjoy the sunshine and the beach.

- **Chimney.** Santa has a big heart. During the night, he climbs onto the roof of a house and drops stockings and presents through the chimney to give people a surprise on Xmas day.

- **Christmas crackers!** Bonbon time! Christmas crackers are paper rolls that when pulled apart make an exploding 'pop'. Inside, you will often find a party hat or a bad joke. For example, Q: How can you tell that Santa is real? A: You can always sense his presents!

- **Gingerbread men and houses.** Gingerbread is Christmassy – these are biscuits that are ginger-flavoured and shaped into a cute human being or house. In the fairytale *The Gingerbread Man*, a gingerbread boy was eaten by a fox.

- **Christmas trees.** People decorate a Christmas tree at home, either real or artificial, and either spruce, pine or fir, with lights, garlands, ribbons and ornaments. Presents are hidden underneath (or hang on) the tree. Check out what Santa has sent you! [≈ What did Santa bring you?]

< Evergreen conifers are often used for Christmas trees. Evergreens symbolise everlasting life because they stay green and retain their leaves throughout the cold winter. They are also believed to keep away witches, ghosts, evil spirits and illness. For some traditions, you don't put up the tree until 1 December and it needs to be taken down by 5 January (Lyall, n.d.). >

# DAY 158
## BONJOUR!

你好. Hello, こんにちは, Ciao

G'day mate! [≈ Good day, mate! ≈ Hello! ≈ Howdy! ≈ Bonjour!] Let's check out various greetings in the office today. Does this sound boring and dry? Have you tried to greet other people in a variety of ways?

< 'Bonjour' is 'Hello' in French, but people sometimes use it to greet in informal settings. The funny thing is that when growing up learning English, our textbook only taught us one version of greeting: 'How do you do?' I've never heard it in any conversation in Australia. >

Here are other ways to say 'Hi!' Quite simply: 'Mate [≈ Hey man ≈ Hi there ≈ Hi dude ≈ Hi English Builder], how are you today [≈ how's it going ≈ how are you doing ≈ how are you going ≈ how have you been]?'

You might respond with 'I'm doing well. How are you?' or 'I'm good, thank you. Yourself?' or 'Pretty well.' or 'I'm doing just fine.'

< Again, my English textbook in China taught me to answer, 'How do you do?' with 'I'm fine. And you?' Locals would rarely reply 'And you?' The same with 'I'm just so-so', which is a Chinglish. As its name suggests, it's not English, but rather, Chinglish is a blending of Chinese and English language. Get to know it for fun – but don't use it. It's not fun at all. >

Remember the expressions from **Day 90 Keep Your Soul Happy**? You can also reply by expressing your happy state, such as, 'I'm in tip-top condition. [≈ I'm tickled pink. ≈ I'm on top of the world.]' Or the very Aussie version, 'I'm bloody well, thanks!' Or even the concise version, 'Epic!'

You can also greet someone with 'What's up? [≈ What's new? ≈ What's happening? ≈ What's going on?]' Responses might be: 'Not much. [≈ Nothing much.]' or 'I'm a bit flat.' or 'Same old, same old.' or 'Nothing special.' To engage with workmates more, you could use, 'I'm hanging in there, been a busy week' or 'Ahh, it's Friday, can't complain' or 'Did you hear about our new product release?'

Greet in a genuine sense and keep a smiling face. That's all you need to do. It's like taking candy from a baby [≈ It's very easy to do ≈ It's that easy], isn't it?

# DAY 159
## SMALL TALK

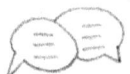

Let's catch up and have a bit of yarn [≈ have a friendly informal conversation ≈ have a chat ≈ have a chit-chat ≈ chat]. We're not going to sweet talk or pep talk [≈ pumping-up talk] or chew the fat [≈ chew the rag] today.

< To 'sweet talk' is to talk to someone nicely so they'll do what you want them to. A 'pep talk' is an emotional talk to encourage someone to do well. To 'chew the fat' or 'chew the rag' is to chat friendly and leisurely, or just gossip at length. >

We're just having some small talk, which is an informal short conversation. It's an opportunity to get to know more about the people who you work with. Small talk can happen any time during the day, and any topic will do.

Which questions (or statements) from the table below can be answered by the following four bullet points?

- It's been quiet. My weekend wasn't long enough though.
- It's been a busy day. [≈ It's been hectic. ≈ It's been manic. ≈ It's been frantic.]
- I'm much better. [≈ I'm on the mend. ≈ I'm recovering.] Or I'm dying.
- Not as much as I wanted to.

| Topic | Small talk example |
|---|---|
| Activities | I'm going to see the new Star Wars movie tonight.<br>Did you read the book you bought last Friday? |
| Clothes/appearance | The dress that you are wearing is pink-ish. [≈ You dressed in pink.]<br>You look sharp [≈ attractive and fashionable] today.<br>You look very suave [≈ smart and attractive]. |
| Family and kids | How's your family? |
| Weekends | What are you up to this weekend?<br>Did you have a nice weekend? [≈ How was your weekend?] |
| Daily commuting | How was your drive to work? [≈ How's traffic? ≈ What was your journey like?]<br>Which train line are you on? |
| Trips | Tell me about your holiday. [≈ Fill me in about your holiday.] |
| Lunch | What's for lunch? [≈ What are you eating for lunch? ≈ What's on the menu today?] |
| Politics and news | Who are you going to vote for? (Though this is sometimes considered a faux pas.)<br>What do you think about the White Island disaster? |
| Show that you care | How are you feeling? |
| Work related | How's your new project going? |

# DAY 160
## SHOOT THE BREEZE

Hey, everyone! How are you? The weather is a popular topic for small talk in the office. Let's shoot the breeze [≈ have a casual and relaxed conversation].

< A 'breeze' is a light wind, but it's also a slang term for rumour in America in the 1900s (Shoot the Breeze, n.d.). The phrases 'shoot the bull' and 'throw the bull' have a similar meaning to chat friendly and chat casually. 'Bull' is a shorten version of 'bullshit' (Shoot the Breeze, n.d.). >

When you walk into the office, you might say, 'Morning! It's freezing. Aren't you cold? You're not wearing enough!' or 'Yep, it's bitterly cold out there. What a misty early morning!'

An hour later, you're looking through the window, you might say, 'Look at the sky. The sun is out. It looks warm out there.' or 'Wow, the sky is crystal clear.'

All of a sudden, it's overcast [≈ cloudy], drizzly and windy. The rain is pouring down [≈ pissing down ≈ pelting down ≈ bucketing down]. You might say 'It's raining cats and dogs.' or 'What a heavy rainfall!' or 'It's torrential [≈ drenching] out there!'

< One of the theories says that 'cats and dogs' comes from Greek expression cata doxa, meaning 'contrary to belief'. So when it's raining cats and dogs, it's raining unbelievably hard (Raining Cats and Dogs, 2022). >

'OMG. The weather is miserable [≈ terrible]! It's wild! What dreadful [≈ dull ≈ fickle] weather! There's a storm on the way. Look at that tree, there are damaging [≈ destructive] winds.'

You check the weather forecast. 'Tomorrow will be sizzling hot [≈ searing hot ≈ boiling hot]. It will be a top of forty. Be prepared for a scorcher.' or 'Hmm, severe heatwaves are coming. We'll be melting.' or 'Stay hydrated. The cool changes won't happen [≈ It won't be cooling down] until late afternoon.'

When you have nothing more to say with small talk with your colleague, provided they're talking something positive, or you'd like to end the conversation, you might say, 'Very good, very good. Let's get back to work.'

# DAY 161
# OFFICE BANTER

You are running 2 minutes late for a casual catch-up meeting. You smile and say, 'Sorry, I'm late.' Your manager pretends to be very serious, 'That's not acceptable.' Then everyone in the room bursts out laughing [≈ suddenly laughs].

Banter is a friendly and playful conversation in which people make jokes with each other. Your workmates and manager may like a bit flirting and joking around. It's a moment for a big laugh, and it takes your brain off any stress.

Other examples of banter could be:

- You can call your boss 'boss' instead of using their first name.
- Your boss might say, 'If you don't work hard, I'll send you to the manufacturing department to fold boxes every day.'
- Your manager or workmates may joke:
    ◊ 'I blame you. [≈ It's all Jessie's fault.]'
    ◊ 'You're a troublemaker.'
    ◊ 'You're a bit cheeky.'
    ◊ 'I'm allergic to you.'
- They could also prank you to 'surprise' you, like putting a fake spider into your drawer or throwing the crumpled paper ball towards your head. My manager once placed a helmet on top of a balloon on my desk after I told him about watching the horror movie *IT*. It scared me when I came back from lunch! It scared the crap out of me!

Of course, they are just pulling your leg [≈ teasing you]. Positive banter can strengthen the bond between people and put a smile on everyone's face. You can do the same with them, creating a pleasant and humorous work atmosphere.

But be alert for people who are more serious and sensitive, who can't take jokes. Your light-hearted jokes could be offensive to them.

Be aware of verbal harassment or bullies and banter. Where's the borderline between humour and bullying? [≈ Where do you draw the line in the sand?] People need to be careful not to be derogatory to others [≈ not to make jokes or comments that put others down] or discriminate against them. Don't cross that line. [≈ Don't step over the line.]

# DAY 162
# CURSE WORDS

'Fuck!', 'Fuck's sake!', 'What the fuck? [≈ What the hell? ≈ What the heck?]', 'Bloody hell!', 'Shit!', 'Bullshit!', or 'Holy crap! [≈ Holy shit!]'

'Excuse my French.'

< 'WTF' is the written abbreviation for 'What the fuck?' and 'WTH' is for 'What the hell?' According to the Urban Dictionary, '#$!&@* the heck?' was first used in a baseball article in 2007, and it was presumed as an editing error (Ortonsault, 2008). >

Don't be surprised if you hear swear words in the workplace. It's often used when people are irritated. It is their way of venting anger, anxiety and frustration.

I understand that vulgar language is easy to remember when learning a second language. Can someone tell me why? In TV shows, a 'beep' sound is used to cover [≈ filter out] the curse words such as 'fuck' or 'shit', which makes you aware that people are saying particular four-letter words [≈ expletive ≈ profanity].

In the business world, I strongly suggest that you clean up your language use. It's best to avoid having a potty mouth [≈ It's best to drop any salty language], although one study shows that those who swear a lot are those who lie the least (Picard, 2017). Swearing at work is not cool. It can be unpleasant to the ears of others. So please consider other people.

But perhaps it's a good idea to know when someone is using bad language. If you hear offensive words from your boss such as, 'Reece is such a jerk [≈ an asshole ≈ a bastard ≈ a dickhead ≈ a wanker ≈ a douchebag]!' then Reece must have done something stupid or annoying that made your boss angry.

< 'Douchebag' is a vulgar slang insult for an arrogant and self-important person. You might also hear people use the word 'bogan' in Australia. It's a slang for an uncultured or unsophisticated person. >

Alrighty, I gotta go. [≈ I've got to get going. ≈ I need to go now. ≈ I'm heading off. ≈ I should get going. ≈ I'm about to take off. ≈ I'm about to shoot off. ≈ I have to dash. ≈ I'm off for the day.] That's too much strong language [≈ foul language] for today for me. Before I head off, do you need anything from me? See ya tomorrow! [≈ See you in the morning!]

# DAY 163
# THE WORD - DOWN

Let's **get down to** business straight away. The word 'down' has a sense of **pushing down, coming down, facing down** or lower. Have a good read of the story **down** below that's jammed with instances of 'down'.

Jenk was **looked down upon** when he was younger. He was always **down** in the bottom three students of the class. One day, he decided to work hard because he did not want to **go down the road** that his parents did, living poor. He started to read a lot.

Nothing is impossible for someone with a willing heart. In his early 20s, Jenk was offered a job after his internship. It **came down** to his decision whether to take it or not. In the end, Jenk **turned** it **down** because he wanted to start his own business. **Deep down**, I felt he was **grounding** himself **down**! But I knew he would achieve big.

Jenk's company profit was **down** 20% on the second year of operating. Jenk had to **cut down** costs anywhere possible. Sadly, three employees were **stood down**. With three employees **down**, Jenk kept himself busier than ever to make up for it. He never **pared down** [≈ **cut down**] his to-do list.

And he was successful after 5 years.

On a hot summer afternoon, Jenk drove me all the way **down** to a white sandy beach. We **sat down** and talked about our future. The sun was about to **go down,** shining brightly upon the clear blue sea, and then it finally **cooled down**. We **walked down** the beach. The sea was perfectly calm. **Further down**, the sky was light blue and pink. All of a sudden, Jenk **knelt down** and asked me, 'Will you marry me?' OMG, I said 'YES'! Tears were **steaming down** my face. He's such a genuine guy, a **down to earth** sort. I love this man so much and this is a new chapter of our 10-year relationship!

Here is Jenk's life motto: **Break down** goals into small and manageable steps. **Calm down** in tough situations. Sometimes, **slowing down** in life is good.

**Write down** your own story using lots of 'down' expressions.

# DAY 164
# INDUCTION

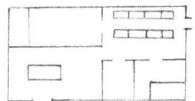

You're all set. It's your first day on the job, so you dress up well, and show up early. Your boss will induct you into the workplace. This brings us to the definition of today's title 'induction': the process of introducing the employee to the company.

Safety always comes first. You'll be shown the emergency exits and emergency assembly areas. When a building's fire alarm system is activated, everyone needs to evacuate. The building's fire extinguishers are located in hallways, meeting rooms, kitchens, electrical rooms and near the exits. Your manager will also tell you where to find the first-aid kits (which include bandaids for any paper cuts and gauze bandages for any major cuts). If you are working for a high-risk role, such as on a construction site or in food production, particular training on how to operate machinery will be provided. Safety manuals will also be provided.

Okay, so you'll be taken to the kitchen areas. Your orientation includes how to use the coffee machine and where to store your food, and heat your lunch meal, and so on. What office kitchen appliances and kitchenware are in your workplace?

| Coffee machine | Microwave oven | Sandwich toaster [≈ press] |
|---|---|---|
| (Cordless) kettle | Fridge | Dishwasher |
| Chopping boards | Cutlery, crockery and glasses | Paper towels and napkins |

< In China, many companies have their own canteens and provide employees three meals a day at a cheaper price. In Australia, I didn't find too many companies that offered this sort of service. So the microwave oven is an important appliance for employees to heat up meals from home at lunchtime! >

You will also be shown where to collect the stationery. Do any of these names roll off your tongue?

| Pencils | Pencil sharpeners | Ballpoint pens | Paper clips | Scissors |
|---|---|---|---|---|
| Highlighters | Staplers | Paper shredders | Envelopes | USB |
| Notebooks | Spiral notebooks | Whiteboard markers | Staples | Stamps |
| File folders | Manila folders | Suspension files | Archive boxes | Bins |
| Label makers | Sticky labels | Rubber bands | Mouse mat [≈ pad] | Printer |
| Trays | Thumb protectors | Transparent tapes | Pinch holders | A3/A4 paper |
| Post-It notes [≈ Sticky notes] | | Whiteout [≈ Correction ≈ Wipe out ≈ Liquid paper] | | |

Your boss will take you to your seat. There are some forms (workplace policies, tax forms, superannuation forms) to read, fill in and sign. You don't have to apply for a new superannuation [≈ super] account for each new job, and sticking to one account reduces administration fees. Now get to know your colleagues. Smile and say 'Hi' to everyone. Introduce yourself when you can. An epic journey has just started just for you.

# DAY 165
# ETHICS

The word 'ethics' is defined as moral values and principles. Use your professional judgement to cross out the below activities that professionals shouldn't do:

- ☐ As an accountant, you give false figures in financial records [≈ fiddle with the books ≈ manipulate the accounting books].
- ☐ As a CFO, you use a company's credit card for your personal activities.
- ☐ As a procurement officer, you receive kickbacks by making payments to a supplier who is a friend of yours.
- ☐ As an HR manager, you ask for money from job applicants in order to hire them.
- ☐ As a designer, you steal the ideas and artwork of others.
- ☐ As a journalist, you write fake news [≈ junk news ≈ hoax news] to deliberately mislead and deceive your readers.

< Talking about the adjective 'fake', are there any other fake things that you can think of?

| Fake news | Fake information | Fake name | Fake smile | Fake person |
|---|---|---|---|---|
| Fake fur [≈ Faux fur] | Fake bill | Fake ID | Fake pass | Fake art |

>

I hope you agree that all the above actions should be avoided at all costs. Don't argue with me that it could be a fine line to walk [≈ a blurred line ≈ a vague line ≈ a grey area], or debate that if other people are doing it, why shouldn't you?

To do the right thing should always be your bottom line. I agree it's not always easy to execute it. You might encounter a situation where you're pushed or intimidated by your workmates or boss to do something against company policy and company laws [≈ protocols ≈ by-laws ≈ checks and balances ≈ boundaries and guidelines].

How would you respond? Will you be caught between two worlds? [≈ Will you be caught between a rock and a hard place? ≈ Will this put you in a position where it's hard to choose?] The question is are you really interested in that kind of short-term benefit? Do you really want to destroy your integrity and damage [≈ trash ≈ sully ≈ ruin ≈ tarnish ≈ dent] your reputation? You could end up in jail with any illegal actions that you take. So think twice before you do!

# DAY 166
# WORK ATTITUDE

Your attitude in today's page is defined as beliefs and behaviours towards your work. Observe yourself and your workmates. Which of the below performances match up with your everyday work attitude? Cross or tick them if they do.

- [ ] Wear to impress. [≈ Dress up in business attire to impress.]
- [ ] Show up in shorts and slippers.
- [ ] You're punctual, and your attendance rate is high [≈ absence rate is low].
- [ ] You arrive about 10 minutes earlier than the work start time.
- [ ] When your boss isn't around, you start to play with your mobile phone or browse websites or perform hobbies.
- [ ] When your boss is around, you pretend to work hard.
- [ ] When the office is experiencing internet drop-outs [≈ out of internet connection], you try to get filing work to do.
- [ ] When you notice the printer running out of paper, you load the paper in for others' convenience as well.
- [ ] You're a gossip. [≈ You're gossipy. ≈ You're a big mouth.] You even spread hearsay [≈ pass on the gossip], adding fuel to the office rumours in a melodramatic manner.
- [ ] You stay true to yourself.
- [ ] You are honest.
- [ ] When you don't know, you don't pretend that you know.
- [ ] You're dodgy [≈ dishonest]. You lie to your customers.
- [ ] You don't really care about the quality of work that you produce.
- [ ] You're completely serious [≈ deadly earnest] about each task.
- [ ] You take initiative and show up with a 'can-do' attitude.
- [ ] You stay late voluntarily to make sure deadlines are met.
- [ ] You spread your love to your workmates by offering to help them and make conversation with them.

Are there any poor behaviours here that you've crossed out or ticked off that you'd like to change? Are there any positive attitudes that you'd like to add here? Don't get the impression that you work for your boss and the company. You work for yourself! The way you utilise every minute or a second will dominate your future career and, of course, future earning ability. Watching the clock ticking, mucking around or making progress every day – that's totally up to you.

# DAY 167
## ACCOUNTABILITY

To learn about the word 'accountability', you first need to identify your job responsibilities. Responsibility is the duty to perform and complete tasks at work. What do you do on a daily basis? What are you responsible for at work?

If the tasks sit [≈ rest] easy with you, you're in charge [≈ you're in the driver's seat]. It's your baby. So please take responsibility. Take ownership.

Accountability is your willingness to accept responsibility for your own actions. When you don't do well [≈ drop the ball], you hold yourself accountable [≈ hold yourself on account ≈ own up to the mistakes ≈ admit that you were in the wrong], like in the example below.

'Bugger! The amount on the invoice is wrong. My bad. [≈ My apologies. ≈ I apologise. ≈ I'm sorry.] I stuffed up. [≈ I blew it. ≈ I botched the whole thing. ≈ I bungled it. ≈ I messed it up. ≈ I screwed it up. ≈ I cocked it up. ≈ I'm totally screwed. ≈ I made a muck of it. ≈ I made a blunder. ≈ I made a mistake.] I'm the one to blame. [≈ It's irremissible of me. ≈ I'm unpardonable. ≈ My mistake is inexcusable.]' Opps! *Mea culpa*! I also just fat-fingered [≈ typed inaccurately] the word 'Oops' here! It should be double 'o' in spelling rather than double 'p'!

< *'Mea culpa'* means 'through my fault' in Latin (Allen, n.d.). 'Fat-fingered' originally meant to accidentally press another button on the phone. It now refers to typing something wrong (Fat-Finger, n.d.). >

< Human errors [≈ Botch-ups] are inevitable at work. To maintain accuracy and avoid making careless mistakes, work in the zone [≈ give your full attention to what you're doing]. Double check, cross check or sense check are techniques to deal with massive amounts of daily data. >

Calm down, admit the mistake and fix it. We all learn from and grow from mistakes. Don't duck out of [≈ abdicate from ≈ shy away from ≈ run away from] the responsibility. Don't pass the buck either: 'This isn't my job.' or 'I'm not responsible for this matter.' or 'That isn't my department.' or 'I don't know much about it.', unless these are true and not related to you at all. Otherwise, own up to it.

# DAY 168
# DEDICATION

The word 'dedication' means that you have a sense of commitment to something. It's the commitment to pour all your energy into your job.

You could end up working at a not-for-profit organisation or a profit-making company. When you get the job, you won't know ahead of time what the work culture might look like. You could come across a workplace like this:

- The place could be full of drama (toxic, unhealthy, shady work environment). Or it's full of love and laughter.
- It could be a place where learning is encouraged (or discouraged).
- You could be lucky to have a manager who takes care of you, or have bad luck if he's a jerk or she's a bitch to you.

These are the things that you cannot control. I remind you again that no job is perfect. But my requirement for you is that from the moment you're committed to the job, treat it as the first day and the last day of your work life. Give 100% effort each and every working day. At the end of the day, you work with people, and for people. Yet, also, you ultimately work for yourself.

< In Australia, it's normal that you could have a huge workload and your day is super busy. There are no jobs that allow you to sit there having an hour-long cup of tea or long lunch to eat and read the newspaper. In my impression, some office workers in China would have the time to do that, and be quite relaxed. People also don't take naps after a lunch break in Australia. Back in China, people normally use a one hour lunch break to take a quick nap.

Overall, it can be more intense working in Australia. You get paid for every minute that you work. But the labour cost is higher as well. The minimum wage by law for employees not covered by an award or registered agreement is $20.33 per hour or $772.60 per week before tax (as of July 2021). The pay rate is reviewed every year. (Minimum Wages, n.d.). Your wage could be paid weekly, fortnightly or monthly based on the frequency of a company's payroll process. >

In the end, remember that you work to live, not live to work. Don't work yourself to the point of illness or exhaustion. It's not worth it. Strike the work-life balance [≈ work-life equilibrium].

Do you know what's one of the biggest regrets from people dying on their deathbed? They wished they hadn't worked so hard.

# DAY 169
## BREAK TIME

It's break time! A break (as a noun) in today's context means a pause at work for a short period of time. You can't operate at your peak [≈ work like a well-oiled machine ≈ fire on all cylinders] all day long like a robot without taking any breaks.

This brings us to our chapter's title – being a workafrolic! What does this mean? To 'frolic' means to behave cheerfully and lively. So, a workafrolic is someone who loves what they do for work, and also has lots of fun. When you're happy and having fun, you work better and you're a ray of sunshine in your work team. And all I want you to do is to get something fun out of your job each day. In reality, an office job could be stressful like this:

Your boss: 'English Builder, the sales report needs to be done in 30 minutes. Where are you at right now?'

Your workmate: 'Hey English Builder, can you please help me out with the Excel formula? I'm stuck here. I really need urgent help.' Your phone is ringing now and you just realised that you needed to go to loo [≈ toilet].

How can I get fun from this?

Take a deep breath. [≈ Breathe deeply.] One thing at a time, please. I suggest getting up for the toilet break first. Don't take your mobile phone on the way. This will give you a chance for a short break. Stop worrying the deadline, your workmate's request, and your ringing phone. What would be the worst scenario if you couldn't do any of them right now? Will it kill you? Nope.

Come back after your break. Tell your workmate calmly if it's not a one-minute job, you'd happy to help later on. Then put on some music on your earphones to help you concentrate on your sales report.

After 30 minutes, the report is all done. Go assist your workmate if your help is still needed. Later on, your phone is ringing again. Pick it up without any pressure! Time for a break again. Blink to avoid dry and irritated eyes. Use eye-drops to lubricate your eyes.

< Other eye symptoms include red eyes, itching eyes, sore eyes, tired eyes and pink eyes. What can you do with your eyes? Blink your eyes, squint your eyes, roll your eyes, rub your eyes, blindfold your eyes. Put down your answers here:

..................................................................................................................................

..................................................................................................................................

.............................................................................................................................. >

Stretch. Recharge your energy with a wander outside [≈ by taking a brisk stroll]. Relax and have fun!

# DAY 170
## PLAYING WELL WITH YOUR WORKMATES

How would you define your relationship with your workmates? As intimate friends, as enemies, or something in-between? We all have different personalities, beliefs, cultures and interests, but the basic principle is to respect everyone in the team. Remember: most of us come to work for that pay cheque.

Have a read of the below conversations. Who is doing the right thing trying to get along with their colleagues [≈ get on well with people at work ≈ play well with their co-workers ≈ rub along with their work pals ≈ get along swimmingly with their teammates ≈ be on good terms with their workmates]?

**Marie:** I'm agitated. How come Brittany did that to me? Enough is enough. I can't put up with her anymore! [≈ I'm fed up with her!] I don't like her. She's dead wood. [≈ She's useless. ≈ She's ratshit.]

**Samantha:** Thanks for that. [≈ I really appreciate your help.] You saved my life! [≈ You did me a big favour!] I couldn't have done it without your help.

Did you like Samantha's appreciation for her co-worker? Did you like Marie's comments? Did she seem to point fingers at Brittany [≈ be personally against Brittany ≈ have a go at Brittany ≈ criticise Brittany strongly]?

< We have five fingers on each hand: a thumb, an index finger [≈ a pointer finger ≈ a first finger ≈ a forefinger], a middle finger, a ring finger, or a little finger [≈ a baby finger ≈ a pinky finger ≈ a pinky]. 'Pinky' comes from the Dutch word pink, meaning 'small'. Pointing fingers here doesn't mean physically pointing an index finger at someone. It means to blame [≈ accuse] someone in this context. >

Does Marie talk behind her co-workers' back and badmouth them? Has she shown any respect? If you were Brittany or another workmate who overheard Marie's conversation, how would you react? What would you do?

Managing workplace relationships is an art and it's one of the most difficult skills to master. But it can be learnt through experience or practice, or reading the rest of the chapter.

# DAY 171
# WORK AS A TEAM

There is no 'I' in team. Am I right? The letter 'I' isn't in the word 'team'. You work together with others to deliver the goal.

You don't have to paddle your own canoe at work. If you're stuck with a task or you're struggling to meet the deadline, don't be afraid to ask for help [≈ don't be scared to request help ≈ don't feel bad about begging someone for help ≈ don't feel guilty turning to someone for help]. 'Can you please do me a favour? [≈ Can you please assist me? ≈ Can you please give me a hand? ≈ Can you please help me out here? ≈ Do you have a moment? I need your help, please.]'

< Did you notice anything in common over the last five sentences of last paragraph? They all have the word 'please' in them. Adding the word 'please' sounds polite. >

The majority of people are happy to assist you if they can. You should do the same for them. The response to this might be, 'Yep. [≈ Definitely. ≈ Absolutely. ≈ Sure. ≈ One hundred percent. ≈ I'd love to. ≈ I'll help. ≈ I'd like to give a hand. ≈ I'd love to lend a hand. ≈ I can assist. ≈ I can be of assistance. ≈ I can be of aid.]'

You should show appreciation when your workmates help you out. Return the favour in the future when you can.

When your workmate covers you while you're on holiday, say 'Thank you so much for stepping in while I'm away.' If they get you out of a difficult situation, say 'You saved my bacon [≈ saved my skin ≈ saved my neck ≈ saved my hide]. Thanks heaps!'

< The idiom of 'save one's bacon' dates back to the 1600s when bacon was a slang term for the human body. So saving my bacon means to save my body from harm (Martin, n.d.). So it's a way to say 'you saved my life'. >

The only trick here is that when you say these words, you should actually mean it. Don't forget to put a big smile on your face. Teamwork makes the dream work. Who doesn't like working in a winning team [≈ a high functioning team ≈ a high-performance team ≈ a team in the groove]?

Bear in mind though, not everyone in the team is willing to do their bit to help each other out. There are people who are hard to deal with. Come back tomorrow to see who they are!

# DAY 172
# CHALLENGING WORKMATES

A workplace is full of personalities. Reflect on the working styles of your workmates. Have you met any of the below people at work yet?

- Victor likes saying, 'Don't bombard me. I'm super busy [≈ crazy busy].' But he's actually not busy at all, just talking the talk. He's lazy and seems not to care about the job much. Others have to pick up his slack [≈ pick up what he left]. Even worse, he's what we sometimes call a hitchhiker [≈ he goes along for the ride].

- Brandon is uncooperative [≈ is unhelpful ≈ isn't collaborative ≈ isn't willing to work with others]. He's such a pain in the arse [≈ a pain in the neck ≈ a pain in the rump ≈ a pain in the backside].

- Heather throws the team under the bus when things fail, and she takes credits to herself when there's success.

- Sean is rude to me, but he's very nice to the upper management and everyone else in the team. What a chameleon!

- Harry likes seeking attention from everyone [≈ stealing thunder ≈ taking centrestage ≈ hogging the limelight].

- Jordan is arrogant, arbitrary, calculating and replies in a crisp [≈ not friendly] manner.

- Jake is a weirdo [≈ is offbeat ≈ is the odd one out ≈ is off the wall ≈ is eccentric ≈ is kooky ≈ is a rebel ≈ is like a unicorn]. He doesn't fit the mould [≈ is a misfit ≈ is the round peg in the square hole].

- Joshua likes rocking the boat [≈ stirring up trouble]. He's mean and tough.

- Finn is nasty [≈ shitty]. He's a bad egg [≈ not a nice person]. He has no class [≈ acts outside boundaries].

The key to dealing with strong personalities is to be objective. Don't cause a fuss. [≈ Don't make a fuss about it.] Take a detached view. Get on with the job and don't go against the person themselves. But you don't have to be overly nice [≈ be a soft person ≈ be a pushover ≈ be Ms SOFT or Mr SOFT] to them.

However, if Finn is offensive to you or bullies you, you can seek help from your manager, the company's HR or even report him to the Australian Fair Work Commission depending on the nature of the behaviour.

# DAY 173
## WHEN YOU'RE BOTHERED

You might have a boss or team member whose behaviour is difficult to deal with, or it could be gobsmacking behaviour from your point of view. Far out!

< 'Gobsmacking' means surprising that you cannot speak [≈ you're speechless ≈ you're lost for words ≈ you can't get words out ≈ you're flabbergasted ≈ you're out of words ≈ you're dumbfounded]. >

< People exclaim 'Far out!' to express that they can't believe something is true or that something happened! It could be something amazing and cool, or it could be something strange and unusual. >

I understand you are bothered. What's wrong with that person? You don't want to work with that person. You don't want to see them at all! Sitting there saying these things isn't fixing anything. You only have one way out of the woods [≈ to get out of difficulties or trouble].

< The phrase of 'out of woods' dates back to Roman times when forests were dangerous for human beings. Imagine: when you got lost in the forest [≈ in the woods] centuries ago, would you be in danger? >

Treat it as a learning opportunity. Below are two things that you can learn:

- **Learn to understand.** The majority of people come to work to earn their 'bread' and pay off monthly bills. We all are the same, aren't we? Think it through. There must be an underlying reason behind a person's annoying behaviours. Take a look from their perspectives and position. It's unnecessary to be harsh to your workmates. Most people don't mean to hurt you. Sometimes, it's just the way they socialise or speak that might conflict with your beliefs and behaviours.

- **Learn to work with the uncomfortable.** Business is business. Get things done. Don't go against anyone personally. Invite the annoying person over for a coffee. Start with a smile and some small talk. What do they like in life? How's their family? Get to know the person first. Don't avoid or refuse to talk to those who you do not like. Doing nothing about it or hiding from them [≈ brushing them off] could only make things worse.

You might think there's another way to escape. There is: to get away from your job immediately! This sounds easier and quicker! But if you quit your job just because of this, and you never make effort to improve your workplace relationships with difficult people, similar issues could crop up again in your next job!

# DAY 174
## SUCK IT UP

After trying out everything you could to fix things at work, you're still unhappy. Do you still give a shit why that person treated you like that? Why did your manager give you the cold shoulder? Why did the credit go to others and not you, the hard worker?

Relax, buddy. You just care too much. It's just a job. Take it seriously. [≈ Do not take it lightly.] But please stop giving a shit about these people and such things!

With those who like interfering in your private activities – the meddlers, do-gooders, busybodies, the nosy – tell them straight away, 'That is none of your business. [≈ Mind your own business. ≈ This doesn't concern you. ≈ It has nothing to do with you.] Curiosity killed the cat.'

< Have you ever questioned why curiosity killed the cat? The original expression is actually 'care killed the cat'. To 'care' meant to worry or grieve in the old days when worrying about others was considered dangerous (Kilmann, 2020). >

Coming across with something unfair, you could tell yourself, 'That is not my concern. [≈ I couldn't care less. ≈ I do not care. ≈ I don't mind. ≈ I don't give a damn about it.] I'm not bothered. [≈ It doesn't bother me.]'

If you really need the F* word to vent, say it out and loud (F*ck! For f*ck's sake!) when you're back home. Or maybe write down what you want to yell right here: _____
_____ !

Or review **Day 106 Manage Your Anger** about being staying calm and **Day 44 Don't Complain** to shift your mindset in this situation. As a reward, I'm going to give you another four words to help you out: 'Suck it up, buttercup.'

< 'Buttercup' is a type of flower with bright yellow colour. It can also be a romantic nickname to call your girlfriend or boyfriend. Why 'suck it up, buttercup' then? It just rhymes with 'suck it up' (What Does Suck It Up, Butter Up Mean?, 2018). >

To 'suck it up' is the ability to accept unpleasant things, to hang in there and deal with them for now. Your boss keeps dumping boring and administrative tasks to you, or even demotes you. Invite them for a coffee and chat with them about your career goals. You can also say 'no' to what your boss has offered (the demotion) (review **Day 42 Be Brave and Say No** and **Day 43 Ways to Say No**). See what'll happen after saying 'no'. If the situation doesn't improve, 'suck it up' (accept this unpleasing situation)! But don't just 'suck it up, buttercup' forever in the job – go get a new job instead!

I know you're talented, and your talent has just been wasted and you deserve better. If your manager is playing favourites, still show your respect to them. I know it's not your fault. If your co-workers seem distant, initiate friendly conversation. I know even smiling at any of them right at this moment is hard.

Pause for a moment. Think about the exciting moment when you got offered the job. Did you promise that you'd do whatever it took to perform well and get along with the team? Deliver on your promise.

# DAY 175
# BE RESPECTFUL

As you can see from last few days, dealing with people at work is indeed hard work because everyone has their own behaviours and perspectives. You can't control how others behave. Again, the basic principle to apply here is to show respect.

The Australian working environment is diverse. Your workmates could wear a face veil, or fast due to religious reasons. They could have tattoos, have a nose ring, write left-handed, or write the number 7 with a small horizontal line in the middle. See how 7 is written by many Aussies in the emotional thermometer in **Day 101 Check Your Emotional Temperature**).

Please respect how everyone looks, and respect their beliefs, choices, sexual orientation, marital status, disability, gender, traditions, life habits, likes and dislikes. Never discriminate.

By saying this, don't judge others [≈ don't be critical of others]. Don't hold prejudice towards someone. [≈ Don't hold biases against someone.] Never look down upon anyone nor speak down to them. [≈ Never put on airs.]

< 'Airs' here isn't the air that we breathe. It is a French word meaning 'look or appearance' (Put On Airs, n.d.). To 'put on airs' means that you behave like you're better than others [≈ you're superior to others]. >

You're not superior to other people. Everyone is equal. So stay humble and treat others as you wish to be treated.

To show [≈ demonstrate] respect, communicate in a friendly manner. Keep eye contact. In western culture, maintaining consistent eye contact [≈ making direct eye contact ≈ looking people in the eye] during a conversation is important. But don't stare at others during the whole conversation.

Listen to what others have to say. Understand other people's perspectives and their needs. Think beyond yourself and your own concerns. [≈ Put aside your viewpoint. ≈ Put yourself in others' shoes. ≈ Stand in others' shoes.]

By being respectful, you'll make your co-workers respect you [≈ earn respect from your co-workers].

# DAY 176
## THE CORPORATE LADDER

The 'corporate ladder' symbolises the employment hierarchy, where an entry-level position is at the bottom, while management and executive positions are at the top. Below is a possible ladder for a career in accounting.

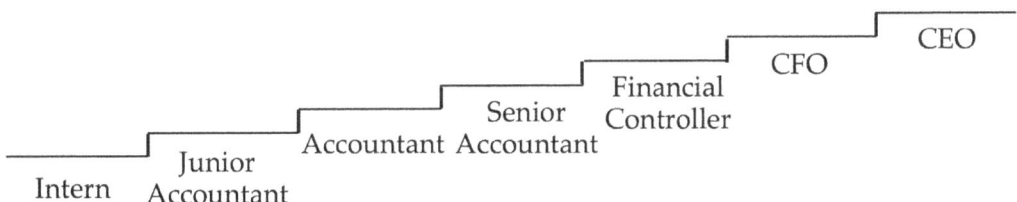

In this chapter, I'll show you how to move up the career ladder [≈ work your way up the ranks], but only if you want to. If you've already reached the pinnacle [≈ the giddy heights ≈ the highest point] of your career or you're happy where you are, congratulations! Go make yourself a cuppa.

Many people start their career at the bottom of the ladder. At such entry-level positions, you're often given repetitive, mind-numbing and monotonous [≈ boring ≈ mundane ≈ lame] tasks to perform, which you might not enjoy doing after a while. You might feel you're overqualified for the role if you have a university certificate. Here, you might say, 'A monkey can do my job. [≈ I could do my job in my sleep.]' or 'I'm not getting paid for what I deserve.' No matter what you're thinking, put in your best effort. Do your best to complete tasks and make continuous improvements for your work.

If you can't even do the small things well, how can you achieve the big things later on? Everyone's job is day-in, day-out, month-in, month-out, year-in, year-out, and everyone shows up day after day, month after month, year after year. It's your work attitude that separates you and the average employee [≈ a rank-and-file employee].

Take a look at the list below and tick which type of employee you'd like to become:

- ☐ You ask for a side project. [≈ You raise a hand to take on projects.]
- ☐ You get involved in [≈ get engaged in] ad hoc tasks.
- ☐ You're willing to undertake outreach work, or be shadowed by a senior.
- ☐ It feels cool to do less work! You even slow down purposely since you're not getting paid for doing more.
- ☐ If you have free time, you'd rather surf the internet or play mobile phones without being noticed by your manager [≈ when unsupervised].

My advice? Try your best at your current role, no matter what level of the ladder you're on. When you're a young, newly minted professional [≈ a fresh graduate ≈ a rookie ≈ a newbie ≈ a green hand ≈ a novice], you should be happy that you have such an amazing job. Because the world is your oyster when you're young! As you gain years of experience and move up to the ladder, you'll only get older!

# DAY 177
# EARN YOUR STRIPES

When you start out learning a new skill or learning about a new subject, you probably can't understand it [≈ can't get a hang of it ≈ can't wrap your head around it ≈ can't make heads or tails of it] right away. Be patient. Sometimes there's a steep [≈ massive ≈ huge] learning curve.

Here are some tips to help you jump through hoops in no time:

< The idiom 'jump through hoops' is derived from the circus where performing animals are made to leap through hoops. Sometimes, the hoops are even set on the fire (Jump Through Hoops, n.d.). In today's context, it means that you perform difficult tasks to achieve your goals. >

**Statement #1:** I don't know how to do the job.

**Response:** Ask questions. There are no dumb, silly or stupid questions. Don't ask the same question many times over though.

**Statement #2:** I don't have skills. I have terrible Excel skills. I'm pretty average at talking to people. I'm not a technology person. [≈ Technology is beyond me. ≈ I'm out of touch with technology.] My SAP system skill is very limited.

**Response:** Do your bit. [≈ Do your part. ≈ Do your fair share.] Pick up the skill. Meet the criteria. Make it into your thing. And you'll be good at it! Then go beyond [≈ go over and above]. Show initiative. Put your hand up. Stand up for advanced duties or onerous tasks.

**Statement #3:** I can't do it. I am incapable of completing it. I can't cut the mustard. [≈ I can't handle the job.]

**Response:** Hey, stop here! Wing it, and fake it until you make it. No job is too difficult. You are able! Practise and keep learning. From unskilled to a professional full of capabilities, you will earn your stripes.

< It is said the phrase of 'earn your stripes' comes from the military practice where someone who has served will wear a service stripe (a cloth in the shape of V) on their uniform. The more stripes that a soldier has, the higher rank they have (What Does Earn Your Stripes Mean?, n.d.). >

After a while, you know how to do the job, you've got the skill. You become capable! Well done! But the tasks are no longer exciting and refreshing (well, the bloom is off the rose). What could you do here? Find out the answer tomorrow!

# DAY 178
## GEAR UP

To fast track your career [≈ upgrade your career ≈ supercharge your career ≈ climb the corporate ladder], you need to consistently upgrade your skill-set [≈ shake up your skills ≈ sharpen your skills ≈ expand your skills ≈ level up your skills].

First, keep updating your professional knowledge [≈ have up-to-date knowledge]. Knowledge is power. This can be achieved through professional development, extensive reading, or talking to senior management. Second, hone your conversational skills. Being concise is the key for effective communication. Most of time, complicated terminologies are not required for an office job. Don't swallow a dictionary! Learn the jargon to make sure you understand them. Meanwhile, develop the ability to talk in a language that others can understand [≈ explain in layman's term ≈ use straightforward language ≈ use plain English].

Avoid using uncertain words (such as might, maybe, perhaps) and reduce the frequency of using filler words (um, uhs, like, kind of), which makes you sound unconfident and hesitant. Eliminate [≈ Get rid of] these unnecessary words from your vocabulary. [≈ Throw these unnecessary words overboard.]

Third, practise being hyper [≈ super] productive [≈ efficient]. Find the means of making your job easier by streamlining the process or grouping work together. Another trick is to clean your desk. When it's all over the place [≈ it's all over the shop ≈ it's really messy ≈ it's a mess ≈ it's a dog's breakfast], it can compromise your work efficiency.

Do you like multitasking? Do you really think it's helpful to get more things done at once? Nope! Studies have shown that juggling many tasks at once [≈ jumping between tasks ≈ flitting from one task to another ≈ keeping several balls in the air] hurts productivity (MacKay, 2021). So please focus on one task at a time.

Work faster! [≈ Be quick! ≈ Speed it up! ≈ Be expeditious! ≈ Let's hurry! ≈ Hurry up! ≈ Get a wiggle on it! ≈ Chop-chop! ≈ Come on. Snap to it!]

Though, don't burn out!

From tomorrow on, we'll learn to write emails, pick up the phone, attend meetings and acquire a couple of other hard and soft skills.

# DAY 179
# A BUSINESS EMAIL EXAMPLE

**From:** jessiegao@theEnglishBuilder365.com

**Cc:** AllEnglishBuilders@gmail.com.au

**Bcc:** AllEnglishBuilders@outlook.com

**Subject:** How are you finding the book?


Good morning English Builders [≈ Hi all ≈ Hi team],

I hope you are well. I am touching base with you [≈ getting in touch with you] to check how you are going with the book.

Feedback is required from everyone. I need your answers by COB [≈ close of business ≈ the end of the business day]. Let me know if you can't by 3 pm today.

- Please complete the survey below.

    1. Are you still actively reading the book and planning to finish it all?
    2. Has the book motivated you to get better at your English skills?
    3. Have you improved in your English so far?
    4. Will you recommend the book to your friends?

- Please share your thoughts and experiences.

    **Sarah** – Go back to Day 43 and let me know your thoughts on how to say no politely.
    **Leah** – What part of the book do you like most? Please specify why.
    **Jonathan** – Which part of the book is the least impressive? Please detail your reason.
    **Everyone** – If you like the book, tell your friends. If you don't like it, tell me.

Please don't hesitate to contact me if you have any concerns. [≈ Please feel free to contact me should you have any further queries.]

Regards [≈ Kind regards ≈ Thanks ≈ Many thanks],

Jessie Gao

Author of *The English Builder!*

Tele: +613 6536 5365

ilovemelbourne365.com

# DAY 180
# BUSINESS EMAIL WRITING TRICKS

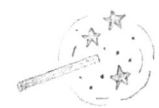

Did you receive my email yesterday? Below are a few bits of information about emails:

- Gmail and Outlook are the two main webmail services.
- In emails, Cc means 'carbon copy'. Carbon copy is a piece of carbon paper coping when writing from one paper to another. Bcc is 'blind carbon copy'. Recipients on the Bcc field are not visible to others.
- On average, a third of an employee's work time is spent processing their email inbox (Dubé, 2017).
- Every second, around 2.7 million emails are sent (Albright, 2018).

Anyway, do you like the email that I sent yesterday? Why? Put down your likes and dislikes in the following table:

| Like (thumbs up) | Dislike (thumbs down) |
|---|---|
|  |  |

Now I'll give you four tricks to write better business emails:

- Your email should be purposeful and meaningful. Otherwise, what's the point in bothering to write it down?
- Keep your writing concise [≈ brief]. Don't be wordy. Cut the fat. [≈ Trim the fat.] Prune away unnecessary words.
- Format and visualise your writing. <u>Underscore</u> important words [≈ Add <u>underlines</u> for key words]. Emphasised words are made *italic* or **bold**, or just highlight them in colour.
- If you want to address a couple of employees or departments (finance, IT, logistics, shipping, etc.) in an email, call people or the department's name out separately like I did yesterday, so each email reader gets a clear sense of what they need to know or need to do.

Here comes another work email. Do you like it?

> Lisa,
>
> Why were invoices missed from sales report? Why were we over accrued $4K for the month? Before fixing problems, ask what and why.
>
> Jennifer

Read through your email draft at least twice before hitting the send button. Consider if it's better to speak over the phone with a situation like this. If so, pick up your phone (the most effective communication method) and make the call right now.

# DAY 181
# MAKING A PHONE CALL

Hey, don't dial the phone number +613 6536 5365 from the email in Day 179 because the number is made up [≈ fake]. But what you do need to know is that the +61 part is the Australian country code. The '3' is the Australian area code for Victoria or Tasmania. See codes for all states in the table below.

**Australian telephone area codes**

| ACT – 02 | NSW – 02 | VIC – 03 | TAS – 03 |
|---|---|---|---|
| QLD – 07 | SA – 08 | WA – 08 | NT – 08 |

Assume you need to make a phone call to this number: +613 6536 5365. If you are dialling outside Australia, press 0011 613 6536 5365. The 0011 part is the international access dialling code. You only need to dial 03 6536 5365 when in Australia. If you share the same area code with the phone number you're calling, you might be able to omit the area code and simply dial the last eight digits directly (6536 5365). Let me ring you. It's easier, more effective and better than writing an email.

**Me:** Good morning. This is Jessie calling from *The English Builder!*.

**You:** Sorry, I didn't catch your name. Who am I speaking to? Can you please spell it out?

**Me:** It's Jessie. J for Jetstar, E for egg, S for snow, another S, I for international, E for elephant.

< This type of spelling method was invented for aircrews to be understood because the sounds of some English letters (such as B, D, M, N) are very similar. The North Atlantic Treaty Organization (NATO) Phonetic Alphabet is commonly used, detailed below:

| A | B | C | D | E | F | G | H | I |
|---|---|---|---|---|---|---|---|---|
| Alpha | Bravo | Charlie | Delta | Echo | Foxtrot | Golf | Hotel | India |
| J | K | L | M | N | O | P | Q | R |
| Juliet | Kilo | Lima | Mike | November | Oscar | Papa | Quebec | Romeo |
| S | T | U | V | W | X | Y | Z | |
| Sierra | Tango | Uniform | Victor | Whiskey | X-ray | Yankee | Zulu | |

An older version of this used A for apple, B for butter, C for Charlie and so on (Phonetic Alphabet: The Story From Alpha to Zulu, 2019). You can create your own alphabet (like what I did for my name just now), such as C for carnival, and M for marry. >

# DAY 182
## THE PHONE CALL CONTINUES

Answering phone calls is not easy because you cannot see the other person's face. Even locals have a difficult time capturing the sounds and inflections of words sometimes. Take the initiative to pick up calls while your colleagues are away from their desks. It doesn't hurt to do so.

Let's resume yesterday's phone call conversation.

(**Me:** It's Jessie. J for Jetstar, E for egg, S for snow, another S, I for international, E for elephant. (our phone call continued))

**You:** Hi Jessie. You're speaking with _____ (put down your name here and below). How are you?

**Me:** Hi _____. I'm doing great, thanks. How are you?

**You:** I'm doing awesome! How can I help you today? [≈ What can I do for you today?]

**Me:** I'm after Tom. [≈ I'm chasing Tom. ≈ Where is Tom? ≈ Is Tom around? ≈ Is Tom available? ≈ Is Tom in the office?]

**You:** Hang on a second. [≈ Wait a sec. ≈ Bear with me for a second. ≈ Can you hold the line?] I will put you through. [≈ I will pop you through. ≈ I will transfer you.]

**Tom:** Hello, you are speaking with Tom.

**Me:** Hi Tom. This is Jessie, the author of *The English Builder!*. How have you been?

**Tom:** Hi Jessie. I'm great. Yourself?

**Me:** I'm well, thank you. Hey Tom. I'd like to inform you that your review about the book is fantastic. You've been selected as one of the most committed English Builders! Congratulations!

**Tom:** I can't hear you clearly. The line is bad. [≈ The line is not stable. ≈ The line is crackly. ≈ The reception is bad.] What's your number? Let me call you back in 5 minutes. [≈ I'll give you a buzz in 5.]

**Me:** No worries. Ring me on my mobile. My number is 04 3653 6536. Talk to you soon. Bye! [≈ Bye now.]

< All mobile telephone numbers start with 04 and have 10 digits in Australia. >

*Brrring, brrring, brrring.* My phone is ringing.

**Me:** Good morning, this is Jessie from *The English Builder!*. How can I help you today?

# DAY 183
## LET'S HAVE A MEETING

Hey English Builders. Let's catch up at 2 pm in the boardroom to discuss how *The English Builder!* book can be further improved.

Now it's 2 pm in the boardroom:

**Jessie:** Good afternoon, everyone. Thanks for your attendance. The purpose of the meeting is to explore your reading experiences and share constructive feedback on the book. Okay, without any further ado [≈ without fanfare], let's get to it.

**Chloe:** I particularly like the author's stories and experiences on the culture clash between China and Australia. But if she can stretch it to other countries as well, it would be—

**Anthony:** Sorry, may I interrupt? I don't agree with you Chloe on talking about the culture in other countries that Jessie hasn't been involved with.

< In the meeting, don't say 'Sorry, may I interrupt?' First, you didn't do anything wrong, and you don't need to be sorry. Second, you don't need a permission to interrupt. 'Hold on [≈ Hang on], I need to interrupt here' will do the work just fine. >

**Bryce:** I love the book. The only suggestion that I have is that the author can make an audio or film a video for each day, it would be more helpful for English learners. People don't tend to read books nowadays.

**Jessie:** Great point there, Bryce. But this will be for the next session of our discussion. Let's not veer away from the topic for now. Let's move on. [≈ Let's keep the ball rolling. ≈ Let's get the ball rolling.] Christina, you've been quiet. What's your opinion?

**Christina:** If the book introduced more origins of interesting idioms and expressions, it'd be more fun to read for me.

**Jessie:** I like the idea, Christina. Okie-dokie [≈ Okay ≈ Alrighty ≈ Righto], let's wrap it up [≈ wind it up ≈ end up the meeting ≈ let's draw this session to a close]. Thanks, everyone. I'll share with everyone my notes here after the meeting. Do you have any questions or concerns?

< Yes, I do have a question: What does 'Keep the ball rolling' mean? What ball does this refer to? What makes the ball keep on rolling? >

# DAY 184
# BECOME A SOLUTION ARCHITECT

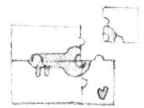

You are hired to solve a problem in the workplace. Tell me what you would do if you came across [≈ encountered ≈ ran into] either of the scenarios below.

**Scenario 1:** The payment didn't go through to your vendor as promised yesterday because your manager didn't release the payment before the bank cut-off time. Your supplier is on the phone with you and angrily questioning why they didn't get the money.

**Scenario 2:** Your boss would like you to have a look at adding some plants to the office.

Here's what I would do:

**Scenario 1:** Apologise to the supplier. Tell them the payment wasn't delivered because the company had a technical or system glitch (it's a white lie here). You'll make sure the payment goes out today as a priority.

**Scenario 2:** Ask Google. Google 'office plant hire' or 'buy corporate plants'. Sure, plenty of ads and websites will come up. Give some of the businesses a call and ask for a quote. Make a list of the quotes and recommend the best option to your manager.

< Google is omnipotent. Anything that you don't know, such as the origin of the idiom 'jump the gun', what is the fastest way to climb the corporate ladder, and how to ask for a salary raise, just do some googling! Of course, you can only Baidu (百度) it if you live in mainland China. Baidu is a Chinese multinational technology company. Its search engine is used nation-wide after Google pulled out of China in 2010 due to government censorship (Sheehan, 2018). Gmail is also banned in China. Of course, you can always grab your workmates for help. Just don't pick others' brains without doing your own research beforehand. >

Solutions for problems are like artwork. There are no absolute right or wrong answers. Develop your problem-solving skills. Where there's a problem, there must be a solution. And there's more than one way to skin a cat. Figure out the best way.

< Is it brutal to skin a cat? With this idiom, we're not literally skinning a cat. We're just sorting out [≈ resolving ≈ tackling] the problem. >

# DAY 185
# BECOME AN IT SUPERSTAR

Computers have become an integral part of modern offices. Mastering technology and computers is a must [≈ a must-have skill ≈ a non-negotiable skill ≈ an essential skill].

Relax. You don't have to complete an IT degree to become a technological know-how expert. For an easy start, learn a few shortcuts, and keep reminding yourself to use them. Turn on your work computer now, and let's play around with your Windows logo keyboard. Do the following:

- Press and hold the Windows logo key and press full stop (.) or semicolon (;) sign on the QWERTY keyboard. What popped up? Was it the emojis window?

- What happens when you press Windows and PrtScn (the Print Screen key)? You'll have saved a PNG file in the screenshots folder in your pictures folder.

- If you want to lock your device or switch users, use the Windows key and press L.

< What is QWERTY? Observe your keyboard layout. Are these six letters (QWERTY) the first six letter keys located on the top left letter row? This is where the name of the QWERTY keyboard comes from.

Now, let's have a read on some symbols on the keyboard:

| , comma | : colon | ? question mark | '' apostrophe [≈ single quotes ≈ single quotation marks] |
|---|---|---|---|
| ~ tilde | ; semicolon | ` acute [≈ back quote] | & ampersand [≈ and] |
| _ underscore | - hyphen | ^ caret [≈ circumflex] | "" double quotes [≈ quotation marks] |
| # hash | * asterisk [≈ star] | / forward slash | \ backward slash [≈ backslash] |
| = equal | . full stop [≈ dot] | ! exclamation mark | \| pipe bar [≈ vertical bar] |
| < less than | ( open parenthesis | { open brace | [ open bracket |
| > greater than | ) close parenthesis | } close brace | ] close bracket |

When your system crashes [≈ stops running ≈ is down ≈ is dead], you can't move the mouse around. The computer is spinning. [≈ It's not responding. ≈ It's thinking.] A quick fix. Hold the Ctrl, Alt and Delete keys. Go to Task Manager and delete any non-responding app. If this doesn't do the job, turn off [≈ shut down] the computer, then restart it [≈ reboot it].

< The three keys 'Ctrl+Alt+Del' were created by programmer David Bradley in 5 minutes. He designed it because programmers back in the old days had to power computers down every time code stopped working. He selected these three keys because it was impossible to accidentally press the combination of keys (David Bradley (Engineer), 2020). But it was Bill Gates who made this 'three-fingered salute' popular (Bishop, 2013). >

# DAY 186
## EXCEL AT EXCEL

Microsoft Excel is one of the most popular tools for processing data for any office jobs. If you know the tricks, Excel can help improve efficiency.

Today, we will not be talking about shortcuts, function keys (F1–F12), macros, formulas, charts, sparklines, tables, conditional formatting, power queries, and so on. We could go on about these for days. Learn about them from YouTube or a Google search, then put them into practice. You will become an Excel guru in no time.

Let's relax and do a fun activity together. Open up Excel. Type the letters from *a* to *z* in each cell. Select all these cells and change the font into Webdings. Did you get the same as me?

Now type capital letters *A* to *Z* in a new row, using the same font. Blimey! [≈ Crikey!] You get a house on the letter 'H' and a heart shape on letter 'Y'.

Did you just manually type each of the letters from *a* to *z* or from *A* to *Z*? There's a better way! Suppose you've entered the letter A in cell A1. In next cell, B1, enter the formula =CHAR(CODE (A1)+1). Did you get letter *B*? Then click on the bottom right of the cell B1. When the cursor turns into a plus sign, drag the formula to the right up to cell Z1. Did you get the letter from *A* to *Z*? Continue to drag across as far as you can. Did you get more exciting symbols? Up to which cell, did the icon stop to change? Now change the font of all letters into Wingdings. Which letters give you a smiley face and a sad face?

It's time to rename your current worksheet to 'History', either in upper case letters [≈ capital letters] or lower case letters, or mixed upper case or lower case letters up. What happened? Did a message box pop out saying 'History is a reserved name'? Huh, you can't assign the title 'history' to a sheet name.

Excel has a bug. It incorrectly assumes that 1900 is a leap year (Excel Incorrectly Assumes That the Year 1900 Is a Leap Year, 2021). A leap year is any year with 29 days in February rather than 28 days. Every year that is exactly divisible by four is a leap year. But century years (divisible by 100, such as 1900, 2000, 2100) that are not divisible by 400 are not leap years, with common 365 days in a year. To verify if the bug still exists in Excel, type 01/02/1900 in any cell. Click on the cell. Move the mouse to the right bottom of the cell until a 'plus' sign shows up. Drag the mouse down to the next 30 cells. Excel automatically fills in a date series, and 29/02/1900 is in there, which is not correct. Why won't Microsoft fix this 1900 leap year bug?

Hang on. Why is it even called Excel? 'Master Plan' and 'Mr Spreadsheet' were considered originally. Excel was chosen in the end, representing that it 'excelled over Lotus 123', expressing the excellence of the program. Plus, it has many cells that make up the spreadsheets (McLean, 2020). There are many cool facts about Excel that you can find online. I'll leave it to you to explore that some more.

# DAY 187
## UPS AND DOWNS

At work, there are times when you need to describe data trends with things like 'rise', 'fall' or 'flat'. Find out similar expressions for today's descriptions on the made-up fluctuation of S&P/ASX 200 share market index between 2008 and 2018, and draw a line on the chart in the space accordingly.

< The S&P/ASX 200 index measures the performance of top 200 stocks listed on ASX, setting the benchmark for Australian share market performance. S&P refers to Standard & Poor's. ASX stands for Australian Securities Exchange. >

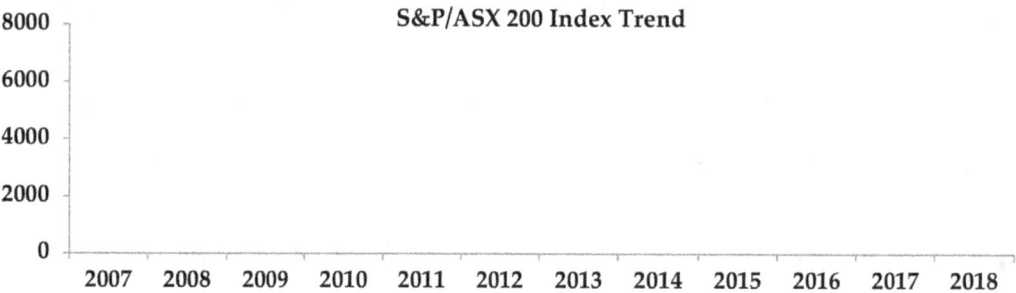

In 2008, the market crashed [≈ collapsed]. The S&P/ASX 200 Index was in decline [≈ had seen a downward slide]. It tumbled [≈ dropped ≈ nosedived ≈ plummeted ≈ plunged] by 10%.

The share market continued to shrink [≈ sink ≈ slump ≈ decrease ≈ reduce ≈ decline] in 2009, which tipped [≈ dipped ≈ slipped ≈ dwindled] further to 1000. At the end of the year it bottomed out [≈ was at its lowest ≈ was at a record low].

The index in 2010 started to rise [≈ climb ≈ grow ≈ increase ≈ jump ≈ surge ≈ ratchet up] again. The next year witnessed a further uptrend [≈ experienced a further uptick]. When the market consolidated its position in 2012, it was 30% up [≈ it achieved increase up by 30% ≈ it was a 30% uplift ≈ it stormed higher by 30%] compared to 2 years previous.

The year 2013 saw an explosion [≈ an upsurge] in price. It grew by leaps and bounds. [≈ It accelerated. ≈ It rocketed. ≈ It skyrocketed. ≈ It roared. ≈ It shot up. ≈ It was speedy. ≈ It sprung up. ≈ It went like the clappers. ≈ It increased dramatically [≈ sharply ≈ swiftly].] It more than doubled [≈ It went up more than twice] towards December of that year. The index then tripled in 2014, quadrupled in 2015 and quintupled in 2016. Does your drawing go out of the vertical axis's maximum bounds (8000)? Is this index going up too quickly? Does it become unrealistic?

In 2017, the index reached a peak [≈ went through the roof ≈ soared to record heights] from where it remained the same [≈ remained flat ≈ stayed stable ≈ was stagnating ≈ stalled ≈ was as flat as a pancake ≈ treaded water]. It didn't fluctuate [≈ change] too much.

These 'up and down' expressions are all yours. Learn all of them and flaunt them [≈ show them off]!

# DAY 188
# WATERWORKS

No-one wants to face unwanted tears at the workplace, but waterworks might be part of your career growth experience.

Perhaps you were bombarded with a heavy work backlog or overloaded with work. Perhaps you lost track of the work. You were behind the eight ball, and stressing out about it.

< One of the versions of the idiom 'behind the eight ball' is derived from the billiards game where the balls must be pocketed in numerical order except for the number eight ball. If the player takes a direct shoot to the eight ball first by using the white cue ball, the game is forfeited and they lose (Behind the Eight Ball, n.d.). So being behind the eight ball leaves you at a disadvantage [≈ in an unfavourable situation]. >

So your boss just gave you another urgent task. You had to chase a tight deadline. [≈ You were up against a strict deadline.] Time was short. [≈ You didn't have much time left. ≈ You ran out of time. ≈ The time was running out.] Even worse, when time got tough, no-one could offer a hand. Even worse, you were in a hurry, and you made a horrible mistake and missed the bloody deadline.

Then one thing after the other: you were criticised by your boss in front of others [≈ your boss yelled at you publicly]. They said, 'Why can't you finish the task?' or 'What have you done?' or 'Why didn't you talk to me in the first place?' or 'Who gave you the permission to open the file?' and so on.

You felt wronged. You felt that you were treated unfairly and differently [≈ you were held to standards that were different from your peers]. You felt your boss was playing favourites. It was unfair!

At that point in time, you broke down and became emotional [≈ broke down in tears ≈ shed tears ≈ burst into tears ≈ got emotional] in front of your boss and everyone else at work.

It's fine getting misty-eyed, red-eyed and red-nosed, or to even cry out loud. We're all human beings with emotions. [≈ We're not emotionless.] It sucks! It was just a bad day at the office. It certainly was. Suck it up. Grow from it. It's just a job.

# DAY 189
## SPEAK TO YOUR HIGHER-UP

In Australia, you are free to speak your mind [≈ express yourself ≈ express your opinion ≈ say your thoughts out loud] to your manager.

Say 'yes' if you agree.

'I agree. [≈ Spot on. ≈ Exactly. ≈ Precisely. ≈ True. ≈ You got that right. ≈ I am on board. ≈ You hit the nail on the head.]'

Say 'no' if you don't agree.

'I disagree. [≈ I don't agree. ≈ I'm against it.]'

We'll exhibit another five scenarios here. Under what circumstances would you talk to your manager like this? Fill in the blanks from Scenario 2 to Scenario 4.

**Scenario 1: When you need to ask a question**

**You:** Do you have a moment [≈ Could you spare a moment], please? I have come across a problem.

**Your manager:** I always have time for you. Shoot. [≈ Fire away.]

**Scenario 2:** ................................................................................................

**You:** I'm on it. [≈ I'll get onto it right away. ≈ I'll do it straight away. ≈ I'll do it instantly. ≈ I'll do it immediately. ≈ I'll do it in a jiffy. ≈ I'll do it in a bit.] I will get back to you in a minute [≈ in a tick ≈ very soon ≈ within two shakes of a lamb's tail ≈ shortly ≈ in no time ≈ in a very short time].

**Scenario 3:** ................................................................................................

**You:** I'll keep a close eye on it. [≈ I'll keep tabs on it.]

**Scenario 4:** ................................................................................................

**You:** Leave this with me. Let me dig into it. [≈ Let me investigate. ≈ Let me find out.]

For **Scenario 5**, you'd like to request a day off because of an illness. You call up your manager and say, 'I'm not feeling well today. May I take the day off?' Oops, the problem here is that you don't have to ask for a permission to be off sick. Asking for sick leave is a work right. You don't need to be overly polite. Let your manager know that you're sick and need to take a day off. This is the same as when you're about to leave the office for the day. You also don't have to ask for permission, 'May I go home now?' Just let your manager know that you are off very soon.

# DAY 190
## ANNUAL PERFORMANCE REVIEW

Are you looking forward to your annual performance review? I bet not. I bet your manager is also dreading this uncomfortable evaluation process. But it's a compulsory process for many businesses that everyone needs to complete each year.

Is a yearly performance appraisal important?

Many studies have revealed that [≈ Study after study has demonstrated that ≈ Evidence has piled up proving that ≈ According to multiple studies,] performance reviews don't serve their purpose well [≈ are useless and pointless] (G., 2020).

I agree. First off, in the one-on-one review meeting, your manager will often reaffirm that you've done well for the past year. Thanks for your efforts, blah blah blah…

< 'Blah, blah, blah' was first used in ancient Greece as 'bar bar bar', which was from the sounds of barbarians, referring to nonsense or meaningless chatter. 'Yada, yada, yada' later evolved to refer to boring or empty talk (Blah Blah Blah Day, 2021). >

Your manager will then point out your weaknesses. And there's always room for you to improve. True but boring! You feel you've given your all. There are always tasks and jobs that you can do better and you just can't reach perfection all the time (your manager's expectation). Overall, managers tend to provide constructive criticism, which is their job. Be aware of your weaknesses, and make improvement. Don't be deflated or take it negatively. I know you've done a super-duper [≈ an amazing] job!

Second, the performance review isn't useful in getting a promotion either. You won't be demoted. But don't hold too much hope that your manager will elevate you to the next level of position. Why? The majority of time, there's no such position available unless company is growing so quickly, someone in that position leaves the company or you have a new boss on board who's changing the whole team structure. Tentatively ask for a promotion. The chances are slim, though.

Third, in the majority of cases the review isn't linked to any financial reward. Let your manager know your achievements and contributions. Don't pin your hopes on the outcome of the review though. Why do we need to do the review then? Is it just to go through the motions? But if you do get good news, share it with me!

# DAY 191
## A BIG PAY RAISE (YOU WISH!)

After a period of time at your work, you've picked things up, exceeded expectations, stepped up in difficult situations, and taken on more responsibilities. Your salary doesn't match what you do now anymore. You've researched industry salary data [≈ market rates] and documented your achievements. You gather your courage [≈ pluck up the courage ≈ muster up the courage ≈ fortify your courage] to negotiate your salary with your boss. Awesome!

You come out the meeting disappointed! Your boss tells you that the company isn't making money or doesn't have the budget this year… You feel that's bullshit!

It is the reality, though? Because there are two ceilings and one floor, as described here:

- **Glass ceiling:** An invisible barrier that prevents women or international employees from moving up to the next level of their career (Kagan, 2021).
- **Bamboo ceiling:** A barrier that prevents Asians from receiving a promotion to a leadership role and a pay-rise (Xiao & Handley, 2019).
- **Sticky floor:** A barrier that prevents women or a particular group of employees from moving from low-paying jobs [≈ low-ranking jobs ≈ low status jobs ≈ low regard jobs] to higher-paying jobs (Spaid, 1993).

For most jobs, certain people can be pigeonholed. Your salary will remain around the range you started, unless you get a big promotion. When a senior role becomes available, the employer prefers to hire someone from outside the company, not you, the 'rookie'.

I'm not saying [≈ I don't mean ≈ This isn't to say] not to ask for a salary bump [≈ a pay-rise ≈ a wage increase]. It's worth trying, and it could be possible. Just don't hold high expectations. If you desire to earn more, develop your skills at your current role and be ready to move up to next level with a new employer who's willing to pay more and appreciate your capabilities and skills.

How much do you make per annum? [≈ What are your annual earnings? ≈ What is your gross annual income?] Hush! Don't answer my question. This is often a private question in western culture. I shouldn't have asked and you should never be curious about how much others are earning either. The same goes for someone's age. Don't ask a person's age unless you're close, but workmates are normally okay with talking about a person's age.

# DAY 192
## WORKPLACE GENDER IMBALANCE

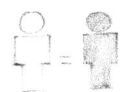

We talked about the glass ceiling yesterday, which is considered a barrier for women and minorities trying to climb further up the corporate ladder.

Unfortunately, even with some changes in the workforce these last few decades, the glass ceiling still exists. Observe closely whether the majority of senior management roles are taken by men in your organisation, with women tending to stay at the lower levels of the ladder like in the below table.

| Gender | Position at the company |
|---|---|
| Male | CEO, CFO, managers, directors, chairmen, senior level positions |
| Female | Receptionists, administrators, contract coordinators, payroll officers, accounts receivable officers, accounts payable officers |

Also, even with a similar level of capability and qualification, are women promoted to the same position as men in the company, or are they promoted as fast as men? The answer is a no, right? By chance a woman is capable and becomes a board member, they will be labelled 'superwomen'. But this word sounds sarcastic.

What about salary? Are women paid equally for the same kind of work as men? The answer is a nope, right? As per the Australian Bureau of Statistics (ABS), women on average are paid 13.4% less per week than men at the same position (The Gender Pay Gap, n.d.). This is the gender salary gap [≈ gender pay gap ≈ wage gap ≈ income disparity ≈ unequal pay ≈ lopsided gender pay].

Often, you hear people say it's a boy's industry [≈ a male-dominated profession], meaning it's hard for a woman to survive in such an industry, not to mention working their way up the corporate ladder.

This is absolutely unfair [≈ definitely outrageous].

As a woman, we need to empower ourselves. Be brave and ask for what you deserve (rights, salaries, positions, promotions). We have our own strengths, often bringing in patience and emotions into workplace, making everyone's job easier and more organised. Men need to get rid of gender bias by understanding women are also challenged with childcare and household responsibilities. Everyone deserves a fair treatment with the same support from the company.

Let's finish up this chapter by keeping something in mind: No matter where you're at on the corporate ladder, no matter if you're happy with work or you're feeling your talent is being wasted, no matter of your salary, your title, your responsibilities, you're so much more than a job. You are also your family, your health, your passions, your big heart, your charisma...! You're an amazing being!

# DAY 193
# THE WORD - THROUGH

Today, let's **go through** [≈ **run through**] stories with the word 'through'. Also, keep an eye **throughout** to look for the word 'throughout'.

First, I'll **walk** you **through** [≈ **take** you **through**] my job-hunting experience. I got a job **through** a recruitment agency. The final round of interviews was a group interview. I **walked through** the door, smiling. I remained calm and wore that big smile **throughout**.

After the interview, I **slept right through** the day.

I couldn't believe I was **through**! I got the job. I'll be working at Expedia. We open every day **throughout** the year. I hope I will **crack through** that glass ceiling and become the CEO in the future.

While this was happening, I had relationship difficulties. I was **through** with my ex. [≈ I was done with my ex. ≈ I no longer had a relationship with my ex.] I regained my freedom, so I started to travel **throughout** the world. Last year, I **passed through** China on the way to Australia.

In many Australian suburbs, you can spot big signs for fast-food places like McDonald's, KFC or Red Rooster and their **'drive thru'**, or sometimes a café, or a car wash.

< A **'drive thru'** [≈ **'drive through'**], as the name suggests, is a service where you can get your fast food, or coffee, or a car washed without having to leave your car. >

If you'd like to visit Crown Casino, remember to bring along your passport. They won't let you **through** otherwise.

After **flicking through** [≈ **skimming through** ≈ **scanning through** ≈ **thumbing through** ≈ **reading through** ≈ **ploughing through** ≈ running your eyes over ≈ casting your eyes over] today's content, what is **running through** your head right now? Let's continue **slogging through** [≈ working hard on] English expressions in this book. I hope you are enjoying the reading process **throughout** this book.

What great effort! You **got through** today's topic, and you are more than halfway **through** this book!

# DAY 194
## TALK THE TALK

Before we ease into the topic of being 'a stellar leader', let's take a look at how a manager talks. Observe the two paragraphs below – which one sounds more like a manager talking?

Paragraph 1: 'Hey Audrey. **Is your report ready?** (a rising tone at the end) Let's **find** the problem. Hmm, we've **found** the issue. The invoices are **missing**. Let's **change** our plan and **complete** it now.'

Paragraph 2: 'Audrey, **is your report ready?** (a falling tone on 'ready') Let's **identify** the problem. The issue has been **flagged**. The invoices **slipped through**. **Modify** your plan. **Knock it out** of the park.'

Does the second one sound better? Did you notice any tricks? Below are three tricks for talking like a manager:

**Play with tones when speaking to establish authority at work.** If you ask your staff questions like 'Is your report ready?' with a rising tone, it makes it sound like the report is not that important. Instead, ask the same question through a falling tone. It makes it sound serious. Your audience will feel the report needs to be done right off the bat.

< The phrase 'right off the bat' is believed to have come from the sport of baseball. When the batter swings and hits the ball, the ball is right off the bat, and the batter needs to run to first base immediately. So the idiom is figurative, meaning doing something immediately (Right Off the Bat, n.d.). >

**Making your speech more formal makes you sound knowledgeable.** Does 'identifying' the problem sound more professional than 'finding' the problem? What about 'flagged' and 'slipped through'?

**Use imperative sentences to show assertion** (for example, modify your plan, knock it out of the park, or you can't…). Other examples could be:

- I want you to complete this by 3 pm today.
- I need you to work 100% today.
- Give them a call.
- Let's park it. [≈ Hold off on it.]
- You can resume work now.
- Go ahead on this project.
- Shut the door.

Keen to see how a manager behaves? See me tomorrow.

# CHAPTER 21 - A Stellar Leader

## DAY 195
## WALK THE WALK

Let's cut to the chase [≈ get straight to the point]. As a manager, you don't just talk the talk, you also need to walk the walk.

< 'Talk the talk, walk the walk [≈ Walk the talk]' is an idiom, meaning what you do should back up what you have said and agreed to [≈ you should put your words into your actions ≈ you should act on what you say]. >

Now cross out the boxes below for the behaviours that a good manager should have. Use your judgement or base your response on any personal experience.

- ☐ I only care about of getting the job done. I never listen to my employees' complaints.
- ☐ I promote teamwork and encourage collaboration by identifying the strengths and weaknesses of each team member and by spelling out each person's responsibilities clearly.
- ☐ I have my favourite employees and have double standards with my employees.
- ☐ I love, care, encourage, challenge and inspire people.
- ☐ I lead by example. [≈ I'm a good example of how to lead.]
- ☐ I can play hardball [≈ be ruthless when making unpleasant decisions].
- ☐ I show no interest in an employee's career development. It's none of my business.
- ☐ I say one thing and do another.
- ☐ I trust my staff. I have their back and they have mine.
- ☐ I don't sugar-coat bad news or hide from it. I'm honest with my staff.
- ☐ I see talented and capable employees as a threat to my position.
- ☐ I hide my knowledge and expertise. I don't want others to steal it.
- ☐ When my team members don't perform well, I'm tough on them. But I identify what the cause is (personal reasons, lack of professional knowledge or experience, or just simply attitude) and I'll help them to improve.
- ☐ I look cool and smile rarely in the workplace. I show a long face when necessary.

< A 'long face' is an unhappy or disappointed expression. Are there other types of faces? Yep. A blank or deadpan face is a face with a lack of emotion [≈ having no expression]. A 'poker face' is also a face that reveals no emotion. This originated from poker games where you would try not to react to give away the cards you're holding (Poker Face, n.d.). A 'stone face' also conceals emotions. >

But a good manager is not the same as an excellent leader. Similarly, an outstanding leader may not be positioned in a managerial role. Someone who is an 'alpha' leads, anticipates, takes risks, lifts the team up and empowers others. This is leadership!

# DAY 196
## LEADERSHIP QUALITIES

Are you leadership material? Observe your workmates around you. Including yourself, write down any names of those who you believe would be a stellar [≈ a prominent ≈ an eminent ≈ an excellent] leader.

...................................................................................................................................

...................................................................................................................................

...................................................................................................................................

What qualities do you see in a leader? Below is my observation. If you have any answers that differ from mine, write them outside of the cloud artwork here.

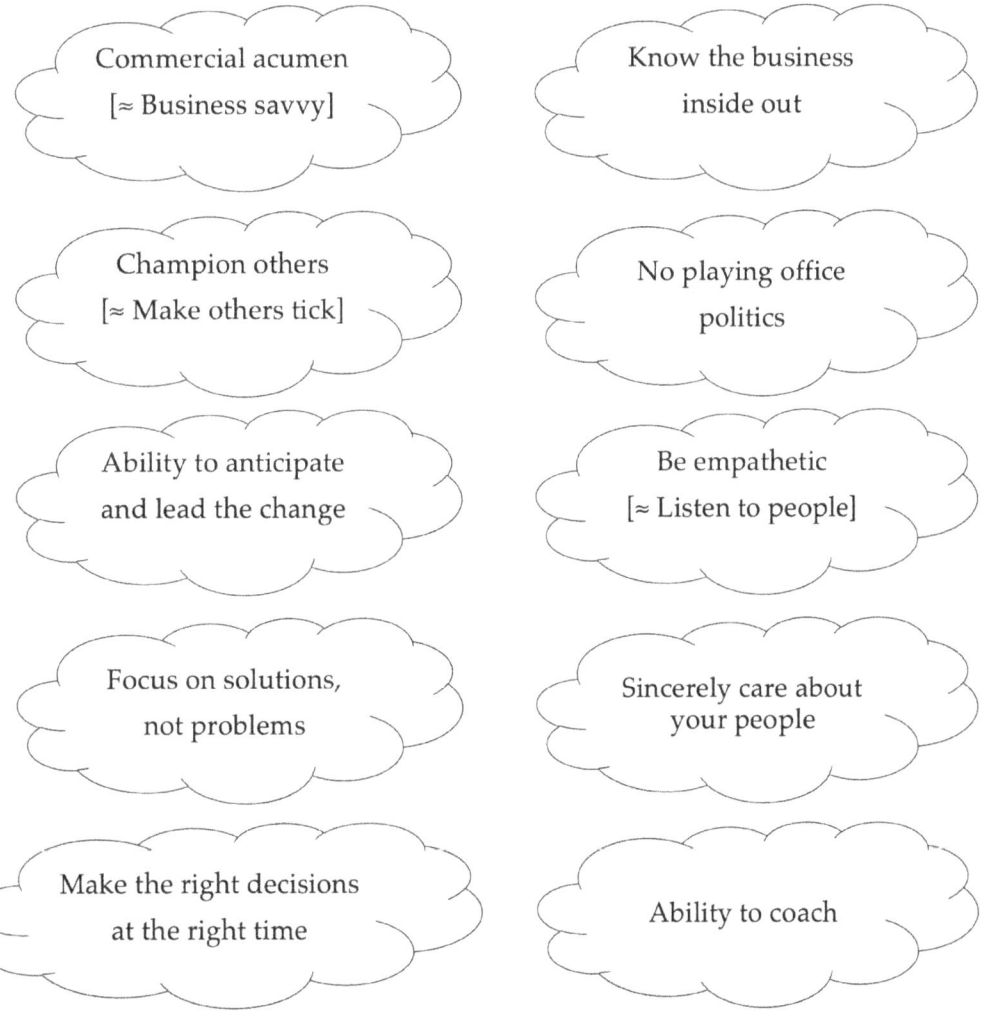

Coaching is similar but not the same as teaching, mentoring, consulting or counselling. As a coach, you should not offer advice telling your people what you think they should do. Instead, you partner with your people, and you guide your people by asking them questions and inspiring them to explore the answers themselves.

I'm giving you advice right now, so I'm not doing the coaching! But I am going to share with you another three qualities of good leadership over the next 3 days.

# DAY 197
## CHECK-INS

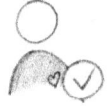

Leadership quality #1: Your people always come first.

As a leader, don't bury your head doing your own heavy workload. You need to step out of the office, talk to your team, and genuinely care about them. Make it day-to-day practice to do so. [≈ Make it into a daily habit. ≈ Integrate it into your daily work life.] Your team will appreciate this and have a higher morale if you care about them more than your team's deadline.

Here are three checks that are worth doing:

**Check on their status:**

- What have you been working on? [≈ What is on your plate?]
- Is everything under control? [≈ Are you on track?]
- How are you getting by? [≈ How did you go?]
- How are you? [≈ How are you travelling? ≈ How's everything going? ≈ Are you winning?]

< In this context, 'How are you travelling?' isn't asking the type of transportation (bus, train, car) that you're taking for your trip. It's just another way of checking in, or 'How are you?' >

**Check on task progress:**

- Where are we at? [≈ Where are you up to?]

< They'll normally respond, 'I'm ahead of the curve. [≈ I'm ahead of time. ≈ I'm ahead of schedule.]' or 'Almost there. [≈ Nearly there.]' or 'Not quite.' or 'I'm miles away.' >

< Something to be mindful about is to check in with them, not check up on them. Say 'What can I do to help out?' or 'Do you need me to help out?' This strategy is quite helpful, especially when you're short-staffed [≈ short of hands ≈ light on staff ≈ have a skeleton staff] and your team is struggling. >

**Check on their career goals:**

- Can you pop into my office? [≈ Can you swing by? ≈ Can you come around? ≈ Can we talk?] I'd like to discuss with you your career goals and work out a development plan for you. Let me know what you would like to achieve over the next year.

What else can you check in with your people to show that they're in a good hand with a caring heart. Put down your check-ins below:

..................................................................................................

..................................................................................................

# DAY 198
# ENLIGHTEN YOUR STAFF

Leadership quality #2: Lift up everyone in the team up to be their best. You can do this through the '3E' strategies below.

**Encourage.** All ideas should be welcomed. If you agree with any of your team members' suggestions and statements, say, 'That's a good point. [≈ Your point is taken. ≈ You're on point. ≈ I take your point.] I'm on your side. [≈ I'm completely with you. ≈ I couldn't agree more.]'

If you'd like them to test data in a testing system, say, 'Go wild.' or 'Have a go.' or 'You can't break it.' or 'You can't do any damage. Go for it.'

When it comes to a tough task, challenge them by asking, 'Is this doable? [≈ Is this feasible? ≈ Is this achievable?]'

**Empower.** Take your team members under your wings and show them the ropes, although shadowing someone all the time isn't your responsibility. This requires you to delegate tasks to them to help them grow and develop. Ask them to hold down the fort while you're away. Give them the autonomy to get things done. Let them shine.

**Engage.** When allocating new tasks to the team members, explain the purpose of the task [≈ why they're performing the task] and what the logic is behind it. Give them the tool, not the completed art piece. Give your staff the chance to speak up. Ask for their thoughts: 'What do you have in your mind? [≈ What are your thoughts on this? ≈ Can I pick your brain? ≈ A penny for your thoughts.]'

You also need to make sure they understand what you're illustrating by checking: 'Does it make a sense? [≈ Am I making sense? ≈ Am I clear? ≈ Am I making myself clear?]'. 'You know what I mean?', 'Do you understand?' or 'Do you follow what I'm saying?' are similar expressions, but to me, these alternative expressions having the word 'you' in the sentence sounds like 'you're not smart enough to understand what I'm saying', especially when you use the wrong emphasis on the word 'you'. This might upset your listener or make them feel inferior. Some people don't even recommend saying, 'Am I making sense?' because it demonstrates your uncertainty about what you're talking about. Instead, ask 'what are your thoughts?' What are your thoughts here?

As a leader, you're there to provide all sorts of support for your employees. Let your employees know that your doors are always open for them, and they've got your trust and your back. Say, 'Yell out [≈ Call out ≈ Shout out] if you have any questions or need anything.'

# DAY 199
## PRAISE YOUR UNDERLINGS

Leadership quality #3: Observe the merits of your team, identify the team's good work and offer praise and rewards at the right moments [≈ at the correct moment ≈ right on cue ≈ at the right time].

This will ignite employee passion and make them more committed to their job. As a leader, have a think now when you might use the below sentences:

- Well done! [≈ Nicely done! ≈ You've done well! ≈ You're too good! ≈ Exceptional job! ≈ Excellent! ≈ Top job! ≈ Great stuff! ≈ Good one!]
- What a ripper! [≈ Quite impressive! ≈ That's brilliant! ≈ That's genius!] Keep up the good work!
- You're a genius! [≈ You're Einstein! ≈ You're the cream of the crop! ≈ You're tip-top! ≈ You're a champion!]
- You're on fire! [≈ You're on the ball!] You're on a roll!
- You smashed it! You knocked it out of the ballpark. [≈ You knocked it out of the park.] It's a knockout [≈ a great success]!
- You've raised the bar [≈ set the bar very high]!
- You're too quick [≈ speedy]!

< 'Ripper' is an Australian slang, meaning something is awesome and amazing. >

< The 'cream of the crop' here means that you're the best of the best in a group. The cream is the richest part of milk. When letting the milk sit, the cream rises to the top (Cream of the Crop, n.d.). >

< To 'knock something out of the ballpark' means that you've done a fantastic job! The phrase stems from the sport of baseball where if a batter strikes [≈ hits] the ball well, they could knock the ball out of the park entirely. This could score your team a home run! >

< When you 'raise the bar', you set the standards higher than the expectations. What type of bar does it refer to originally? It's the bar in pole vault or high jump sports. You need to jump over the bar. The bar is raised each time and you'll win the competition and set the bar if you've jumped the highest. >

Wow! You've almost reached Day 200 of the book. You're phenomenal! [≈ You're a rock star!] I'll give you 10 out of 10!

< '10 out of 10' is a perfect score, indicating that you've done extremely well. Well done! >

Stop for a moment. You deserve a pat on the back and a bottle of champagne. Cheers! But it's unfinished business. Continue on. There's more to come!

# DAY 200
## IDIOMS ABOUT FOOD

We've been talking about idioms for quite a while, but we haven't even explained much about what an idiom is. Well, idiomatic expressions are words or phrases that you don't take literally. They contain a figurative meaning. Today's activity is a made-up story [≈ an unlikely story] filled with common idioms with food.

Julianna was my former colleague [≈ used to be my colleague], a well-known **apple polisher** [≈ brown-noser]. It was so obvious that she **buttered** my boss **up** [≈ massaged my boss's ego]. As a result, she became **the apple of** my boss's **eye** [≈ was loved by my boss]. Let me be honest. This **bad apple** [≈ **bad egg**] was a **fruitcake** [≈ crazy], **driving** me **bananas** [≈ **driving** me **nuts** ≈ driving me crazy ≈ driving me bonkers ≈ driving me up a wall]!

< A 'bad apple' means a bad person. The proverb 'One bad [≈ rotten] apple spoils the whole barrel' means a person in a group who has bad influence. Does one bad apple really spoil the whole barrel? The answer is yes. When the apple is overripe [≈ mouldy], it generates ethylene gas, which causes other apples to start ripening, and too much ripening can spoil them too quickly (Thomson, 2016). Hang on. Why are you assuming apples are bad? Could it be a bad barrel or a bad barrel maker? >

In the end, I couldn't put up with Julianna anymore. I couldn't **give a fig** [≈ couldn't care]. She wasn't worth my time working with her. I knew I **had bigger fish to fry** [≈ had more important thing to do]. I quit my job without finding a new one, which indeed put me **in a pickle** [≈ in a difficult situation] for a while. I felt I was **treading on eggshells** without any financial income.

Luckily, I nailed a **plum job** [≈ a highly coveted job] after 5 months! My new workmates are just **peachy** [≈ good]. I'm glad that my rash decision didn't **go pear-shaped** [≈ didn't go wrong]. With 2 years' efforts, I've become the **top banana** [≈ the **big cheese** ≈ a very important person] here at my current company. Some of my projects have started to **bear fruit** [≈ yield positive results]. These are the **fruits of my labour** [≈ the result of my efforts]. And this job turned out to be **the greatest thing since sliced bread** [≈ the best thing]!

This is **food for thought** [≈ is thought-provoking ≈ gets you thinking ≈ provokes you into thinking seriously ≈ stimulates your mind]. Take a risk. You never know what awaits you.

# DAY 201
## TIME TO QUIT?

Nowadays, no-one wants to stick to just one job for life. My principle to you: start looking for new opportunities when you start to question whether you should quit your job. Some symptoms of needing to consider changing jobs might include:

- You feel a sense of stress on a Sunday night. [≈ You have the Sunday nights blues.]
- You dread having to get up on a Monday morning.
- You slog to work every day and feel trapped there.

The real reason behind any of these feelings could be that the pay is a shit [≈ the pay sucks] compared to your skill level; your potential is wasted, and you are not fully engaged [≈ you are disengaged]; the company has no further career growth opportunities; you have a tough, abusive manager or an annoying workmate that you've tried everything to deal with but the situation doesn't improve.

Fair enough. The job probably isn't for you anymore. It's time to make the move! Here are two types of actions you can take:

The first move is to walk out of the door without a new job lined up. It's not a bad thing if you do need a break and have a certain amount of savings. The move is risky. If you don't get anything after a few months, will you get through? But if you work hard enough, there's always a position out there that is designed just for you.

The second move is to start quietly looking for a new job while keeping your current one and still being active and proactive on what you do. You could then resign from your current job after getting the new job offer.

If you're unwilling to make the effort to find a new job, you just have to stay with the current job that you don't like anymore. Well, this is your choice. But don't think: Why do I have to suffer in a job that I'm unhappy with? Why can't I have a job that I love?

Admittedly, searching for job can be like looking for a needle in a haystack. But it's a 'short-term pain, long-term gain' process, billion dollars worthwhile. You'll find that 'needle', for sure, as long as you make sure the process is working! Imagine the moment you're given a job offer with better conditions! Are you ready for that?

# DAY 202
## SHOULD I QUIT?

Are you still in two minds whether to quit your current job? I understand, your job is your bread and butter [≈ your job is a means to an end ≈ you are doing your job to make a living ≈ you work to pay your mortgage and bills ≈ you work to keep a roof over your head]. Like it or hate it, you just need the job.

Apart from this, what other parts of the job do you still love? It could be some of these?

> great perks, flexible work hours, a good boss, supportive colleagues, growth opportunities, work culture, close to home, challenges, work-life balance, variety of work

What things make you feel miserable right now? List this in the blank area below.

The question is: are you happy with your current job? Only you have the answer. When you're not doing what you love [≈ When you're unenthused about what you do], you run out of gas [≈ run out of steam ≈ lose enthusiasm], and your happiness level is reduced.

< Imagine an old steam engine. When the fire powering the boiler is too low and it's unable to produce steam, the engines will lose energy and slow down steadily and stop (Run Out of Steam, n.d.). So when you run out of steam, you lose your interest and motivation to continue doing what you're doing. >

A third of a day's time has to be allocated to a full-time job and, on average, 90,000 hours could be spent at work in a person's lifetime (Goudreau, 2010).

Do you really want to continue to suffer for most of your daytime, or even the rest of your life? How desirable is it that you want to [≈ How bad do you want to] regain your happiness? Make the move right now. It's going to be tough, for sure. But, if you stay put, you'll feel even more miserable after a couple of years. You'll only get older, and the longer you leave it, the harder it is to quit.

Put effort in. Get a better job with better salary package and better work conditions. All you need to do is to complete the whole job-hunting process. Go back to review **Day 111 Embrace Change** to get the motivation you need.

Are you all in now?

## CHAPTER 22 - A Job Exiter

# DAY 203
# I QUIT

If you're still unconvinced on your next move, let me share my story.

In my late 20s, I quit my job without having a new one lined up. My workmates said that I was silly. My boss asked me to stay while searching for new opportunities. My parents attempted to persuade me to do the same. (Mum and Dad disagreed with my approach, but they sent me money afterwards, although I told them I had my own savings for a couple of months. That's parent love. Love you, Mum and Dad!)

I quit anyway because I asked myself many times: is this what I wanted to do for the rest of my life? The answer was definitely no. I went all in to seek out a new job that I really wanted.

To be honest [≈ Frankly speaking ≈ Frankly ≈ Point blank ≈ Candidly ≈ In all seriousness ≈ In all truthfulness ≈ Let's not mince words], the whole process was tough. **Day 104 I'm Desperate** was what I experienced during that period of time.

But I nailed a fantastic job in a Fortune 500 company after 3 months' job searching full-time. It totally altered the course of my career. And it was a job in which almost all of my workmates were Aussies. We talked about Aussie sports, food, cooking, travelling and gardening quite often. They actually taught me almost everything about Aussie! We went to pubs, had poker nights, played lawn balls and attended industrial conferences after work. (See, the work environment can be quite laid-back.) That's why I have all these things to share with you in the book. It's like an adventure, isn't it?

Luckily, my job-hunting process has become easier and quicker since that job search experience! It took me less than a month to secure the job offers for my recent two jobs, just by using all the methods I've shown you in this chapter!

So advice from me: Sometimes you'll go to the same workplace day in, day out and feel like a robot doing the same thing over and over again. And you don't want to feel like a robot! If you can't afford to quit your job without lining up new work, take action by throwing yourself into the job market. Talk to recruitment agencies. Putting yourself out of your daily routine can give you a fresh view. When you get a new job offer, the new position could broaden your horizon (and, hopefully, the pay is better!)

Now, can you tell me any reasons that you shouldn't start looking for a new job when you're stagnating in a job or suffering (overworked, underpaid, underappreciated, unhappy…) in your current role?

A perspective from me: Your employer and your boss are not responsible for your career. You need to take ownership. Plot your next career move. [≈ Map out the next step for your career.] Change your job when it's time. Jobs are like your shoes: whether they're comfortable to wear or not, only you know. When the shoes stop fitting, or get broken, it's better to find a new pair of shoes!

# DAY 204
## LEAVING YOUR JOB

Once you've signed off on the new job offer, or whenever you're 100% ready to quit, tell your boss that you're leaving [≈ you'll no longer be working there].

Then submit [≈ hand in] your resignation letter giving 4 weeks' notice (depending on your contract). Once the decision is made, don't accept any counteroffers from your current employer. You should be adamant on this. That's my point of view, at least.

Now that you're hitting the road, your boss might disseminate an email to all employees about you leaving the role. What would normally be written in this farewell email? Let's have a look:

'We regret [≈ apologise] that Leilani has resigned from the company to pursue other interests. Thank her for her dedication and contribution over the last 5 years. Leilani's last day with the company will be Friday next week. We'll throw a farewell party. She will be sorely missed.'

Your workmates will secretly prepare a farewell card [≈ a 'you will be missed' card]. They will possibly write words like:

'It's been a great pleasure working with you. Thank you for all your help. We will miss you. Enjoy your new adventure! All the best!'

< Food for thought: Great staff tend to jump the ship when their needs can't be met. In business, companies tend to hire the best staff, but how do they maintain their top talent? >

What if you are made redundant [≈ fired ≈ sacked ≈ laid off ≈ let go ≈ given the boot ≈ dismissed ≈ kicked out ≈ bundled out] at work?

If your boss sends you home [≈ you get a pink slip], never mind. You might be eligible for a redundancy [≈ severance] pay out. The amount is calculated based on your continuous years of services. Better opportunities will be out there. Basically, you won't lose anything! It's your employer's loss. Get yourself ready to serve your next employer, hopefully someone who will value your worth. It's also a chance for a bit of a break.

# DAY 205
# ENJOY A CAREER BREAK

Dreaming of a bit freedom? While you're out of work between jobs [≈ out of the job ≈ unemployed ≈ jobless ≈ on the off-ramp from the workforce], it's the perfect time for you to do the things that you've always wanted to try. Appreciate this period of time – the sort that people holding a full-time job just don't have.

Great! I congratulate for you for the short break!

Have a think about what you'd love to do in this break. List a few things. This might include:

- Using the break to travel around the world. Backpacking is one popular option when you travel (often literally with a backpack with all your stuff). Australia also offers working holiday visas for people at a certain age. You can make a living by being a boat crew, a fruit picker [≈ harvester], a hotel worker. Or any other eligible profession, all the while experiencing the culture of other countries.
- Learning a new skill you've desired to pick up.
- Spending more time with your partner and kids.
- Being social. Catch up with old friends and make new friends.
- Doing something new and challenging.
- .................................................................
- .................................................................
- .................................................................
- .................................................................
- .................................................................

By doing all these things, your career isn't disintegrating [≈ isn't down the hill ≈ isn't stagnating ≈ hasn't stalled]. The loss of employment actually gives you time to refresh yourself [≈ gives you a breath of fresh air].

To give yourself a break isn't a bad choice at all. So just simply enjoy it, please! As long as you don't end up doing nothing [≈ sitting idle at home] all the time, you will come back with a boost of energy, with new knowledge and with a new perspective. You could even land a higher position job! Who knows?

One thing that I'd like to bring up is to make sure that you can be self-sufficient [≈ self-contained] during this period. Your financial independence lays the foundation for you to survive and do things that you love during such a period of time. So it's quite important to save money for a 'rainy day' for when you're unemployed.

# DAY 206
## ARE YOU AN ENTREPRENEUR?

You might feel that you're not made for an office job. The idea of setting up a company geminates in your mind. Before you bravely quit your 9-to-5 job, test yourself with the seven questions below. Do you have what it takes to become an entrepreneur [≈ a starter ≈ a creator ≈ a founder] of your own business?

- Are you self-motivated to work hard?
- Are you a risk taker instead of being risk averse [≈ a person avoiding risks]?
- Can you lead?
- Can you work outside the box?
- Can you live with uncertainty?
- Can you take responsibility when things go wrong?
- Are you able to consolidate success and cope with failure?

These questions do not determine and predict if you can set up and run a successful business. But they are basic qualities that an entrepreneur should have or develop in the course of time. Are you physically and mentally ready for this?

Even if your answer is yes, just hold on a moment. Before you become your own boss [≈ start your own business], do you know what could be ahead of you being a freelancer or an entrepreneur? Seth Godin explained the difference: a freelancer is someone who gets paid for their own work (writing, cleaning, tutoring, doing taxes) while an entrepreneur uses their ideas to hire others to build up a business bigger than themselves. Apparently, entrepreneurs can even make money when they're sleeping [≈ they're asleep]! That sounds cool!

You won't become a successful entrepreneur and get rich without putting in money, time and effort. You can start with being a freelancer by turning your hobbies into a business and scaling up the business when the time comes.

So start with expanding your social network and finding some clients. Perhaps talk to a mentor.

Wait, don't drop the day work just yet [≈ still keep your day job]. You need be self-sufficient [≈ self-sustaining] until your business generates a decent income.

# DAY 207
# BUSINESS IDEAS

Let's brainstorm some great business options today. Add in your ideas to the blank spaces in each box.

Let's start with some professions:

> tailor, seamstress, photographer, consultant, bookkeeper, tutor, podcaster, SEO (search engine optimisation) freelancer, personal trainer, hairdresser, café owner, app developer, cleaner

Now put down some ideas for a business (each starting with a verb of some kind):

> buy an IGA supermarket or buy a 7-Eleven franchise, craft jewellery to sell, become a cupcake queen or king, write a blog, open a food truck business, provide a moving service

< IGA and 7-Eleven are both convenience grocery stores. IGA stands for Independent Grocers of Australia. 7-Eleven stores are open 24 hours a day, seven days a week. The 7-Eleven stores were called Tote'm initially! The name changed in 1946 to 7-Eleven to notify customers that their operating hours changed from 7 am to 11 pm, seven days a week (Lammle, 2018). I noticed there were once some milk bars (convenience stores) on corner streets in Australia many years ago, but I rarely see them these days. >

< *Shark Tank Australia* is a great TV program that you can use to seek out ideas on what people are doing in business. Five entrepreneurs and business leaders, Steve Baxter (internet pioneer), Janine Allis (Boost Juice), Andrew Banks (Talent 2), Naomi Simson (RedBalloon) and Glen Richards (Greencross Vets) assess candidates who aim to grow their business but are short of money and mentors. If any of the interviewers love the business ideas and see a potential growth in a candidate's business, they will negotiate any investment fund and any expected equity percentages with the interviewee. >

Whatever the business you're planning to set up, make sure it is legitimate. In Australia, you can't sell dumplings or cakes through WeChat without a health permit. You can't become a money transfer dealer without registration. Is ticket scalping [≈ becoming a ticket scalper] legal in Australia? The Victorian Government declared that selling or advertising tickets for resale for more than 10% above face value was illegal when an event was declared as a major event. If you do scalp tickets, you could face penalties anywhere from $806 and up to $483,500 (Ticket Scalping FAQ, 2019). So you need to do your research to correctly set up your business and make sure that your business isn't illegal.

Have you decided what kind of business you want to start yet?

Kickstart your business! [≈ Commence your entrepreneurship journey!] How exciting!

# DAY 208
# TURN YOUR BUSINESS IDEA INTO REALITY

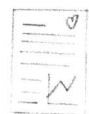

Great, so you're on the right track to start your business. What's the next? Make it happen! How? Let's go through three steps right now.

**Step 1: Write down a business plan.** A business plan is the foundation of your business. It's the roadmap for your business. This plan should include an executive summary, market analysis, an overview of your product or services, milestones, budget and forecast, and financial planning. Don't ignore [≈ Don't overlook] this very important step.

It takes time to complete a business plan, but it also gives you a chance to review if your business idea is viable [≈ feasible] and if you're starting the business just on a whim [≈ based on a sudden decision] or whether it's something more credible.

**Step 2: Choose a business structure.** In Australia, there are four main legal business structures (sole trader, partnership, trust, and company) that you can set up. Get to know the pros and cons of each type. Once you've decided which structure to set up and figured out your business name, apply for an Australia Business Number (ABN) on the ATO website, which is a unique 11 digit number for each business entity. It will make it easier for you to keep track of your business transactions for tax purposes.

< In Australia, it's totally free [≈ it doesn't incur any charges] to register on the ATO website for an ABN. Be vigilant though. Some tax agency websites look like the ATO's website and prompt as advertisements on the very top of a Google search. They'll charge you service fees after you go through the application for the ABN. >

**Step 3: Start doing the work.** Work out your financials; find [≈ source] your customers; pitch [≈ explain and sell] your product or service; promote your brand; set up an accounting system and hire employees, if needed; manage your cashflow... Phew! That's a lot of hard work!

If your business goes like clockwork [≈ happens as planned] and grows, that's awesome! Well done! If it doesn't go like clockwork, find ways to fix the issue or adjust your plans. You'll learn from failure and mistakes. You're definitely not back to square one [≈ not going back to the drawing board], so keep putting in the hard work and commit to the business.

# DAY 209
# TAX BASICS IN AUSTRALIA

Today, we'll be looking at some basic tax knowledge for setting up [≈ registering] a sole trader business structure in Australia.

A sole trader is an individual running a business. You need to have your tax file number (TFN) ready. Applying for a TFN is free via the ATO website. If you were eligible at the time, you normally would have applied for a TFN when you arrived in Australia.

As mentioned yesterday, you also need to apply for an ABN. If you don't, your clients must withhold 47% of their payments to you for tax purposes. But there are situations where you're not entitled to an ABN. For example, a residential property investor may not need an ABN, or you're not eligible for an ABN for any work carried out as an employee – including apprentice, trade assistant or labourer.

You might also need to apply for licences and permits, pay your employees' payroll tax, PAYG (pay-as-you-go) and superannuation, and purchase insurance.

At the end of each financial year (starting 1 July and ending 30 June), you use your TFN and ABN to lodge your income tax return to the ATO. You report business income on your individual tax return and pay tax at the individual income rate. Below are the brackets for income tax rate for the financial year 2021–2022.

| Annual income | Rate | Tax payable |
| --- | --- | --- |
| $0–$18,200 | 0% | Nil |
| $18,201–$45,000 | 19% | 19 cents for each $1 over $18,200 |
| $45,001–$120,000 | 32.5% | $5092 plus 32.5 cents for each $1 over $45,000 |
| $120,001–$180,000 | 37% | $29,467 plus 37 cents for each $1 over $120,000 |
| $180,001 and over | 45% | $51,667 plus 45 cents for each $1 over $180,000 |

The rates above do not include the Medicare levy of 2%.

If your business is registered for GST, you need to lodge a BAS (business activity statement) monthly, quarterly or yearly. Please note that all information that I've provided here cannot be used as tax advice for your business. These are just some tax rules that you need to comply with in Australia.

Does it sound too complicated to you? [≈ Does it confuse you? ≈ Does it baffle you? ≈ Is it over your head? ≈ Is this Greek to you?] Get a registered tax accountant to do the work for you. A small-sized tax accounting firm could charge you over $300 or more for a business income tax return. And you need to keep all business-related invoices on record.

Is it expensive? Is it too much work already? Well, this is just the beginning of your entrepreneurial journey! Get it all set up, and show me your passion for your business!

# DAY 210
# THE WORD - IN

Let's dig into the word 'in' today. I don't encourage you to **cut in** while others are talking. But if you can **add in** proper phrasal verbs to today's conversation between Luke (a new employee) and his boss, Daniel, feel free to **butt in**.

< Phrasal verbs are phrases made up of [≈ consisting of ≈ combined by] a verb and another word or two (preposition or adverb) such as **drop in** and **stand in for** someone [≈ do someone's job while the person is away]. They're used everywhere in everyday conversations. Go back and review previous days' activities with 'The Word' in title to see if lots of phrasal verbs have been used in there. >

**Daniel:** Hey Luke. **Come on in** [≈ **Step in** ≈ **Pop in**] (to the office). Let's pin down a time and schedule [≈ set up] a meeting to discuss business development. What about 10 am on 17 October?

**Luke:** Sounds good.

**Daniel:** Cool, let's **pencil** it **in**. I'll book the time **in** my diary. Are you **settling in**?

**Luke:** Yes, I am.

**Daniel:** I notice you were working at night. Thanks for **stepping in** while Mark is away. You're doing well. Keep it up. All reports must be **in** by next week. Remember to **turn in** your reports on time. Hey, **fill** me **in** on your new project.

**Luke:** The proposals have just been **filled in**. I'm still picking up the new system.

**Daniel:** That's brilliant. **In light of** gaining a new skill, practice is definitely the key. You'll get there. I trust you. You can **bring in** changes to the team. You **fit in** with the work. By the way, Gunner is leaving us. We're buying a gift for him. Are you going to **pitch in** [≈ **chip in** ≈ **join in** ≈ **take part in** ≈ participate]?

**Luke:** Yes, **count** me **in** please [≈ **I'm in**].

Is this a lot to **take in**? I'm just **checking in** with you.

# PART 3 THINK BIGGER

The quality of your house is decided by great, big ideas. What style do you want your house to have? Do you want a European style or Chinese style? Or do you want a South-Asian, American, Brazilian or even Antarctic style to your house? You do the thinking!

Part 3 of *The English Builder!* guides you on essay writing while raising your awareness on various social problems facing us humans.

For each topic discussed in Part 3, ask some questions: Why is this happening? What is the impact of this? What are the solutions? What's your opinion? Are you in support of the issue? Are you against the issue or neutral to the issue? You might even propose your own questions and raise your own concerns to further explore the issue.

Make sure you give answers of your own because, after all, it's your house! The rule: There are never stupid questions or dumb answers.

If the space I leave for you isn't big enough for your creative ideas and arguments, write it all down in your notebook.

Let's dive in!

# DAY 211
## ESSAY WRITING – WHAT NOT TO DO

Writing is a process of communicating your ideas with your readers, just as I'm doing right now.

Essay writing is a type of formal writing that presents a point of view on a particular topic. Let's summarise what not to do in essay writing.

- Do not use contractions (isn't, can't, doesn't…). When writing academically, write in a formal way and deliver your opinions seriously. So 'It's unlikely that…' should be changed into 'It is unlikely [≈ It seems not likely] that…'

- Do not use emotive language. 'This essay is wonderful and useful!' Would you use a sentence such as this in the academic style? No. Not only is it a biased opinion, but also the exclamation mark (!) used here is too emotional. You are supposed to be objective, not subjective about your topic. The alternative way to deliver the same idea, but more formally, could be 'This essay is relevant.'

- The use of analogies [≈ metaphors] should be minimal. Melbourne's weather is like a chameleon changing colours [≈ unpredictable]. Liam's choice dropped like a bomb. Stephanie's full of sunshine. These are sentences that describe how the weather looks, what the result of a person's actions is, and what the person's personality is like. They are not essay writing standard.

- The first person singular POV (point of view) (I or me), first person plural POV (we or us) and second person POV (you) are best to be avoided.

< Here's a summary of some punctuation marks you can use: full stop [≈ period] (.), comma (,), colon (:), semicolon (;), question mark (?), apostrophe ("), forward slash (/), hyphen (-), en dash (–), em dash (—), ellipsis (…), brackets [ ], parentheses ( ), quotation marks (' ' or " "), exclamation mark (!). >

< What's the difference between en dash and em dash? As you can see, en dash is about the length of the letter *n* while em dash is longer, about at the length of letter *m*. Generally, an *en dash* can be used to express ranges between dates or numbers. For example, go read pages 1–365. An *em dash* can be used to separate a phrase from a sentence to emphasis or sudden change the thoughts, or in dialogue to represent an interruption. For example, English language, western culture, the author's experience—they're all written about in the book. >

< Depending on the style, sometimes spaced *en* dashes are used to separate a phrase from a sentence or for a sudden change of thoughts – this can be the difference between different publishers, or sometimes between American and Australian punctuation styles. >

The content in Part 1 and Part 2 of this book is written in a light and friendly way, so they're not academic writings. Do you agree?

# DAY 212
## ESSAY WRITING – WHAT TO DO

Yesterday, we got a feel for what types of language should not appear in an essay. So, what are the rules of thumb [≈ fundamental rules ≈ general rules ≈ ground rules ≈ basic principles] for essay writing then?

< A 'rule of thumb' is a rule that is based on experience rather than theory. Many believe that the phrase originated from an English law of the 18th century that permitted a man to beat his wife with a stick no wider and thicker than his thumb (Shapiro, 1998). >

**Rule 1: Answer the essay question.** Stick to the question. [≈ Answer what is asked.] This is very important; otherwise, your argument will be pointless. Spend some time unpacking and analysing the question carefully and establish your point of view.

**Rule 2: Set a clear structure.** Start an essay with the introduction, follow this with a body of argument and finish off with a conclusion. I'll give you a sample of a complete essay writing in Day 217. The main purpose of Part 3 of *The English Builder!* is to get you think big and form the opinion of your own.

**Rule 3: Use inspiring ideas.** Let your mind wander and persuade readers with your insights. Don't pad out your essay with irrelevant ideas and details though.

**Rule 4: Upgrade your language.** You don't want to turn your readers away by having the same words or phrases appearing many times throughout the essay. If your essay talks about 'improving health', for example, work out other ways to express it. Perhaps use 'enhance health level', 'stay healthy', 'health improvement'. Put down your alternative expressions here:

..................................................................................................................................

..................................................................................................................................

..................................................................................................................................

**Rule 5: Use logical argument to support your ideas.** Link all parts of the essay together by applying logical argument skills. Examples, statistics, and historical data can support your stance.

**Rule 6: Come back and reflect.** Review and refine your writing by reading essays written by others and ask someone for feedback who might be at a higher writing level than you.

Stick around. We'll dissect Rule 3 to Rule 5 over the next four days.

# DAY 213
## WRITE TO INSPIRE

What is the purpose of writing an essay? You might never write an essay for fun. You might only write it for the sake of passing an exam.

To score high on an essay, you need to answer the essay question and be straight to the point. Your ultimate goal should be to inspire your readers and engage them to think on a deeper level. This requires in-depth thinking skills and critical thinking skills.

< Here are other types of thinking: lateral thinking, forward-thinking, blue-sky [≈ creative] thinking, divergent thinking, black-and-white thinking [≈ all-or-nothing thinking]. Put down your type of thinking here: ................................................

..........................................................................................................................................

.................................................................................................................................... >

*Q&A*, *The Drum*, *The Project* and *A Current Affair* are TV programs that discuss current affairs and issues. Along with ABC News, 7NEWS and 9News, these programs are all a great source for ideas and inspirations for essays.

You can also use everyday objects around you for inspiration on an essay topic. Right now, you probably have your phone nearby. Have you ever considered any problems associated with your smartphone before? Have mobile phone manufacturers created a safe working environment for employees and complied with environmental laws and the *Modern Slavery Act*? Why are people nowadays attached to this device all day long? Can we go back to life before cell phones [≈ days when smartphones haven't been invented]? Is technology a boon or a bane [≈ a blessing or a problem ≈ a good thing or a bad thing]?

When there's a plate of beef tenderloin or roast lamb on the dining table, what goes through your mind? The livestock that makes its way to your plate are bred and fed at feedlots and on farmland, then killed, processed and cut up in the slaughterhouse [≈ abattoir]. Although farmers and manufacturing companies keep improving animal health and welfare, occasionally there's still footage of filthy and crowded sheds for animals, poor handling and inhumane treatment. What can we do to help?

When you hear a story on TV, consider why those events would happen. Should these problems be solved [≈ resolved] by individuals, businesses or governments? You might also consider whether there are any biases in the news and whether it's fake news, or twisted news by journalists, news reporters, or even the government.

Now, look around you for some objects that might inspire you to write an essay. Tell me what you spot and what you would like to write about.

# CHAPTER 24 - An Essay Writer

## DAY 214
## AVOID REPETITION

In your essay writing, is there a lot of repetition of certain words? Do you tend to repeat the same words or phrases again and again [≈ write down a word or phrase repetitively]? Do you like your repetitive expressions?

What are we doing? In the above paragraph, which word has been written in its noun, adjective, verb, and adverb forms. Put down your answer here:

.................................................................................................................................

.................................................................................................................................

This is actually one of the secrets to make your writing stronger: vary your words – extend your thinking to all forms of a word and use them in an appropriate context.

The second secret is to vary your phrases and sentences. Let's experiment together! Want to express that something or someone is important? You don't have to limit yourself by just rephrasing 'important' with 'integral', 'key', 'essential', 'crucial', 'paramount', 'vital', etc.

Below are some examples:

The CEO is the brain behind the business. The administration roles of a company are its backbone. The chef is truly the heart of any restaurant. The curriculum is the nervous system of the school. Communication is the lifeblood of a good relationship. Computers are the meat and potatoes of a business. Research is the cornerstone [≈ the keystone] of the academic profession. Tourism is regarded as the engine room of the Australian economy. The arts reveal the mind and soul of a nation.

Now try expressing things that have become popular. Write these below:

.................................................................................................................................

.................................................................................................................................

Here's mine:

The avocado has become a trendy fruit [≈ has become tipped to trend] in the Asian market. Mobile phones are catching on. [≈ Mobile phones are sweeping the world.] Due to the popular demand, Samsung, Apple and other mobile phone manufactures have increased production volume. Meditation and mindfulness have picked up steam [≈ gained traction ≈ started rolling] in recent years as a way to manage stress. Driverless cars are an up-and-coming product [≈ likely to become a popular product]. A growing number of English learners are using the thesaurus (a reference book that has lists of synonyms of words or phrases) as a tool to avoid repetition in their writings. (I made this up (i.e. the 'An increasing number of people' part!) But a thesaurus is indeed a handy tool for you to look for synonyms!)

# CHAPTER 24 - An Essay Writer

## DAY 215
## STRENGTHEN YOUR ARGUMENTS

It's not enough to just have a perspective on a subject and apply the language well, you need to use logical argument skills to make your ideas convincing. The logical connection between parts of your essay can be established within the one sentence and between sentences.

Identify which logical function (**cause-effect**, **addition**, **concession**, **illustration**, **restatement**) is used in each of the seven paragraphs below. Apply these methodologies to your essay argument.

**Due to** [≈ **Thanks to** ≈ **Because of** ≈ **Owing to**] foreign exchange noise, gross margin goes down. Drugs are **the bane of** the city. The careless worker is **partly to blame**. The adequate food supply is **a driving factor behind** growing population. Alcohol consumption **contributes to** many road tragedies.

**Even though** students often forget the details of what they learn at school, what they have gained are critical thinking abilities, people skills and a sense of fun. **In spite of** strict copyright laws and intellectual property (IP) protection, there are many cheap software knock-offs and counterfeits on the market. The company has been consistently outperforming in the market **despite** the fact that its competitors [≈ contenders ≈ adversaries] have reduced product prices. **Although** feminists greatly promote gender equity, society is still far from gender equality [≈ parity].

**In addition** [≈ **Additionally** ≈ **Besides** ≈ **Moreover** ≈ **Furthermore**], honesty is always the best policy [≈ it is best to be true and honest all times]. **An additional** approach is to charge council rates based on how much rubbish a household throws in the bin. Those who see international travel as a negative are **also** encouraged to look at this from an economic perspective.

**In other words**, real talent [≈ exceptional talent] is predetermined by genes [≈ generic inheritance]. **To put it another way**, watching TV for a long time stifles creativity [≈ discourages creativity ≈ kills innovation ≈ is a creativity killer].

**Take** the Great Barrier Reef **as an example**. The Australian Government has launched the Reef 2050 Long-Term Sustainability Plan because the overwhelming number of travellers and climate change have caused damage to the natural environment there.

You can use news and events happening around you to help support an argument. **For example**, while arguing that traditional values are not fading away, you can use this true story: when a homeless fight against the terrorist attack in Melbourne, strangers raised the money for his kindness.

Making things that are general more specific is also a way to support an argument. **For instance**, in your example when talking about artists [≈ art creators], you can be specific about what type of artist they are. Use one of the examples from the table below:

| Fine artists | Painters | Sculptors | Dancers | Songwriters | Poets |
| --- | --- | --- | --- | --- | --- |
| Illustrators | Singers | Actors | Writers | Musicians | Printmakers |

# DAY 216
## TIGHTEN YOUR LOGICAL ARGUMENTS

Let's continue to identify some of other logical functions that can be applied to your writing: **comparison and contraction, chronological ordering, information prioritisation, conclusion, emphasis** and **scientific research or statistics**.

The wildfires [≈ bushfires] in California in 2018 were destructive. **This is the same with** the Australia bushfires in 2019. **In contrast**, those who work 4 days per week are able to work more creatively and effectively with work-life balance better managed.

For the sake of public safety, **the most direct method** is to keep felons (murderers, robbers and terrorists) in prison for longer periods. **More importantly**, patients should be aware of the potential harmful consequences of cosmetic surgery.

**According to scientific research**, the level of global warming caused by animal farts and poop has been underestimated (Lemonick, 2017). **A study found that** depression cases could have dropped by 12% if participants attended 1 hour of physical activity a week (Cook, 2017).

**First**, a lack of privacy is one disadvantage to becoming a celebrity. **Second**, celebrities are often followed by stalkers and the paparazzi. **Third**, famous people sometimes cannot lead a normal life like the average person.

**Without a doubt** [≈ **Undoubtedly**], some human activities (wet markets illegally selling wildlife, poaching of endangered animals, hunting and killing wild animals) are forcing wild species to go extinct quicky. **Unquestionably**, all wildlife has the right to coexist peacefully on this planet with human beings.

**Therefore**, everyone shoulders the responsibility to protect wildlife from dying out. **In brief** [≈ **In short**], over-tourism has created a burden on local attractions and the natural environment [≈ over-tourism has overwhelmed the location]. **As mentioned above**, education is the most cost-effective way to curb the already high recidivism rate. **To summarise** [≈ **To conclude**], it is up to the audiences to apply critical thinking skills when they interpret news reports, half-truths or downright lies.

Great stuff. With all these powerful weapons you've been given (answering the topic spot on, establishing a clear structure, exhibiting in-depth ideas, showing off your ability to vary language, crafting airtight arguments), you should be confident dealing with any writing topics thrown at you. You can't fail to master the essence of essay writing.

Don't go away. There is some more exciting content to come! For the rest of Part 3, you'll participate in some role-playing as an expert in many fields!

# DAY 217
## REGULAR EXERCISE IS IMPORTANT

As we all know, there are a host of [≈ a myriad of] benefits in engaging in regular physical activities. It can reduce the risk of heart attack, diabetes and cancer. It aids in weight loss. It can even make you smarter, happier and improves your wellbeing.

**Write down your questions and thoughts as a physical health adviser:**

| Your questions | Your thoughts |
|---|---|
|  |  |

**My question is 'Is regular exercise the best way to keep fit?'**

Would you now like to answer my question in your notebook? Your time starts now.

(After 30 minutes) Woohoo! It's self-evaluation time for the essay. Read through my essay today and compare it against yours. Where did you do better? Were there any areas to improve on?

My essay: Albeit medical advances, a substantial number of patients suffer from and die from cancer and other diseases each year. The health of an individual has become a big concern. Gym instructors and personal trainers often claim that a workout is the most effective way to maintain a person's fitness level [≈ keep control of a person's health].

Admittedly, regular exercise does wonders for a person's mind and body [≈ works wonders for the body ≈ is great for physical and mental wellbeing]. Sweating in the gym or jogging in the park strengthens the immune system and prevents cardiovascular disease. Not only that, the body of a regular yoga-practitioner is flexible. Yoga includes a meditation process that can reduce stress. Scientific research has shown that those who engage in physical exercises a couple of times per week outlive those who live a sedentary lifestyle.

However, this does not necessarily mean that exercise is the best option in terms of improving wellbeing. A well-balanced and wholesome diet is equally important. Incorporating fresh vegetables, high-protein meats and seasonal fresh fruits in everyday meals provide all sorts of nutrition that the human body requires, whereas eating rubbish food all day every day wrecks a person's metabolism. Further, sufficient high-quality sleep ensures that someone can be full of energy the next day. An ongoing lack of sleep will put the body at risk, resulting in an increased chance of heart attack and high blood pressure no matter how hard a person has been exercising. Mental health is also closely associated with physical health. For example, long-term depression and stress increases the risk of heart disease, diabetes and other illnesses.

In conclusion, the abovementioned factors are intertwined in keeping fit [≈ staying at peak health]. Day-to-day health can be improved when a person increases their healthy habits and gets rid of unhealthy habits.

# DAY 218
# MENTAL HEALTH IS ALL IMPORTANT

Stress has become a normal part of life in this fast-moving world. A small amount of stress motivates a person, while living under constant pressure can cause chronic mental illness (anxiety, depression, distress), which is also detrimental to physical health.

**Write down your questions and thoughts as a mental health expert:**

| Your questions | Your thoughts |
|---|---|
|  |  |

**What factors contribute to increased stress of day-to-day life?**

Work stress [≈ A stressful work life] is the main trigger [≈ the main driver ≈ the driving force ≈ the root [≈ direct ≈ underlying ≈ primary] cause] for many workers suffering day-to-day stress. For example, endless deadlines and high expectations require an employee to perform at peak level consistently [≈ at optimum levels all the time].

Furthermore, when an individual feels unhappy and is stressed in their daytime job, they could bring this back home with them – possibly depression or anger. This in turn could lead to damaging relationships at home, which could possibly further increase an individual's stress level at work.

Another source of high-level stress comes from the comparative nature of human beings. Some people constantly put pressure on themselves to achieve personal goals by working long hours, but they forget the importance of other little things in life, such as practising self-care, meditating, and spending time with family and relaxing.

**Are there any solutions?**

First, employers should set reasonable work targets and genuinely care about the wellbeing of each employee. Good policies to help achieve a healthy work-life balance include 20-days or more annual leave per year for full-time employees, and days in lieu for any overtime worked.

Second, anyone suffering from stress should talk to a mental health professional. Some people are not even aware that they have been stuck in a stressful situation for a long period of time. Physical exercise releases chemicals like endorphin and serotonin that improve mood and reduce stress – and reduce the symptoms of mental health problems. Regular meditation and healthy meals can also help to improve mental wellbeing.

# DAY 219
# EXAM-ORIENTED EDUCATION

An exam-oriented education system has long been applied in many counties around the world. This is used to test how well students have mastered knowledge and to distinguish top students and students performing poorly. Parents and teachers alike, especially in China, purely focus on the exam results for students. Many Chinese students, especially high school students, cannot even take a break over the weekend. They need to use the time to brush up textbooks, finish up assignments and take on many extracurricular activities.

Therefore, in recent years, a heated debate [≈ a hot-button topic ≈ a major talking point ≈ the talk of the town ≈ a barbecue stopper] has become whether schools should scrap [≈ remove] exams entirely or not.

**Write down your questions and thoughts as an educator:**

| Your questions | Your thoughts |
|---|---|
|  |  |

**What are the benefits a student gets from preparing for and taking exams?**

Exams prepare students for an adult world. That is, only when they are willing to work hard towards a goal, can they get excellent results. Exams also force a student to learn something specific (history, language, math and music, to name a few). In an exam, students will practise how to make decisions and react under pressure. Most importantly, exams can offer a certificate and qualification that a student will need to survive [≈ make a living] in a competitive world.

**What can't students learn from exams?**

Students reading a textbook or sitting an exam do not develop the other skills that a student needs in life. For example, to become more social, students need to talk to people in a workplace and nurture workplace relationships. To grow plants, they need to physically go buy seeds from a shop, bury them into the soil and water regularly. All of these skills cannot be acquired by preparing for academic-style exams.

Hence, exams exist to serve a purpose. But pushing students to solely focus on exam results is short-sighted. It can backfire as to the true purpose of education – enrich a student's knowledge and develop their personal character. Students themselves need to be aware that life is so much bigger than preparing for and passing exams. Non-academic learning does not stop at the point of finishing school.

# DAY 220
# KIDS STUCK INSIDE

Kids who grew up before the 1990s spent a lot of time playing outside. Nowadays, they tend to stay at home playing electronic devices and watching TV. Many kids have become housebound.

< When I was a kid, there were no pagers, MP3 players, walkmans, mobile phones or computers. My childhood friends and I spent a lot of time outside playing soccer, basketball, hide-and-seek, hopscotch and tug of war, or rubber band jumping, throwing beanbags, roller skating, and even making snowmen and having snowball fights [≈ throwing snowballs] when it snowed in winter. >

**Write down your questions and thoughts as a parent:**

| Your questions | Your thoughts |
|---|---|
|  |  |

**Can kids benefit from playing electronic games at home?**

Contrary to the traditional belief, studies have found that playing video games [≈ indulging in console games] will activate the brain cells of young children (Granic, Lobel, & Engels, 2014). While immersing themselves in video games, children have to strategise and find out ways to survive. This actually builds up innovative and creative thinking. The creativity and imagination of young players are better stimulated than those who do not play at all. Some kids become an expert in designing these kinds of games or mobile phone applications in adulthood. Under the right circumstances, working in these areas can earn them a fortune.

**Should busy parents engage their kids more often in outdoor activities?**

Parents should regularly take their kids out of the house for fun activities. This is a better way of spending time with kids than only letting them plug into a PlayStation or TV with some animated cartoons – these sorts of activities can lead an inactive lifestyle.

Outdoor activities strengthen [≈ encourage] the family bond. By partaking in various outdoor recreations (such as having a picnic or BBQ in the park, punting on the lake, picking cherries at the farm, and trekking [≈ hiking] in the mountains), kids can get fresh air while exploring and appreciating the beauty of the Mother Nature.

Research has shown that children who are involved in outdoor activities [≈ play outdoors] tend to be more confident, positive, enthusiastic and determined. They are more likely to stay calm and find solutions in the face of unexpected situations. Such interpersonal skills are crucial throughout their study and working lives [≈ make them better prepared for their adult life].

# DAY 221
# CHAMPION DRIVEN

Young kids at school these days compete fiercely against each other for academic results. They are made fully aware of the significance of performing exceptionally well from an early age. TV programs and sports also promote championship. From watching these sports or TV programs, children might get the impression that whoever wins gets the biggest rewards, and who also gets the most attention from media reporting.

**Write down your questions and thoughts as a parent or a teacher:**

| Your questions | Your thoughts |
|---|---|
|  |  |
|  |  |

**Should younger generations be taught to compete to win to be the champion?**

Admittedly, learning to compete to win is an important lesson for youngsters. By participating in sports, for example, they will know what types of preparation needs to be done to win a competition. Such an experience can boost [≈ enhance] children's confidence and help give them a sense of achievement.

However, the concept of 'losing is also okay' is too often ignored by parents and teachers. After all, there is only one first place in every competition, and no-one can stay at the very top for all things all the way through life. Hence, children should also be taught to embrace failure. Being a 'loser' is not something they should be ashamed of. Instead, kids should be praised for taking part in a competition and respecting all other players, as long as they have tried their best. The key point is to help them identify why a goal was not achieved and how to overcome any difficulties and build up resilience.

Meanwhile, schoolchildren also need to establish an awareness of the cooperation. Through group activities at school, children will learn how to work with people from a variety of backgrounds or with different characteristics, how to get along with peers, and how to encourage team members to achieve their objectives. This will prepare them well for their future work life.

Thus, kids should be encouraged to experience both individual work and group projects with both competitive (winners or losers individually) and cooperative awareness (winners or losers as a group).

# DAY 222
# FUERDAI

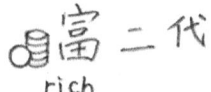

In China, fuerdai (富二代) refers to the sons and daughters of the super-rich families [≈ heirs to the nouveau rich ≈ second-generation rich]. They represent an emerging new social class in China. The generation born in the 1980s (and after) is perceived to as 'the generation born with a silver spoon in their mouth'. They are wrapped in cotton wool.

< What are the most recent seven generations and what are their birth years? Please refer to below list.

- The Greatest Generation (1901 to 1927)
- The Silent Generation (1928 to 1945)
- Baby Boomers (1946 to 1964)
- Generation X (1965 to 1980)
- Millennials (1981 to 1996)
- Generation Z (1997 to 2010)
- Generation Alpha (2011 and after)

The year for each of these generations could vary depending on the source. >

**Write down your questions and thoughts as an educator:**

| Your questions | Your thoughts |
|----------------|---------------|
|                |               |

**How do the super-rich kids behave?**

Some super-rich kids probably have never thought about the source of their wealth [≈ never realised where the money comes from]. They spend frequently and irresponsibly to show off their wealth on social media platforms. Even worse, they disobey the law, doing such things as drink-driving and trafficking drugs without feeling any guilt just because they naively think their parents can clean up everything with money.

**Why is this happening?**

It is a reflection on the gain of wealth followed by years after years of poverty. These parents have suffered a lot to get where they are today, so they do not want their offspring to experience what they had to go through in life. These wealthy parents have been accused of being overly permissive. To please their kids, pampering parents have let their kids have whatever they want [≈ have spoiled their children]. Without discipline, the pampered kids cannot understand how hard it is to make a living. Furthermore, the super-rich parents are tied up with work and social activities. They spend no time with their kids and give them money to do whatever they want.

# DAY 223
# THE WORD - ON

Hi Builders. How are you **getting on**? Today, let's **focus on** the word 'on' or any phrases that use 'on'.

I **took on** a fantastic job 3 months ago. I'm **on** a good salary. Our managing director Carlin is always available and approachable [≈ amiable]. He could **go on and on** about his views **on** the global financial status. He likes **turning on** the radio in his office. Carlin says he can **rely on** me [≈ **count on** me]. I **get on** well [≈ have a good relationship] with him and the team.

Anyway, after a few setbacks, I **pressed on** with my work. I **took on** more hours over the weekend. Carlin said to me, 'Mate, you are **on fire**!' He gave me days off in lieu.

< 'In lieu' is a French expression, meaning 'instead of'. When you work extra hours, your boss gives you paid time off in the near future instead of paying you for additional work hours. This is called TOIL (time off in lieu) (Lesiuk, 2021). >

I **went on** a cruise trip with my family. All the drinks were **on the house**. [≈ The cruise company would pay the bill for the drinks. ≈ Drinks were at the expense of the cruise company.] I'm fully **switched on** after the holiday. Now I need to **focus on** my work. The management report showed that our sales were **on target**. The issue that persisted, however, was how to **save on** the freight cost. I don't have the tax invoices **on** me. **Come in on** Monday to discuss it. We need to draw our own conclusions. **Pass on** the information to the team. [≈ Get the message across the team.]

How are you **getting on** with reading the above story? I believe you've **gotten off on the right foot** [≈ you're making a good start]. And you've **built on** your success so far.

< One of the origins for 'get off on the right foot' suggests that people tend to associate left with wrong because we have right and left, and right and wrong. So 'get off on the wrong foot' is an idiom with the opposite meaning, 'making a bad start by doing something in a wrong way' (On the Wrong Foot and on the Right Foot, n.d.). >

Let's **carry on**. [≈ Let's **go on**. ≈ Let's **keep on**.] You are a precious diamond! Come back to **brush up on** these interesting expressions any time you like!

# DAY 224
# HIGH TECH

Technology has revolutionised the way we live and work. People can do everything from their laptop and other portable electronic devices. Paying bills, shopping, and chatting with overseas friends are all possible on the information highway. Technology such as washing machines and vacuum cleaners can relieve people from laborious household chores.

Technology also allows small business to operate with global reach and lifts productivity. The latest wearable payment technology means that consumers can even make their purchases on watches or mobile phones.

**Write down your questions and thoughts as a technology user:**

| Your questions | Your thoughts |
|---|---|
|  |  |

**Are there any negative impacts of modern technology?**

Too much exposure to high-tech machines could cause chronic laziness and illness, and it could also reduce social interactions. For example, the overuse of calculators and Excel sheets gradually weakens the ability to calculate. Playing computer games for long periods causes obesity, stress and sleeping issues (Peter Grinspoon, 2020). Children who spend a lot of time on digital devices [≈ use electronic devices frequently] often feel isolated and lonely. This has a negative impact on their social skills (Beurkens, 2020). Families who lean too heavily on technology develop poor communication skills with each other.

To some extent, technological advances are a threat to privacy [≈ weaken privacy]. Personal information can be easily leaked or hacked online. Google tracks all searches by the internet users.

However, it is impossible to completely eliminate the use of mobile phones and other technology from our life. We should keep ourselves vigilant about the negatives that technology brings in and use technology wisely instead of going overboard with it. If we are not careful, our lives could be taken over by advanced technology [≈ cutting-edge technology ≈ state-of-the-art digital technology ≈ innovative technology].

# DAY 225
## SOCIAL MEDIA AGE

Social media has transformed the way that we connect with the world. It provides a playground for people expressing opinions and emotions. Facebook, Twitter and WeChat are social media applications and platforms for expressing our thoughts and showing off the activities in our lives. Blogs also provide treasure trove of information on such things as sports, travel, personal growth, today in history and many other topics.

The widespread use of social networking sites brings people together. Users can follow or 'like' anyone, including celebrities on Twitter around the world just with the click of a button. In the past, people would have no chance to communicate with anyone outside of their immediate circle. Video meetings, Skype and Yammer online groups also promote effective communication for workplaces.

**Write down your questions and thoughts as a social media user:**

| Your questions | Your thoughts |
| --- | --- |
|  |  |

**Is social media too noisy?**

Social media is a crutch. From the moment we wake up to the last minute before sleep, mobile phone users are constantly checking Instagram, Snapchat or other social media platforms. This can be a giant waste of time. Being attached to a mobile phone or tablet screen for a prolonged period of time can cause both physical and psychological effects in a user.

One of the effects of increased social media use – with users frequently staring at the screen – is that this has had a dramatic decrease in face-to-face conversations. As a result, family cohesion becomes weaker.

Most of time, people post all kinds of wonderfulness on their social media. And when other people read this, they start to compare themselves. This comparison lowers a user's self-esteem and reduces happiness. Isolation and disconnection are also a result of overly using the social media. [≈ Those who use social media too much often feel isolated and disjointed.]

Staying online too much can impact someone's mood. There is often violence and negativity on mainstream websites – viewers are likely to be exposed to a great deal of such content.

# DAY 226
# WILL ROBOTS TAKE YOUR JOB?

The prevalence of artificial intelligence (AI) is creeping up on us [≈ sneaking up on us]. It is predicated [≈ anticipated] that some professions around the world are doomed to be replaced by robots – both highly-skilled positions and positions held by low-wage employees could be under threat.

< Are you worried that your job or profession will disappear with the emergence of super smart robots? Jump onto [≈ Hop onto] the website **https://willrobotstakemyjob.com**, enter your job title, and discover what is predicted! >

**Write down your questions and thoughts as a technology futurist:**

| Your questions | Your thoughts |
|---|---|
|  |  |
|  |  |

**Will all jobs eventually be done by artificial intelligence or robots in the coming years?**

With IT languages processing data faster and more accurately than human beings, accountants have been predicted to have a 95% chance of losing their jobs (Jones N., 2020). Similarly, call centre jobs are projected [≈ expected] to be replaced since robots can be programmed to answer customer questions and deal with complaints – this has already been happening in some companies. Transport jobs could be in jeopardy due to the invention of driverless vehicles.

The use of AI is also creating new jobs such as cloud architects and data scientists, positions that did not exist decades ago. The statistic shows that AIs could help to create 97 million new jobs by 2025 (Ascott, 2021).

As we can see, some types of repetitive jobs might be taken over by smart machines with the rise of AI, but automation will not eliminate all jobs [≈ not all jobs will be completely robotised].

Certain creative jobs might appear in the digital world and still require human involvement – jobs such as designing programs for robots to better serve our purposes.

With humans still in charge, robots can be used to relieve humans from laborious work and give them extra time to put into the brainwork. Thus, the education system needs to be transformed in a way that students are empowered the abilities and skills that computers simply do not have.

# DAY 227
# DRIVERLESS CARS

The first robot car was invented in the 1970s [≈ Self-driving cars first came onto the scene in 1970s] (Townsend, 2020), but it is still at the testing stage even now. Driverless cars are currently being tested by Tesla, Google, Uber, Ford and other global companies. They are predicated to be sold within the next few decades.

**Write down your questions and thoughts as a technology innovator:**

| Your questions | Your thoughts |
|---|---|
|  |  |

**What benefits do driverless cars provide?**

Driverless cars are lighter and more fuel-efficient. More importantly, it is predicted that drivers will be able to read newspapers and make phone calls without having to worry about putting on the brakes or watching for traffic lights all the time. This means travelling in driverless cars can free up commuter time in traffic [≈ save valuable time for the passengers of driverless cars]. In theory, car accidents could be eliminated through the use of smart computer programming. In addition, all driverless vehicles on the road could run more smoothly, easing traffic congestions.

**Why are autonomous cars not available yet?**

Although computer chips are smart enough to sense their surroundings, how driverless cars with these chips respond to an emergency in complex traffic environments is still unknown [≈ uncertain]. In a test on public roads in the United States, a woman was struck and killed by a self-driving car. The car showed no response to the woman who was approaching (McCausland, 2019). Therefore, safety is a main concern. Furthermore, how often the software needs to be upgraded with information about new roads or roadworks has not been answered.

In the short term, testers, inventors and engineers should ensure that the right safeguards are in place for driverless cars while they are still being tested. No-one knows when self-driving cars will be the norm [≈ become commonplace ≈ be ready] for public use, and if such fully autonomous vehicles will be affordable or feasible.

# DAY 228
## YOUR NEIGHBOURHOOD

In this modern age, nearly a third of Australians don't see or hear from their neighbours regularly. Almost half of Australians don't call on their neighbours for help when they might need it (6 Ways to Be a Better Neighbour – and Why It Matters, 2019).

**Write down your questions and thoughts as a local resident:**

| Your questions | Your thoughts |
|---|---|
|  |  |

**Why are neighbourhood relationships not as strong today as they have been in the past?**

Today's super busy lifestyle is one of the main factors in the loss of neighbourhood communities. An individual's daily life is often filled with an overload of work, household chores and childcare. Hence, not too much time is left after all these activities. It is even rare to bump into [≈ come across ≈ fall over] neighbours and have a conversation on the front doorstep. City-dwellers living in high-density areas are even less likely to get to know their neighbours because they tend to move out after living in one area for a short period.

Social media has changed the way people live. Even family members nowadays have reduced the amount of time they communicate face-to-face compared to a decade ago, let alone interact with their neighbours. Even though neighbours might tend to know each other by sight, no-one really connects with conversation anymore.

**Are there any solutions to help build a sense of community with neighbours?**

To strengthen relationships with neighbours, small acts like lending a hand for lawn-mowing and childcare can make a huge difference. Communities can organise activities such as a neighbourhood BBQ, pet care, kids playing together at the playground, or music festivals for those who live in the area. Even joining Australia's annual Neighbour Day is a perfect opportunity to connect with those who live in the neighbourhood.

# DAY 229
## ONLINE EDUCATION IS HIP

In recent years, online education has become more and more popular [≈ has become enormously [≈ hugely] popular ≈ has gained ground ≈ has gone mainstream].

Write down your questions and thoughts as an online course student:

| Your questions | Your thoughts |
|---|---|
|  |  |

**Why has online education been welcomed?**

Online learning is self-paced, which means an individual can study anywhere and anytime [≈ at any given moment]. Unlike traditional places of learning with course shortages or limited places, students are offered a variety of courses, or even courses from overseas universities. In addition, a full-time worker with family commitments can save travel time to the campus [≈ shave hours off their commute ≈ save time travelling back and forth to campus]. Online education services are also much cheaper than for study in brick-and-mortar classrooms. Many courses are even free.

**Are traditional universities being replaced by online education?**

Although studying remotely is handy and trendy nowadays, programs held in a traditional campus have advantages. Conventional education [≈ In-class setting] requires students and teachers to physically sit together in a classroom. While students acquire knowledge, they are also learning how to interact with others in social environments. Communication skills developed here cannot be achieved through online learning. Attending school in person provides a more disciplined environment where students are more easily motivated through structured learning schedules.

In conclusion [≈ All in all], online-learning programs cannot replace face-to-face education [≈ traditional classrooms are irreplaceable]. But the online education system can provide a supplemental learning environment for the traditional classroom. These two education systems could even be combined to form a model for 'blended' education and learning. Crash courses [≈ Rapid and intense study] or business conferences and certificates could also be organised more easily online. For those who are studying full-time, learning on a campus is still an excellent option.

CHAPTER 28 - A Lifestyle Change Analyst

# DAY 230
# ONLINE SHOPPING

Ecommerce (electronic commerce) is growing rapidly worldwide. According to Australia Post, 82% of Australian households shopped online in 2020 (Inside Australian Online Shopping, n.d.). In China in 2020, the special shopping day Double 11 made over US$116 billion of sales for Alibaba, Tmall and JD – all in one day (Team, 2020).

< Double 11 takes place on 11 November each year. It is also called Bachelors' Day or Singles' Day. Why? Because the number 1 looks like a bare stick. A bare stick stands for guanggun (光棍) literally in Chinese. Guanggun in Chinese is interpreted as a person who is single and hasn't been married. There are four 1s on 11 November (11th of the 11th) – a group of guanggun! >

**Write down your questions and thoughts as an online shopper:**

| Your questions | Your thoughts |
| --- | --- |
|  |  |

**What are the advantages and disadvantages of online shopping?**

More and more consumers choose to shop for goods and services over the internet because of convenience. No matter where they are, all a customer needs to do is 'click and pay' [≈ it's just the touch of a button ≈ it's just one tap of the button away]. Food and other products can be delivered to a customer's door without them physically travelling. With the access to the internet and global logistics, even international purchases are more easily accessible.

In addition, not having a shopfront means that the cost of running an online shop is much lower. Therefore, online items are sold at a relatively low price [≈ the price tags marked online are more attractive]. Many ecommerce businesses even offer free delivery. Thus, it is more cost-effective for a customer to shop online than in a brick-and-mortar store [≈ shoppers can purchase products for less than those who buy at a physical store].

Furthermore, ecommerce per se can create more job opportunities. Alibaba, Amazon and other online retailers have significantly increased demand in the logistics industry over recent years.

While online businesses have been thriving recently, customers are often still searching for the face-to-face contact experience in physical stores. Australians still prefer to shop in stores with families during holiday seasons. Often, the quality of a product is hard to identify through online pictures or videos. An image on screen can differ from the actual colour or dimension of clothes. With online shopping, there is also a chance of personal private information being hacked due to online security issues.

# DAY 231
## GOGGLE-BOX

The goggle-box [≈ idiot box ≈ telly] is a great tool.

< *Gogglebox* is a hilarious TV program in Australia. The show is about TV viewers who watch the latest news, current affairs or other TV shows and comment on these in a hilarious way. >

Television provides a window to the world. Up-to-date news keeps viewers informed with global events. Educational programs are packed full of information. High-quality shows such as *Sesame Street* and *Ask the StoryBots* improve a child's cognitive abilities. Children who watch educational programs tend to read more books and have better grades (Rumana, 2019). Talk shows like *The Graham Norton Show* and *The Ellen DeGeneres Show* give their audiences a laugh and help audiences to escape a busy life.

**Write down your questions and thoughts as a TV viewer:**

| Your questions | Your thoughts |
|---|---|
|  |  |

**In my opinion, this great invention can cause trouble. Why?**

Firstly, excessive viewing of TV [≈ too much screentime] has a detrimental effect on the viewer's health. Habitual [≈ Regular] TV viewers [≈ TV watchers] are found to have a higher risk of developing short-sightedness and obesity, heart attack or even a stroke.

Furthermore, binge-watching TV shows offers no stimulation of people's mind [≈ is junk food for the mind ≈ keeps the mind zombie-like ≈ dulls and rots a person's brain]. Scientific research has proven that watching the boob tube [≈ mindless TV ≈ brainless TV] for too long kills creativity and imagination since audiences passively receive information all the time.

To enhance their ratings, TV producers often create poor quality, shallow entertainment programs and commercials. Watching such programs all the time is a giant waste of time, time that could be spent with family members for other activities.

# DAY 232
## TO EAT OUT OR EAT AT HOME?

Nowadays, people often find themselves time-stressed [≈ time-poor]. Being super busy with work and social activities has resulted in increased use of dining out or takeaway dinners.

**Write down your questions and thoughts as an everyday eater:**

| Your questions | Your thoughts |
|---|---|
|  |  |

**Is cooking at home better than eating out at a restaurant?**

< This is a trick question. You need to go deeper and give a reason for which of eating at home or at a restaurant is healthier or cheaper or better. Discuss! Use a star to mark the fronts of the sentences of the paragraphs below where a comparison is used. >

Modern and upscale restaurants offer a relaxing environment and fine-dining setting with high-quality food dishes and astonishing services, which cannot easily be achieved by simply cooking at home. Even eateries, corner stores and fast-food takeaway outlets have menus with a variety of selections. Restaurants run by immigrants give opportunities for people to try exotic of foreign foods that would rarely be cooked at home.

However, food served in a restaurant can contain higher amounts of fat, salt, calories, and even be overly oily. Although they are tasty, these can all impact health in the long term. Hygiene is another major concern in some cases since some restaurant owners are irresponsible for the freshness of their food.

In contrast, the cost of a homemade meal is much lower than dining out [≈ eating out]. Honest-to-goodness home-cooking is healthier and the food is more packed with nutrition since the home cook has choices in what to put in a dish. Furthermore, cooking with other family members can strengthen the family bond. Children's interests in cooking will be raised if they are engaged. Preparing a meal, though, can be a time-consuming and cumbersome process. And dishes prepared at home might not be as flavoursome as those cooked by a professional chef.

Hence, there are both pros and cons for eating away from home and cooking at home. Meal kits are changing the way people cook and live. Fresh ingredients are delivered to a customer's home along with simple but tasty recipes. These can save time for families since they do not have to all travel to a restaurant or race to the supermarket to look for ingredients.

# DAY 233
# ADVERTISING BOMBARDMENT

Nowadays, modern advertising (billboards, TV commercials, pamphlets and digital advertising) seems to be all over the place: from commercials that keep interrupting TV programs every 10 minutes, to videos or promo images on the web that spoil the enjoyment of online users.

**Write down your questions and thoughts as an advertising audience:**

| Your questions | Your thoughts |
|---|---|
|  |  |

**What should be done to reduce the noise that advertising has created?**

Overwhelming and intrusive advertising can waste people's time. The frequency of broadcasting ads during TV programs should be reduced. Similarly, those who manage webpages should consider placing ads somewhere to catch a reader's eye, but which does not spoil a reader's browsing experience. (Pop-up ads every second can cause the audience to shun a webpage quickly.)

In addition, advertisers should produce bold [≈ creative], genuine and interesting content. This will inspire rather than be annoying to consumers. Most importantly, advertisers should make sure the right customers are targeted.

**Is advertising harmful?**

In this digital world, good ads are still welcomed by audiences. Ads can be used to inform, educate and entertain. Customers sometimes dive headfirst into new products after they are advertised and promoted. A billboard at a train station can truly be informative for an audience. Commuters can get information quickly on a university's open day, a low price for an internet provider, and many other consumer products.

Non-profit organisations who advertise can inspire people and arouse their awareness in such things as making the planet greener or appealing for donations for needy children. Moreover, such advertisements are often attractive and create a charming source of entertainment.

# DAY 234
# AIR POLLUTION

In the past two decades, we have witnessed the boom of the aviation industry, with more frequent global travel. But the air quality in many cities around the world has steadily been getting worse.

< In recent years, air pollution has been severe in China, especially in winter in the northern part of the country. Heavy sandstorms sometimes engulf lots of cities. You can't even see objects and other people within 10 metres. [≈ Visibility is reduced to 10 metres.] It's sad to think that the blue sky that I used to see most days when I was younger isn't that blue anymore. >

**Write down your questions and thoughts as an environmentalist:**

| Your questions | Your thoughts |
| --- | --- |
|  |  |

**The aviation industry might pose a severe threat to the environment. Is restricting air travel the only way to prevent air pollution?**

Fuel combustion is one of the primary drivers for air pollution and aircraft engines emit heat, particulates and gases with every trip, and at large volumes for especially long-distance flights.

However, airflights cannot be considered to be the number one cause of excessive carbon dioxide release. Billions of cars and trains also burn fossil fuels and generate greenhouse gases on a daily basis, contributing to acceleration of global warming. Therefore, limiting and prohibiting the number of the flights around the world will not put an end to air pollution because of the volume of fuel consumption from vehicles on the roads.

Furthermore, restricting air travel does not necessarily mean that the environment will be better off. Industrial activities that emit toxic gases into the air has previously threatened people's health. For example, a chemical factory explosion in Western Melbourne in 2019 released thick smoke into the air for hours and caused breathing issues for nearby residents.

To make our planet cleaner, individuals are encouraged to reduce their carbon footprint as much as they possibly can. Eco-friendly vehicles (such as Tesla cars) have been invented and manufactured. Governments should be working shoulder to shoulder [≈ side by side] with local residents to reduce air pollution and protect public health. The key lies in developing new energy sources and devising vehicles that do not produce air pollution.

# DAY 235
# DEFORESTATION

Forests are the lungs of the earth. Forests give humans fresh air, clean water, precious wildlife and calm and peaceful [≈ tranquil ≈ serene ≈ placid] surroundings (7 Products You Didn't Know Come From Trees, n.d.). The tree-felling industry plays an indispensable part of modern life. Wood is used as raw materials to construct houses or manufacture furniture (such as double beds, dining tables and bookshelves). The production of paper involves the use of trees. Other everyday household products also made from trees include brooms, wine corks, sponges and rubbers.

**Write down your questions and thoughts as a forester:**

| Your questions | Your thoughts |
|---|---|
|  |  |

**Illegal logging is still often seen in many countries. What are the consequences of abusive logging of forests?**

Extensive logging can lead to the loss of habitat and species extinction. Seventy percent of land animals and plants live in forests, and they would not survive deforestation if their homes were destroyed (Civic Issues - Deforestation, 2016). Trees also provide oxygen. Excessive land-clearing means increased greenhouse gases are released into the air, and this results in climate change.

Therefore, removing forests [≈ chopping down trees indiscriminately and arbitrarily] destroys the ecological balance, thereby threatening wildlife habitats and the environment that humans depend on.

**What can we do to protect the forests?**

All governments around the world shoulder the responsibility to stipulate the best season, exact location and upper limits for logging. For example, logging activities are prohibited in the areas where endangered species live. In Victoria, native forest logging will be phased out by 2030 and transition to a plantation-based timber industry will take its place (Cox & Butler, 2019). Companies involved in the forestry sector should be socially responsible and plant tree saplings and seedlings to replace the trees they use. A replanting program can make sure there are adequate tree stocks [≈ sufficient trees regrown ≈ tree supplies stay sufficient ≈ native forests are managed sustainably].

# DAY 236
## PLASTIC EVERYWHERE

At least 3.5 million tonnes of plastic is generated every day globally (Leahy, 2018). It is estimated that up to 2.4 million tonnes of plastic enters the ocean each year (The Great Pacific Garbage Patch, n.d.). Many whales have reportedly died from swallowing plastic bags that are dumped into the sea by human beings.

**Write down your questions and thoughts as an environment advocate:**

| Your questions | Your thoughts |
|---|---|
|  |  |

**What can we do to reduce the use of plastic products and protect Mother Nature?**

The general public at large should change their mindset on [≈ switch their mindset on] using non-biodegradable plastic bags and product packages. Some alternatives could be jute bags [≈ reusable bags ≈ forest-friendly bags] and baskets. Individuals should do their bit to classify and properly dispose of their waste, and reuse [≈ recycle] plastic packing items where possible.

It would be more effective if manufacturers put a stop to the production of plastic bags, bottles and other plastic products. For example, coffee cups and lids should be manufactured with compostable materials only. A Melbourne café shop has even introduced drinking coffee with edible cups that are made of wheat and grains. In situations where plastic production is still necessary and unavoidable, the production volume should be reduced as much as possible.

Retailers also play a big role in promoting consumer awareness of using reusable bags. Even since Australian supermarkets have phased out single-use plastic bags, customers have modified their behaviour by bringing in their reusable bags for grocery shopping.

All governments around the world should spare no effort to advocate the use of green products. They should also shoulder the responsibility for funding development of biodegradable containers and bags. If plastic bags are not going to be banned completely, a tax should be imposed for their production and use.

# DAY 237
# THE WORD - OFF

Let's **kick** it **off**. **Switch off** your phone. Let's run a self-reflection. What have you achieved so far this year? Check your bucket list [≈ wish list] and **tick off** [≈ **cross off**] any activities once you've done them. I believe your hard work has **paid off**. Anything unfair, unhappy, or unexpected, just **laugh** it **off**.

Let me share my recent unlucky experience with the word 'off'.

My boyfriend **stepped off** the plane and onto Australian soil a month ago. He **dusted off** his English before coming here. I thought we were going to **pick off** where we left things. But he started to **brush** me **off** [≈ ignore me] and wanted a break. We **called off** our relationship. I was heartbroken and didn't sleep well lately. I've been **nodding off** in my classes and keep **putting off** doing the assignment. I just can't **shake off** the sadness and depression! The other day, while I was **off** to the café to grab a coffee, the wind was horrible. My beanie was **blown off** the top of my head! Later on, I **headed off** to the supermarket, wanting to get **peel-off** face masks, and **skin-off** Tasmanian Atlantic salmon fillets but they were sold out. Then I found out I was **ripped off** for the pair of shoes that I'd bought on eBay. Back home, while I was cutting watermelon, my roomie screamed, '**Hands off**! That knife is sharp! Watch out! You're bleeding!' I later found out that the milk that I drank earlier in the day had **gone off**!

At 3 am in the morning, the fire alarm **went off**! It woke me up. I **got off** the bed and rushed outside.

< In Australia, fire alarms are installed in each office building and apartment. They are sensitive. If the smoke alarm detects any thick smoke, this will trigger the alarm. When it **goes off**, you need to evacuate from the building. The Metropolitan Fire Brigade [≈ MFB ≈ The fire truck] will arrive in minutes. If you are responsible for the fire or for calling the MFB, you might have to pay over a thousand dollars if you don't have a valid reason to let them **wave off** the bill. >

< Back home in China, we don't have this kind of domestic smoke alarm system installed in apartment buildings, or at least I haven't experienced alarms being activated while cooking or smoking in China, which happens from time to time in Australia! >

My story is **off the table** now. [≈ There is no more discussion on my story now.] This has just not been my day. As I said, **laugh** it **off**. Good things will happen. Okay, we've **finished off** today's topic. You are **off the charts** [≈ beyond expectations]! **Off you go**. [≈ You can leave now.]

# DAY 238
## MUSEUMS ATTRACT LOCAL VISITORS

Museums play a crucial role in inspiring and educating people. A national museum traces the rich history of a nation. A science museum and planetarium provide visitors with multisensory and hands-on experiences to explore the wonders of science, technology and the universe. Art galleries showcase artworks of the past, present and future. How often do you go to your local museum? Have you noticed that museums today are mostly visited by tourists rather than local residents?

**Write down your questions and thoughts as a local culture promoter:**

| Your questions | Your thoughts |
|---|---|
|  |  |

**What can museums do to bring in more local visitors?**

One of the strategies to reach out to locals in order to draw them to museums would be to reduce the price on entry tickets [≈ entrance fees] or even scrapping fees for locals. Other ways to bring in local tourism could be to have discounted annual fees for families, time-limited offers or special events such as night functions and parties.

Museums can also add in mixed functionality (such as opening a small-scale movie theatre or hosting meeting places for community groups), making visits more entertaining and functional for visitors.

Another strategy would be to ask for the feedback from locals and listen to their voices.

In addition, museums can engage with families, particularly kids through activities such as origami or colouring activities. Hosting educational research and volunteer programs can also draw in attendees from local schools and universities.

Furthermore, museums can pique the interest of locals through cooperating with other museums around the world and host international exhibitions and valuable artefacts. For example, the Tutankhamun exhibition from Egypt came to Melbourne Museum in 2011 and attracted nearly 8000 visitors daily – so many Victorians were able to visit this international exhibition at their doorstep (Tutankhamun Exhibition Breaks Records, 2011).

# DAY 239
## ENDANGERED MINORITY LANGUAGES

Today, many minority languages are struggling to survive and are endangered of becoming extinct [≈ teetering on the brink of extinction ≈ on the verge of extinction ≈ at the edge of extinction ≈ being wiped out ≈ being neglected ≈ disappearing ≈ vanishing].

**Write down your questions and thoughts as a culture promoter:**

| Your questions | Your thoughts |
|---|---|
|  |  |

**Why are minority languages struggling?**

This is primarily because these minority languages are not being taught in schools, and as a result, they are not being applied in daily conversation. Young adults tend to speak the mainstream language of a given country, and whatever language is taught at school. Furthermore, social media and TV programs saturated with the national language also drown out of the use of minority languages.

**Why is protecting indigenous languages important?**

Language is central to human beings. We are intimately bound up with the culture handed down from our ancestors [≈ forebears]. Once lesser-known languages go extinct, they will likely never be revived. As a result, the traditional arts of ethnic groups could also gradually fade away, further jeopardising these cultures. In addition, if some indigenous languages died out, it would also mean that some professions (such as translators, linguists and even archaeologists) could disappear.

**What can we do to keep endangered languages alive?**

In order to save endangered languages, authorities need to establish schools and classes that educate in various native languages and cultures. At the same time, there needs to be increased awareness in the general public through school curriculum or TV programs about these cultures and their languages, particularly to the younger generation. Both print media and digital media should use these minority languages to help keep them alive. Finally, individuals and family members should also commit to using minority languages or dialects in order to help their survival.

# DAY 240
# ENDANGERED HERITAGE BUILDINGS

In recent years, property developers and local governments have demolished historical buildings in the city business centres and the city fringes. These important heritage buildings are being torn down [≈ knocked down ≈ pushed down] so that skyscrapers can be built to accommodate new office spaces and residential spaces.

**Write down your questions and thoughts as a culture protector:**

| Your questions | Your thoughts |
|---|---|
|  |  |

**Should old buildings be razed to meet the needs of economic development?**

Admittedly, some old buildings can spoil a city view [≈ wreck the city spectacle]. Unlike contemporary apartments and business blocks with stunning looks, houses built a century ago are becoming an eyesore [≈ hideous ≈ ugly ≈ unsightly ≈ unpleasant to look at]. In terms of functionality, modern architecture is more light-filled and comfortable, and features modern sewage systems. Houses that were built hundreds of years ago are often left to go to rack and ruin [≈ wither on the vine]. The maintenance cost for ratty houses is high. In this sense, buildings founded centuries ago can get in the way of economic development.

However, historical buildings are part of a nation's history and culture heritage. In the long run, protecting these historical buildings offers plenty of benefits for a community and its people. For example, the Melbourne Open House event gives attendees the opportunity to look inside buildings they might not ordinarily visit and provides the chance for visitors to appreciate the history of a city and building architecture. Iconic buildings such as St Paul's Cathedral and the Royal Exhibition Building give Melbourne a mix of modernisation and the past, attracting tourists, and hence bringing in significant revenue for local government.

< For me, the Royal Exhibition Building (REB) is such a special and memorable place. Most of my exams during my Master's studies were held there. It has a big hall that can accommodate many students taking exams together. The REB hall was used as a COVID-19 vaccination centre in 2021 during the pandemic. >

Furthermore, saving [≈ preserving] old buildings does not drag the economy down. Many of these buildings do not just exist as purely historical sites. Businesses such as bookshops and neighbourhood pubs thrive in old buildings (Rocchi, 2015).

# DAY 241
## CRIME ON THE RISE

A house was broken into and robbed; a jewellery store window was smashed; a woman was stalked and attacked in the park; a man was found growing poppies on a property without a cultivation licence… Every year, the crime rate continues to increase: everything from international scam calls to theft to assault and murder.

**Write down your questions and thoughts as a criminologist:**

| Your questions | Your thoughts |
|---|---|
|  |  |
|  |  |

**Why do people break the law?**

Poverty and economic deprivation are the main factors in the increasing frequency of criminal acts. Those living below the poverty line have to battle with survival on a daily basis. With little education, such poor citizens are more likely to treat stealing as an easy way to get money, even with the risk of being caught by police or facing prison time.

Unemployment further contributes to wrong doings [≈ misdeeds]. When a person lacks competent skills to find a job to financially support themselves, they might take risks that lead to crimes such as drug smuggling, fraud, and even human trafficking in the hope of making money.

Experiencing extreme stress and depression in life can also lead to some people committing crime. Revenge and anger are also motives for someone to flout the law [≈ to have a brush with law ≈ not to comply with the law].

Some young criminals violate the law because of influence from peers and because of neglect from their parents. Drug and alcohol overuse can further trigger criminal behaviour.

# DAY 242
## CYBERCRIME

Cybercrimes are those crimes that take place primarily online. Increasingly in today's modern world, many individuals and organisations are becoming the victims of cybercrime.

Hackers are able to break into personal computers and obtain personal information. Global companies have had their business severely affected with cyber-attacks. In some of these cases, their computers could not be used and the hackers demanded a ransom to allow the companies access to their computers again.

< One of the companies that I worked for was cyber attacked once. Everyone's computer turned into a black screen with instructions to get the computer decrypted. It said 'We guarantee that you can recover all your files easily and safely. All you need to do is to purchase the decryption key by sending $300 worth of bitcoin to a specified address, and sending your bitcoin wallet ID and personal installation key to a specified email address.' Our IT department worked all day and night for over a week to get all the computers recovered. >

**Write down your questions and thoughts as a cybercrime detector:**

| Your questions | Your thoughts |
|---|---|
|  |  |

**How can we address cybercrime?**

Internet hackers are technology gurus. They should be made aware that, while creating ransomware seems to be a quick way to generate money, what really awaits is a life behind bars.

Individuals should be vigilant with [≈ take precautions with ≈ be on the lookout for ≈ exercise caution on ≈ prevent exposure to ≈ not be lulled into] email scams and inappropriate online content. They should avoid using public networks, clicking on unusual links and filling out private information on untrusted websites. Antivirus software can be installed on personal digital devices to prevent cyber-attacks. Users should perform regular scans for viruses or malware.

Companies can ensure the latest software and antivirus software are installed on their computers. Emails could be circulated to each employee with information about watching out for phishing attempts. Employees can be educated to not open untrusted emails nor to click on links from unidentified email addresses.

Governments should establish a strong cybersecurity to protect personal information and national security from being attacked by the cybercriminals. Creating a national internet crime website is an effective method. The Australian Cyber Security Centre website is a great example where individuals or companies can report suspicious behaviour. Support for the victims of cybercrime is also provided by the centre.

# DAY 243
# MEDIA VIOLENCE

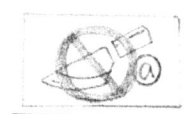

There is too much violence portrayed in the media in today's society: violent shootings, assault, cyberbullying, and sexual harassment through email and text messages, unwanted profanity, nudity, child abuse, and other shocking content…

In 2014, two pre-teens from the US lured their best friend into the woods and then stabbed her 19 times. They claimed that it was the internet meme 'the Slenderman' that drove them to do so (Meredith E. Gansner, 2017).

**Write down your questions and thoughts as a person against social media violence:**

| Your questions | Your thoughts |
|---|---|
|  |  |

**Does violent content in the media lead to real-world crime?**

Violent content in the media can act as a trigger for actual crime. Intense scenes and strong language in the media can impact the viewer, making it hard to get out of the viewer's mind the content they witnessed (such as examples on how to bully, harm or even kill others). This can lead to subsequent aggressive behaviour. In fact, research has shown that the exposure to the social media violence is associated with increased aggressive and violent behaviour in real-life, which could cause long-term mental health impacts on the viewers, especially young children (Huesmann & Taylor, 2006).

**What are the solutions?**

To prevent such violent tragedies from happening, it is necessary for governments to censor content on mass media before releasing it to the general public. All TV programs and movies should have content warnings and be graded for particular audiences. The studios behind various media can provide reminders or warnings when violent content or swearing will appear in a program. All website, app and video game developers should take responsibility for creating a safe environment for the content that they produce.

Additionally, parental guidance and supervision is one of the most overlooked steps in moderating content. Parents can use filtering software to get rid of any unsuitable programs or website contents before allowing their kids sit in front of the TV or a screen. Parents can also supervise their children's viewing throughout a show, app use, or website access.

# CHAPTER 31 - A Crime Detector

## DAY 244
## TRAGIC SHOOTINGS

In 2017, in Las Vegas, 58 people were killed and hundreds were wounded by a mass shooting during a live musical performance. In 2019, a gunman killed 49 people at mosques in New Zealand. This event was even live-streamed on social media. In 2020, in Vienna, a shooting left 5 dead and 15 injured.

**Write down your questions and thoughts as a firearms expert:**

| Your questions | Your thoughts |
|---|---|
|  |  |

**If you were in a gun support group, what would be your debate for gun use?**

Pistols can be used in self-defence in the event of unexpected situations. The shootings [≈ massacres] described above might have been avoided if the general public were allowed to carry guns. Gun violence is not a major source of crime and violence. Terrorist attacks [≈ Acts of terrorism] occur more often – acts such as hijackings, sieges, riots, bombing or even driving cars ploughing into crowds [≈ mowing over crowds ≈ barrelling towards pedestrians]. Furthermore, owning a gun is a civil right. Hunters and weapon collectors use them for their hobbies.

**If you were against gun ownership, what would be your argument against gun use?**

It is true that guns can be used for personal protection. But allowing everyone to own a gun poses great risk to the community. First, if a person has not been trained properly in the use of firearms, it could lead to fatal or injurious consequences to themselves and others. Second, when gun ownership is made legal [≈ guns are made accessible], domestic crime and suicide rates increase dramatically. Last but not the least, citizens would feel insecure and live in panic every day in the fear of gun violence – such as a shooting at a school, or on a subway. This might result in increased mental stress in the populace in the long term.

# DAY 245
## SEXUAL HARASSMENT

In 2020, a Melbourne University professor was accused of having inappropriately harassed his female students (Houston, 2020). Sexual harassment also exists between workmates in the workplace. One-third of Australians have experienced sexual harassment in some form in the workplace over the last 5 years (Croxon, 2020).

Write down your questions and thoughts as a sexual harassments lawyer:

| Your questions | Your thoughts |
|---|---|
|  |  |

**Why is workplace sexual harassment so prevalent?**

Sexual harassment occurs in the workplace mainly due to gender inequality. Position power dynamics at work is one of the key drivers in sexual harassment. In many situations, managers abuse their power to harass their subordinates (Huber & Bean, n.d.). Although more women have become managers than ever before, men still account for 60% of managerial positions (Sherman, n.d.). With men being the main perpetrators, women are more likely to be victims of sexual harassment with their insecure and vulnerable positions, and possibly their lower level of self-confidence. (Sexual Harassment, n.d.).

**What are the impacts of workplace sexual harassment?**

Sexual harassment impacts the victims emotionally, leading to stress, anxiety and depression. Such experience lowers a person's confidence and self-esteem. As a result, the vulnerable are often found absent, distracted, and unable to concentrate on the job. This will jeopardise their career and mental health in the long run.

If victims and bystanders fail to report sexual harassment or the company does not deal with it, team performance will suffer. A high absenteeism rate, high employee turnover and low work productivity are often seen as a result of workplace harassment (Funk, 2016).

**What can employers do to prevent this from happening?**

Companies should make policies clear to specify what types of behaviours are intolerable and against the law [≈ illegal ≈ unlawful].

Management needs to help to create a harassment free work environment. They can lead by example. Mandatory training programs can be held regularly to educate each employee that sexual harassment is not only just inappropriate, but a crime that could put the harasser in the jail. Everyone should be made fully aware of the consequences of using offensive language and unwelcomed physical and sexual contacts with others.

Employees are all encouraged to stand up and speak up on inappropriate behaviour and report such behaviour to the relevant authorities (while all relevant parties keep it confidential). A process should be set up to provide support for any victims of sexual harassment.

# DAY 246
# DOMESTIC VIOLENCE

Queenslander Hannah Clarke and her three children were allegedly to set alight in her car by Rowan Baxter, her estranged husband and her children's father in February 2020. Before the fatal incident, Clarke had been emotionally, physically, sexually and financially abused by Baxter (Murder of Hannah Clarke, 2021).

Domestic abuse is never okay. It can take the form of emotional, physical and financial abuse. White Ribbon Australia collected data that showed that 25% of women since the age of 15 have experienced emotional abuse by a partner at some point in their lives (Prevalence, n.d.). And it is not just women: men can also be the victims of intimate partner abuse.

**Write down your questions and thoughts as a domestic violence caseworker:**

| Your questions | Your thoughts |
|---|---|
|  |  |

**Family violence is a crime and the abuser is breaking the law. Why do people still commit this kind of abuse?**

From a psychological perspective, abusive partners believe that they have the right to control, manipulate and restrict the activities of their partner. Some even enjoy the feeling of power over another person (Why People Abuse, n.d.). What is more appalling is that abusers often see themselves as the victim.

**Are there any solutions?**

Putting those who commit domestic abuse in jail is only a temporary solution. This can even lead to greater violence after the perpetrator is released from prison (T, 2021).

Education programs and resources should be made available for domestic abusers so that they can be made aware of the effect of their violence and the consequences following. They should learn that a healthy relationship is all about taking care of the other person and showing respect to their partner. Love is not possessiveness, jealousy, control, or violence in any form.

In addition, domestic violence helplines should not just provide counselling services to those who need help, they should also provide financial support and emergency housing to those who are suffering in a destructive relationship.

< Many hotlines have been created to provide family violence support services in Australia. Here are a few hotlines: 1800RESPECT 1800 737 732, Lifeline 13 11 14, Relationships Australia 1300 364 277. >

# DAY 247
# COVID-19 OUTBREAK

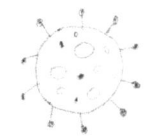

The sudden outbreak of novel coronavirus in 2019 had a global impact.

Millions died, and hundreds of millions fell ill. Frontline health workers risked their lives every day to help save the lives of others from COVID-19. Hospitals became overcrowded. [≈ The health system was overrun. ≈ Inpatient bed demands overtook ICU capacity.]

The world ground to a halt. Cities and countries entered lockdown and closed their borders. Many non-residents were banned from entry into some countries. Mass gatherings were banned. Social distancing rules were introduced, meaning people in some environments had to be a certain distance apart (which was 1.5 metres in Australia). International sports and local sports and events were cancelled. Airline companies [≈ Air carriers] grounded international fleets and slashed domestic services. Global cruise ships stopped running. City CBDs emptied. Streets became deserted. Local museums, gyms, libraries, restaurants and pubs also closed.

As virus panic took hold, shoppers emptied [≈ cleared] supermarket shelves of toilet rolls, tissues, rice, flour, meat, hand-sanitiser, nappies – almost everything!

< Why did panic buyers stock up on toilet paper? [≈ Why did shoppers stockpile toilet paper? ≈ Why did people hoard toilet paper?] Niki Edwards from the Queensland University of Technology explains that we use toilet paper to tidy up and clean up, which symbolises control (that is, controlling our tidiness and cleanliness). Human beings are afraid of losing control of their environment, so when many people heard about the coronavirus outbreak and lockdowns, they might have been attempting to control their environment more (Ketchell, 2020). >

Education went online. People started working remotely. [≈ People worked from home.] Home office supplies also flew off the shelves. Companies collapsed. Pay rates were cut off. Millions of workers lost their jobs suddenly. This was just the tip of iceberg. The world fell into chaos. There were probably only two good sides to the pandemic:
- Pollution and greenhouse gas emissions fell [≈ Pollution dropped] across the world.
- Washing hands became habit for many.

**Write down your questions and thoughts as a person experiencing the global pandemic:**

| Your questions | Your thoughts |
|---|---|
|  |  |

# DAY 248
# CONTAINING THE VIRUS

As of 4 May 2022, over 515 million cases of coronavirus, with more than 6.3 million deaths had been confirmed worldwide (COVID-19 Coronavirus Pandemic, 2022). Vaccines and booster shots have been rolled out in many countries.

**Write down your questions and thoughts as a government official:**

| Your questions | Your thoughts |
|---|---|
|  |  |

**How did the Australian Government respond to the crisis in 2020?**

To stop the virus from spreading [≈ halt the spread of COVID-19 ≈ tackle the virus ≈ eradicate the virus ≈ combat the pandemic ≈ flatten the curve], Australia, like many other countries, took various measures, establishing testing clinics, making more hospital beds available, ordering more medical supplies, and so on.

To protect the health system and save lives, various restrictions were imposed and police were given the ability to issue on-the-spot fines for whoever flouted physical-distancing rules or other compliance rules.

Individuals faced over $1000 in fines for gathering in groups, and businesses copped penalties of up to tens of thousands of dollars for not following compliance rules.

However, the Australian Government also needed to balance public health with economic growth.

To support the Australian economy, the Australian Reserve Bank cut rates to a record low. The federal government spent billions of dollars to stimulate the economy, including introducing JobKeeper payment plan to keep businesses affected by COVID-19 alive. When restrictions lifted in Victoria, the Victorian Government also introduced a regional $200 travel voucher scheme.

< China used a different strategy. When numbers surged, residents of each household were only allowed to come out to buy food every two days. Those coming back from overseas were required to quarantine for 14 days at a hotel in the city where the airplane landed, another 7 days quarantine at local hotel at hometown city, plus another 7 days of self-isolation at home. Based on my observation, contact tracing was quicker and more effective than Australia and case numbers were much lower than Australia's numbers. >

The COVID-19 virus is the enemy of all human beings, no matter where we are. But we are all in this together. Let's finish this passage of history and overcome this tricky virus together.

# DAY 249
## POST COVID-19

From the start of 2021 and onwards, COVID-19 case numbers were not in as many news headlines. Case numbers had dropped significantly. We could almost call it a post-COVID-19 normal life.

**Write down your questions and thoughts as an epidemiologist:**

| Your questions | Your thoughts |
|---|---|
|  |  |

Before vaccines were fully rolled out to most of the population, we saw changes in the way we were living. Some of these changes were:

- Long-distance business trips were reduced. Work meetings and conferences moved online.
- Supermarkets put up transparent screens at the check-out counters.
- The most hated seats on the airplane were kept empty (those middle seats in-between the window seat and the seat along the aisle).
- When crossing the road, many pedestrians no longer had to press [≈ push] the button to stop traffic. Many traffic lights and pedestrian crossings were set to automatic.

< At many road intersections in Australia before the COVID outbreak, pedestrians needed to press a button at the traffic lights to interrupt traffic to cross the road. Once the traffic light becomes green, it activates a *tick-tock-tick-tock* sound, which means the pedestrian is safe to cross the street. This isn't something that we have back in China. >

However, new Delta strain of coronavirus appeared around the middle of the year in 2021, followed by the Omicron variant towards end of the year (and then Omicron's sister variant followed quickly and spread even faster than other variants). At the beginning of 2022, Victoria cases increased up to over 50K a day. Citizens were encouraged to get their booster shots. We continued to guess:

- When was the virus going away? [≈ When would the pandemic end?]
- How long would travel restrictions between countries last?
- Was another financial crisis approaching?
- Would the pandemic transform the way we live permanently?

Only time would tell. The year 2020 was tough – 2020 is the Chinese year of the Metal Rat, which happens every 60 years. Something bad has always happened in the year of the Metal Rat: the First Opium War (1839–1842), the Boxer Rebellion (1899–1901), the Great Chinese Famine (1960), and the COVID-19 pandemic (2020). Is all of this a coincidence?

Many of the topics explored in this book, or any arguments or advice were written before the global pandemic occurred.

# DAY 250
# FARMERS NEED HELP

Agricultural businesses play a vital role in feeding over 7 billion people each year (More on Feeding Nine Billion People by 2050, n.d.). But our society doesn't give too much attention [≈ pay enough attention] to farmers living in remote areas.

Most farms are family run. Many smallholder farmers live in poverty. Their harvests are largely affected by the climate, which is out of control of human beings. Without financial support from other sources, it would be hard for the farmers to beat extreme weather conditions (drought, extensive rainfall or other production threats).

**Write down your questions and thoughts as an agriculturist:**

| Your questions | Your thoughts |
|---|---|
|  |  |

**How can the government and communities help farmers?**

In terms of drought conditions [≈ dry weather] or other damaging weather, direct financial support from the government can help farmers to rebuild their homes and remedy any loss of crops and stock. This could help farmers get out of the woods in any bad years. In the longer term, the government can make a levy on profit-making agriculture companies. The fund can be used in agriculture research and to provide financial support to farmers after any natural disaster.

Rural communities can bring local farming residents together to discuss how to quickly recover from damage to agriculture and how to manage and reduce risk in the future. Insurance company can design products and premiums that will suit farmers. When natural disasters strike, the insurance claims should be able to help farmers through the tough times. The general public can also become active participants [≈ great contributors] to the agriculture industry. For example, the supermarket giant Coles previously launched a campaign to charge an extra 30 cents for each bottle of milk. This was to raise money to help farmers more directly in summer drought conditions.

# DAY 251
## URBANISATION

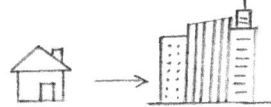

Many rural areas have been experiencing the phenomena of the 'brain drain' where people move from regional areas to the cities to pursue big dreams. Such movement is referred to as [≈ termed] 'urbanisation'.

**Write down your questions and thoughts as an urban developer:**

| Your questions | Your thoughts |
|---|---|
|  |  |

**What are the problems with urbanisation?**

In developing countries, citizens are suffering from starvation due to insufficient food supply. Farmers from developing nations have been flocking to bigger cities where natural resources are rather restricted. As a result, already overcrowded cities are experiencing water scarcity, housing shortages, traffic congestion, a competitive job market, and increased crime. Massive immigration to cities is the culprit here, leading to lower crop yields and food security issues. This is a vicious circle.

**What are the solutions?**

First, governments should allocate funding to scientific research in order to advance cultivation techniques and technologies. This could help improve agriculture and work towards better feeding the global population.

Second, urban expansion should be made more feasible. Designing better road systems, constructing more residential complexes, and creating more job opportunities can alleviate urbanisation problems.

However, the most effective method is to balance both urban and rural development. Local governments can spare no effort in establishing schools in regional areas – ranging from elementary education to tertiary education. This will help to retain graduates in regional areas. Productive crop-cultivation methods and subsidising farmers can help to increase revenue for farmers. The private and corporate sectors can entice and encourage workers moving to regional areas, and this would create employment in countryside locations. Building community centres, shopping malls and hospitals in regional areas can make them more attractive to live in.

# DAY 252
## ANIMAL EXPERIMENTATION

Every year, millions of mice, Guinea pigs, rabbits, hamsters and other animals die from medical testing in barbaric ways [≈ in savagely cruel ways].

**Write down your questions and thoughts as an animal rights activist:**

| Your questions | Your thoughts |
|---|---|
|  |  |

**Should animal testing be prohibited?**

Non-human primate experimentation involves ethical and moral issues. Animals are enough like human beings that they can be substituted for testing the safety of cosmetics and medical products.

However, animals have a sense of self, and they should not be treated with such brutality. They only have one life, and they deserve to be respected and protected from harm. For example, a pig used for the testing of new drugs might never leave their tiny enclosure in the research laboratory (Animal Experimentation, n.d.). What is even more inhumane is that the animals are often burned, poisoned and killed in painful experiments.

The company Lush previously launched a campaign for customers to sign a petition against animal testing [≈ to stand up for animal rights]. This campaign has helped customers to become more aware of purchasing cruelty-free products only.

On the other hand, those who support the use of animals in research argue that there is no alternative way at this stage to make sure that new drugs and cosmetics are safe for use by humans. In fact, the invention of new drugs for the treatment of cancer, AIDS and other diseases in the near future [≈ in years to come ≈ in the not-too-distant future] could be lifesaving.

Even though many countries have introduced legislation to ban animal testing for new cosmetics, some companies still use animal testing (Cosmetics Testing FAQ, n.d.). This proves that no better way has been found to replace animals in the development of cosmetics and medicines.

Until medical technology develops further, animal testing must only be used as a last resort, and they should be protected from any mistreatment.

# DAY 253
## SMOKING

As we are all aware, smoking is detrimental to health. Those who inhale toxic substances found in cigarettes are prone to severe diseases, such as heart attack, lung cancer and bronchitis. Colleagues and family members of smokers [≈ Second-hand smokers] are also likely to suffer from these smoking-related diseases.

**Write down your questions and thoughts as an anti-smoker:**

| Your questions | Your thoughts |
|---|---|
|  |  |

**What can we do to protect public health if smoking isn't prohibited entirely?**

First, the public should be made adequately aware of the detrimental and irreversible impact of heavy smoking. The global Body Worlds exhibition shows visitors what a smoking lung looks like. This sort of education hopefully encourages smokers to toss away their cigarette packs.

Second, smoking should not be made accessible to young children at all [≈ tobacco products should not be sold to persons under 18-years-old]. Too much inhalation of cigarette smoke can severely jeopardise children's health.

Third, public spaces (such as workplaces, hotel rooms, public transport and beaches) should be made smoke-free. For those who breach the rules, a heavy penalty should apply. Banning tobacco advertising and branding is also an effective method to regulate the smoking industry. Cigarette packets are designed with dark colours, graphic health warnings and prominent words such as '**SMOKING KILLS**', '**SMOKING DAMAGES YOUR GUMS AND TEETH**', and '**SMOKING CAUSES BLINDENSS**' to make smokers vigilant of the harm that cigarettes can cause.

< Don't overuse capitals in your writing. This can come across as rude. Capital letters should only be used when starting a sentence, mentioning proper nouns, titles of books and movies, or giving emphasis on particular odd words. Am I using capital letters right in the above paragraph? Lots of signs for small shops in Australia are written in capital letters. Get yourself used to that. >

# DAY 254
# DISCRIMINATION OF IMMIGRANTS

Amid the coronavirus outbreak, graffiti such as 'Shame on China. Go home yellow dog' was painted on the walls by racists. Chinese international students wearing masks in public were verbally abused, or even physically assaulted. The Asian-Australian community suffered unfair treatment in this time. This behaviour is unacceptable and intolerable, and against the law.

Even if the coronavirus health emergency had not happened, racism and discrimination exist in many aspects of life. For example, many employers pay attention to the surname of job applicants on resumes in the screening process. Some Asian restaurants only hire students from Asian countries so they can secretly underpay staff. Some real estate agents or landlords have refused to lease properties to people from overseas (Rabe, 2019).

**Write down your questions and thoughts as an immigration lawyer:**

| Your questions | Your thoughts |
|---|---|
|  |  |

**What should we do to eliminate discrimination?**

All the above examples show there is a trust gap between immigrants and non-immigrants in Australia. For locals, they need to understand that it is immigrants who give the country its rich diversity [≈ have made their home country into a multicultural and multiracial society]. Every individual should be respected and should have equal rights, regardless of skin colour and background.

Nonetheless, racism does persist. Apart from making laws against discrimination to deal with racism, anti-immigrant bias could also be reduced if those who discriminate travel overseas themselves and throw themselves into the culture of other countries. This helps to increase understanding of the culture of immigrants. Mindsets can be changed: those coming from other countries deserve respect and should be welcomed.

# DAY 255
## TRAFFIC ACCIDENTS

Here's a TV ad: A journalist interviews a man on the street. The journalist mentions that in 2016, Victorian road toll reached 291. He asks the man what would be a more acceptable number in his opinion. The man thinks for a while and says hesitantly, 'Maybe seventy?' Then the journalist sends in 70 of the interviewee's family. The man looks at them, becomes teary says, 'Zero. Zero.'

**Write down your questions and thoughts as a responsible driver:**

| Your questions | Your thoughts |
|---|---|
|  |  |

**Why does the man change his mind on the number of fatalities?**

High-speed crashes and some other serious road incidents can be lethal. Victims could end up with serious injuries and even lose their lives. Drivers and passengers being killed in traffic accidents would leave a family grieving for their lost ones.

**What are the other impacts of traffic accidents?**

Accidents can have effects other than injury and death. They can cause traffic jams and delays. In severe cases, roads become closed and drivers have to make detours. This wastes everyone's time. For offenders or victims, collisions often result in high repair costs, or the car could be totalled. Those who cause accidents could receive fines and have demerit points deducted from their licence. Their licence could also be suspended or revoked.

Offenders sometimes flee the scene of an accident. Those who are involved with hit-and-runs like this could land themselves in jail or be issued with a large fine.

**What are the causes?**

There is far more traffic – cars, trucks and public transport – on the road than ever before. Irresponsible and careless drivers are those who are not vigilant [≈ do not keep their eyes on the roads] all the time. Unlicenced driving, speeding, drink-driving or even drug-driving still occur even with strict traffic law and regulations. Unthoughtful road design can sometimes also lead to deadly crashes.

# DAY 256
## REDUCING ROAD ACCIDENTS

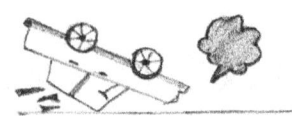

Nepean Highway head-on car crash. Single vehicle accident on Central Road. A trio of crashes on the Monash Freeway. Truck on fire near Toorak Road. V/Line train hit a car [≈ A vehicle was struck by the V/Line train] in Bendigo... Such traffic accidents are reported in Melbourne in the news every day. Melbourne is not alone – this happens in all other cities around the world.

**Write down your questions and thoughts as a road accident reporter:**

| Your questions | Your thoughts |
|---|---|
|  |  |

Today, let's brainstorm some solutions to help people travel safe on the roads:
- Roads should be well designed, and maintenance needs to be conducted regularly.
- Clear signage should be installed for building construction areas, road bumpers, roundabouts and road-crossings.
- Rigid driving tests should be implemented to reduce the risk of accidents caused by new learners.
- Strict punishments should be implemented for major driving offences.
- Police officers should issue heavy [≈ strict] fines for speeding and unruly driving. [≈ Aggressive drivers and unruly drivers should face stiff charges. ≈ Hash penalties should be given to traffic offenders.]
- Drivers who are caught using phones or drink-driving should cop more demerit points, potentially facing months of suspension of their licence.
- Drivers themselves should remain vigilant for road hazards and follow all traffic rules. Bad driving habits such as tailgating and running traffic lights should be punished.
- Car manufacturing companies can focus on improving the safety and quality of their cars.

Here are three more solutions for improving road safety that I've seen in Victoria:
- Train station level crossing removal projects have helped improve the safety for both drivers and pedestrians. These projects aim to remove the shared crossing between trains and other road users.
- Traffic conductors are assigned to help coordinate busy traffic, especially school crossing supervisors during school hours to help with the safety of school kids.
- VicRoads enforced a new rule to help protect emergency workers: drivers must slow down to 40 km/h when they pass stationary law enforcement or emergency vehicles with flashing lights.

Are there any other solutions or strategies that you've observed in your local region that have helped to reduce road accidents? Put them down in your notebook.

# DAY 257
# PAYING TAX

Australia has claimed that the country has a world-class social security and welfare system. However, people consistently complain about high tax rates (See **Day 209 Tax Basics in Australia**).

Write down your questions and thoughts as a tax agent:

| Your questions | Your thoughts |
|---|---|
|  |  |
|  |  |

Where does the government spend taxpayers' money?

| | | | |
|---|---|---|---|
| Education system | Childcare | Employment sector | Housing and community |
| Medicare | Space exploration | Industry assistance | Recreation and culture |
| Infrastructure | Public safety | Immigration | Foreign affairs |
| Aged welfare | Public health | Disability | Economic aid |
| Natural disasters | Defence | Veteran support | Freeway/highway expansion |

What if no-one paid their taxes?

If no-one paid their fair share of tax [≈ If nobody filed their income tax ≈ If people stopped paying tax ≈ If there was no tax], the government would not collect as much money. The federal government would lose power and not be able to help those in need and improve welfare in the society. As a result, the government would have to borrow money from other countries. Furthermore, the wealth gap would widen further. Additionally, public servants working in the Treasury, or tax agents, could lose their jobs.

What should government and individuals do about their taxes?

For the betterment of society, everyone should pay taxes to the government. Anyone who earns income and every business that earns income should be a part of the tax system. Some taxpayers complain about high tax rates. Although the government has designed the tax system so that higher income earners pay higher tax, unfortunately, the ultra-wealthy always find ways to take advantage of tax laws to lower their effective tax rate. Each individual is responsible for managing their earnings at the most effective tax rates. Meanwhile, the government should use the income from taxes effectively for its citizens. A system of transparency should be established to reveal where all government money is spent, and a rationale for expenditure should be provided.

# DAY 258
## AGEING POPULATION

People are living longer lives than ever before. [≈ The average human lifespan is increasing. ≈ Individuals can enjoy longer lives.]

In Australia, although there are no laws dictating when a person can retire or should retire, many people choose to continue to work into their 60s. The retirement age keeps going up, and one of the reasons could be that there are conditions for a person to access their super and for them to be eligible for the age pension. So the question is: are we living better?

**Write down your questions and thoughts as a gerontologist:**

| Your questions | Your thoughts |
|---|---|
|  |  |

**What problems could an ageing population cause?**

The increasing ageing population means that labour forces are declining [≈ working-age population is in decline]. A shortage of qualified workers will result in a decline in productivity and higher labour costs, which will further diminish profits and cause a negative impact on a country's economy (Borji, 2016).

Retirees need financial support from the government. If the pension for the retired [≈ the elderly ≈ the over-65s ≈ retired workers ≈ senior citizens] is insufficient, this means they will have uncertainty with their lifestyle.

An ageing population also challenges [≈ burdens ≈ puts pressures on] the healthcare system due to the increased demand.

**How can businesses and the government help?**

Companies can create job opportunities for the elderly who desire to contribute to the workforce later in life. Wherever possible, their wisdom and life experiences can be a great contribution to businesses. The health care sector and nursing homes can invest in new technologies to assist the elderly. Nurses, doctors and home-care personnel should be trained to best support the wellbeing of ageing individuals, both physically and emotionally. Having underqualified staff in some nursing homes can be detrimental to the health of the elderly.

The government should have the plan in place to make sure sufficient funds are allocated to pension based on longer life expectancy. The aged care sector should also be supported financially by the government to upgrade infrastructure and improve general living environment for the elderly, as well as lowering their living costs.

# DAY 259
# FOOD SAFETY

'Gutter oil' is illegally recycled waste cooking oil. Some restaurants in China have been found using gutter oil. Australia has previously reported food safety issues, with several incidents of needles found hidden in bananas and strawberries.

There have been reported cases of fast-food workers spitting on customer burgers before serving. A proportion of fast-food delivery drivers admitted that they'd eaten food from a customer's order during a delivery run (Gilbert, 2019).

**Write down your questions and thoughts as a food hygiene officer:**

| Your questions | Your thoughts |
|---|---|
|  |  |

**Why is food safety important?**

Food safety directly affects health and quality of life. Food poisoning can result from bacteria from poorly handled and prepared food. In a worst-case scenario, food poisoning could even cost a person's life.

Contaminated food puts a burden on the public health system.

When food safety standards are not followed by a business, their reputation can suffer. In 2008 in China, melamine (a chemical is used to make plastic) was found added into Sanlu (三鹿) milk powder. Hundreds of thousands of young children were poisoned. This tragedy has made Chinese domestic customers wary of local formula even over a decade later.

**What can we do to ensure a public food safety?**

First, food safety laws and regulations should place the obligation on food businesses to produce food that is safe and suitable to eat. A whistleblowing policy can be established to encourage reporting those food processors and restaurants conducting businesses unethically.

Second, food manufactures and restaurants should follow correct food handling processes. Training should be provided to staff to make sure the hygiene procedures are all followed thoroughly. Such businesses should also have a crisis management plan in place to specify how to respond in the event of a food safety crisis – such as when a foreign object is dropped into packaging or when a worker is affected by hepatitis.

Third, consumers themselves also need to be responsible for their own food safety. They should make sure they read the labelling on food packaging to help manage food allergies, consume food before the use-by-date, and follow the instructions on how to store food products correctly.

# DAY 260
# WEALTH INEQUALITY

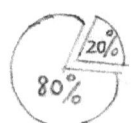

The 80/20 rule (Pareto principle) for wealth inequity is as follows: 80% of the wealth is owned by 20% of the population. The gap between the rich and the poor [≈ the haves and have-nots] is becoming wider [≈ is widening ≈ keeps growing]. [≈ The rich get richer while the poor get poorer. ≈ The world is becoming economically polarised. ≈ Wealth inequality is soaring.]

< Vilfredo Pareto developed the concept for his principle when he was working in his garden and observed about 20% of the peapods in the garden contained 80% of the peas (Tardi, 2020). This rule can be applied to time management and many other aspects of life. >

**Write down your questions and thoughts as an economist:**

| Your questions | Your thoughts |
|---|---|
|  |  |

**What can be done to reduce the wealth gap?**

To shake off poverty and austerity for those underprivileged [≈ lift the poor out of poverty], the government should help raise the minimum wage.

Imposing progressive tax rates is also a good alternative to narrow [≈ bridge ≈ bring down] the wealth gap. The tax system can also be redesigned to support lower class families, providing tax credits for childcare and low-income support.

Those who are better off [≈ The better-to-do ≈ The well-to-do ≈ The upper class] can be encouraged to donate to charities, recycle second-hand items for those on the poverty line, and help to support poorer families through various initiatives.

Education is the key to breaking social barriers and lifting the poverty line. Adults who have difficulty finding work should be supported to receive relevant training courses and helped to find a job through the government Centrelink system. Schools should focus on developing skills that could help students with future careers. Personal finance courses can be set up to help students establish better money-management awareness. All of this kind of education can eventually give students the chance to get out of the poor living conditions.

# DAY 261
## UNAFFORDABLE EDUCATION

Tertiary education is considered a launchpad [≈ launching pad] for a person's career. The harsh reality is that not all families are wealthy enough to afford for their children to study at university.

< A 'launchpad' is a platform that a rocket or a missile sits on before launch. >

**Write down your questions and thoughts as an education minister:**

| Your questions | Your thoughts |
|---|---|
|  |  |

**Should the government pay for tertiary study course fees for everyone?**

For families living below the poverty line [≈ living on the dole], receiving an education is one of the best ways to break out of the poverty cycle. But these disadvantaged families often cannot afford university learning for their kids. So the government should pay for tuition fees for students from these families.

However, not everyone has a genuine interest in university study. Supporting such students could be a waste of government money and a giant waste of time for some students. Only students who are keen on learning, but cannot pay out university fees, should receive the free funding.

It is also unrealistic for the government to support each student financially [≈ bear all the costs]. Back in 1974, the Whitlam Government abolished university fees in the hope that all Australians would access tertiary study. It failed because it put too much burden on the federal budget. So the HECS (Higher Education Contribution Scheme) system was introduced where the Australian Government provided students with interest-free loans for tertiary study (Should We Bring Back Free Tertiary Tuition?, n.d.). On this scheme, individuals do not need to repay their student loan until they have started working and earning income above a certain threshold. The government and the university can also provide grants for outstanding performers as motivation for students who pursue academic success. Many world-renowned universities charge a much higher tuition fees for overseas students than for local students. This helps relieve the financial pressures for local students. After all, the government and universities are not charities.

# DAY 262
# OTHER BIG ISSUES

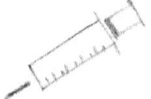

In Part 3 of *The English Builder!*, we've discussed problems and challenges facing nations around the world, such as health, education, poverty, crime, firearm control and carbon emission.

There are other big issues ringing alarm bells around the world, and some of these cannot be glossed over [≈ fobbed off]:

- **Refugee rights.** Each year, asylum seekers pay people smugglers to help transport them to safer countries or attempt to travel by boat to safer countries at the risk of dying during the journey. Whether the Australian Government should welcome refugees, where refugees should be settled, whether the detention centre facilities are good enough, and how to help refugees overcome language barriers have all been controversial issues.

- **Euthanasia.** Euthanasia is also known as assisted suicide. When patients fall seriously ill and suffer a great deal of pain, euthanasia is intentional action to end their life painlessly. Should it be legalised and become a voluntary personal choice? Many argue that people should have the right to select how they are going to leave the world. But if euthanasia is made legal, there is concern that it could be abused, resulting in vulnerable people ending their lives prematurely. So what should the government do here?

- **Housing affordability.** Housing prices have been growing rapidly while wages have lagged behind. It makes it hard for families to keep up with the rising prices of consumer goods, let alone find ways to afford their own home with the increasing house prices. There is regular industrial action from unions every year because wages have shown no sign of increasing. The government needs to find a way to support those who are struggling to buy a home. One example of the Australian Government successfully doing this is for Australian first homeowners – when they satisfy eligibility criteria, they can apply for financial relief in the form of a one-off first homeowner grant.

The government deliberately shutting their eyes to the problems will not solve them. Governments need to take actions in many areas, such as helping to eliminate starvation, cracking down on stock and real estate speculators, creating jobs [≈ increasing the employment rate ≈ decreasing the jobless rate] and curbing corruptions. Citizens can cast votes to elect government officials [≈ policy makers] who act on their interests. At the same time, each member of a community is also responsible for many things: obeying laws, loving Mother Nature, protecting wild animals, respecting people's sexuality…

So please think big and be socially responsible.

# DAY 263
# THE WORD - WITH

Let's have a look at a fun-packed conversation full of the preposition 'with'. Highlight any phrasal verbs that use 'with' for the meaning 'having a lot of something' or 'to be completely full'.

**Ruby:** What's up **with** you? You look concerned. Are you still **with** Samsung? [≈ Are you still working at Samsung?]

**Mario:** Yep. I've been **with** the company more than 10 years. I've been so anxious about an upcoming project, which seems to be **bristling with** challenges. Anxiety really **messed with** me lately. How about you? Are you still **with** Bruce?

**Ruby:** Yes. He **quarrelled with** me last time. He apologised afterwards and I forgave him. I'm in love **with** him. I can be myself when I'm **with** him. I like his oozing confidence.

**Mario:** That sounds great. I'm **with** you. [≈ I **agree with** you. ≈ I **side with** you.] It's quite important to **live with** someone who you love and who loves you back.

**Ruby:** True. It's so warm out there. I feel like going to Brighton beach. Would you like to **take a ride with** me? I just bought a new car.

**Mario:** Wow! Congratulations! It sounds like a great idea! Let's go!

**Ruby:** Hey, I've been reading a book called *The World **Loaded with** Problems*.

**Mario (bursting with** curiosity): What is the book about?

**Ruby:** It talks about how our world is **fraught with** various problems. Tropical forests no longer **teem with** wild animals. The ocean is **awash with** rubbish. Public transport is **crammed with** [≈ **jammed with**] commuters. Our culture is **saturated with** television and advertising. Our days are **laden with** endless work. The streets are **equipped with** surveillance cameras. Fast-food restaurants **with** fat-laden food seem to be in every nook and cranny [≈ in every part] of the city… It **struck a chord with** me. [≈ It **resonated with** me. ≈ I **identified with** the authors. ≈ The opinions in the book **chimed with** me. ≈ The book **echoed with** me.]

# PART 4 SHINE BRIGHT

Hey English Builder, your dream house is almost here. Great effort!

The very last part of this book aims to help you create your own style of living. Porch, stylish. Bedrooms, calming. Living areas, inviting. Cushions on sofa, warm colours. Dining room, brilliant. Kitchen, modern. Bathroom and powder room, extravagant. Laundry, well-organised. Rumpus room, playful. Garage, spacious. Front yard and backyard, an oasis. Swimming pool, attractive…

Your house shines bright, and you shine bright too!

Let's rock and roll!

# DAY 264
## THE PLANE TAKES OFF

What's life in Australia look like? Get your passport and visa ready. Book your ticket and let's fly there. Your trip will involve a lot of different kinds of actions, so pay attention to the verbs!

Before travelling, pack your luggage. Don't place bottles with liquids in your carry-on baggage. Mark or tag your luggage in some way that's noticeable so that it will be easier to spot at the luggage carousel. Weigh your luggage beforehand to ensure your bag is no heavier than the weight limit. This is to avoid overweight baggage fees. Check that you have your passport, visa, and air ticket (or e-ticket) with you. You're all set.

Arrive at the international terminal 3 hours earlier than taking off. Find the check-in counter [≈ check-in desk]. The staff will ask you some questions: 'Where are you flying to?', 'Are you carrying any firearms or flammable materials?', 'Would you like a window seat or an aisle seat?' Put your bags on the scale and they will then be tagged and sent to your destination. You will be given a pass with the boarding gate number on it for your plane.

Now it's time to say goodbye to your parents [≈ wave to your parents at the departure gate], or whoever takes you to the airport. Listen to their parting words and feel the love. Once you're on your own, you'll start to realise how much unconditional love and care that they've been giving you your entire life.

Now proceed to the security check. At the screening point, empty out your pockets. Take out any mobile phones or other electronic devices and metallic objects. In China, you're required to take your umbrellas out. Put them in the tray. Airport officials will use a metal detector to check over you. If the detector doesn't beep, collect your stuff and head to your departure gate.

For international travel, you need to pass through customs before heading to the boarding gate. Listen to the announcement when the gate is open. Walk onto the plane when the instructions are given. Find your seat. Place carry-on bags in the compartment overhead. Switch off any mobile devices. Fasten your seatbelt. Listen to the safety instructions, then 3, 2, 1, 0! The engine revs. You are off! Fly safe!

# CHAPTER 33 - An Aussie Life Starter

## DAY 265
## THE PLANE LANDS

The airplane is now entering the stratosphere. You're in the air. The flight attendants will serve you some food and drinks. You could end up flying for over 10 hours if you're travelling from China to Melbourne. Oops, a long-haul flight! If you're struggling with sleep and get bored watching in-seat movies, circle all verbs you can find on this page.

The next day, when you wake up, you might look through the window and see the clear blue sky and white fluffy clouds. You're flying above Queensland!

The flight attendant will give you an incoming passenger card to fill out with accurate information such as your name, passport number, flight number, and the intended address that you'll be staying at while in Australia. You also need to declare if you're bringing particular items into Australia, such as more than 2250 mL alcohol, more than 25 cigarettes or 25 g of tobacco products, illicit drugs, cooked food, or $10K or more in Australian dollars or foreign currency equivalent. You must declare all of these honestly.

< $10K stands for $10,000. In Australia, big numbers are arranged into every 3 digits with commas. But in China, we tend to use ten thousand (wan 万) and hundred million (yi 亿) as units, arranging numbers into chunks of four digits in spoken language. So we say 'ten thousand', 'yi wan (一万)', 'hundred million', 'yi yi (一亿)'. '一' in Chinese is 'one' in English. >

Finally, the plane has landed! An announcement: 'Welcome to Melbourne. The current local temperature is 23 degrees. There is a sunny day ahead. Again, thank you for taking Star Alliance airplane. We hope you enjoy your trip.' Take a few stretches. Take your carry-on bags out with you. Time to get off the plane.

Walking along the signage, you'll pass through customs. Show your declaration card and passport to the officer. Then pick your luggage up at the conveyor area. Join the queue where a detection dog is assigned to sniff your bags for any drugs or other illicit substances. If you're not intercepted by the authorised officer, you can head out to the arrival area.

< *Border Security: Australia's Front Line* is a TV show documentary of how Australia's border is protected. In one episode, a Chinese student tried to bring in 7 kgs of Chinese traditional food zongzi (粽子) without declaration and was fined a few hundred bucks. In the same episode, an Indonesian girl was declined entry to Australia because she was lying about the address she was staying at and the real purpose of her arrival in the country. So you *must* give true information on the card. >

Welcome to Australia – it's a new world! If you've got someone to pick you up, the person will be waiting outside the exit gate. Otherwise, head to the Uber and taxi rank for a lift or take the Skybus to Southern Cross Station.

# DAY 266
# FIND A ROOF

Arriving in Australia, if you haven't already, you'll have to arrange your own accommodation. Rental is not cheap in Melbourne. A one bedroom apartment close to Melbourne's CBD (central business district) is listed at around AUD $350 per week (or more) in recent years.

If you're an international student under 18 years of age, you must live with a homestay family, on on-campus accommodation or reside with a parent or relative approved by the Department of Home Affairs.

< A homestay is a private house where the local host family offers accommodation and cooks for you. The Department of Home Affairs plays a big role [≈ a key role] for everyone who wants to come to Australia and stay here. You need to submit your visa, permanent residency, and Australian citizenship applications to them. >

Otherwise, you can find a place to rent through websites such as Gumtree and YeeYi (亿忆). Rooms are often furnished, but you normally have to share the dining room, kitchen and bathrooms with other flatmates. A contract with the sublessor is essential in case of any conflict arising while living there.

< YeeYi.com is a website platform providing all sorts of information for Chinese people living in Australia or those who can read Chinese, including news, rental services, job and business opportunities, car dealings, airport pickup, dating – just about everything! >

Renting through a real estate agent is also a popular option. Download the Domain or RealEstate apps. Set up your renting criteria (location, weekly rental range, and number of bedrooms, bathrooms and car parks). Check out the inspection times and head on over for an inspection of the property. If you like the place, send an offer to the agent who will do a reference check on you.

Once your offer has been accepted, you can move in. If you find a spot this way, you need to buy furniture because it's not provided by the landlord. You need to pay a bond, which is a deposit that's equal to the amount of your monthly rent – this money sits with the government.

A condition report of the property needs to be filled out. This is to make sure that you report any pre-existing damage and ensures you do not vandalise the owner's property. When you stop leasing the property, pay for a vacate clean. If the property has stayed in good condition, you can get the full bond back from the government.

You normally need to give notice at least 28 days before you vacate [≈ move out from] a property. The number of days may vary depending on the rental agreement for your property with the real estate agent.

# DAY 267
## LOOKING TO BUY YOUR OWN PROPERTY

Are you planning to settle down in Australia? With sufficient funds and a stable monthly income, you can buy your own house to live in. In Australia, eligible first homebuyers are granted a tax deduction on purchasing a property, while non-Australian residents [≈ offshore buyers] are subject to an FIRB application.

< The 'FIRB' is the Foreign Investment Review Board, who reviews and decides if a foreigner is entitled to buy a property locally (FIRB Approval, n.d.). >

But first, there's some other research and preparation to do before buying your home.

The first step is to find a broker who will get pre-approval for you for a home loan application. This will give you a rough idea on your maximum loan amount and the maximum property value that you can purchase.

The next step is to decide which suburb and location you prefer to live in. Will it be inner city, city fringe [≈ the vicinity of the city] or the outer suburbs? In Melbourne, the east side is well developed but the prices are also too high! Some old houses can be priced up to hundreds of millions and some are not allowed to be knocked down because they are heritage listed. The houses are newly built and much cheaper in the western suburbs – some people don't like living on this side, feeling public transport, schools and other infrastructure are yet to be developed. Also consider whether you want to live close to a school zone [≈ school catchment zone] for your kids' education. Do you need your home close to a shopping centre? Does the property adjoin to a train station or is it on a main road? Noise is expected when cars or trains are close by.

The third step is to decide what type of property you'd like to buy. Will it be a house, a townhouse, a unit or an apartment?

< In Australia, buying a house means the land is permanently yours [≈ you own the land under your house permanently]. That's why you'll be called a landowner or a landholder! But you need to pay an annual council fee. Townhouses could either be freestanding or attached (sharing a wall with other townhouses). The courtyard for a townhouse might be smaller than the yard for a house.

Units and apartments are buildings with multiple units in them. Strata and annual body corporate fees could cost you thousands of bucks – these are used to maintain shared garden areas, possibly also a gym, swimming facilities and car parks. >

# DAY 268
## BUYING YOUR OWN PROPERTY

Once you've found a property you like in the area that you're interested in, contact the agent [≈ realtor] for an inspection. Check out the floor plan. Ask questions like:

- What is the size of the land and the building area?
- What is the orientation of the property?
- Does the property have a big backyard or a swimming pool?
- Will the property be sold on the market or is it an off-market property sale? Does the seller prefer to go through auction or through private sale? [≈ Will the property go under the hammer or not?]

< In Australia, squares might be used to measure the size of a place. One square is equal to 9.290304 square metres. If we say something like: the land size is 500 m² (square metres) and the building area is 40 squares, how big is the living area in square metres? >

< A north-facing house is the best choice in Australia. This is the opposite in China where a south-facing property is preferable. West-facing rooms get natural light in the afternoon but get really hot in summer. >

< Having [≈ Owning] a swimming pool at home sounds wonderful. But you also need to consider the maintenance costs – regular cleaning including using the chemicals to keep the water pH (potential of hydrogen) level balance right, cleaning the filters, taking out fallen leaves, and so on. It can require hours to clean a pool! >

Before making any offer on the property, get a solicitor or conveyancer to go through the sales contract with you, especially Section 32. A solicitor is a type of lawyer who will give legal advice about the contract (and they charge more than a conveyancer).

< *Buying Blind* is an Australian reality TV show about agents and experts who look for properties, then purchase and design the rooms based on a homebuyer's requirements and budget. The property itself is bought blind by the homebuyer and not revealed to the buyer until it is all done. Basically, buyers have no idea of what they're buying beforehand. >

The settlement date normally takes up to 1 to 6 months. In-between, prepare documents and be ready for land and property ownership transfer, which your solicitor or conveyancer will assist with. You can also start to look for home and contents insurance, in case of a hurricane damaging the building or a burglar breaking into your home.

Once everything's settled, go get the house key from the agent, and the house is yours! Congratulations!

# DAY 269
## GET CONNECTED

Before moving into a new place, you need to do some extra homework.

**Homework #1:** Reach out to electricity and gas companies (Energy Australia, AGL, Origin, etc.) to get your home utilities connected by your moving date. Whether you also need to get water connected depends on where you live and how your building is designed.

The energy company might offer a lock-in contract [≈ bundle contract]. For this, you are locked in with their company for a period of time (say 1 to 2 years). An exit fee will be incurred if you terminate the contract [≈ breach the contract] early. You don't have to read the electricity meter yourself, but make sure you understand your energy plans. Below is an example of an energy contract and rates.

| Gas | Electricity |
| --- | --- |
| Winter rates:<br>• Usage per day: 2.09 c/MJ<br><br>Non-winter rates:<br>• First 200.000 MJ per day: 2.992 c/MJ<br>• Balance of daily use: 1.87 c/MJ | Variable cost:<br>• Usage: $0.2774 per kWh<br><br>Fixed cost:<br>• Charge rate: $1.16 per day |

**Homework #2:** Inform the local water utility company of your new address. If you're a tenant, you'll only be charged for the water usage, whereas the landlord and house owner need to pay an annual fee, sewage, and waterway and drainage charges.

**Homework #3:** Call up a telecommunication company (Telstra, TPG, Optus, Belong, Dodo, etc.) for a home internet connection (ADSL, NBN or Cable). Sign up for a fixed GB (gigabyte) or an unlimited data plan.

< 1 PB (petabyte) = 1024 TB (terabyte) = 1024 × 1024 GB (gigabyte) = 1024 × 1024 × 1024 MB (megabyte) = 1024 × 1024 × 1024 × 1024 KB (kilobyte). Wi-fi is an Australian invention. Over time, it has improved from 2G (2nd generation) connections to 5G connections. What does wi-fi stand for? Nothing! [≈ Wi-fi doesn't mean anything. ≈ There's no meaning.] It's not an acronym and it's just a nonsense word. >

< What are other inventions from Australia that have changed our lives? Ultrasound scanners, Google maps, wine casks, black box flight recorder, RaceCam, electric drill, polymer banknotes, etc. >

**Homework #4:** Book a professional mover to transport any furniture and boxes of your possessions to the new property.

# DAY 270
## HANDPICK YOUR FURNITURE

When moving into the new place, you might have old furniture to dispose of. Simply arrange a time with your local city council or hire a professional rubbish removalist (or even if the timing lines up, use the local council's hard rubbish collection service).

It's the time to think about new pieces of furniture for a new home. I recommend getting high-quality furniture, but within your budget. Well-made, durable furniture can last you a long time. Then, based on any theme for your home, decide on furniture materials (such as oak, redgum, jarrah, cherry, mahogany, rosewood, redwood, birch, messmate, maple, walnut or others) to best reflect your personal style and preference. Now I'll give you three tips for selecting furniture for both large and small living spaces.

For a big house, go for a generous size of furniture. Otherwise, your rooms will look empty or out of proportion. Consider:

- Placing a king-sized bed along with bed stands in a spacious master room with a walk-in closet.
- Choosing an armchair, a TV stand, a leather or fabric sofa, a love seat, a coffee table, a side table and a lamp for your spacious living area.
- Getting a set of four bar stools for the open-plan kitchen, dining and living area.

< What is a love seat and why is it called a love seat? The name comes from the idea that it's primarily designed so that couples can sit intimately with each other (so basically a comfy two-seater couch). >

For a shoebox apartment or a cramped and poky house, choose multipurpose furniture in a light colour to maximise your space. Consider:

- Buying a queen-sized bed, a double bed or a single bed, a loft bed, a sofa bed, or even a bunk bed, depending on the size of the bedrooms.
- Choosing a foldable dining table and stackable chairs without armrests for a high traffic kitchen [≈ heavily trafficked kitchen]. This helps save some space.
- Installing a mirror across a wall to expand the look of the place.

IKEA is a furniture store full of different styles and with relatively low prices. It offers collection and delivery services. But IKEA furniture comes in flat packs, which means you have to assemble on your own unless you're happy to pay for an assembly service (for example, for a product worth between $600 and $1499, the assembly fee is $199 in Victoria). How expensive! Get a combination toolkit (drill, wrench, spanner, hex key, hammer, screwdriver, plier, clamp, etc.). Do it yourself! Have fun!

# DAY 271
# FILL YOUR HOME WITH ART

Decorating your home can be an artform of itself – creating a comfy, cosy, inspiring and artsy living environment. It doesn't have to be the job for an interior designer. Take a look for yourself to see how you can add extra charm to your house.

You can start with a wall decoration in your entryway. This can also improve a living space. Adorn the wall with [≈ Hang] modern fine art prints or frame some family photos.

Scatter cushions [≈ Accent pillows ≈ Throw pillows ≈ Toss pillows] give the sofa accent features. Hue match your cushions too. Go for playful colours [≈ bold colours ≈ bright colours ≈ eye-catching and cheerful colours].

Fragrance around the home can add a personal touch too. Ignite some candles, use oil diffusers [≈ oil burners ≈ aroma diffusers] or use some air fresheners.

An elegant table centrepiece is a soft touch in the room. Some fresh flowers on display are also a great choice. Consider how to look after the flowers and make them last longer [≈ keep them at their freshest]. You could:

- Cut the stems at an angle, allowing the flowers to better absorb water.
- Half fill the vase with clean water.
- Keep the bouquet away from hot spots. [≈ Place the floral arrangement under cool conditions.]

Indoor plants [≈ House plants] can also brighten up your room. Green leaves make a stunning statement.

Install a fireplace [≈ hearth] in the living room to add warmth, cosiness and comfort.

< *The Living Room* is a popular TV show that involves a wide range of hot topics, ranging from home maintenance to pet raising and cooking, from travelling to photography. 'Is it hot or not' is one of the main questions asked by host Amanda Keller to audiences after the three guests (Dr Chris Brown, Barry Du Bois and Miguel Maestre) introduce their inventive home products or high-tech gadgets. This show is fun to watch. >

Do you have any other splendid ideas to keep your space fresh and help to make it best suit your style and taste?

# CHAPTER 33 - An Aussie Life Starter

## DAY 272
## BUYING HOME APPLIANCES

From robot vacuums to large refrigerators, range hoods [≈ overhead fan] and air conditioners, you will need home appliances in your new place.

Go to places like Myer, David Johns, JB Hi-Fi, Harvey Norman or The Good Guys to bring home top of the range [≈ good quality] appliances within your budget. Don't go for tacky [≈ cheap with bad quality] ones for the sake of saving money. Let's take a look at four different appliances below, with descriptions, specifications and price.

| Samsung 8.5 kg QuickDrive Front Load Washer | Bosch 60 cm Series 6 Freestanding Dishwasher |
|---|---|
| • Hygiene steam cycle<br>• 39 minutes super speed<br>• Simply add items during wash<br>• Energy efficiency: 4 stars<br>• Manufacturer's express warranty 24 months<br><br>AUD $1499 | • Regulate water usage depending on the size of each load<br>• Colour: stainless steel<br>• Child lock [≈ Parental lock] system<br>• 6 wash programs and 4 wash options<br>• WELS water efficiency: 5 stars<br><br>AUD $1299 |
| Hisense 630 L French Door Fridge with LED Display | LG 65-inch 4K Ai ThinQ Smart TV |
| • Adjustable glass shelving<br>• Humidity controlled crisper drawer<br>• Door open alarm<br>• Three-tier freezer drawers<br>• Energy efficiency: 3 stars<br><br>AUD $1475 | • Quad core processor: dynamic colour<br>• Cinema experience<br>• Google assistant, Apple Airplay 2<br>• Screen type: LED/LCD<br>• Resolution 3840 × 2160<br><br>AUD $1255 |

< Talking about the dishwashers, back home in China, dishwashers aren't in every household. I have dishwasher installed at home in Australia. Almost everyone does here. Dishwashers are also an essential appliance in the workplace. And even though I have one, I still prefer to wash some dishes by hand. It's a habit that I formed back home in China that's hard to get rid of. >

Now put down above four consumer goods into the correct category based on the definition below:

- White goods. Normally in white colour and difficult to move [≈ not portable]. Examples could be dryers, air conditioners, stoves and _____.

- Brown goods. As opposed to white goods, brown goods are electronic goods that come in a small size and are relatively cheap. DVD players, radios, computers, and _____ are typical brown goods.

< 'White goods' got their name because the home appliances were originally only available in a white colour. 'Brown goods' were termed because the electronic products used to be packed in black or dark cases. These nicknames were actually defined by economists, allowing them and companies to track consumer goods for a specific purpose (Vitez, 2012). What are red goods, yellow goods, and orange goods then? >

# DAY 273
## YOUR KITCHEN ESSENTIALS

Myer and David Jones are places to shop for premium kitchenware, from cheese boards, cutting boards, storage containers, canisters, kettles to coffee machines. The cookware, utensils and tools available today are extensive. Please tell me what else is in your kitchen!

< '-ware' is a suffix that refers to objects that have the same kind of use, so you can have tableware, homeware, glassware, bakeware, software, giftware, etc. >

Let's fill up your cabinet or cupboard with pots and pans. You could have some of the following in your kitchen:

| Frying pan [≈ Frypan] | Rice cooker | Wok | Deep fryer | Slow cooker |
|---|---|---|---|---|
| Saucepan | Induction cooker | Crepe pan | Air fryer | Toaster |
| Steamer | Pressure cooker | Skillet | Fondue | Casseroles |

A complete cookware set isn't necessary. Look for heavy-gauge cookware. They deliver heat more evenly [≈ manage heat better]. Copper and aluminium are the best conductors of heat [≈ are responsive to temperature]. Stainless-steel is more durable, but it lacks a non-stick coating. You also need smaller-sized cooking utensils for your bench [≈ scullery]. You might find some of the following utensils in a kitchen:

| Measuring cups and spoons | Citrus squeezer | Paring knife | Tongs | Corkscrew |
|---|---|---|---|---|
| Can or bottle opener | Ice cube tray | Spatula | Timer | Soup ladle |
| Fine-mesh sieve | Meat thermometer | Meat tenderiser | Sifter | Bag clips |
| Garlic crusher [≈ Garlic press] | Potato masher | (Balloon) whisk | Funnel | Pepper mill |
| Pestle and mortar | Salad spinner | Peeler | Cleaver | Cookie cutter |
| Muffin tin | Kitchen scissors | Pastry brush | Grater | Baking tray |
| Silicone oven glove | Tea infuser | Pizza cutter | Colander | Kitchen scale |

Please note: You must be 18 years or over to purchase knives or knife blades. Proof of age may be required.

Don't spend money on cheap culinary appliances (hand mixer, blender, food processor, pasta and noodle maker) for your pantry. Get high-performance brand appliances (Kenwood, Breville, KitchenAid, Sunbeam, Bosch, Vitamix, etc.). If you get a good quality product, you'll use them again and again over many years.

# DAY 274
# LIVING IN YOUR HOUSE

You've finally settled down! Take us for a tour around your house.

In front of your house, there's a nature strip between your property boundary and the road, which is owned by your local council. The council could make it into a lawn and plant a tree there. But it's your responsibility or whoever lives in the house to maintain it (remove the weeds, mow the lawn, and make sure it's rubbish free). If you don't keep it neat, council might issue you a fine.

You will find two or three rubbish bins in different lid colours. Normally, yellow lids (sometimes red lids) are for general landfill garbage, blue (sometimes yellow in some municipalities) lids are for recycled waste. Green waste can be put in the green lid bin, which is an optional choice. Find out on which day of the week that the council collects the bins. Pull them to the curb in front of your house a day before or in the early morning on that day. Your rubbish will be taken away!

Now take us to your rumpus room. It is a family recreation room. What do you have in there? Did you create a reading corner, make it into a family theatre room, or even place a pool table there (if you're a pool shark)?

A good thing about living in Australia is that each household has accessible cold water and hot water. This means that you can enjoy a spa at home! You don't have to go to a public bathhouse!

< Public bathing actually isn't common in Australia. In North-east China, it's still quite popular because many apartments don't have hot water systems built in. Without installing a hot water heater at home, you might end up becoming a regular bathhouse customer. You'll enjoy showers, saunas, pool, whole body cleaning and even massage services! >

It's time to make yourself a cup of tea and curl up or sprawl out on the couch, cover yourself with a throw, and enjoy *The Block* on Channel 9 while learning some home improvement skills!

< *The Block* is a reality TV show where four or five couples renovate and decorate houses or apartments with a given budget over 12 weeks. At the end of the show, the property goes to auction. The couple will be given any profit made above the reserve price of the property that they've renovated and designed. An additional $100,000 prize money is awarded to the couple with the highest profit. >

# DAY 275
## A FEW LIVING TIPS

In Australia, labour is expensive. It's much cheaper to fix any problems in your house yourself.

For example, when your toilet doesn't flush [≈ your toilet is clogged ≈ your toilet backs up ≈ the drain is blocked], you could unclog it with a plunger or just use vinegar! If the tap is dripping or the showerhead is leaking, check for leaks and then soak it in vinegar for 20 minutes.

< The above methods might be called life hacks. They're tricks and tips that help you to complete tasks easily. Here is another one: baking soda and vinegar is an easy cleaning solution [≈ a terrific deep-cleaning cleanser ≈ a natural cleaning product]. It helps to get rid of the mould in your bathroom, remove stains on carpet, clean a stainless-steel kitchen sink, and the like. >

For some problems such as rot, rattling or drafty windows, sinking floors, cracking walls and weak ground, you'll need plasterers and crack repair specialists to help with the issues.

If you have any of the below pests in your house, call up a local pest controller [≈ expert] for a pest control service. Your kitchen, wardrobes or toilets can become infested with pests in no time.

The following household pests can cause health problems too:

| Ants | Bed bugs | Birds | Cockroaches | Fleas | Flies |
|---|---|---|---|---|---|
| Mice | Mosquitoes | Rats | Centipedes | Possums | Silverfish |
| Spiders | Stink bugs | Termites | Textile pests | Ticks | Wasps |

< One of the scary things about living in Australia is that there are venomous snakes and spiders. It's quite common if you find spiders inside your home – and various types of them too! Some Australians have spider phobia! Snakes? Occasionally on the news snakes are reported hidden in someone's home. What should you do if that happens? Keep an eye on them, but don't catch them yourself. Call a licenced snake catcher immediately! >

To revamp [≈ renovate] your kitchen, spend some time first to design your kitchen. Then: paint the wall; replace the cabinet doors; get your appliances, fittings and fixtures; pay a tradie [≈ an electrical contractor and plumber] to connect all the power points, switches, sinks, and lighting for you. Then you're all set! You'll have an upgraded, happy new look kitchen!

The very last tip for today is to go to Bunnings to get whatever hardware and tools you need for your home makeover. Get what you need for the garden, blinds, wallpaper, flooring, cleaning, and so on. You can even get home DIY advice at the hardware store.

# DAY 276
# OBTAIN AN AUSTRALIAN DRIVER'S LICENCE

In Australia, driving is a must-have skill. To get your driving licence – either a red P [≈ provisional] plate, a green P plate, or a full licence – you need to pass three tests with VicRoads if you live in Victoria.

The first one is the learning test, which is about basic road rules and safe driving awareness in the form of multiple-choice questions. Once you've passed this test, you'll be issued with a learning permit card, allowing you to drive under supervision. This learning permit can also be used as an ID card [≈ identity card].

The hazard perception test comes next. This is a mock driving test on the computer [≈ on screen] to check your reaction time for potential hazards. Click the mouse when you should slow down, overtake, stop or give way. Or don't click if there's no action required.

The road test is the final test. If you are new to driving [≈ have no driving experience], I recommend enrolling in some driving lessons with an accredited driving instructor beforehand. If you're under the age of 21, you need to log 120 hours of supervised driving experience before taking the drive test. This includes 20 hours of driving at night.

Now fasten your seatbelt. Turn on the ignition. The examiner will call out some of the parts of the car, and you need to indicate where they are. Some of these might be:

| Windshield [≈ Windscreen] | Accelerator | High beam | Fog light | Air bag |
|---|---|---|---|---|
| Windscreen wipers | Foot break | Low beam | Hand brake | Boot |
| Steering wheel | Emergency lights | Indicators | Bumper | Bonnet |

Put your foot on the brakes. Pull the handbrake. Shift the gear stick into drive position. Make sure the surroundings are clear. We're ready to go! Take your foot off the brake.

Listen to the directions from the examiner: 'Turn right at the traffic light. Please continue driving along the street. Make a U-turn or a three-point turn at the end of the road. Pull over to the kerb and stop. When you are ready, please make a reverse parallel park.'

Keep in mind, driving is never easy. There are always hazards on the road. Stay focused and keep safe.

# DAY 277
# DRIVING IN AUSTRALIA

Driving can be different between China and Australia. Here are my observations:

In Australia, beeping the horn [≈ horn blaring] is not that common. You are beeped at only when the other driver feels you are driving dangerously. Most drivers are polite. When another vehicle indicates to merge into the lane, the driver already in the lane behind will allow the vehicle to enter smoothly. When a vehicle wants to move into another lane, and cars are moving slowly, another driver would wave a hand to let the turning vehicle in. The turning vehicle driver will wave a hand back to show appreciation. As a driver, you should always give way to pedestrians, letting them across the road.

While wearing helmets is compulsory for bike riders – as are lights on a bike at night – you have to watch out for them because many roads are shared between bikes and cars. You can't overtake a bike unless it's safe to do so. Be cautious with motorcycles on the road too. They are often speedy with loud, annoying noises (*vroom, vroom...*)!

In China, drivers seem to honk their car horns all the time. We have give-way rules, but it seems just to be a written rule – whoever is 'better' or 'faster' with driving skills wins the race. The car in front of you could hit the brakes out of nowhere, so please stay focused! While driving, watch out for pedestrians since not everyone follows the traffic rules. In northern China, you also have to look out for driving on ice in winter. This rarely happens in Melbourne. Also in China, bicycles, electric bikes and motorbikes are thick on the road, and riders don't have to wear a helmet.

Once you get to know the road rules in Australia and have driven more, I feel it's enjoyable to drive here. On country roads, the sun is bright, the skies blue, the clouds white, the farms green. Take some day trips into the countryside and play some music you love while you drive. Look out for kangaroos – slow down and give way to them if you see some!

Wherever you are, please drive safe. A split-second's inattention could change a person's life. [≈ A person's life could change in a matter of seconds [≈ in a heartbeat ≈ in an instant ≈ instantly ≈ quickly].] So please follow the local driving rules at all times.

# CHAPTER 34 – A Qualified Driver

## DAY 278
## PLEASE FOLLOW THE ROAD RULES

I'll reinforce this: please follow the road rules in Australia. Failure to do so will put you in danger. I'm not kidding. In recent years there have been several severe car accidents caused by Chinese travellers driving in Australia. The driver and passengers either died on the scene or became injured and fighting for the life. Catastrophic! [≈ Calamitous!]

Here are some common practices that you need to remember:

- Australians drive on the left side of two-way roads.
- Stay focused while the car is in motion [≈ when the car is moving]. Don't use your phone. Don't drink, eat, smoke and drive!
- Cars turning right or left must give way to oncoming cars. Normally there's a clear 'Give Way' or 'Stop' sign to guide you.
- When approaching a roundabout, slow down. Check for cars coming from your right side. Don't move if other cars are already in the roundabout. [≈ Don't enter the roundabout until the cars are clear.]
- When merging or changing lanes, don't miss indicators and don't miss a shoulder check! Enter from the dotted lines, not the solid lines.
- At a zebra crossing [≈ rumble stripes ≈ sleeper lines], a driver must give way to pedestrians.
- Reduce the speed in school zones at specified hours (in most cases, 40 km/h). In Victoria, it's from 8 am to 9.30 am and from 2.30 pm to 4 pm during school days.
- In the Melbourne CBD, when you see the hook turn sign 'RIGHT TURN FROM LEFT ONLY', you need to drive towards the left of the lane to perform a hook turn to turn right at the intersection.

Please refer to the Australian Government road rules for further information. Bear in mind: a full licence holder can only accumulate up 12 demerit points within any 3-year period. Traffic infringement penalties are hefty. For example, you'll get fined $363 and 3 demerit points when driving a non-heavy vehicle over the speed limit by 10 km/h to 24 km/h (Fine Amounts & Demerit Points, n.d.). The most important thing is to drive safe. I have to say this once again: please follow the road rules. Driving is not a game. Cats have nine lives, but you only have one life.

< Is it true that cats have nine lives? Well, in reality, cats can't have nine lives. Scientists do, however, believe that cats can survive falls from the high places because of their reflexes – they can balance their body out and land on their feet, which human beings can't do (Bicks, 2019)! >

# DAY 279
# ROAD SIGNS

Today, we'll have a look at some traffic and road signs in Australia. Please feel free to colour the demonstrated signs as indicated. I'll warn you one last time: stay focused on road at all times.

**Regulatory signs**

Drivers must obey all instructions on the road signs. The signs are normally in black and white with red to indicate danger.

 When driving towards this octagonal-shaped stop sign, you must stop completely, and give way to all traffic until it's all cleared.

 You must give way to any vehicles entering or approaching the intersection on your right when you spot this sign.

 There's a roundabout ahead. Decide which exit you'd like to take and move to the correct lane. Stop your car when you're about to enter the roundabout. Give way to all vehicles coming from your right. Some lanes will require an indicator.

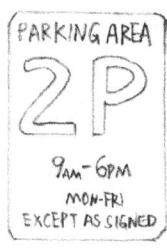 This parking sign means that you can only park 2 hours in the parking area except as signed (disability parking or loading zones) between 9 am and 6 pm Monday to Friday. This type of parking sign is often marked in green. If the sign is also marked METER or TICKET, you need to pay the parking fee at the meter nearby. Park your car into the parking bay [≈ parking spot].

**Warning signs**

Drivers are normally warned with yellow signs for a change of road conditions ahead.

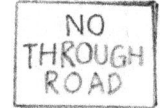

A speed bump is coming up.

The road is closed [≈ blocked off]. Please detour.

You're driving into a no-through road [≈ dead-end road].

**Freeway signs**

Drivers are guided by green signs with directions and are informed when the freeway starts and ends. Toll roads are signs in blue. You can set up a Linkt account for auto-payment for any toll road travel.

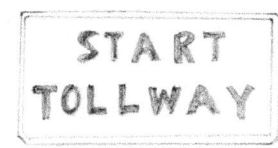

# DAY 280
# GET A CAR

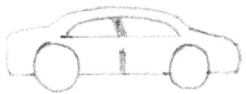

In Australia, you basically can't go anywhere without a car. The majority of residents live in the suburbs where shopping centres are not in walking distance and where you can't rely on public transport as much as in the city. On weekends, in some areas you could be waiting for up to 40 minutes for a bus service. Any disruptions where buses replace trains due to roadworks could also increase your journey time.

So what would be the smart thing to do? Get your own car!

There are things to consider before visiting a car dealership:
- Do you prefer a brand-new car [≈ a new car] or a used car [≈ a second-hand car]?
- Are you going for an economic car, a sporty car, a SUV, an off-road car, a 4-wheel drive, a performance car, or a limousine?
- Will you buy a sedan or a hatchback?
- How are you going to pay for the car? Through car financing, or stump up the cash all in one go?
- Most importantly, which brand would you buy?

| Mazda | Tesla | BMW | Kia | Maserati | Lamborghini |
|---|---|---|---|---|---|
| Toyota | Honda | Lexus | Fiat | Mitsubishi | Mercedes-Benz |
| Porsche | Volvo | Jeep | Ford | Land Rover | Rolls-Royce |
| Subaru | Audi | Buick | Suzuki | Alfa Romeo | Jaguar |
| Nissan | Acura | Hyundai | Cadillac | Volkswagen (VW) | GMC |

< A quick test: Which of these brands are from Japan? Which are European cars? Are there any car brands made in Australia? Which are the American brands? And which are the luxury brands? >

Shop around. Take a test drive. Kick the tyres. [≈ Kick the wheels.] Then decide. Negotiate the price patiently with sales staff. The price might go back and forth several times, but stick with your budget.

< To 'kick the tyres' means to examine or test something carefully before you decide to buy it. Where did this phrase originate from? In the early days, the tyres of automobiles were made of thin rubbers. So people normally would kick them to inspect if they were thick enough or if they would deflate before buying a car (Payes, 2013). >

< In Australia, the car dealers promote drive away prices for new vehicles. That means the price includes the stamp duty, dealer delivery, third party insurance, and registration. So you pay for the car and drive away the same day. Drive away prices are negotiable. >

A car can get you almost anywhere you like. Fantastic. Keep in mind though, there are ongoing costs for owning a car. You will need to pay an annual vehicle registration fee, car insurance, and service and maintenance fees. You also need to fill your car with petrol regularly. Make sure you don't mix up diesel and unleaded petrol though!

# DAY 281
## WHAT'S AN AUSSIE'S LIFE LIKE?

No matter where you are, we all have similar routines: work, home, gym, supermarket, shops, bank, etc. What's an Aussie's life look like? Let's take a quick look today at some things you might get up to at the gym and pharmacy.

When visiting the gym (Snap Fitness, 24-7 First Fitness, Anytime Fitness, Jetts, F45…), you can exercise with a range of exercise equipment. Below are the names of some pieces of equipment:

| Treadmill | Spin bike | Gym cross trainer | Rowing machine [≈ Rower] |
| Kettle bells | Dumbbells | Abdominal bench | Lat pulldown |

Bring a towel and drink bottle. Work out and sweat. Wipe the equipment after use. Once you're a gym member, it should be free for you to join in any group class. Below are some group classes you might take:

| Cycling | Boxing | Pilates | Zumba | Yoga | Body attack |
| Judo | Karate | Pump | Squash | HIIT | Cardio box |

When you're a gym member, you can meet with a fitness adviser [≈ a personal trainer] who will assess your fitness level, test your blood pressure, check your height, weight, BMI and such and help design a customised exercise program for you (from warming up to weightlifting, stretching, biking, to cooling down), and give you advice on food and carb intake to keep your health in check.

Now it's time to visit the pharmacy to get some health products or medicines. You might head to My Chemist, Pharmacy Warehouse or Priceline. At some pharmacies, Asian 'daigou' shoppers are nabbing [≈ raiding ≈ quickly grabbing ≈ snapping up ≈ hurriedly buying] health products (Blackmores Odourless Fish Oil, Swisse Chlorophyll, GO Healthy Propolis, etc.), skincare products (Lucas Papaw Ointment, Thursday Plantation Tea Tree Medicated Gel for Acne, Healthy Care Lanolin with Sheep Placenta, etc.) and baby formula (Aptamil Gold + 1 Baby Formula, a2 Platinum Premium Follow-on Formula Stage 2, etc.).

< A daigou (代购) is known as a surrogate shopping. This is a phenomenon that's been emerging in recent years. Surrogate shoppers buy various products from overseas and sell them back to customers in China, taking advantage of the price discrepancies to make money. >

In Australia, most shops are closed by about 6 pm during business days. Almost all banks are closed on weekends. Only ATMs (automated teller machines) operated 24-7. The post office is open on weekdays with some open up to midday on Saturday.

< I found the opening hours for shops in Australia a bit inconvenient. In China, lots of shops close at 9 pm or even later, and you can go to the bank or post office on both Saturday and Sunday. >

Are you curious about exploring life in Australia? Let's sneak into a few more places over the following 17 days.

# DAY 282
## AT THE SUPERMARKET

Many working Australians prefer to go shopping on weekends. They buy food at places like Coles, Woolworths (colloquially 'Woolies'), Aldi or Asian grocery stores for the next week. Let me take you to Coles today.

One experience that's different between Australia and China is that in Australia you can bring in any bag you want into the supermarket. In China, you have to check in your bags either in the cloak room outside or let the shop assistant seal your belongings into a bag before entering.

Grab a trolley at the entrance. The trolleys might be secure, so you'll need to insert a coin to get the trolley out. If not, you can get a token from the supermarket assistance desk.

You'll enter straight into the fresh vegetable and fruit areas. Vegetables are washed clean without dirt (though you might find unwashed potatoes for cheaper than washed potatoes). They are either sold in kilograms (broccoli $5.50/kg, garlic $25.00/kg, apricots $6.90/kg) or per each or bunch (cauliflower $3.50 each, avocados $3.00 each, limes $0.90 each). Some vegetables loved in Asian cooking (chives, garlic shoot, cowpeas) are not available at Coles, Woolies or Aldi. They are sold only at Asian grocery shops. There's a basket filled with fresh fruit that's free for kids until all have been eaten.

Alongside the fruit and veg section are the meat, seafood and deli [≈ delicatessen] areas. Grab a ticket around the deli counter. When the shop assistant calls the number on your ticket, it's your turn to order: 'Can I please get a dozen oysters?' or 'I'd like to have four pieces of snapper, please.' or 'I want 100 grams of ham. Can you please slice it for me?'

Around the freezer section, you'll find different types of meat by cut: pork loin chops ($15.00/kg), beef porterhouse steak ($35.00/kg), lamb shoulder ($13.00/kg), chicken thigh fillets ($14.50/kg), turkey mince ($12.00/kg) or even ham, bacon and plant-based sausages.

Eggs are sold in cartons of 6 or 12 or more and categorised as free-range [≈ cage free] or caged eggs. Proteins and milks have much shorter expiration date, and yoghurt in Australia is thicker than yoghurt in China. When products are on sale, a yellow sticker with a dropped price will be attached to the product. Quick sales are often put on products that are expiring soon.

# DAY 283
## STILL AT THE SUPERMARKET

Our shopping trip continues. Let's go aisle by aisle. Grab whatever you'd like and put it in your trolley. Here's what you might find in each aisle:

| Aisle no. | Popular items |
|---|---|
| Aisle 1 | Bread and bakery, muesli bars, spreads, gravy and stock, salad dressing… |
| Aisle 2 | Long-life milk, canned food, desserts, cookware, breadcrumbs, baby food… |
| Aisle 3 | Snacks, biscuits, coffee and tea, crackers, diced fruit in juice, jam, peanut butter… |
| Aisle 4 | Honey, seasonings, dips, pasta sauce, ice cream cones, energy drinks… |
| Aisle 5 | Cosmetics, hosiery, napkins, razor blades, toothpaste, vitamins, hair care… |
| Aisle 6 | Dishwashing liquid, scourers, laundry, air freshener, deodorant… |
| Aisle 7 | BBQ and picnic, portable coolers [≈ ice boxes ≈ eskies], party supplies, serviettes… |
| Aisle 8 | Cat food, tissues, pest control, power boards, international travel adaptors… |

< I'd like to recommend some popular snacks: Parker's Baked Twists Pretzels for $2.50, Smith's Twisties Cheese for $2.00, Cadbury Cherry Ripe chocolate bar for $2.00, Arnott's Chicken Crimpy Shapes for $3.20. >

< What is an esky? Yep, they're plastic tubs where people put food or cold drinks in to keep them cool on hot summer days. Why do Aussies call them an esky? Esky is actually a brand name, an abbreviated version for Eskimo. Back home in China, I haven't seen these kind of ice boxes in ages! >

The layout of each supermarket might be different. Looking for something in particular? The store directory is hung up at the side of the shelves, which helps you to quickly locate in which aisle the product is placed. Or you can just simply ask for help from a shop assistant.

Let's proceed to the checkout now. You can self-serve by scanning the barcodes on product packages. Welcome to the express counter if you've picked 12 items or less. If you've observed closely while browsing, you'll see that some products are marked with prices in cents (e.g. $1.75 for 700 g Coles Soft White Toast bread loaf, $1.17 for a 1.25 L Pepsi Cola soft drink when it's on special). But Australia only has five-cent coins as the lowest coin currently. So your total purchase amount will be rounded up or rounded down to the nearest five cents when paying with cash.

When spending $30 or more in store (excluding some purchases like gift cards or tobacco), you'll receive a 4 cent off per litre discount on petrol at Shell and Coles Express petrol station, which shows at the bottom of your receipt. Don't miss out a voucher with alcohol drinks on there as well! Alcohol is not sold at Coles or Woolies directly, but at nearby liquor shops instead. Liquor shops like Liquorland for Coles or BWS (Beer, Wine, Spirits) for Woolies, are normally next door to the supermarket.

We've done our shopping. Put your groceries in the car. Now return the trolley and pull your coin (or token) out.

# DAY 284
## AT THE SHOPPING CENTRE

Today, I'll take you to Chadstone (colloquially known as 'Chaddy'), the Fashion Capital. It claims to be the largest shopping centre in the Southern Hemisphere, situated in Malvern East, Victoria. You are going to love this place, I promise!

Here, you get everything under one roof: clothing stores (Lululemon, H&M, SABA), shoe shops (Wittner, Foot Locker, Aquila), jewellery retailers (Angus and Coote, Bevilles, Tiffany & Co), the Apple store, bookshops, luxury brands, a Build-a-Bear Workshop, food courts, a cinema… Chadstone has over 500 stores. You could just stay there all day long. We'll be visiting three places today, which can be found at most shopping centres in Australia.

**Kmart**, **Big W** or **Target**. These department stores have a good variety [≈ a good selection] of products at affordable prices. Here, you might find bookshelves, rocking armchairs, coat racks, car accessories, cookware, clothing, etc. There is normally a shop assistant at the entrance who has the right to check your bag when you exit the shop. The interesting thing here is that Kmart now keeps cash registers [≈ checkouts] at the centre of [≈ in the middle of] the store. Is it a creative design or does it attract a customer's attention to grab something on the way out?

**Flower shop.** The florist [≈ floral designer ≈ floral artist] is here to cater to your floral needs. Do you need a stunning bouquet or a bunch of flowers to surprise a friend or send flowers for a particular occasion? Pick one of the below flowers:

| Rose | Forget-me-not | Daisy | Carnation | Sunflower | Tulip | Dandelion |
| --- | --- | --- | --- | --- | --- | --- |
| Orchid | Chrysanthemum | Daffodil | Lily | Peony | Iris | Camellia |

< A daffodil is a trumpet-shaped flower with tube-shaped in the middle, predominately in yellow. They first bloom in spring and represent rebirth, hope and new beginnings. The Cancer Council in Australia launches campaigns in August each year to fundraise for those whose lives are affected by cancer. This fundraising takes place during the Daffodil Day Appeal. >

**Key-cutting shop.** Here, you can get shoe repairs, engraving, car key replacement, watch repairs, garage remotes clone. I was once wanting to get an extra apartment key as a back-up but was told that the key wasn't allowed to be copied and that I needed to contact the apartment building manager to get one extra key. Interesting to know. This actually can be easily done at key-cutting shops back home in China!

Tomorrow, I'll bring you to some clothing shops where you can enjoy a shopping spree [≈ enjoy binge shopping]!

# DAY 285
## STILL AT THE SHOPPING CENTRE

Let's check out some discounts offered by retailers today! You might find some goods marked down. Some sales might have up to 50% off on selected goods. Maybe a clearance sale will have up to 70% off RRP (recommended retail price). Some shops might have 30% off storewide. There might also be some EOFY (end of financial year) sales. At some shops you can take 40% off a second item that you purchase, or receive a buy one, get one free [≈ one-for-two] deal.

Entering into the store, a salesperson just greets and asks how you're doing and whether you need any help. Sometimes, there's no-one greeting you. You just take along whatever clothes you like to try on in the change rooms.

Below is an Australian women's clothing size guide with the international size conversion. Australian size is similar to size in the UK. The size and measurement could be slightly different between each brand.

| Size | US Size | AU/UK Size | EU Size | Bust (cm) | Waist (cm) | Hips (cm) |
|------|---------|------------|---------|-----------|------------|-----------|
| XS   | 2       | 6          | 34      | 78        | 63         | 86        |
| S    | 4       | 8          | 36      | 83        | 68         | 91        |
| M    | 6       | 10         | 38      | 88        | 73         | 96        |
| L    | 8       | 12         | 40      | 93        | 78         | 101       |
| XL   | 10      | 14         | 42      | 98        | 83         | 106       |

The sales assistant will give you a numbered tile to indicate how many pieces of items that you're bringing in to try. Mirrors are inside the fitting rooms so you can see what you look like when trying something on. If nothing suits, just put it back or tell the sales assistant, 'I don't like it' or 'It doesn't fit' or 'That's not for me', or even 'That's no good on me'.

< In China, some sales assistants can be overwhelming. The moment you step into the shop, they greet you, ask what you would like to buy and recommend clothes for you. Mirrors are placed outside the fitting rooms. The moment that you step out of the fitting room with the clothes you're trying on, they start their complimentary, 'It looks fantastic on you. You should get it.' Even if you feel it's not a fit [≈ it's not for you] at all. >

If you like it, just go to the counter to make your purchase. The clothing is now yours! Lots of shops offer 'afterpay' services [≈ 'no upfront payments and free interests' service ≈ 'own [≈ get ≈ enjoy] it now, pay later' service].

If you love the dress, jacket, jeans or any other outfit that you're going to buy, but it has some faults (for example, the jacket has snagged on something, or the edges of the jean are a bit frayed) and it's the last one in their stock, ask for a discount. You might be offered with a further 5% to 10% off for slightly faulty items.

# DAY 286
# AT THE BANK

We need to go to the bank at some point in time. When stepping into the bank, the security guard might assist you to get a ticket number by selecting the service that you need at the ticket machine.

When the number on your ticket is called, proceed to the corresponding counter. The teller will greet you and say, 'How can I help you today?'

- **I'm here to deposit a cheque.** You can fill out the deposit slip yourself or let the teller do it for you. A cheque normally takes 3 business days to clear. You can also cash a cheque (that is, exchange the cheque for the cash value).

- **I'd like to exchange coins for banknotes.** Once you've been living in Australia for some time, you probably have a whole lot of coins sitting around at home. You can bring these into the bank and swap them into notes or deposit the value directly into your bank account.

- **I need to open an account.** You'll be asked what types of account you need. Will it be a Savings, Debit, Credit (Visa, MasterCard, American Express [≈ Amex]), Joint Account, Business Transaction Account or an Offset Account?

- **Can you please help me remit funds overseas?** For an international transfer, you need to provide the recipient's bank details, including account name [≈ beneficiary name], account number or IBAN (International Bank Account Number), SWIFT (Society for Worldwide Interbank Financial Telecommunication) code, beneficiary's bank name and address including country's postcodes.

- **I have queries about home loans.** The broker, financial adviser or personal consultant will help you. When you're ready to apply for a home loan, they'll go through a series of questions for assessment. The bank will then assess predominate factors and risks to decide how much to lend to you.

< For the third bullet point above, I find Australian offset accounts interesting. I'd never heard of them in China. It is an account linked to your home loan to offset your mortgage interest. Your loan interest is calculated based on the difference between the total loan and the money you put in the account. So the more savings in the offset account, the less interest you will need to pay on your home loan. >

< For the fourth bullet point, do you know some countries don't have postal codes? >

# CHAPTER 35 - A Down Under Navigator

## DAY 287
## AT THE LIBRARY

Libraries are open to the public in Australia. You can access any library in any community or university campus during open hours. You can also apply for a library card for free, which allows you to borrow books and DVDs (digital versatile discs or digital video discs). This will give you free access to the library wi-fi and unlimited access to online materials, such as ebooks or ejournals.

Libraries hold regular activities, such as the 'World of the book' tour at the State Library of Victoria, language groups run by volunteers at the City Library, art exhibitions from the Fitzroy Library and a book fair event at the Richmond Library. Most events are free! Just check out the library's website. Wow, so many freebies! I like that. Let's take a peek at libraries now.

Some libraries have vending machines where you can purchase bottled spring water, sparkling water, Coke Cola, Pepsi, chips, energy bars, and so on. Drinking fountains [≈ Water fountains] are also installed in many libraries.

< Water bottle refill stations are also often located on many streets in Australia and these are free to use. Such refill stations aren't often found in China. >

Books are sorted and shelved by genre and by author name. Comfy chairs and sofas are arranged in the quiet study area [≈ quiet zone] or group work areas, or scattered around bookshelves.

Self-help borrowing and renewing services are provided. Friendly librarians can also lend a hand. The librarians sit at an information desk at the entrance to the library.

Set up a reminder for the due dates for your books. Otherwise, you'll be fined for not returning the book on time. When returning books, place them in the chute outside, which is a 24-hour service. Librarians will put the books back onto the shelves.

< A 'chute' is a sloping channel where things can slide down to a container below. Do you know what a rubbish or water chute is? >

Of course, libraries will also have facilities like male toilets, female toilets, ambulant toilets [≈ wheelchair accessible toilets] and even baby change rooms.

# DAY 288
## AT THE HAIR SALON

Snip, snip, snip... Do you need a hair service? Book a time slot with local barbershop [≈ beauty salon ≈ hairdressing salon ≈ hairdressers].

< Did you spot anything wrong in the above sentence? Bingo, the alternative expressions are not quite the same. A barbershop [≈ barber] is only for men. Beauty salons [≈ Beauty parlours] offer extended services such as nail manicure, facial treatment and foot care compared to the services at a hair salon. >

Here are some prices and services from a hair studio in Melbourne:

| Haircuts/blow waves | Styling/style cut |
|---|---|
| • Female dry cut from $35<br>• Fringe trim from $20<br>• Cut & blow wave from $55<br>• Men's style cut from $30<br>• Clipper all over/head shave from $20 | • Shampoo & dry off from $25<br>• Blow wave long from $55<br>• Braids from $20<br>• Hair ups from $70<br>• Curls from $30 |
| **Tint/highlights** | **Foils/treatment** |
| • Regrowth from $65<br>• Full colour from $75<br>• Ammonia free roots from $75<br>• Half head of foils short from $130<br>• Full head of foils long from $190 | • Partline foils from $120<br>• Balayage/ombre from $160<br>• Bleach bath from $95<br>• Perms long from $145<br>• Keratin treatment from $199 |

Please take a seat. Let your hairstylist know what you would like to do with your hair:

- I only need to shampoo my hair [≈ clean my hair] today.
- I'd like to have my hair cut up to my collar and have my fringe trimmed.
- I'd like my hair thinned.
- Can you please make my bangs short?
- I want to bleach and colour my hair [≈ dye my hair].
- I want loose curls with big waves all over or medium curls. What do you reckon?

Okay, the service starts. What tools and products might your hairstylist use?

| Comb | Clippers | Curling iron | Neck duster | Shaver |
|---|---|---|---|---|
| Scissors | Trimmers | Hair dryer [≈ Hair blower] | Pomade | Mousse |
| Shear | Razor | Shampoo & conditioner | Brush | Hair-dye |

# DAY 289
# AT THE MEDICAL CENTRE

Are you feeling sick? Call up the bulk-billing clinic to seek medical attention [≈ medical advice]. Find out when your GP (general practitioner) [≈ family doctor] has an opening. With a Medicare card [≈ When you are on Medicare], you'll receive a free consultation.

When visiting the doctor, how would you describe your symptoms [≈ feelings of discomfort]?

- I have a fever. [≈ I'm running a fever. ≈ I've got a temperature.] My head is very hot. I'm also short of breath.
- I have a runny nose. I'm sneezing again. The headache doesn't go away.
- My stomach has been unsettled [≈ I've had an upset stomach] for a couple of days.
- I'm constipated lately. I can't poop.
- I think I've got food poisoning. I'm feeling nauseous. I have a loose and watery bowel.
- I can't feel my legs [≈ I have numbness in my leg] sometimes when awake in the morning.
- I passed out the other day. I had no strength, and I'm feeling fatigued. I'm afraid it was low blood sugar or an iron deficiency.
- My back pain comes and goes.

< Do you find it hard to describe your pain? You could use some of the following to describe a particular type of pain:

| Aching | Burning | Dull | Hot | Intense | Nagging |
| Sharp | Shooting | Stabbing | Tender | Tingling | Throbbing |

How bad is the pain? On a scale of 0 (no pain) to 10 (severe pain), how would you rate your pain? >

Here in Australia, you need to make different appointments for specialist doctors and equipment. Your GP can refer you for an X-ray, CT scan, MRI, ultrasound, bone densitometry (DEXA) scan, lateral cephalogram, etc. Specialists could include an orthopaedic surgeon, a gynaecologist or other type medical practitioner. The waitlist can be quite long in Australia (I don't why) – and it could take months for a specialist appointment in a public hospital. Back home in China, we don't even need to make any appointments. We can just walk into the hospital asking for a specialist doctor. We can get a special examination on the same day!

# DAY 290
# AT THE DENTIST

Do you have a phobia of dentists? [≈ Do you have dental anxiety? ≈ Do you dread the dentist? ≈ Do you have an intense fear of visiting the dentist? ≈ Would you rather avoid the dentist]?

Like it or not, we need to have a routine dental check-up at least twice a year. Consider some other reasons to make an appointment with your dentist:

- I need to clean and polish my teeth.
- I have stains on my teeth. I'd like to whiten [≈ bleach] my teeth.
- I have a toothache and swollen gums.
- I have a cavity [≈ a hole] in a back tooth. It's begun to rot. It gives me a bad breath. It needs drilling and a filling, probably a root canal.
- I've got a chipped tooth [≈ broken tooth]. I probably need to take out that tooth. Should I fit in a false tooth or go for a dental implant?
- I want to have a crown fitted.
- My teeth are crooked. I want to straighten them. I need to see an orthodontist [≈ a specialist dentist]. I'll have to wear braces [≈ put braces on my teeth] for a while.
- My wisdom teeth did not come out properly. They have to be removed.

< Most adults have 32 teeth, 12 more than their baby teeth. There are four types of teeth:

| Type | Location | Function |
|---|---|---|
| 8 incisors | Front part of your mouth | Cut food |
| 4 canine teeth (aka cuspids) | Next to incisors | Tear food |
| 8 premolars (aka bicuspids) | Between canines and molars | Crush and grind food |
| 12 molars, including 4 wisdom teeth | At the back of the mouth | Break up food |

>

Like it nor not, your dentist will ask you to take a seat and lean back [≈ recline]. They will ask what brings you there. Then the examination starts, 'Pop open your mouth. Open wide. [≈ Say 'Aaaaaah.'] Chin down. Bite together. [≈ Put your upper teeth and lower teeth together.] Please take a drink and rinse. I'll give you an X-ray [≈ a radiograph].'

# DAY 291
## AT THE OPTOMETRIST

To stay eye healthy, it's best to get your eyes checked [≈ tested ≈ examined] at least once a year by a qualified optometrist. Book an appointment for an up-to-date script [≈ prescription] with your local optometrist (OPSM, SpecSavers, Oscar Wylee, etc.).

Bring in your Medicare card and private health insurance (Bupa, Medibank, Australia Unity, etc.) card. In Australia, a Medicare card covers the cost for eye tests. But purchasing any lens or frames comes out of a customer's pocket. Private health insurance might only cover a portion of it, depending on your insurance policy.

Your optometrist will bring you into the eye-testing room: take a seat and relax. Tell them what you'd like to check on or what your eye problems are. 'I'm mildly [≈ moderately] short-sighted.' or 'I have a severe eyesight problem. I'm near-sighted with 6.5 diopters. I'm astigmatic and was born with cataract.' or 'I'm far-sighted [≈ long-sighted]. It's getting worse. I'm colour-blind too.'

< Astigmatism is a condition where your eyes are not completely round. You could have trouble seeing under lights at night, have blurred or distorted vision, but this could be easily fixed with glasses. >

Take it easy. You'll be asked to read the letters on the projector, or 'Which one is clear? Number one or number two?' while your optometrist tries out different lenses.

< One thing that I found interesting is that we use the tumbling E chart (optotype in four different directions – up, down, left and right) in China for eye tests, while Australia uses the Snellen eye chart (different letters with different thickness on the chart). >

You will come out of seeing the optometrist with a prescription. The sales assistant will help you select which frames and glasses (either reading glasses or near-sighted glasses) to go with.

< One thing that I don't like about getting glasses in Australia is that most of frames here are designed for westerners with a higher bridge nose fit. I have a flatter nose (like many other Asians). Such frames are not suitable for us to wear because glasses would be too close to our eyes! There are not many options for Asian-fit glasses, and they don't look fancy or pretty compared to what's sold in China. How annoying! >

As for lenses (thin, ultra-thin, high-index, bifocal, ultra-light or contact lens), I suggest getting good quality ones, although it could cost up to a few hundred bucks. The cheap ones could smear easily or fog up a lot.

It's a free of service to book a session with your optometrist to learn how to put in and take out content lens. It's also free to have your glasses cleaned and tightened [≈ adjusted ≈ reshaped ≈ modified ≈ bent].

# DAY 292
## AT THE BAR

Before we go to the bar for a drink, we need to understand the concept of a standard drink. A standard drink is any drink containing 10 grams of alcohol. If you hold a full driver's licence, you are allowed to drink up to one standard drink of alcohol before driving on the road. The calculation is as follows:

**Standard drinks = 0.789 × the volume of container (litres) × the percentage of alcohol volume**

The density of ethanol at room temperature is $0.789 \text{ kg/m}^3$. For example, a bottle of 375 mL beer with 5% alcohol volume will have 1.5 standard drinks (0.789 × 0.375 × 5). Check at the bar if you're unsure how much alcohol you can consume. If you want to have a blast [≈ have a ball ≈ have a great time ≈ enjoy yourself], just don't drive there.

If you'd like to buy drinks for your friends, say 'I'll shout you a drink.' or 'My shout!' If you buy particular drinks during a 'happy hour', you'll get a discount (or two drinks for the price of one). Cheers! [≈ Cin-cin! (pronounced 'chin-chin')]

< In Australia, we order drinks at the bar, then mingle with friends or strangers while holding the drink. We could clink the glasses and say 'cheers', and drink as we please (either fast or slow). Back home in China, we often drink while having a get-together lunch or dinner at a restaurant. We rarely have bars or pubs in small cities. Chinese baijiu (白酒) and beers are popular options. We also say 'cheers' but we could say 'bottoms up' to drink the whole glass of alcohol in one go! It's more like drinking it bottom up – ganbei (干杯) in Chinese. By doing so, it shows that you're genuine in establishing and developing a deep relationship with others at the table. >

< Chinese 'baijiu' normally contains a high alcohol volume, which could be between 35% and 60% (or sometimes higher). So far, I haven't seen any of my local friends enjoy drinking this spirit! >

Let's order some drinks at the bar [≈ tavern ≈ pub]. A 'pub' is short for 'public house', but no-one in Australia really uses the full name for them!

| Drink order | Explanation |
| --- | --- |
| Can I please have a single gin and tonic? I'd like a double vodka cranberry. | A single is one shot of alcohol. A double means two shots of alcohol. |
| May I have a martini and two Bacardis? | A martini can be ordered with or without olives. Bacardi is one of the popular rum brands. |
| Two pints of Guinness, please. A pot of Stone & Wood, please. A schooner of apple cider, please. | We're ordering beers on tap. A pint glass = 568 mL (British) = 473 mL (America). A pot glass = 285 mL, approx. ½ imperial pint. A schooner = 425mL (15 fl oz) (in all Australian states except SA where schooner is 285 mL (10 fl oz)). |
| I'll have a lemon lime bitters on the rocks. Give me a whiskey, neat. | 'On the rocks' refers to drinks with ice. 'Neat' means a drink served without ice [≈ at room temperature]. |
| I'd like to try out the house wine, please. | The house wine is an inexpensive option offered by the bar. |

# DAY 293
## AT THE RESTAURANT

Whoo-hoo! We're dining out at a restaurant today! What differences are there in dining experiences between China and Australia?

| China | Australia |
|---|---|
| • Share dishes [≈ Eat communally] <br> • Round tables [≈ Lazy Susans] <br> • Spoons and chopsticks <br> • Prone to drinking heavily to show friendship | • Prefer individual servings <br> • Square tables <br> • Knives and forks <br> • Eat and talk elegantly |

Now let's hear a conversation between a waitress (Tamara), two guests (Nigel and Julie), and a stranger (Louise) at the Meat & Wine Co Steakhouse Restaurant.

### Scene 1: Nigel and Julie have just entered the restaurant

**Tamara:** Good evening. Have you made a booking?

**Nigel:** Yes. A table for two, under Nigel.

**Tamara:** This way please. I'll bring you the menu.

Julie is going to show us how to order some food. Quite simply, if you want to try out the below entrée on the menu, just read out the name of the dish to order: **'I'd like to have baked potatoes, please.'**

| | |
|---|---:|
| **Baked Potatoes (V)** <br> Garlic crème fraiche, pancetta & chives | **12** |

The dish's name consists of the hero ingredient (potatoes) and how it's cooked (baked). The details on the menu indicate elements on the plate (garlic crème fraiche, pancetta and chives).

The letter V on the menu is the abbreviation for vegetarian. You may also spot other abbreviations: BYO (bring your own), GF (gluten free), DF (dairy free), R (raw), VG (vegan), pp (per person).

Allergy warnings are often seen on menus, such as 'Food prepared may contain or have come in contact with tree nuts, peanuts, soybeans, milk, eggs, wheat, shellfish or fish.' or 'Certain items may contain traces of allergic ingredients. Please notify our staff and ask for our allergy menu.'

# DAY 294
## STILL AT THE RESTAURANT

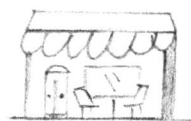

Our dining experience continues.

### Scene 2: Julie is ready to order their food

**Julie:** We'd like to have garlic bread and the Portuguese prawns as entrees. One medium-rare New Yorker steak, with creamy mushroom sauce. One rib-eye steak with blue cheese sauce. Make it medium. One garden salad, and one strawberry crème brûlée for dessert. One Peroni Italian beer, please. Thank you.

### Scene 3: Louise would like to borrow the extra seat from Nigel's table

**Louise:** Can I grab this seat? [≈ Can I borrow this chair? ≈ Is this seat available?]

**Nigel:** Go for it. [≈ Take it.]

### Scene 4: The food is now served

**Julie:** I'm hungry. [≈ I'm starving. ≈ I feel like I can eat a cow. ≈ My stomach rumbled.]

**Nigel:** Let's tuck in. [≈ Let's dig in.]

### Scene 5: Julie and Nigel have now finished the dinner

**Tamara:** Can I take the plates away?

**Julie:** Go for it.

**Tamara:** Can I get you something else or are you alright?

**Julie:** I'm good. Can I please have a takeaway box [≈ a doggy bag ≈ a take-out container]?

**Nigel:** Can we also have the bill, please? It's my treat. [≈ Dinner's on me. ≈ Let me pay for the bill. ≈ Let me get this. ≈ I will take the cheque.]

< If Nigel would like to share the bill, he would say, 'Let's go Dutch. [≈ Let's go halves. ≈ Let's split the bill.]' Oodles of restaurants don't allow splitting the bill. Some fancy and classy restaurants don't offer plastic containers [≈ don't offer to bag up what's left on your plate ≈ refuse a diner's request for takeaway containers]. >

By the way, Nigel and Julie could tip the restaurant staff, but it's not compulsory in Australia. Giving tips isn't a custom in China.

In Australia, if you dine out during a public holiday, a surcharge fee will apply. Many restaurants remain closed during public holidays.

# DAY 295
# AT CHURCH

Are you religious? If so, fill in your religion below. You might be Christian, Catholic, Buddhist, Hindu, Sikh, Islamic, any other religions or non-religious.

I'm ........................................................................................................................................... .

Most Chinese people don't belong to a religion [≈ don't practise a religion ≈ don't believe in a religion], and they've never been to church. For me, religion was a mystery. I had little knowledge about what people would do in church service. To complete today's topic, my friend Annabelle took me to the Bridge Christian Church in Richmond on a warm winter day.

This church service is held in a modern theatre. Before the service starts, lots of people are chatting and getting to know each other outside.

Entering into the theatre, performers can be on the stage singing, dancing and playing musical instruments. It's more like a musical festival, a celebration or a concert. Then the sermon starts. The pastor shares stories, explains one chapter in the Bible associated with modern life in a funny but sensible way: 'The fathers have eaten sour grapes. And the children's teeth are set on edge. You cannot blame your bad to your parents. You actually can be the great one in your family tree.'

Listening to the stories opens my mind. Newcomers are given a welcome pack. Later on, a small bucket or bowl is passed around to everyone. Put your pocket money in if you'd like to donate to the church – this money will be used for church expenditures and helping those living in poverty. The donation is voluntary. Prayer follows, and the service ends with gospel music.

After the service, the volunteer Brendon approaches to us to check how we're doing and if we'd like to join their life groups. The life group is a small group of people gathering outside of church service hours on a regularly basis to pray together, discuss the Bible, and support each other. Evangelisation [≈ Persuading people to become Christians] is considered the responsibility of all Christians. Brendon lives 50 km away and has been in the service of the church for more than 4 years. What a commitment! Free drinks and desserts are provided to attendees too.

For some westerners, attending church regularly is part of their life. People who share the same beliefs gather each week to pray, learn, share and grow. A devout Christian will be baptised with water. This is Christian tradition – immersing yourself in water is a symbol for new life and spiritually cleanses you. Christians spread kindness in God's name.

# CHAPTER 35 - A Down Under Navigator

# DAY 296
## AT THE CASINO

If you're coming to Melbourne, you can't miss out on heading to Crown Casino, which sits in the business distinct, along the Yarra River. Let's sneak in there for two games for today's fun. Remember to bring your photo ID to get into the casino.

The slots games are super easy. You can start small, even one dollar. Just insert [≈ drop] coins into a slot machine. Select the credit level and pay-lines to play. Hit the button and repeat. The machines use random number generator software, which means the symbols popped out on the screen are random. If you win, the machine will tell you. Otherwise, keep spinning the reels until you run out of money to bet.

But a kindly reminder [≈ a special reminder ≈ a friendly reminder]: the slot machines [≈ fruit machines ≈ poker machines ≈ pokies] will swallow your money quickly! That's probably why the slot machine in China is called a tiger machine (lao hu ji 老虎机)! The tiger just eats up your money swiftly! On a very slim chance, you might strike the jackpot (the tiger will throw up all money).

Let's move to the baccarat table, a very popular game. The tables here are always full. You put your wager on the player side, the banker side, or bet on a tie. The player or the banker are not real people in this case. They're just the names on the baccarat table for you to decide which side to put the bet on. It's a poker game playing with a total number 9. Ten, Jack (J), Queen (Q) and King (K) do not have values and are calculated as zero. The rests of cards have their face values (Ace (1), 2, 3… 9).

The dealer deals out cards face-up, two each for the player side and the banker side, whichever hand side totals closest to nine wins. The picture below is an example where the player gets a total hand value of 3 and the banker gets a total hand value of 7.

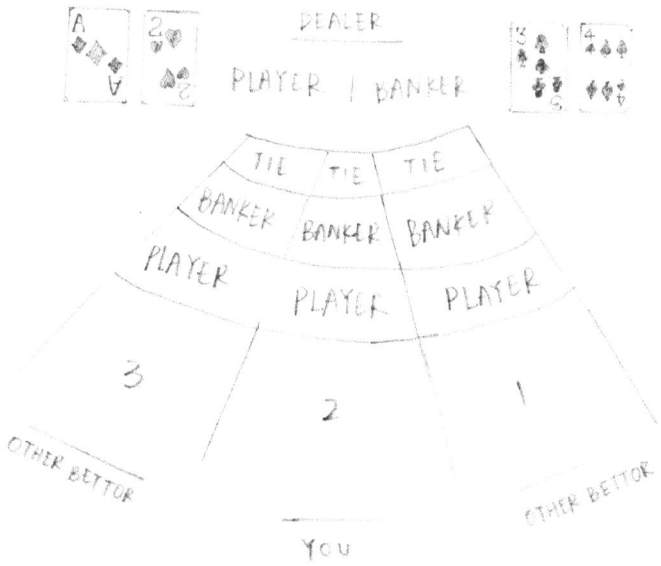

The banker is closest to 9, so if you put the bet on the banker side, you win? In theory, yes. But there's a rule: if the player has two initial cards with a total of 5 or less than 5, the player must draw an additional card. So we can't decide yet who wins in this example.

The payout for the player and the banker is 1:1, and the payoff for the tie is usually 8:1 or 9:1 depending on the casino house rules. But a 5% commission needs to be given to the casino for a winning bet on the banker.

There are also rules for when a natural 8 or 9 appears on one of the cards, when two cards are worth more than ten, and when the third card is handed out… Don't get addicted! Under Australian taxation law, income from gambling winning is taxable only if gambling is your business or profession. On this basis, you don't have to pay taxes on your winnings if it's just an occasional entertainment activity. Good luck!

# DAY 297
## AT THE CITIZENSHIP CEREMONY

Australia welcomes people from all over the world. If you'd like to become an Australian citizen, and you are eligible [≈ you meet criteria], apply online or in hardcopy through paper documents. Australia allows dual citizenship, but if your birth country doesn't allow it, you'll have to give up your original citizenship.

Once your eligibility has been checked, you'll eventually be invited to the interview and the citizenship test. The interview is as easy as one-two-three. The interviewer will confirm your identity to make sure that you're eligible for the test. The test is as easy as shooting fish in a barrel!

< Are there any other ways to express something is easy? Refer back to **Day 2 Noun Is a Thing** and **Day 3 Adjectives Describe Things** if you get stuck. Are you craving more expressions? Here are some: it will be child's play; like stealing candy from a baby. Or just: simple. >

You need to answer 20 multiple-choice questions and get at least 15 questions correct (75% pass mark). But you need to be correct on all 5 questions related to Australian values. Questions could be like what's Australia's national gemstone, national flower and national colours? Who is Australia's Head of State? What are your responsibilities and privileges as an Australian citizen?

The booklet *Australian Citizenship – Our Common Bond* will be posted to you before the test. Read it through and you can pass the test easily, as long as you have basic English language skills. (This could be one of many reasons that you learn English!)

Suppose you've passed the tests. You're now invited for the ceremony by law. How exciting! You are encouraged to wear smart casual or cultural dress. Invite your guest. Bring your letter of invitation and official ID. Arrive early to register. If you're over the age of 18, you're required to add your name to the electoral roll [≈ enrol to vote].

Once everyone has been seated, the minister will deliver a formal introduction and a speech. The presiding officer will ask attendees to repeat the pledge of commitment. Pledge 1 is a pledge under God, and Pledge 2 is secular.

Stand up to make Pledge 1: *'From this time forward, under God, I pledge my loyalty to Australia and its people, whose democratic beliefs I share, whose rights and liberties I respect, and whose laws I will uphold and obey.'* Afterwards, it's time for those who have chosen to make Pledge 2. The difference is that Pledge 2 doesn't use *'under God'* in the wording.

Congratulations! You are now an Australian citizen who's committed to showing loyalty to Australia and accepting the responsibility and privileges of Australian citizenship.

The Australian National Anthem, *Advance Australia Fair*, will be played next. Sing the anthem.

Let's proceed to the front stage to get your citizenship certificate, take a photo with the minister and your guest. Let's celebrate! Some councils organise light refreshments and a native Australian plant (a wattle tree) as a gift.

# DAY 298
# NAVIGATING DOWN UNDER (CONTINUED)

Let's go somewhere else today to explore some places that haven't been covered.

| Where are we going? | What can we do there? | Notes |
| --- | --- | --- |
| Costco | Do some grocery shopping (food, alcohol and homeware). Have eye and hearing tests. Upgrade tyres for your car. | You need a Costco member card ($60 annual fee for a household card and $55 per year for a business member) to enter into this big wholesale warehouse with great savings. Products and packaging are huge. |
| Vodafone, Telstra, Optus | Work out your mobile phone and tablet plans, prepaid phone plans and broadband plans with store assistants. | When applying for a mobile phone number, you normally pick any last four digits you like, and the system will randomly pop out several phone numbers, from which you can pick one. But if you'd like to cancel your phone number, you have to call up the customer service team yourself! |
| Village, HOYTS, Lido, Cinema Nova | Eat popcorn and enjoy a movie! | An adult ticket is around 20–25 bucks. Students can get a discount. Don't come right at the start of the movie screening if you dislike advertising and trailers before the film starts. They can last 20 minutes or even longer! |
| Spotlight | Shop for fabric, craft, curtains, party supplies and other home interior decorations! | There are a wide range of colours for fabric and thread here. Get some and make clothes at home yourself with a sewing machine. |
| Bunnings Warehouse | Get hardware tools and garden stuff! | The store's famous slogan of 'lowest prices are just the beginning' was ditched [≈ dropped] in 2020. But they still offer a low-price guarantee: if you find any products you buy at Bunnings higher than their competitors' price, they'll beat it by 10%. (Terms and conditions apply.) |
| Officeworks | Shop for stationery, printers and other office products; scan documents; photocopy; print photos. | I found ink for printers expensive in Australia! A value pack of Brother brand ink cartridges with four colours is marked over $190 at Officeworks. |
| National Gallery of Victoria (NGV) | Appreciate ancient artefacts and modern art from all around the world. | The NGV is a weekend go-to destination for Melburnians. Keep an eye out for their pop-up exhibitions. They change regularly. You might find any of these: A Golden Age of China: Qianlong Emperor; Van Gogh in Melbourne – A Multi-Sensory Art Experience; Gabrielle Chanel – Fashion Manifesto… |

Up to this point, our mission to explore Aussie life definitely hasn't finished yet. There are too many exciting places worth travelling to, too much food to try, and too many fun sports for you to engage in. So stick around!

# DAY 299
# THE WORD – AROUND

I'm glad that you're still **around**. Here comes a story with a lot of uses of the word 'around' – all marked in bold.

I was on a project with my workmate, Toby. Soon I found we were **going around** in circles. So I asked Toby to **pop around** [≈ **come around** ≈ come over] to the office to discuss the issue. Since then, we have been working **around the clock** [≈ nonstop], **batting around** ideas [≈ discussing ideas]. It led to frustration **all around**.

Finally, we **got around** the problem [≈ solved the problem]! The good news eventually **got around** the entire company too. Those issues were not **buzzing around** my head anymore.

My friend, Kyle, who I met while I was **touring around** Europe this time last year **came around** to my place over the long weekend. It's easy to **get around** town. I **showed** him **around** a few of my favourite places. We **browsed around** [≈ **walked around** ≈ **traipsed around** ≈ **milled around**] the shopping centre. Kyle bought a souvenir, a boomerang made by the Aboriginal and Torres Strait Islander Peoples.

< As mentioned in **Day 156 Public Holidays**, any weekend with a public holiday on the adjoining Monday or Friday is called a long weekend. It means people can rest for three consecutive days! >

< The Aboriginal and Torres Strait Islander Peoples used boomerangs for hunting, as weapons thrown at the target to hit and kill. Many people think boomerangs used for hunting were meant to return after throwing them, but this is a common misconception. Nowadays, boomerangs are sold as works of art, with paintings featuring Aboriginal and Torres Strait Islander traditions. >

Kyle **foraged around** in the bag and found his credit card and bought the souvenir. He was still **scouting around** for a place to live. I invited him to stay with me. I ensured there were enough drinks to **go around** for us so that we could chat all night.

Hey English Builder, **stick around** for a bit. The moon **goes around** the Earth, and the Earth **goes around** the sun. Whether you are here or not, the world keeps spinning. **There's no getting around** the fact that everyone will get old and retire one day. So stop **mucking around** [≈ **messing around**].

# DAY 300
## IDIOMS ABOUT ANIMALS

Congratulations! You've made it through to another milestone, the 300th day! Yay! I'll be **a monkey's uncle** [≈ I'll be very surprised] if you haven't progressed on your English by this stage. You'll be one step further along after reading today's story brimming with idioms about different animals. Come on! **Keep an eagle eye** [≈ an observant eye ≈ a watchful eye] on them.

I'm an **eager beaver** [≈ a hard-working person]. I love reading so I decided to open a bookstore before graduating from college. My parents scoffed at this idea and said it would happen **'when pigs fly'** [≈ would be a pipe dream ≈ would never happen]. I was **pig-headed** [≈ close-minded] back then and insisted I would go ahead, because I believed having the bookshop was the **cat's meow** [≈ excellent and wonderful].

I had **ants in my pants** [≈ felt anxious] at the start [≈ at the outset] of the business. I was like **a fish out of water** [≈ uncomfortable] when negotiating with banks, publishers and other third parties. My business was initially a success, but I got into trouble with the rise of internet shopping.

**Holy cow!** [≈ Wow, I'm surprised!] At the lowest point of my life, I met my lovely wife Renei, who's a website designer. She **loves me, loves my dog**. She's very kind and wouldn't even **hurt a fly**. She **eats like a bird** [≈ eats very little]. But during **dog days** [≈ hot days], she likes **pigging out** on [≈ eating a lot of] ice cream!

I was planning to close down my bookstore that was no longer profitable. Renei encouraged me to **hold onto my horses** [≈ be patient] with the shrinking business. With her help, we started to sell books online, and extended our online platform for buyers and sellers to exchange almost anything. We **killed two birds with one stone**! I'm now an IT expert. See, you can **teach an old dog new tricks**!

We've now turned into a **cash cow** business, earning $50 million per year globally. Renei gets the **lion's share** [≈ the major share]. She deserves it. Of course, we've saved enough for our **nest egg** [≈ superannuation]. We are glad that we got out of the **rat race** in today's **dog eat dog** [≈ competitive] world. Now, we are free to travel around the world! For all those years, reading was such a big part of my life. It always will be. My advice, keep reading!

# DAY 301
# WHERE IS HOME?

Home is where the heart is. It could be a place where you've travelled to, a house that you are living in with your loved one, or any other place you are. But today we'll be talking about your hometown, a place where you were born and grew up.

I'm from China. [≈ I'm Chinese. ≈ I'm Chinese by descent.] My hometown is Chaoyang (朝阳), a small city in north-eastern China, Liaoning (辽宁) province.

< I'm proud of my country. Our 9.6 million km² land feeds a population of over 1.4 billion. We have 23 provinces, 5 autonomous regions, 4 municipalities and 2 special administrative regions. We have 56 ethnic groups. Our country has over 5000 years of history. Our ancestors invented papermaking, printing, gunpowder and the compass. Our people are diligent and brave. >

< In English, the way to write an address is from street to city to province or state to country, which is the opposite to how it's written in China. For example, the address for the Melbourne Immigration Museum is 400 Flinders Street, Melbourne Victoria 3000 Australia. If written in the Chinese way, it would be Australia Victoria Melbourne Flinders Street 400, Zip Code 3000. >

Chaoyang is largely unknown [≈ is unheard of ≈ is off the beaten path ≈ is off the beaten track ≈ isn't largely known]. The population is 3 million.

< If you mention a city with 3 million people, an Aussie would be amazed. It doesn't sound small to them. Australia, the whole country, only had a population of around 26 million in 2020 (Population, n.d.). Over 27 million people were living in Shanghai (上海) in that same year (Shanghai, China Metro Area Population 1950-2021, n.d.). >

My hometown has a rich history [≈ has a great deal of history ≈ is soaked in history ≈ is steeped in history]. Dinosaurs lived in the area billions of years ago. Human beings only started to live there thousands of years ago. It's not a metropolis, like Beijing (北京) or Tianjin (天津), but it has it all – restaurants, shopping malls, schools, etc. The locals there enjoy a peaceful life.

What's your home like? What excites you most about your native city? What's the weather like down there? What would you miss the most if you were not living there anymore?

After answering these questions, you're all set. Let's start a global tour tomorrow!

# CHAPTER 36 - A Global Traveller

## DAY 302
## DOWN UNDER HISTORY AT A GLANCE

Before visiting a country, get to know its history. Let's explore Down Under today.

About 60,000 years ago, the Aboriginal and Torres Strait Islander Peoples [≈ Indigenous Peoples ≈ First Nations Peoples ≈ First Peoples ≈ Traditional Custodians] arrived onto this island. It's believed that the Aboriginal Peoples came from Africa and Torres Strait Islander Peoples are of Melanesian decent, from the islands of the Torres Strait (between the tip of Cape York in Queensland and Papua New Guinea).

< Have you worked out which country we're talking about? Gee, your drawing has indicated it is Australia! Yes, we'll be introducing Australia today, but New Zealand sometimes is also referred to as the land Down Under. The name is self-explanatory, right? Both countries are located in the Southern Hemisphere, below the equator, as are many other countries around the globe. >

After Captain Cook from Britain encountered the island in 1788, the Europeans arrived, and settlers rapidly dominated the land. Colonial life began. Criminals from England were sent here. Port Arthur in Tasmania, remote and isolated, is one of the iconic historical sites where criminals were exiled. There was no way prisoners could escape from there.

< The name 'Australia' was suggested by British explorer Matthew Flinders. It is the abbreviation of a Latin term *Terra Australis Incognita*, meaning 'unknown southern land' with the belief back then the Earth was a sphere and there must have been a land in the south (How Was Australia Named?, n.d.). >

< Please note that the above fact of the origin of Australia name is mentioned only to help increase your knowledge about history Down Under. For us immigrants, we are probably not aware that this content could be sensitive. Why? During the colonial era, the Aboriginal and Torres Strait Islander Peoples suffered a lot. Continue to read through to find out why they suffered. >

In 1850s, the Gold Rush started when gold was discovered in Australia. People travelled to Australia in search of the gold and wealth, often risking their lives to try to make their fortune. These newcomers boosted the population.

Between 1910 and 1970, the children of Aboriginal and Torres Strait Islander Peoples were forcibly removed [≈ taken away ≈ separated ≈ torn apart] from their families as a result of government policies. These kids were forced to adopt white culture and reject their own heritage. They are the stolen generations.

Today, Australia has become a multicultural melting pot with immigrants from all over the world.

< Have you heard the melting pot theory? It started in America where they believed when people from different cultures 'melted' together (like metals melted in a pot), they would create a stronger and cohesive society. What is salad bowl [≈ tossed salad] theory then? >

# DAY 303
# DOWN UNDER EXPLORATION CONTINUES

Let's continue to get to know more about Down Under from four experts.

From a geographer's perspectives, ages ago [≈ forever ago], the Australian landmass drifted [≈ became adrift] from European and Asian lands.

Today, Australia has six states (NSW, VIC, SA, WA, QLD, TAS) and two territories (NT, ACT). Question: Which Australian states are these people from? Sandgropers, crow-eaters, banana-benders, cornstalks, gumsuckers, apple islanders, top-enders and roundabout-abouters.

The country sits 8 to 11 hours ahead of GMT (Greenwich Mean Time). Victoria and NSW have daylight savings starting at 2 am on the first Sunday in October. Here, you need to put your watch forward by 1 hour. The clock changes back at 2 am on the first Sunday in April.

What will a vexillologist tell you? The Australian flag was first flown in 1901. The flag contains three elements: the Union Jack, the Commonwealth Star and the Southern Cross. The Union Jack is also called the British Union Flag. The red cross [+] on the flag represents St George for England. The white saltire [X] is for St Andrew's Scotland while the red saltire symbols Ireland and is called St Patrick's Cross (Union Jack, 2021). The Union Jack represents that Australia is associated with Great Britain.

< 'St' stands for 'saint'. In Christianity, a person who has been very good or holy will be given the title 'saint' by the church after they have died. >

A zoologist will probably let you know that the emu and kangaroo are native Australian animals. Neither of these two animals can move backwards. They are chosen on the Commonwealth Coat of Arms, symbolising Australia is a nation moving forward.

What would an anthropologist say? Melbourne was crowned the most liveable city for 7 consecutive years [≈ 7 years in a row ≈ 7 years running]. Native trees (wattle, eucalypt, kangaroo paws, jacaranda) are planted along the roads. Parrots build nests in trees. Ducks, swans and pecans swim in the lakes. Seagull and sparrow walk around in the parks. Be aware that magpies and seagulls could attack people! Birds may poop on your head. (This happened to me once!) Many people suffer from hay fever in spring due to the high coverage of vegetation.

Now it's time to reveal the answer! Sandgropers, crow-eaters, banana-benders, cornstalks, gumsuckers, apple islanders, top-enders and roundabout-abouters, where do these people come from? In order: they are Western Australians, South Australians, Queenslanders, residents of New South Wales, Victorians, Tasmanians, Northern Territory, and those who inhabit Australian Capital Territory. Did you get them right?

# DAY 304
# A TOUR IN MELBOURNE CBD

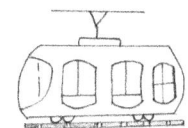

Melbourne is a modern and vibrant city. It is developing fast. [≈ It is a fast-growing city.] More and more high-rise buildings [≈ skyscrapers] have been erected in recent years.

I'll usher [≈ shepherd] you over to the banks of the South Yarra River first. The Yarra River runs for about 242 kms, from Mt Baw to Port Phillip Bay at Newport. It was used primarily for agriculture by early European settlers. The name is derived from Wurundjeri words, meaning 'ever flow' (History of the Yarra River, n.d.).

Not far from you is Crown Casino. On your right, you will see the West Gate Bridge. The bridge is over 2000 metres long. It collapsed in 1970 during construction and 35 workers were killed (West Gate Bridge 50th Anniversary, 2020). It is a vital link between the western suburbs and Melbourne CBD.

< It can take ages for Australians to complete a road or a building project! Take Melbourne airport rail project for example. The construction is expected to commence in late 2022 and be completed in 2029! It's so Aussie style. In China, without exaggeration, we might finish such a project in a much shorter period of time. >

If you look up, you will notice one of the highest apartment buildings in Melbourne, Eureka Tower (mentioned in **Day 113**). In a few minutes, we will be passing a bridge, and South Wharf DFO is just a minute away. DFO is the abbreviation for direct factory outlet. You can buy famous brands there at cheap prices.

Now let's hop on the Melbourne Yarra Heritage Tram Route 35 [≈ board the City Circle Tram ≈ catch the free tourist tram ≈ get on the free of charge service tram ≈ take the zero-fare tourist tram]. The route runs in two directions, clockwise and anticlockwise. There is informative recorded audio commentary about each stop as the tram moves about. The next stop is Parliament Station. Let's hop off here [≈ get off here ≈ alight here ≈ step out of the tram here].

< If you get off a ship or aircraft, you can use the verb 'disembark'. For example, let's disembark at Docklands Harbour. >

For other tram routes in Melbourne, you need a valid myki card to board unless you are in the free tram zone (on many tram lines in the inner city). You can top up a myki at 7-Eleven stores, train stations or tram stops. Anyway, on your right, there's Parliament House. When the Victorian Parliament is not sitting, tours are available (and free). Let's go inside to visit this landmark architecture…

# CHAPTER 36 - A Global Traveller

## DAY 305
## A TOUR IN MELBOURNE CBD (CONTINUED)

Our tour today starts at Melbourne Central. This shopping centre is located in the centre of the city. [≈ It is situated in the city centre. ≈ It sits in the heart of city. ≈ It is in the commercial hub. ≈ It is in the CBD.] The giant gold fob watch [≈ pocket watch] inside has a show on the hour, playing 'Waltzing Matilda'.

The State Library Victoria is a stone's throw away [≈ a short distance ≈ within walking distance ≈ nearby ≈ close by ≈ on your doorstep ≈ down the road ≈ across the road ≈ in close proximity ≈ around the corner ≈ not that far].

< If the distance is long, you can say 'It's far away. [≈ It's a million miles away.]' >

Between Melbourne Central and State Library Victoria is Swanston Street. Let's walk along this main street towards Flinders Street Station. We'll first pass by the Emporium, a modern shopping centre, which adjoins to [≈ is beside ≈ sits alongside ≈ is next to] Melbourne Central.

Further down, you can see Chinatown on your left, down Little Bourke Street. Chinatown dates back to the 1850s where Chinese immigrants came to Victoria during the gold rush. Lodging houses were built in the area, providing convenience for the Chinese community. In 1901, the 'White Australia Policy' restricted immigration and caused a decline in Chinatown's businesses (About Chinatown, n.d.). Many Chinese and Asian restaurants are now clustered around Little Bourke Street. The modern dim sim recipe was actually invented and developed here in 1945 by William Wing Young (Dim Sim, 2021). There is a Chinese museum here too, which tells the history of Chinese migration in Melbourne.

< A 'dim sim' (dubbed as 'dimmy') is steamed or deep-fried dumplings with a thick skin and filled with minced meat, cabbage and other ingredients. >

Continuing on, we'll arrive at Bourke Street, a busy [≈ bustling] shopping strip. You can get everything here. It has it all: graffiti, fashion, the Royal Arcade, restaurants and cafés – you name it. Art performers also love the area. While immersing yourself here, I encourage you to dig into your pockets for a little money for the buskers, even just a few cents.

Collins Street, a luxury brand street, is just over in the next block. Anyway, I hope you've enjoyed the tour.

# DAY 306
# PLACES TO GO IN VICTORIA AND BEYOND

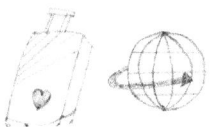

Living in Victoria is such a blessing. Drive along the Great Ocean Road to the Twelve Apostles, go to the Mornington Peninsula for hot springs, take the ferry from Queenscliff to Sorrento for stunning sea views, complete the 1000 steps in the Dandenong Ranges, head to white soft sand at Squeaky Beach, seek wildlife at the Grampians National Park…

Beyond Victoria, you've got Kangaroo Island in SA, Cradle Mountain in TAS, Uluru [≈ Ayers Rock] in NT, Darling Harbour in NSW, Lake Burley Griffin in ACT, the Pinnacles Desert in WA…

< When planning a trip in Australia, it's best to have yourself and the car insured while on the trip. Why? With travel insurance, you won't have to pay out of your own pocket for any sky-high bills when calling an ambulance for an emergency, or medical expenses for unexpected incident. Also, in Australia, it could cost up to thousands to repair a car [≈ do the bodywork]. With car rental insurance, you only need to pay the excess amount and the insurer will pay the rest. >

Travelling is a real eye-opener [≈ opens your eyes ≈ blows your mind ≈ broadens your horizons ≈ expands your outlook ≈ widens your perspective]. It is a life-enriching experience. [≈ It enriches your life. ≈ It adds to your life experience.]

There are 195 sovereign states or nations in the world today that are officially recognised by the United Nations (14 countries in Oceania, 44 in Europe, 48 in Asia, 54 in Africa, 23 in Northern America, and 12 in South America) (All Around the World How Many Countries Are There in the World?, 2021).

Are you hankering for around-the-world trips? I encourage you to. I always have itchy feet. I finally started to plan a global trip in 2020. However, COVID-19 hit, and international travel was put on pause. So a lesson learnt from me: if you want to do something, do it as soon as you can. Don't wait.

We are fortunate enough that we can do virtual trips around the seven continents of the world. So let's go out, escape from the everyday life [≈ break free from the norm], and feel the world over next 7 days!

# DAY 307
## GOING TO OCEANIA

Oceania consists of thousands of islands. It is the smallest continent in the world by land area (with Australia being part of Oceania and often referred to as the continent). Kiritimati Island is host to [≈ is home to] the world's largest atoll. Papua New Guinea is the country that has the world's highest number of languages – over 800. Nauru is the world's smallest island nation without an official capital.

We've toured around Australia in last few days, so let's put a foot in some other countries that belong to Oceania.

**New Zealand**
New Zealanders call themselves Kiwis.

< The name 'kiwi' comes from the little flightless bird from New Zealand. New Zealand's indigenous Māori people have always had a great respect for the kiwi bird [≈ held the kiwi bird in high regard] (New Zealand People, n.d.). >

Come to the Remarkables ski field in Queenstown to spend time in the snow and have some skiing lessons.

**Fiji**
Looking for picture perfect mesmerising beaches and sea views? Fiji is best known for [≈ boasts] its tropical islands, Viti Levu, Vanua Levu, Wakaya Island… it's quite a roll call.

**Kiribati**
Capitan James Cook found Christmas Island (also known as Kiritimati) on Christmas Eve. You'll be amazed by watching red land crabs migrate from the forests to the coast in late October and November.

**Samoa**
How about delving into authentic Samoan foods (Oka, Panipopo, Panikeke, Sapasui, Palusami), while exploring Polynesian culture (dance, music and even tattoo ceremony) and discovering natural wonders (beautiful beaches, caves and wildlife)?

**Tonga**
The Vava'u islands are calm and peaceful. The waters are crystal clear [≈ are translucent ≈ resemble cut glass]. Walking on the powdered soft white beach, there's only you and the world.

**Tuvalu**
On Fongafale islet, you'll see WWII relics. Hire a motorcycle to travel around the islet.

**Tahiti**
Hop on board on a Bora Bora romantic cruise, swim and snorkel under the green and emerald ocean with sharks and stingrays. It's a true paradise.

# DAY 308
## TAKING A TRIP TO EUROPE

Europe, the second smallest continent in the world, is described as the 'peninsula of peninsulas'. It has the smallest [≈ tiddliest] country in the world, Vatican City, which is only 0.49 km² in size. European explorers and navigators discovered much of the 'New World', and they became settlers of many of these countries, bringing western culture with them. We'll be visiting seven famous [≈ iconic] landmarks across Europe today. Let's go!

**Moscow, Russia**
St Basil's Cathedral is one of the not-to-be-missed icons. You'll feel blessed standing in front of this Russian architecture: the colours, patterns and shapes are all eye-catching.

**Barcelona, Spain**
La Sagrada Familia ('Basilica of the Holy Family') is a magnificent temple. It was initially designed to be a simple Roman Catholic church, but was redesigned by architect Antoni Gaudi a year later. The foundation stone was laid in 1882 but construction is still in progress and due for completion in 2026.

**Bavaria, Germany**
Neuschwanstein Castle, built in the 19th century, is a fairytale style palace nested on a hilltop. The castle inspired some of the designs in the Disney movie *Sleeping Beauty*.

**Rome, Italy**
The Colosseum, a large [≈ an enormous] amphitheatre, was built between 72 and 80 AD to hold entertainment for the Roman people.

**Paris, France**
Built in 1889 to commemorate 100 years of the French Revolution [≈ celebrate the French Revolution's centennial], the Eiffel Tower wins rave reviews for its modern artistic design.

**Athens, Greece**
The Parthenon, an old temple, sitting on the Acropolis hill, was completed in 438 BC. 'Acropolis' in Greek means 'highest point'.

**Wiltshire, England**
The prehistoric monument Stonehenge is massive. It's believed this stone circle was constructed between 3000 and 2000 BC. The stones attract hundreds of thousands of tourists each year.

< AD stands for 'anno domini' in Latin, meaning 'in the year of the Lord', which refers to the birth of Jesus Christ. BC stands for 'before Christ'. BCE (Before Common Era) and CE (Common Era) have been suggested to replace BC and AD respectively in the modern world (BC and AD, BCE and CE: What's the Difference?, 2017). >

# DAY 309
## TRAVELLING IN ASIA

Asia is the world's largest continent. It has Earth's highest mountain, Mount Everest; the largest lake, the Caspian Sea; the tallest building, Burj Khalifa. The Asian population is roughly 60% of the entire world's population (Asia Population, n.d.). So don't be surprised if there are people everywhere [≈ here and there] when you visit the countries on this continent.

**Beijing, China**
The Great Wall is a must visit. He who has never been to the Great Wall is not a true man (Chinese saying: 不到长城非好汉).

**Nara, Japan**
Mount Yoshino for the cherry blossom in the spring is worth visiting.

**Bangkok, Thailand**
The Grand Palace, the home of the Thai king, is spectacular.

**Ha Long City, Vietnam**
Ha Long Bay, dotted with over a thousand limestone islands, is a nature wonder.

**Seoul, South Korea**
No trip to Seoul is complete without visiting Bukchon Hanok Village, featuring traditional Korean architecture.

**Ifugao, The Philippines**
The Banaue Rice Terraces, built a thousand years ago, are magnificent.

**Mondulkiri, Cambodia**
Come here to bathe and feed the majestic beasts – the elephants. Welcome to the Elephant Valley Project!

**Singapore**
The gardens by the bay, a futuristic botanic garden, are breathtaking.

**Langkawi, Malaysia**
Langkawi Island is a beautiful archipelago. Head to Pulau Beras Basah for sandy beaches, azure blue water and palm trees.

**Mumbai, India**
The Gateway of India, a starting point for visiting Mumbai, is a monument built to commemorate the landing of King George V and Queen Marry in 1911.

**Dubai, United Arab Emirates**
Souks are part of Dubai's history and culture, which is one of the big draws [≈ a draw card] here. At Deira, you can shop for gold, spice, perfume and textiles! Do not miss out! [≈ Do not overlook it!]

**Bali, Indonesia**
Tanah Lot Temple is built on a massive rock in the sea. Surrounded by the waves, it's prefect to walk around during sunset.

# DAY 310
## JETTING AWAY TO AFRICA

Africa, the world's second largest continent, is the 'cradle of humankind' where human beings lived about 3.5 million years ago (Cradle of Humankind, 2021). What are three world facts about Africa?

- The Nile River is the longest river in the world.
- The Sahara is the largest hot desert in the world.
- The Great Rift Valley is the longest rift in the world.

**Cape Town, South Africa**
The Victoria and Alfred Waterfront has a lot to offer [≈ has plenty on offer]: shopping malls, restaurants and bars, food markets, views of the harbour and Table Mountain, and more!

**Giza, Egypt**
Come along on a camel ride for the ancient architectural marvel, the Pyramids of Giza and the Great Sphinx of Giza.

**Coast Province, Kenya**
Let's go on a safari at Tsavo East National Park! It's home to large mammals: dust-red elephants, lions, buffalos, rhinos and leopards.

**Mara & Simiyu Regions, Tanzania**
The Serengeti National Park should be at the top of your travel list. It offers classic African scenery and unprecedented natural beauty. If you come around the Serengeti Great Migration season, you can watch wildlife (wildebeests, gazelles and zebras) making their journey to Kenya's Masai Mara Reserve.

**Mauritius Island, Mauritius**
You'll absolutely fall in love with Mauritius Island, surrounded by turquoise blue water and lush rainforests. It's a dream getaway destination [≈ dream escape].

**Merzouga, Morocco**
The Sahara Desert is reputedly scorching [≈ super hot]. Come along and immerse yourself in the gorgeous golden sand dunes.

**Kilimanjaro Region, Tanzania**
Mount Kilimanjaro is the highest [≈ tallest] mountain in Africa. It's one of the Seven Summits. It's also a snow-capped volcano. Make sure you're physically fit if you want the challenge of trekking to the Uhuru Peak (which is 5898 metres above sea level). Stay safe and healthy!

# DAY 311
# FLYING TO NORTH AMERICA

North America is the world's third largest continent in size. It has the world's largest island (that is not a continent), Greenland; the world's longest highway at the length of 30,000 km – the Pan American Highway; and the world's longest known cave, Mammoth Cave in Kentucky.

Let's make our way to North America now!

**New York City, United States of America [≈ USA]**
The Statue of Liberty [≈ Liberty Enlightening the World] is a national monument, sculptured by French sculptor Frédéric Auguste Bartholdi. It was given by France as a gift to honour the relationships between the two countries. It is iconic [≈ a landmark ≈ an iconic attraction] to the city.

**Viñales, Cuba**
Go to Viñales National Park to get a hands-on experience seeing how cigars are made by hand and how to smoke like a Cuban.

**Honolulu, Hawaii**
Take a hike to Diamond Head, a dormant volcano, for the best views of Honolulu.

**Mexico City, Mexico**
El Zócalo Public Square should be on your bucket list. It has a giant Mexican flag at the centre, which Mexican soldiers march out to raise up at sunrise and take down at sunset.

**Port-au-Prince, Haiti**
Jalousie, the neighbourhood on the hills behind Petionville, has houses painted with a rainbow of colours. This pretty façade, sadly, hides the kind of poverty that can be found in much of the country.

**Ottawa, Canada**
A maple leaf is on Canada's national flag. Parliament Hill is home to Canada's federal government and is one of the most visited destinations here. An unforgettable spectacle.

**Panama City, Panama**
Panama Viejo, the remaining part of the original Panama City, holds a great deal of charm for visitors. It was founded by Spanish in 1519, and it's known for being the first European settlement on the Pacific coast of the Americas.

**Puntarenas, Costa Rica**
Monteverde is a must-see ecotourism destination for rainforests and for a wide range of flora and fauna.

**Ilulissat Town, Greenland**
Visiting Ilulissat Icefjord is such a spectacular experience. Not only will you see the stunning natural beauty of the glacier, you'll also be inspired to raise concern about global warming.

# DAY 312
# TOURING SOUTH AMERICA

This part of the world has the Andes Mountains, the longest continental mountain range in the world; the Amazon River Basin, which has the largest tropical rainforest in the world; and Salar de Uyuni, the largest salt flat on Earth.

Welcome to the fourth largest continent in the world, South America!

**Rio de Janeiro, Brazil**
The Christ the Redeemer statue is perched on top of [≈ sits atop] Corcovado Mountain. The statue is 30 metres high.

**Medellin, Colombia**
Guatapé Lake artificially made as part of the hydroelectric dam complex. This lake is gorgeous. Admire and climb the huge rock Piedra del Penol nearby to get 360 degree views.

**San Pedro de Atacama, Chile**
Valle de la Luna (Moon Valley) is a moon-like landscape, located in the Atacama Desert. The view of the sunset there is stunning!

**Galápagos, Ecuador**
The Galápagos Islands are home to an array of wildlife: seabirds, giant tortoises, iguanas, lava lizards, sea lions, fishes – you name it.

**Rupununi, Guyana**
At the pond of Karanambu Ranch, spot Guyana's national flower, the world's largest water lily, *Victoria amazonica*.

**Misiones, Argentina**
The highlight of Iguazú National Park is Iguazú Falls, which is the largest waterfall system in the world. It's a natural wonder and just so beautiful.

**Bolivar, Venezuela**
Head out to the world's highest uninterrupted waterfall, Angel Falls, which is a jaw-dropping experience to behold.

**Cuzco, Peru**
Machu Picchu, the symbol of the 15th century Incan Empire, is unmissable.

**Ingavi, Bolivia**
The ruins of Tiwanaku are a must-see historical site. It's a pre-Columbian archaeological site that's also designated as a World Heritage Site by UNESCO.

# DAY 313
# CRUISING TO ANTARCTICA

Our last stop is Antarctica, the end of the Earth [≈ the bottom of the globe]!

Unlike other continents where there are countless people [≈ a sea of people ≈ a river of people ≈ a ton of people ≈ a flock of people ≈ a mass of people ≈ loads of people ≈ hordes of people ≈ swarms of people], Antarctica is all about vast white wilderness (glaciers, icebergs and wildlife).

What are you waiting for? Ahh! Wait for late spring to come. The best time to visit the coldest and windiest continent is between the Southern Hemisphere's late spring and early autumn (which falls between October and March). Wait. You should also check your wallet. How much do you have to pay [≈ How much does it cost] to travel there? Depending on the package, the ship and days that you'd like to go for, it could vary from roughly AUD $5000 to $40,000 per person.

Are you ready now? Let's board the cruise ship and set out!

While crossing the Drake Passage, you might get seasick. Keep yourself active on the deck by keeping an eye on a variety of seabirds (such as the petrel and albatross) gliding alongside the ship.

< The Drake Passage is about 1000 kilometres wide. It was named after Englishman Francis Drake, who sailed there in 1578. It marks the Antarctic Convergence [≈ meeting point], where the cold polar water collides with the warm seawater from the north, creating powerful eddies (Drake Passage, n.d.). >

Wow! The pristine snow, icebergs and snow-capped mountains are just in front of you. We're reaching the South Shetland Islands. At the Antarctica Peninsula, watch penguins waddling [≈ tottering] and seals resting along the shore. Head to Scotia Sea to witness a solar eclipse [≈ the eclipse of the sun], then visit South Georgia, a bird paradise.

Now it's time to say goodbye to this southernmost continent. As the white wonderland disappears, we've completed the ultimate voyage, with our around-the-world adventure! I hope you've enjoyed the journey with an unforgettable experience.

# DAY 314
## SURVIVAL TOOLKITS

Are you terrible with direction? [≈ Do you have bad sense of directions?] Are you worried that you'll get lost when travelling? Don't panic. I'll give you four tools to help you survive.

First up, the compass. It functions with north at 0°, east 90°, south 180° and west 270°. You can use it to find your way while hiking.

Your second tool: ask a random passer-by for direction, saying, 'Excuse me, how can I get to the Sanctuary Lake shopping centre?' They will direct you if they know how to get there. 'Turn left on the next block. Go straight [≈ Head straight] until the end. Keep going until you see the traffic light, then turn right. As you reach the red brown brick house, you will arrive at your destination. It's just off to the left.'

Your third tool: by looking at the place's name on a map, imagine what it looks like: Parliament **Rd** [≈ **Road**], Church **St** [≈ **Street**], Haze **Dr** [≈ **Drive**], Bickhams **Ct** [≈ **Court**], Central **Blvd** [≈ **Boulevard**], Bayside **Ave** [≈ **Avenue**], Saltwater **Promenade**, Marlin **Crescent**, Flinders **Ln** [≈ **Lane**], Lincoln **Square**, Ocean **Grove**, Nest **Pl** [≈ **Place**].

< A **road** is a place that connects two points. A **street** normally runs from east to west. A **drive** is a private and winding road. A **court** ends with cul de sac [≈ is a dead-end street]. A **boulevard** is a wide road with trees and vegetation along the sides. An **avenue**, normally leading north to south, is a road that has buildings on one or both sides. A **promenade** is a wide road close to the beach. A **crescent** is a street with a curved shape road. A **lane** is a narrow road in the countryside or in a city. A **square** is a wide-open area in a square shape. A **grove** is a street sheltered by thick trees. A **place** is a road or street that has no throughway. Now find out what Eugene **Terr** [≈ **Terrace**], Village **Mews** and Orana **Way** might look like. >

Your fourth tool: Google Maps. With it, you can get directions to anywhere in the world! So you won't get lost at all!

Hopefully you're now pumped to see a city renowned for a rich history and culture, a picturesque island, World Heritage Sites, and the great wonders of the world. Have a map in your head. 'Have a suitcase heart, be ready to travel', as Gabrielle Zevin says. Take footsteps in a new country! Where is your next destination [≈ next go-to destination] going to be?

# DAY 315
## THE PURSUIT OF BEAUTY

Who doesn't like feeling pretty or handsome? Pursuing beauty is the nature of human beings. Now tell me, which parts of your body are you satisfied with? Write down what you're happy with after the examples provided in the table below.

> double-fold eyelids [≈ double eyelids], gorgeous eyes, thick brows, dimples, straight and sharper nose [≈ having a high nose bridge], clean and shiny teeth, pale peachy skin, bright white skin
> 
> ......................................................................................................
> ......................................................................................................

< Overall, Asians like bright white [≈ pale] skin while westerners like tanned skin, believing that tan coloured skin is more attractive and healthier. >

Do you have any insecurities about your appearance? Are you annoyed with any minor physical defects: either something you've had since birth or developed later in the life? Put them down in the below blank areas if there are any.

> dark circles under eyes, wrinkles, bags under eyes, panda eyes, puffiness, crow's feet, pimples, dry lips [≈ chapped lips], moles, freckles, dark spots or blemishes on the skin, a flat nose, small eyes and single-edged eyelid, shot eyelashes, yellow spots on teeth, double chin, dandruff [≈ dry and flaky scalp], a bald head, hunched back, armpit or underarm odour, foot odour or athlete's foot, eye gunk, earwax, boogers
> 
> ......................................................................................................
> ......................................................................................................

< A person who loves popping pimples [≈ squeezing stuff out of pimples] is called a 'popacholic'. Squeezing blackheads or even watching them be popped is so satisfying. It brings pleasure because it releases dopamine, but it could leave a scar and even lead to infection if you're not careful. Do you still want to do it? >

Some people prefer surgery [≈ prefer to go under the knife] to enhance their looks and get a perfectly shaped body through liposuction, facelift, rhinoplasty [≈ nose job], chin implants, or breast enhancement. Be mindful: when plastic surgery goes wrong, it's irreversible. I'm not one for cosmetic surgery. I encourage you to appreciate your unique genes and appearance (review **Day 36 Have Faith in Yourself**). But you can always put in extra effort for your appearance by taking care of your skin, wearing make-up or just dressing up.

# DAY 316
## MORNING SKINCARE ROUTINE

Good morning, English Builder! Time to get out of bed and start your day with a six-step gentle skincare routine. Also, circle or highlight all verbs shown on today's page.

**Step 1: Brush your teeth**

Squirt a small amount of toothpaste on the toothbrush. Open your mouth. Tilt the brush 45 degree angle against the gumline. Gently move back and forth, inside and outside surfaces, upper and lower, for 2 minutes. Once finished, rinse your mouth with water.

< Should you brush your teeth before or after breakfast? Well, the answer is totally up to you, or google to check out the 'correct' answer. But the key word here is to 'brush'. You need to brush your teeth every day. >

**Step 2: Wash your face and neck (L'Occitane Foaming Cleanser)**

Work the cleansing foam with a little water between your hands. Gently massage onto your face and neck with circular movements. Rinse thoroughly.

**Step 3: Apply toner (Chanel Anti-Pollution Invigorating Toner)**

Saturate [≈ Moisten] a cotton pad or a cotton ball with a facial toner. Gently press the pad around your entire face, starting from your T-zone and moving around in an upward and outward motion.

**Step 4: Apply eye cream (Kiehl's Eye Treatment with Avocado)**

Apply a pea-size amount of eye cream onto your ring finger. Gently tap small dots [≈ dot the cream] under your eyes and pat the cream into your skin. Let it absorb for about 30 seconds. [≈ Wait about 30 seconds to let the cream fully absorb.]

**Step 5: Apply serum (Estée Lauder Perfectionist Pro Serum)**

Apply a few pumps [≈ Use several drops] of serum onto your skin. Pat it on and smooth it out gently all over your face and neck. Don't rub it in.

**Step 6: Apply day cream (Clarins Hydra-Essentiel Silky Cream)**

Warm a small amount of [≈ a small dab of] cream between your palms. Then distribute the cream evenly over your face and neck. Massage it in an upwards sweeping motion.

Oh dear! Too much work! Don't rush. Take your time with your skincare routine in the morning. Start your day with a clean face and moisturised [≈ hydrated], radiant, luminous, smooth, glowing skin.

# DAY 317
# WEAR SUBTLE MAKE-UP

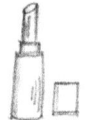

A light application of make-up can help your appearance shine. It can make you more confident! So let's get practical. Select the verbs in the table below and put them down on the blank line of each of the make-up steps. You can use each of the verbs or phrasal verbs twice. Feel free to write down any verbs if your answers differ. Any make-up or skincare products are marked in bold.

| Pop | Rub | Apply | Use | Give | Complete | Put on | Dust with | Fill in |

The process starts:
- .................. the morning skincare routine I showed you yesterday, cleaning [≈ washing] your face and neck, and applying **day cream**.
- .................. **sunscreen** over your face to keep off the UV lights.
- .................. a small amount of **primer** on your finger, and apply a thin base on your face, which helps make your cosmetics last longer.
- .................. **concealer** under the eyes, or on any redness or flaws on the skin or where needed before blending it in.
- .................. your fingers, a sponge or a brush to apply **liquid foundation** all over your face. It can even out your skin tone.
- .................. **loose powder** or **pressed powder** by using a **brush** to set the foundation.
- .................. **eyeliner** to create and enhance the shape and colour of your eyes.
- .................. **eye shadow**.
- .................. your brows by using either a **brow gel**, **pencil**, **powder** or **pomade**. A **Q-tip** [≈ **cotton tip**] can help to blend out if needed.
- .................. both of your upper and lower eyelashes a bit of curl by using **eyelash curler**.
- .................. **mascara**.
- .................. **lipstick** onto the lips to add colour. Finish by dabbing a pinch of **blush** along the cheekbones.

< 'SPF' marked on a sunscreen product stands for 'sun protection factor'. SPF50 means it can block [≈ filter out] 98% of UVB rays (About SPF50+ Sunscreen, n.d.). Exposure to the sun's UV (ultraviolet) rays can make your skin darker [≈ darken your skin]. >

Phew! The morning make-up process ends.

Now you are all set for the day. Carry a **toilet bag** [≈ **cosmetic case** ≈ **make-up bag**] because you might need to touch up your foundation during the day. When you're back home, the very first thing to do is to use your **make-up remover** to take off your make-up after a long day. Today's topic is more or less for girls. But boys, you now understand why your girlfriend spends a fair bit of time in the bathroom every morning, right?

# DAY 318
## NIGHT-TIME ROUTINE

After a long day's work, you get home exhausted. You postpone night-time skincare just before bedtime. You might not even bother washing your face.

Oh no! Night-time skincare is essential to rejuvenate your skin. Suggested below is some skincare routine you could undertake as soon as you hit home. You've learnt how to use some skincare products for a morning routine. Now see if you can complete Step 4 to Step 7 in the table below.

| Step | Action | Skincare product | How to use |
|---|---|---|---|
| Step 1 | Remove make-up | SKII Facial Treatment Cleansing Oil | Dispense 1–2 pumps of the cleansing oil onto your palms. Gently massage over your face with circular movements. Be gentle on your eye areas. Emulsify the oil by adding warm water. Massage again and rinse thoroughly with water. Pat skin dry with facial tissues. |
| Step 2 | Exfoliate | Dior Le Sucre De Gommage Exfoliation | Exfoliate two or three times a week. Apply the product evenly to your cleansed face and lips. Avoid eye areas. Let it sit for a minute before exfoliating your skin using circular motions. Rinse off with tepid water and gently dry with a soft cloth. |
| Step 3 | Apply face mask | La Prairie Cellular Hydralift Firming Mask | Use a face mask twice weekly. Use your paintbrush or your finger to spread the mask generously over your face, avoiding the immediate eye and lip areas. Rinse thoroughly with lukewarm water after a couple of minutes and pat dry. |
| Step 4 | Use lotion | Clinique Moisture Surge Hydrating Lotion | |
| Step 5 | Put on eye cream | La Mer The Lifting Eye Serum | |
| Step 6 | Apply serums | Lancôme Anti-Ageing Advanced Genifique | |
| Step 7 | Apply a night cream or moisturiser | Jurlique Nutri-Define Supreme Restorative Light Cream | |

Whew! Again, quite a lot of hard work!

Please don't be slack! Make this into your nightly routine to keep your skin plump and baby-soft, especially after a good night's sleep. Who doesn't like waking up with nourished skin?

# DAY 319
# IT'S NOT JUST ABOUT SKINCARE

You have probably noticed that a wide range of skincare brands have been recommended over the last three days. In the beauty section of a shopping store, these particular brands are often demonstrated.

Disclaimer: I'm not making any profits by mentioning skincare and beauty brands and their products. But I'd be glad if they paid me a commission [≈ kickback]! It's just a joke! [≈ I'm kidding!]

I'm not suggesting that you should include all these different brands into your skincare list. You need to know your skin type to choose the right products. Is your skin seasonally dry? Is it oily? Is it a combination of these? Is it sensitive? Is it acne-prone? Or is it normal?

To make yourself look more attractive, you also need to find the right hairstyle (short hair, straight layered hair, a bob, beach-wave, textured braid, bangs, etc.) and the right colour through trial and error.

What is your natural hair colour?

| Blonde | Fair-haired | Brunette | Ginger red | Chestnut brown |
|--------|-------------|----------|------------|----------------|
| Copper | Titian | Natural black | Grey and white | Light brown |

At home, you can use a ceramic curler or hair straightener [≈ straightening iron] to create a hairstyle that you like.

Don't forget to maintain your personal hygiene. Clean your teeth thoroughly, day and night [≈ at least twice a day]. Wash your hands after using the toilet. Wash your hair regularly. Put on body lotion after a shower. Apply deodorant to your armpits. Put on some perfume or aftershave. Clip [≈ Cut or trim] your nails.

< The tool that's used to clip your nails is called a nail clipper or nail scissors. You could have a round-blade clipper or a compound lever clipper. Do you know what hangnail is? >

To upgrade your beauty routine to the next level, you could get yourself a manicure and a pedicure.

# DAY 320
# EXAMINE YOUR WARDROBE

Is your wardrobe [≈ closet ≈ dressing room] filled with clothes but you still feel like you have nothing to wear? Are you dreaming of a wardrobe full of fashionable clothing that also meshes with your personality? It's not that hard to do.

Let's check out what you've got in your wardrobe. Highlight any of the below items that you don't have in your collection.

> jackets, coats, outerwear, dresses, jeans, tops, T-shirts, sleepwear [≈ pyjamas ≈ nighties ≈ nightclothes], activewear [≈ sportswear ≈ athletic clothing ≈ tracksuit], knitwear [≈ sweatshirt], baggy attire [≈ loose [≈ shapeless ≈ loose-fitting ≈ oversized] clothes], skirts, pants, jumpers, hoodies, loungewear, jumpsuits, shorts, polos, cardigans, suits, blazers, blouses, thermals, leggings, denims

Now, describe each of your clothes items by adding some of the adjectives below. I'll give you some clues.

What colours are your clothes?

| Black | Light grey | Violet | Beige | Pink | Navy |
|---|---|---|---|---|---|
| Off-white | Mustard | Olive | Turquoise | Vibrant lemon | Plum |

What types of materials are your outfits made from?

| Flannel | Acrylic | Polyester | Silk | Cotton | Polyfill |
|---|---|---|---|---|---|
| Rayon | Nylon | Hemp | Linen | Fur | Boucle |

Were your clothes expensive? [≈ Were they pricey? ≈ Did they cost an arm and a leg?] Or were they dirt cheap [≈ were they a snip ≈ were they a dozen a dime]?

Has the attire become outdated [≈ gone out of the date ≈ gone out of the style]? Or is it still trendy?

You could also tackle this from a style angle. Let me know your clothes by type. For example, what types of jeans do you have? You might have low-raise jeans, mid-waisted skinny jeans, high-rise cigarette jeans, boyfriend jeans, wide-leg jeans, straight-leg jeans, cropped jeans, cut-up jeans, ankle fray jeans, relaxed jeans, bootcut jeans…

# DAY 321
## SHOES, BAGS AND ACCESSORIES

It's time for another activity. Go to wherever you store your bags, shoes and accessories at home and tick any of the below items that you have.

**Bags:** tote bag, pouch, overnight bag, sling bag, minaudiere, cross body bag, athletic bag, backpack, weekend bag, muff, handbag, clutch bag, fanny pack, doctor's bag, messenger bag, satchel, wristlet, bucket bag, envelope bag.

< A doctor's bag is also known as a Gladstone bag. It was named after a UK prime minister, William Ewart Gladstone, who liked carrying it because of its lightweight nature. Soon doctors started to use such bags to carry equipment when visiting patients (All You Need to Know About Leather Doctor's Bags, n.d.). >

**Shoes [≈ Footwear]:** crocs, ankle boots, army boots, sandals, flats, flip-flops, galoshes, earth shoes, heels, court shoes, sneakers, monks, loafers, slippers.

< Why are they called flip-flops? Imagine: when you're walking while wearing flip-flops, do the rubber material making a slapping ('flip-flop, flip-flop') sound against the ground? This is where the name came from! Aussies call flip-flops thongs. >

**Accessories:** necklace, hat, sockette, sunglasses, hair clips, scrunchie, bracelet, anklet, earrings, belt, gloves, jewellery, hair tie, keyring, kaftan, scarf.

< The scrunchie was invented by Rommy Revson, a nightclub singer and pianist. She created it in 1986 because she wanted to have a gentler alternative to metal hair ties (Granero, 2019). >

For every item that you've ticked, describe each of them. I'll give you an example. I love my pink-ish Furla's mini-cross body bag. The bag features a metal chain strap and has a small inner pocket. I have a pair of soft leather ankle boots from Tony Blanco. This features squared toes and block heels and is very comfy to wear. I also have a Swarovski necklace with two entwined hearts. It's so beautiful and sparkly... Be quick, it's your turn.

You really don't have to go for luxury brands if you have a limited budget. You can always find something affordable [≈ at a fair price ≈ that is labelled at a reasonable price ≈ that doesn't break your bank] that also suits you and makes you look fantastic. Knockoff [≈ Shanzhai (山寨)] products are never a smart choice. Please think twice before buying.

< 'Shanzhai' is a Cantonese term referring to counterfeit consumer goods. The phenomenon of manufacturing and selling such products exists in China. You can get clothes, bags or other items looking quite similar to luxury fashion brand (such as Louis Vuitton, Chanel and Gucci) at a relatively low price. In Australia, you won't find any shop that sells such products similar to the big brand names. This is the infringement of trademark, and the regulations are tight. >

# DAY 322
## INVEST IN YOUR WARDROBE

Every day before work, you find yourself struggling with what to put on, even if your wardrobe is already full. You wonder how your friends and workmates always know how to wear the right clothes to make them look stunning. You hope that you can afford as many as stylish clothes, shoes and bags as they can. Of course, you can.

The key here is to create a 'capsule' wardrobe, which is a collection of a few essential items that don't readily go out of fashion, such as skirts, dresses, trousers and coats. These items can be mixed and matched easily. And they can last a lifetime.

Before doing this, first clean up your closet.

Throw away clothes that:
- have stains.
- have holes or are damaged beyond repair.
- don't fit you anymore, or are too tight or too large or simply ill-fitting.
- you don't imagine you would wear anymore (not even once).

Get rid of pairs of shoes or handbags that:
- are dorky and you haven't worn or carried once.
- are uncomfortable to wear or not functional to put stuff in.
- have scuffed or scratched leather and can't be repaired anymore.

Or, if possible, give any clothes a second life by donating them, or repurposing them into kitchen rags. As you remove them from your collection, you will realise you probably wasted a lot of money on unnecessary items. So keep educating yourself on fashion and dress style.

< What are other ways to give a second life to your old clothes? Write down your sparkling ideas here:

..................................................................................................................................

.............................................................................................................................. >

Don't throw out your good quality items just because they've gone out of fashion. They probably won't be dated too much. You might even buck the trend [≈ be a throwback ≈ be the fad] a decade afterwards.

You now have room for new fashion pieces, maybe even some classics. So, go get them! Get what you love to wear, not just anything that's just *alright*, or get anything for the sake of a sale! Don't forget to peel off the price tags from the bottom of the heels or on your clothes!

# DAY 323
# WEAR TO IMPRESS

In this chapter, we've talked enough about beauty and fashion. You really don't have to jump [≈ climb ≈ get ≈ leap] on the bandwagon to become a hipster, a trendsetter, or chic.

< The phrase 'jump on the bandwagon' means that you join others for a popular activity. The word 'bandwagon' is simply the name for the wagon that carried a circus band. It was a term coined by Phineas T Barnum, a circus owner (Jump on the Bandwagon, n.d.). It's said the phrase was first used in 1848 when Dan Rice, a famous clown used his circus bandwagon to attract attention for a political campaign (Jump on the Bandwagon, n.d.). >

You are a unique individual, different from anyone else. Dress in your signature style with your own confidence. Get disciplined in your wearing habits.

Keep your outfits pristine. Wearing dirty clothes is not a good look. Wearing shirts inside out, backwards [≈ front to back] is not a good fashion choice either.

Here are a few trendy or easy outfit ideas:

- Half tuck a T-shirt into jeans or tie a knot on your shirt and throw on a pair of elegant heels. Add a motorcycle jacket.
- Roll your sleeves [≈ Cuff your sleeves] up your arm.
- Wear at least one statement accessory, whether that's putting on a hat, giving your trench coat a belt, adding some jewellery (earrings, necklace) or sunglasses, or applying lipstick in a bright colour.
- Add a silk neck or head scarf to make a huge [≈ a world of] difference to how you look.
- Go bold [≈ Be innovative] with colours. But your shoes match [≈ coordinate with] your clothes.
- Go monochrome [≈ one colour]!
- Wear black – it's a simple look, but it's a classic look.

# DAY 324
## LET'S TALK ABOUT SPORT

Do you love watching or taking part in sports? Can you distinguish any of the following as summer sports and winter sports in the Olympic Games from the list below?

| Archery | Judo | Athletics | Ice hockey | Speed skating |
| --- | --- | --- | --- | --- |
| Trampoline | Fencing | Gymnastics | Canoe slalom | Wrestling freestyle |
| Shooting | Diving | Equestrian | Freestyle skiing | Synchronised swimming |
| Luge | Triathlon | Taekwondo | Ski jumping | Nordic combined |

If you are a huge sports fan, what's your favourite sport, and why?

Table tennis is my jam. I trained seriously for a while many years ago. [≈ I was a semi-professional player.] I love table tennis because there are so many ways to play the little ping-pong ball (chop, spin, push). Different types of rubber on the bats – short-pimpled rubber and sandwich rubber – can also make the ball behave differently. They say that table tennis is like a mix of martial arts and Chinese chess. You have to think two or three steps ahead of your opponent/s. Because of table tennis, I've met many enthusiastic players, and we've become great friends along the way. I just love it!

There are other ball sports (and related sports), such as:

| Water polo | Handball | Beach volleyball | Shot-put | Basketball |
| --- | --- | --- | --- | --- |
| Billiards [≈ Pool] | Snooker | Ice hockey | Hockey | Badminton |
| Gateball [≈ Croquet] | Bowling | Volleyball | Netball | Golf |
| Foosball [≈ Table football] | Football | Hurling | Squash | Softball |

Wait a minute! The object in hockey and ice hockey games is not a ball. It's called a puck. Similarly, with badminton, the object is called a shuttlecock.

In China, table tennis, badminton, football, volleyball and basketball are extremely popular sports. They're often broadcast live on TV. We grow up playing these fun sports. We don't get too much of a chance to watch or partake in sports like golf, rugby or cricket favoured by western countries.

If you're in Australia for long, gaining some knowledge in such sports won't hurt [≈ won't be harmful]. You'll be able to talk their game and use their language. Hopefully you'll have some more engaging conversations!

I benefit a lot from playing sport. Participating in a social tennis group gives me the chance to make friends with different backgrounds playing tennis, all the while improving my tennis skills – tennis can be such a physically demanding sport sometimes! I also run weekly with a bunch of lovely people in a local running club. A lot of them have done many half marathons, marathons, ironman races and triathlons – what a commitment!

Let's decode a few sports that Aussies love over the next few days and become part of the sports culture here!

# DAY 325
## FORMULA ONE RACING

Mercedes, Red Bull, McLaren, Aston Martin, Alpine, Ferrari, Alfa Romeo, AlphaTauri, Hass, Williams… It's time to raise the curtain. Buckle up! Cars can reach speeds of up to 280 km/h. [≈ The cars could roar past at 280 km/h.]

< To 'raise the curtain' or 'lift the curtain' means to begin something, or to reveal the truth. In today's context, it means to begin a race in Formula One (F1)! >

Formula One is an international form of motor racing. The races are called Grand Prix. A Grand Prix is a series of races for racing cars. The Grand Prix starts in Australia (at Albert Park in Melbourne) in March and ends in Abu Dhabi in November each year. The Australia Grand Prix is currently under contract to host Formula One until 2023 (Balfour, 2019).

The 'formula' in the name refers to a set of rules with which all participants and cars must comply. For example, helmets are compulsory for driver safety. A head and neck support (HANS) device is attached to the seatbelt in the cockpit. The 107% rule means that a driver can't participate in a race if they exceed 107% of the fastest time in the first phase of qualifying session. F1 cars were previously banned from refuelling during the race. This rule was reintroduced in 2010. Penalties will be given out for jumping the start, causing collisions, blocking a rival driver, etc.

Different colour flags are waved to send out messages to drivers. Below are some examples:

| Racing flag | Message |
| --- | --- |
| Green | Race can resume. |
| Red | Session has been stopped or suspended. |
| White | There's a slow-moving car ahead. |
| Single waved yellow | Hazard on the track and overtaking is prohibited. |
| Double waved yellow | Marshals are working on or near to the track. |
| Yellow and red striped | There's a slippery track ahead. |
| Black with orange circle in the middle | The car is damaged, and the driver must head to the pit immediately. |

Car racing is a very challenging sport! A driver could lose about 2 to 3 kilograms in a single race! How do they do this while sitting down the whole race? This is due to extreme heat in the cockpit, which could reach 40 to 50 degrees Celsius! Imagine: with several layers of clothing and other gear head to toe, F1 drivers have to consistently battle extreme dehydration and the heat for the entire race. Every racer gets weighted pre-racing and post-racing.

A home straight! Max Verstappen is the winner! Congratulations! Now it's podium time. Let's call it a day!

< The 'home straight' is the final straight stage of the racecourse. In today's context, it also refers to the last part of today's activity. >

# DAY 326
# TENNIS

Tennis is one of the most popular sports in Australia. The Australian Open, one of the Grand Slam tennis tournaments, is the highlight. The prize is massive. For the 2020 Australian Open, the purse was AUD $71,000,000, out of which the champion [≈ the titleholder ≈ the grand finalist] received AUD $4,120,000 (Record $71 Million in Prize Money for Australian Open 2020, 2019).

The Australian Open is held at Melbourne Park normally in January each year. A ground pass ticket sold for $64 in 2020, for which you can watch games in any outside courts for the entire day. Don't wait until the last minute to buy tickets for the semi-finals and finals held at Rod Laver Arena or Margaret Court Arena. They are sold out super quick.

Let's go watch a game between ageless veteran [≈ seasoned player] Roger Federer and unseeded Australian player John Millman. The toss of a coin decides who serves first. The game starts. The court goes quiet. No noises or flashlights are allowed while players are in the game. You are not allowed to enter the court or leave until there's a short break. Federer starts with an ace! Fifteen–love (15–0).

< Why is zero points called 'love'? One of the theories is that 'love' arose from the French word *l'oeuf* (egg), because zero looks like [≈ resembles] an egg (Tennis "Love" and the Love of Tennis, n.d.). >

It's a let. First serve. John pushes up the line. What a sweet play. He puts in an excellent point. But Federer returns with a great serve… It's a game. A strong hold [≈ An easy hold ≈ A big hold] for Federer.

< When a 'let' is called in tennis, the players shall replay the point. Most of time, a let is called when a player is serving, and the ball touches the net but still lands on the correct serve box of their opponent. But it could also be called when a game is interrupted. >

< A tennis match consists of points, games and sets. To win a game, you must win at least four points. To win a set, you must win at least six games. >

Both players are now reset for a new game. The serve was weak. First serve. Second serve. Double fault. Mr Federer challenging the ball on the left hand of the service line. It's in. John missed it! Deuce. Advantage to Roger. The ball-kid just caught the ball! Fifth set. Roger's upped his game. Look at that smash! What a volley! The end is near. It's a super tie-break. Out! It's long. Come on, Roger, come on! It's coming from the crowd. Now match point. Federer finds a way! The Swiss goes into the fourth round of the Australian Open 2020!

What a thriller! The audience all stands up, clapping as John leaves the court. Now here's the top-player [≈ the great legend ≈ the classy player ≈ the big-time player] himself. Listen to Roger's after-match interview…

# CHAPTER 38 - A Sports Enthusiast

# DAY 327
## GOLF

In China, small cities like my hometown don't have a golf course. In Australia, golf courses are easily accessible, and the price is more reasonable.

As a golf 'dummy' [≈ a new golfer], I enrolled in a basic group clinic at Albert Park, Melbourne in 2018. So come with me and my coach Kevin to the driving range to have a swing [≈ have a hit of golf].

< A driving range is a big area for golfers to practise their golfing strokes. There are tap-and-go machines where you can get 100 golf balls for about $20. Once you've collected golf balls in a bucket, walk to a driving range bay. >

Which is your dominant hand [≈ lead hand]? If you're left-handed, get the right-hand glove, and vice versa. Put it on. Let's first identify the parts of a club. See the below picture. Different driving clubs have different angles.

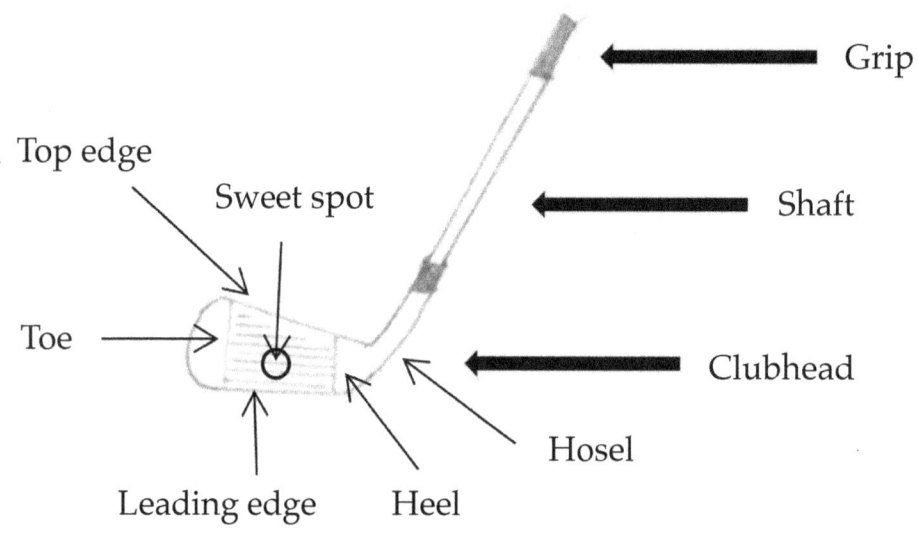

Now lie the ball on the tee. Your grip is crucial. Don't grip [≈ grasp] your club too tightly [≈ firmly]. It won't give you a good shot. Relax a little! Turn the club around the body. Look at the ball all the way through. Hit the ball. Wow! That's a good swing! [≈ That's a perfect shot!]

Obviously, we cannot cover everything in just one page. Jump online to get to know more golfing basics, such as putting, chipping, par, birdie, bogey, fairway, sweet spot, 18 holes, and so on. Let's tee off now.

< To 'tee off' means that you hit the golf ball from the tee towards a hole for the first time each game. In American English, if you 'teed me off', you made me angry and you irritated me. 'To tee off' someone in this situation is an alternative for 'to piss off'. >

# DAY 328
# CRICKET

Below is some information about Australian cricket. Cross out anything that you already know.

- ☐ The popularity of cricket in Australia is the same as the popularity of table tennis in China.

- ☐ The Test Match starts on Boxing Day each year at the MCG (Melbourne Cricket Ground). It's a cricket tournament for two teams played over 5 days. Each team has two innings.

- ☐ A test match is a sporting contest between national representative teams for sports such as cricket, rugby, netball, and so on. Test cricket is the highest level of cricket in the world. Also, popular forms of cricket are 20/20 and 50 overs (aka: One Day International). The Cricket World Cup is played in the 50 overs format.

- ☐ The waiting list for becoming a MCC (Melbourne Cricket Club) member is long. Lots of parents register their kids even before they're born.

- ☐ In 2018, the Australian cricket team was involved in a ball-tampering scandal during the third test match against South Africa in Cape Town. The reputation of Captain Steve Smith and his team was in tatters. It was a dark day for the Australian cricket team. Australia is normally considered a country that likes to win fair and square [≈ win without cheating].

- ☐ 'Ball-tampering' is a term for when the cricket player alters the conditions of the ball illegally, such as through scuffing the ball. The ball could be altered to be faster or to change direction unexpectedly.

- ☐ Is there such a thing as legal ball-tampering? A fielder [≈ fieldsman], one of the players who tries to catch the ball in a game of cricket, can dry the ball with a towel when it is wet, remove any mud under supervision, polish the ball without use of an artificial cleaning substance, or rub the ball against their clothing (Ball Tempering, n.d.).

- ☐ The Ashes is a test cricket series played between England and Australia. The trophy was first crafted in the shape of an ash urn.

- ☐ Ian Chappell, Don Bradman, Ricky Ponting, Michael Clarke, Shane Warne, Steve Smith, Tim Paine are all huge names in cricket. Talk about these big stars with your local friends. Trust me. They have a lot to share on the topic.

< Was the phrase 'win fair and square' a grammatical error? Shouldn't it be 'win fairly and squarely'? >

< Sadly, Shane Warne, one of the finest bowlers in cricket history, died of heart attack at the age of 52 in March 2022. The Great Southern Stand at MCG was renamed as the Shane Warne Stand. *No Spin* is a book that highlights the career and life of this cricket legend. >

# DAY 329
# FOOTY

AFL is short for the Australian Football League. Aussies call the sport 'footy'. This is one of the most popular sports nationally. [≈ This is an Aussie game that most locals love. ≈ Footy is like a religion in Australia.]

The shape of the football is not round like a soccer ball. Instead, it's oval-shaped. When it falls to the ground, the ball can bounce in unexpected directions, making it hard to catch. Eleven players from two teams each play on a field. A game of football can show off the Australian fighting spirit and good teamwork.

Here were the teams that played in the 2021 AFL [≈ that were on the 2021 ladder]. Each club has a city's (or place's) name and the club's moniker.

| Adelaide Crows | Essendon Bombers | Port Adelaide Power |
| Brisbane Lions | Fremantle Dockers | St Kilda Saints |
| Carton Blues | Greater Western Sydney Giants [≈ GWS Giants] | Sydney Swans |
| Gold Coast Suns | Melbourne Demons | West Coast Eagles |
| Richmond Tigers | Collinwood Magpies [≈ the Pies] | Geelong Cats |
| Hawthorn Hawks | North Melbourne Kangaroos | Western Bulldogs |

Which team do you barrack for? [≈ Which team do you cheer for? ≈ Whose side are you on? ≈ Who do you support?] Pick one team to support if you don't have one already.

I barrack for the Tigers. [≈ I'm a Tigers supporter. ≈ The Tigers is my team. ≈ I'm a Tigers fan. ≈ I like Richmond.] We won three premiers in four seasons. The team's colours are yellow and black. Richmond champion Dustin Martin won the Norm Smith Medal in 2020 (which was his third medal). The medal is awarded to the best player on the ground in the Grand Final. The Brownlow Medal is awarded to the fairest and best player in the AFL home-and-away season. This award was created by Charles Brownlow, a former Geelong Football Club footballer. Port Adelaide's Ollie Wines won the Brownlow Medal in 2021. [≈ Ollie Wines from Port Adelaide was the 2021 Brownlow Medallist.] Each year, the winner is announced on the Brownlow Show, which is broadcasted on TV by Channel 7 in Melbourne.

The AFL store has team merchandise, including jerseys, beach towels and thongs. The money made from any purchases with team logos goes to that team. Whenever I have my Tigers cap on, a random stranger might either say 'Go Tigers!' to me or tell me that they're also a big fan of the Tigers!

# DAY 330
## AFL GRAND FINAL – FIRST HALF

Wind back to the 2020 AFL Grand Final. The Tigers versus the Cats!

< Due to the coronavirus outbreak in Melbourne, the Grand Final was moved from the MCG to the Gabba in Brisbane. The attendance was only at 70% due to COVID-19 social distance requirements (Voss, 2020). Normally, it would be a full house [≈ you wouldn't spot any empty seat ≈ all seats would be filled to full capacity] when held at the MCG in Melbourne. >

After singing the Australian National Anthem, toss the coins (heads or tails) to decide who gets the first choice of which end of the field. The game starts!

Just a couple of minutes in, Gary Ablett from the Cats was tackled by Richmond Captain Trent Cotchin. Ablett's shoulder was injured…

< In AFL, a player can tackle the opponent when they have the ball, but they cannot have body contact with the opponent in the back or above the shoulders. >

The ball is out to Patrick Dangerfield. It's a high ball. Dylan Grimes catches it – it's a mark!

< A 'mark' is when the player catches the ball 15 cm above with both hands after it has been kicked by another player but before it has touched the ground. When getting a mark, you can kick from the spot where the ball is caught. This is called free kick. >

What a nice curve kick! Dion from the Tigers kicked the opening goal of the match!

< A goal is worth 6 points. Goals are when the team kicks the ball through the middle goalposts. A behind is only worth 1 point and is when the ball is kicked into the side goalposts, or the football touches a goalpost. >

At the end of first quarter, the Cats lead by one point (14 vs 13). At the end of the second quarter, Geelong dominates the game, leading by 15 points (35 vs 20).

< Each game has four quarters. Normally, the playing time for each quarter is 20 minutes plus additional time-on [≈ extra play time]. The break time for first quarter and third quarter is 6 minutes and half-time is 20 minutes. There's also a 50 second break after a goal is kicked. In 2020, the quarter length was reduced to 16 minutes due to COVID-19. >

# DAY 331
## AFL GRAND FINAL - SECOND HALF

It's so hard to watch the game when the team you support is behind. But do you reckon the Tigers can turn it around in the second half?

The third quarter begins. Go, go, go! Go for it! Tigers! It's a make-or-break [≈ a do-or-die ≈ a sink-or-swim ≈ an all-or-nothing] situation now.

The Tigers are finally on the attack. Jack Riewoldt gets a free kick from 20 metres early on. It's a goal! Jason Castagna kicks another one! The Cats are struggling, but they score a goal! The Tigers return another two goals straight after! The Tigers lead [≈ hit the front] for the first time in the game.

In the fourth quarter, Richmond comes back even stronger! Bring it on, Tigers! The Tigers keep getting goals. The Cats are feeling the pressure. Only 8 minutes away from the end of the game, Richmond is up front by 16 points (60 vs 44)! The Tigers kick 10 of the last 12 goals!

What a sensational [≈ a magnificent ≈ an epic] comeback! Wow, it's never over until it's over [≈ it's not over until the fat lady sings]! This is the charm of sport. You fight until the last second to win the game [≈ seal the win ≈ claim victory]!

The crowd goes nuts! [≈ The onlookers go nuts! ≈ The spectators go nuts!] I jumped and yelled in front of the TV!

The siren ends. Full time. Tigers (Goals 12, Behinds 9, **Points 81**) vs Cats (Goals 7, Behinds 8, **Points 50**). The Tigers team song 'We're From Tigerland' plays…

< I wrote down the full lyrics for the Tigers' song here originally, and also the Australian National Anthem in **Day 297 At the Citizenship Ceremony**, just simply wanting to share these beautiful songs with you in English. I wasn't aware song lyrics were copyrighted unless they were in the public domain or the copyright had expired (like the 'Jingle Bells' song cited in **Day 157 Santa Is Here!** and which was written in 1857), or unless you had permission to use. You can get permission, but often this has a cost involved. Credit to my editor Scott who pointed this out.

What a bummer! But we can take a look at the song titles of some other AFL club teams: Geelong – 'We Are Geelong'; Essendon – 'See the Bombers Fly Up'; Brisbane Lions – 'The Pride of Brisbane Town'; North Melbourne – 'Join in the Chorus'. Which one do you like best? >

Now there's an interview on the grass with some of the players: 'What a game, Dustin!'

Then it's time to lift [≈ hoist] the trophy and celebrate! The Richmond skipper [≈ captain] Trent gives his speech, 'Full credit to Geelong. They challenged us, but credit to our boys. They showed the resilience that we know they can.'

< Why do people call the captain of a team a skipper? It comes from the Dutch word, schipper (literally 'shipper' – a person who is in command of a ship). >

# CHAPTER 38 - A Sports Enthusiast

# DAY 332
# RUGBY

When talking about Rugby in Australia, you should know that there are two versions in total – Rugby League and Rugby Union. The rules between League and Union are similar but there are differences. Even the ball shapes are slightly different. It's said Union is more brutal than League.

The table below shows 16 National Rugby League (NRL) team names. How many of them are named after an animal?

| Melbourne Storm | Sydney Roosters | Gold Coast Titans | Canterbury-Bankstown Bulldogs |
| Newcastle Knights | Brisbane Broncos | New Zealand Warriors | Cronulla-Sutherland Sharks |
| Parramatta Eels | Penrith Panthers | South Sydney Rabbitohs | St. George Illawarra Dragons |
| Wests Tigers | Canberra Raiders | North Queensland Cowboys | Manly Warringah Sea Eagles |

In Australia, many young kids train to play rugby and dream of becoming a professional player. It is a rough physical game. Rugby players often have a large body size and big muscles. Most players end up with cauliflower ears [≈ ears swollen into a cauliflower-like shape]. This is caused by injuries.

Let's get to know some basic Rugby League rules by watching the 2020 NRL Grand Final between Melbourne Storm and Penrith Panthers!

The game is on. Just 3 minutes in, Justin Olam gets the ball to the goal line. He scores a try for Melbourne! And Storm makes it into a goal! Six points go to Storm!

The ball rolls into touch. [≈ The ball is out. ≈ The ball goes wide.] Now the **scrum**... Panthers loses the ball. Storm Suliasi Vunbivalu catches the ball. He's on the run! Down 20 metres, no-one can catch him! Yes! That's another try for Melbourne!

At half time, Storm leads by 22–0!

In the second half, Panthers is catching up but it's too late! My favourite team Storm won the premiership and the trophy with the score of 26–20! What a gallant game! It's dreamland rugby and insane stuff!

< The scrum is when the players all push together in a circle, with their heads down, and try to get the ball. A try equals 4 points, when a player places the ball on the ground in the opponents' in-goal area. Following a try, 2 points is given if the team kick the ball from the position where the try was scored through the posts and above the crossbar. Half time is at 40 minutes and full time is at 80 minutes. >

These basic rules will come together once you've watched a couple of games. To me, the essence of Rugby League is that you can only pass the ball to the player behind you. Each team only gets six tackles to pass the ball to the teammates to score... But you have to take the ball to the finish line to score a try!

# CHAPTER 38 - A Sports Enthusiast

## DAY 333
## HORSERACING

When springtime arrives in Australia, the racing season goes into full swing. Derby Day is a major event for horseracing on the first Saturday in November. Melbourne Cup takes place on the first Tuesday in November. It is the race that stops the nation. On this big day, racegoers dress up nicely or extravagantly and gather at Flemington Racecourse. Pubs, bars or the TAB are also popular destinations for horse betters [≈ punters ≈ wagers].

You can also wage [≈ have a punt ≈ place a bet] through apps, such as BetEasy, Sportsbet, PointsBet and Ladbrokes. There are numerous ways to set up bets via bookies [≈ bookmakers], such as Each Way, Exacta, Quinella, Trifecta, Frist 4, BIG6, Double, Flexi, Flexi Quaddie. I like Win, Place and Show Bets.

- **Win:** The horse you select must be the first past the post. The payoff is determined by the odds of them winning. For example, a $100 bet on a 10-1 horse would pay you back $1100 ($100 × 10 +$100 of your investment).
- **Place:** Your horse must finish in either the first or second spot.
- **Show:** Your horse must finish in the first, second, or third position.

The chances of winning for Place and Show are higher than for Win, but the payoff is lower.

Giddy up! The carnival starts!

< The term 'giddy up' is said to make a horse start moving faster! You can also ask a person to 'giddy up', meaning for them to move faster. A carnival is a public event with people playing music, everyone dressing up nicely, and dancing. >

Let's watch the 2015 Melbourne Cup together. The race distance is 3200 metres.

And they're off! **Trip to Paris** jumps well, followed by **Max Dynamite**. **Excess Knowledge** is on the outside of the field. **Quest for More** isn't too far away. **Big Orange** at a good spot... With 300 metres to go, **Prince of Penzance** for Michelle Payne coming out, taking the lead! It's **Prince of Penzance**!

Michelle Payne created history, being the first female jockey [≈ rider] to win the Melbourne Cup when she rode Prince of Penzance!

< Horseracing is very male dominated. Women were not allowed to join the race many years ago. Nowadays, female jockeys can compete against males in a race. Michelle's winning was quite inspiring. The movie *Ride Like a Girl* was released in 2019 and based on her story. Like she said, 'Keep working hard and trying hard, and your dream will come true.' >

Michelle Payne won against the odds (100-1)! Winning the race won the horse owner about $3.6 million of prize money! If you placed $1000 on Prince of Penzance, you would have picked up $101,000 on the day (Nine Things You Need To Know About the Michelle Payne Story, n.d.).

Did you know that the phrases above in bold are the names of the horses in the race?

# DAY 334
# FISHING

Hey, how would you like to relax *and* play a sport at the same time? Have you watched *IFISH* TV show? Have you gone fishing at Cape York in Queensland, or at Broome in Western Australia? Would you like to become an angler? Haha! Don't answer my questions! I'm fishing!

< Fishing in the context of 'I'm fishing' here doesn't mean to actually catch a fish. It more means that I'm 'fishing' for information about you with my questions. >

Relax. I'm not really fishing here. There are no games and competitions today. I'll take you out fishing. Before we go, we need to purchase a valid recreational fishing licence online.

Next, let's get some fishing tackle [≈ fishing gear] and accessories ready: fishing rod, fishing reels [≈ spinning reels], swivels, hook, fishing lines [≈ trace lines], sinkers, fishing lures [≈ baits], waders, torches, lights, polarised sunglasses, and a bobber.

< If you are caught 'hook, line and sinker', you have probably been tricked into believing a lie completely. >

Now let's anchor up, anglers and fishers!

While our boat moves far from the shore, tie the hook onto the fishing line. Attach weights and a bobber. Bait the hook and cast the line. Let's keep the line vertical. Wait patiently! There he is. Reel it in. Stop winding. Swing him over. I got him! [≈ I hooked the fish!] A monster! [≈ A thumper! ≈ That's a big catch! ≈ Look at the size of that!] That's a weighty trout!

What other fish can you hook in the waters around Australia (either the ocean or freshwater)?

| Salmon | Giant trevally (GT) | Bass | Murray cod | Bream | Flathead |
|--------|---------------------|------|------------|-------|----------|
| Snapper | Parrot fish | Mullet | Red emperor | Redfin | Whiting |

Under law, some fish (those fully protected species and fish more than the legal permitted length) need to be released back to the water after catching them.

'A little fella [≈ Mate], back you go [≈ back to the sea ≈ it's time for you to go home ≈ see ya]!'

My question now: is fishing considered a competitive sport or a recreational [≈ leisurely] activity?

# DAY 335
## EXTREME SPORT

Adventure sports are extreme sports. They can be dangerous. You put yourself and your body on the line. The risk is real. In return, you get an adrenaline rush and get your pulse racing.

First things first. Safety is paramount. You can only perform extreme sports like abseiling, cliff diving and ice climbing in remote areas. Let your family members know where you are heading to and what you'll be doing. When in danger [≈ in trouble], stay calm and protect yourself from injury or death. Dial triple zero in Australia in case of an emergency (police, fire or ambulance).

To start, I recommend Russell Coight's TV show, *All Aussie Adventures*. Russell (played by comedian Glenn Robbins) is an Australian outback [≈ countryside ≈ remote area] expert who will show you survival skills for the wilderness in a funny way. You can share a laugh or two with Russell!

< A laugh or two, a thing or two, a day or two, a decade or two, a shower or two, a drink or two… do you see anything in common between these phrases? >

Up next: are you a daredevil [≈ an adventurer] wanting to try an extreme sport (flying fox, trekking, street luge, zorbing, caving, flyboarding, whitewater kayaks, river rafting, paddling down a waterfall, rock climbing, parkour and free-running, freefall [≈ bungee jumping], parachute jumping, skydive, tandem skydiving, hot air ballooning [≈ hot air balloon rides])? My advice: don't perform any extreme sport unless you are under instruction and training from a professional.

Still to come. Do you dare to dive with sharks? Big sharks can be up to 3 metres in size! I've never done that. It's said to be an experience that you'll never forget [≈ like no other]. Safety briefing: Don't dive if you suffer from medical conditions such as diabetes, epilepsy and heart disease. Don't touch the shark when you're in the water!

Let's wrap up with the SOS, a distress signal in Morse code. This is often seen in films where people are in danger and desperately in need of help. It doesn't stand for 'Save Our Ship' or 'Save Our Soul'. It's not an abbreviation of anything (Soniak, What Does SOS Stand For?, 2012).

# DAY 336
# WATCHING SPORT

We already got to know a couple of Aussie sports. I also want you to get familiar with the nicknames of 10 Australian national sports teams.

| Sport | Men | Women | Sport | Men | Women |
| --- | --- | --- | --- | --- | --- |
| Baseball | Southern Thunder | Emeralds | Basketball | Boomers | Opals |
| Rugby Union | Wallabies | Wallaroos | Water Polo | Sharks | Stingers |
| Rugby League | Kangaroos | Jillaroos | Fistball | Wombats | Possums |
| Field Hockey | Kookaburras | Hockeyroos | Soccer | Socceroos | Matildas |
| Softball | Aussie Steelers | Aussie Spirit | Volleyball | Volleyroos | Volleyroos |

If you're going to attend a sports event at a stadium, show good etiquette by minding your manners. Here are the don'ts:

- Don't block the view of others.
- Don't shout '*boo*' and respond with catcalls.
- Don't spit.
- Don't leave rubbish, cans, and plastic bags behind.
- Don't brawl [≈ Don't squabble over ≈ Don't battle] with others over whose team is the best.
- Don't punch others. [≈ Don't hit others. ≈ Don't bash others. ≈ Don't give others a whack.]

< The 'catcall' originated from a noisy squeaking instrument, which was used to express dissatisfaction. It sounded like an angry cat (Catcall, n.d.). A catcall in today's context is a loud noise from the audience because of something they disapprove of, such as the unfair referee decisions or unethical attacks from players against other players. >

Some sports like golf tournament, billiards, and tennis matches require silence during specific times. Don't make any sudden sounds. Keep your voice low. When a player gives a fantastic shot, just put your hands together [≈ clap your hands ≈ give them a big hand ≈ applaud].

If you're watching sport at home, be considerate of your neighbours. Tone it down a little when your team is winning. Hopefully, I've turned you into a sports-lover if you haven't been into it before.

# DAY 337
# THE WORD - BACK

Hello English Builders! **Welcome back!** **Looking back** over the last 11 months, how have you been going with your English studies? Please **get back** to me.

Okey-doke, let's **get back** to business [≈ **go back** to today's topic] now. You'll get some general life wisdom from me, all brimming with the word of 'back'. Let's do this one last time: identify each part of speech that includes the word 'back' in the sentence.

At work, don't **hold back**. It's always your time to shine. But think before you speak. You can't **take back** what you have said. You need to keep **watching your back** as well because your workmates could be secretly jealous of you.

If you've borrowed money from your workmates [≈ your workmates have lent you money], please **give that back** as soon as you can. Overall, Australians are easy to work with. If they accidentally wear the sweater **back to front**, tell them and get a laugh from them.

Be professional. Be concise and articulate on what to say to avoid **going back and forth** in the conversation. If you've failed a project or made a mistake, learn your lesson. You can **bounce back** from adversity. **Backing up** your files is always a wise option. Never do anything unethical. Your boss could **send you back** home straight away for being dodgy.

If you're experiencing any **back pain**, get a **back massage** at the physio.

No matter how busy you are at work, remember to **call** your parents **back** regularly. If you were **back** home now, you would have their **back** if there were any difficulties. Sending them old family photos can **bring back** [≈ **cast back**] happy memories. **Roll back** the years, you'll appreciate your folks' unconditional love, which they'd never expect you to **give back**. When you **come back** home from a holiday, **bring** them **back** some Australian wines, Tim Tams, opals, kangaroo leather, macadamia nuts, an Akubra hat or some emu oil…

Now tell me what's **at the back of your mind** now. When you **get back** to this book tomorrow, observe the **back cover** of the book. Tell me how many buildings do you see in there?

# DAY 338
## A FOOD LOVER

I'm a foodie. [≈ I am a food lover. ≈ I love food from all countries. ≈ I'm a food nerd. ≈ I love to eat. ≈ I'm a food-driven soul.] Awesome. Enjoy some cuisine from around the world, and while you do so, get to know the origin or any other interesting details behind these foods. So, dig into some foods with me.

**Cheese.** I don't mind cheese, but it is rare to find much cheese in Chinese cuisines. No Australian dislikes cheese. Cheese comes in the form of slices, blocks, shredded, grated, or shaved. Refer to the below table for some common types of cheese. There are about 1800 types of cheese around the world (Roos, 2021).

| Brie | Blue cheese | Camembert | Cheddar | Feta | Gouda |
| Goat cheese | Mozzarella | Mascarpone | Parmesan | Ricotta | Bocconcini |
| Colby | Burrata | Emmental | Romano | Swiss | Cottage cheese |

**Buffalo chicken wings.** Why are they called 'buffalo' wings? The food doesn't contain buffalo, that large animal of the cow family. The term originated at the Anchor Bar in Buffalo in New York City (Chicken Wing History, 2017). The sauce coating the wings is a hot sauce with cayenne pepper and melted butter (or margarine).

**Chicken parma [≈ Chicken parmigiana ≈ Chicken parmesan].** This is a dish with chicken breast coated in breadcrumbs, covered in tomato sauce and mozzarella cheese (sometimes with ham under the cheese too). You will find a chicken parma at most pubs in Australia, or in Italian restaurants, along with other dishes such as risotto, lasagne, ravioli, pizza, spaghetti bolognaise, or other kinds of pasta.

**Vietnamese beef pho.** Pho was first made in Northern Vietnam in the mid-1880s. It was heavily influenced by both Chinese (rice noodle and spices) and French (red meat) cooking. Pho is derived from a French soup, called 'pot au feu' (The Origins of Pho, n.d.).

**Fortune cookies.** Fortune cookies originated in California. They are served in many Chinese restaurants in western countries. But they are definitely not a traditional food in China.

**Tempura.** Tempura is a deep-fried seafood or vegetables with a special batter. While the dish is actually a classical Portuguese dish, it was made famous in Japan (Burrows, 2020).

Let me also share some food names that I find odd or funny: Eton mess, ladyfinger, pigs in a blanket, toad in the hole, spotted dick, rocky mountain oysters, century eggs [≈ 100-year-old eggs ≈ 1000-year-old eggs], Dutch baby pancake, Juicy Lucy burger. Do you know what each of these are? How did they come up with each name? Have you tried any of these dishes?

# DAY 339
# A FOOD CRITIC

Want to know how to describe food like a food critic? Cooking shows such as *MasterChef Australia*, *My Kitchen Rules*, and *Zumbo's Just Desserts* could help. Explore food with me: from presentation, smell, and taste to texture.

The soup is spoilt [≈ is off ≈ has gone bad ≈ has turned sour]. Yuck! [≈ Puke! ≈ Disgusting! ≈ Gross!]

This beef is undercooked. It's still raw and blue. This lamb is overcooked. It's too tough and too dry. It's rubbery [≈ chewy]. Plus, it's bland [≈ tasteless ≈ unsavoury] and tastes like cardboard.

This lemon tart looks like a lemon disaster. It's nothing special [≈ not impressive] in term of tastes. These cookies are stale. The cake is soggy [≈ mushy ≈ wet and soft].

Finally, I'm served more pleasant-looking food! Staring with the entrée, we have the Oysters Kilpatrick. I love the crispness of the bacon. The oysters are plump and briny, and with a smoky sauce. This is just a heaven on a plate.

The main dish for today is Mediterranean grilled chicken salad. Look at that shining colours on the dish. It's vibrant and inviting [≈ attractive]. It smells so freaking good! I salivated. Let me tuck in. Yum! [≈ Yummy! ≈ Delicious!] The chicken breast is succulent [≈ juicy and tasty], moist and tender. The salad has loads of flavour. [≈ The salad is flavour packed.] The flavour is bang on. [≈ The flavour is spot on.]

Wow! [≈ It's the bomb! ≈ It's scrumptious! ≈ The dish is divine!] My mouth is singing. [≈ My taste buds are dancing.] It satisfies my cravings.

My lemon lava cake is mouth-watering and irresistible!

Eager to try it out?

# DAY 340
# FOOD TRIVIA

The word 'trivia' means matters and details of little importance. A trivia game or trivia quiz is often used as a game where [≈ in which] players are challenged with questions about miscellaneous facts around many topics. Let's boost your food trivia knowledge by answering the below questions:

1. Are chicken thighs juicier than chicken breasts?
2. I see BLT on the menu. What does it mean?
3. I'm sitting in a restaurant where ramen, soba [≈ buckwheat], bento boxes, katsudon, yakitori chicken, udon, unagi, onigiri, gyoza, takoyaki are available to order. Which country's cuisine am I most likely having?
4. What is some Australian bush food [≈ bush tucker]?
5. I'm about to order Wagyu rump (MB +6) 500 g for $58 at a steakhouse. What does MB +6 mean?
6. Why is a pound cake called a pound cake?
7. Australians love to spread Vegemite on their sandwiches. What is Vegemite?
8. Brothers Frederick and Louis Rueckheim introduced the Cracker Jack snack at the World's Fair in Chicago in 1893. What were the three main ingredients?

All the above questions are answered below. Match them to each of the questions.

A. It stands for bacon, lettuce and tomato! It's a type of sandwich with these three ingredients.

B. The name comes from its original recipe, which is one pound of butter, one pound of sugar, one pound of eggs and one pound of flour!

C. 'MB' is a marble score. In short, marbling is the white fat within the meat muscle, especially red meat. Australian grading standard goes from 0 (marble-free) to 9. The higher the score, the higher marbling the beef has. And the juicier and more flavoursome the beef is!

D. Popcorn, peanut and molasses.

E. They are any foods that are native to Australia, such as native plant foods (Davidson's plum, finger lime and quandong) and native spices (lemon myrtle, mountain pepper, and the kakadu plum).

F. It's a dark brown thick paste. This savoury spread is made from leftover brewer's yeast. It's salty and has an umami flavour. It's an iconic Australian food.

G. Yes.

H. Japan.

# DAY 341
# MELBOURNE RESTURANT RECOMMENDATIONS

One thing that I love about Melbourne is that you can dine in at many restaurants with cuisines from all over the world. Let's explore a few restaurants, and recommend them to your friends!

**Chin Chin, 125 Flinders Ln, Melbourne**
This Asian fusion restaurant is very popular. I highly recommend the pad thai noodles, butter chicken curry and crispy duck. Great food and service!

**Vue de Monde, Level 55 Rialto Towers, 525 Collins St, Melbourne**
This is a contemporary fine-dining restaurant that uses native Australian ingredients. The view is amazing [≈ spectacular]; the food is insane [≈ blows you away]; the staff are welcoming [≈ inviting ≈ friendly].

**Secret Kitchen, 222 Exhibition St, Melbourne**
This is a great place for the Chinese yum cha experience. I love all the food here and rave about their attentive service. I've been there a couple of times and will definitely revisit.

**Radio Mexico, 11–13 Carlisle St, St Kilda**
A busy [≈ bustling] restaurant with a wide range of taco flavours. It's worth trying the BBQ pork belly, cochinita pibil, and grilled fish. They're all delicious. Don't miss out on the cocktail margaritas made with fresh, cold-pressed lime!

**The Railway Club Hotel, 107 Raglan St, Port Melbourne**
If steak is your preference, head to this restaurant. This place is rated highly. They have high-quality beef (rump, porterhouse, scotch fillet, eye fillet, rib eye). They chargrill the steak to your liking.

< Steak can be normally grilled as **blue** (sealed, very red in the centre), **rare** (red in the centre), **medium-rare** (pinkish-red), **medium** (pink), **medium-well** (very little pink), or **well-done** (no pink, brown in the centre). >

**Subway, found in many suburbs and shopping centre food courts**
Subway is a fast-food sandwich chain. Pick the bread size (6-inch or footlong), the bread type (white, 9-grain wheat, honey oat, Italian herb and cheese…), any protein (chicken schnitzel, meatball melt, tuna and mayo…), how you want it cooked (toasted or fresh), any toppings (cheese or fresh veggies), the sauce (honey mustard, garlic aioli…) and salt and pepper, or not?

# CHAPTER 39 - A Holistic Foodie

## DAY 342
## MELBOURNE'S COFFEE

Melbourne claims to have the best coffee in the world. Tasty coffee shops are everywhere in the city (making Starbucks a less popular option for coffee). Coffee is life here, and it has become part of my life here. Ground coffee is loaded with flavour, bitterness and sweetness. It's just too good to resist. I've turned into a coffee lover [≈ a coffee aficionado ≈ a coffee purist].

Let's get to know two types of coffee beans: Arabica and Robusta.

| Coffee bean type | Arabica | Robusta |
|---|---|---|
| Caffeine content | Less caffeine | Caffeine almost double |
| Taste | Smooth | Bitter |
| Price | More expensive | Cheaper |

Most instant coffee uses Robusta beans. Coffee beans ground in a coffee machine normally have the two types of beans combined.

Let's dive into some common coffee drinks now. I can't wait!

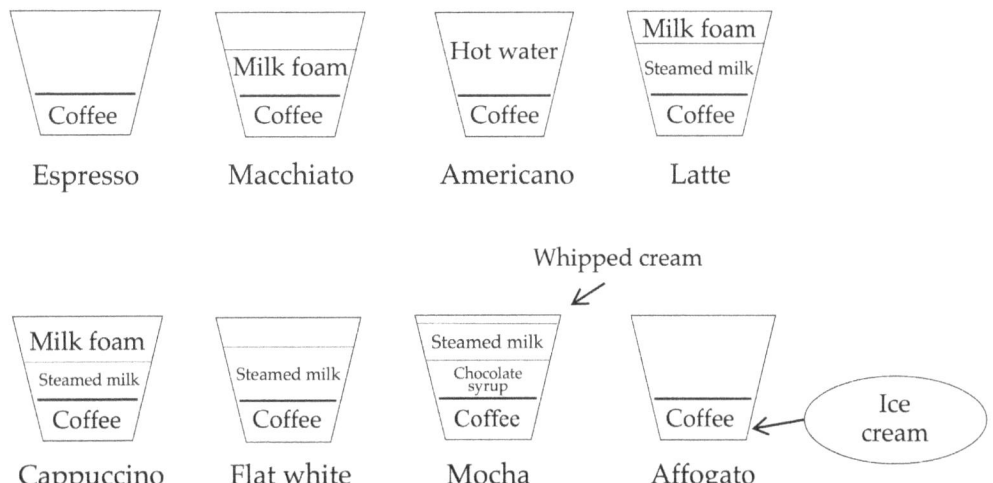

Wait! You haven't made your order yet. Here are some examples:
- 'Can I please grab a regular cappuccino?'
- 'Can I have a tall macchiato, please? To have here.'
- 'I'd like to have a large mocha with skimmed milk to go. Two sugars, please.'
- 'A regular skinny latte. Takeaway, please.'
- 'A soy flat white to have here.'

Let me know what you would like.

If the takeaway coffee is too hot, ask for a cup sleeve [≈ a cup holder]. Drink coffee when it's warm to hot (just not too hot). This gives you a better taste than a tepid coffee [≈ a lukewarm coffee]! Wow, it's wonderful – smooth, light, and refreshing!

# DAY 343
# YUMMY DESSERTS

Today, let me take you to Brunetti, a café with heaps of sweet delicacies on Lygon Street in Carlton, Melbourne. Whenever I step in the store, I feel like a kid in a toy store [≈ my eyes light up like a kid's on Christmas morning]. There are countless cakes and pastry options. It's so hard to choose!

Let's start with French macaroons. Almost AUD $3 each. They're soft, colourful, light and airy! So many flavours are available – passionfruit, tiramisu, salted caramel, lavender, pistachio.

Next, let's look at some mignons [≈ bite-sized sweets]. Lemon meringue tart, royale, French custard, rum baba, chocolate mousse, strawberry tart, éclair, millefoglie, pretzels and more. The cakes are also exquisite: blackforest cake, New York cheesecake, sachertorte, choux, opera, you name it.

All the desserts I've tried here suit my palate [≈ tickle my palate].

Now I'd like to introduce you to two popular, yummy desserts (pavlova and lamington) that both Australia and New Zealand argue they invented. Pavlova is a creamy and fruity meringue. It was named after the Russian ballerina Anna Pavlova who visited Australia and New Zealand in the 1920s (Saurine, 2020). A lamington is made from a sponge cake, sliced into square shape, then dipped in the melted chocolate and sprinkled with fine desiccated coconut.

On a hot summer day, pop into an ice cream or gelato shop where you can enjoy refreshing icy treats either in a cone or a cup.

Ice cream is made of milk, cream, sugar and egg yolk and is creamy and fluffy. Gelato is the Italian word for ice cream, which is derived from Latin word *gelātus*, meaning frozen (Gelato vs Ice Cream - What's the Difference?, n.d.). Gelato doesn't use egg yolks, and it uses more milk and less cream than ice cream, resulting in it being lower in fat. There is also sorbet and sherbet. Sorbet only contains fruit and sugar, and it doesn't contain dairy ingredient [≈ it's dairy free]. Sherbet is also a fruit-based dessert similar to gelato but has an additional bit of milk or cream.

# DAY 344
## TWO CHOCOLATE BOXES

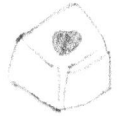 

Are you a chocoholic [≈ a chocolate lover]? Pana Chocolate, Koko Black, Haigh's Chocolates, Cacao Lab, Lindt are all crowd-pleasing chocolate shops in Australia that can sate your sweet tooth!

I'm going to get you a nine-piece assortment of Koko Black's most loved pralines at $24.90 (only on this page, sadly) as a congratulation gift for you getting this far in the book. So what's in the box?

| Milk sienna strawberry | Dark salted caramel | Almond praline |
| Dark hazelnut cluster | Hazelnut crisp | Baileys |
| Café latte | Caramelised coconut | Milk salted caramel |

You can personalise the box and make your own chocolate selection. There are so many flavours: lemon myrtle gin, macadamia and wattleseed, dark raspberry ganache, dark pistachio, apple pie moonshine, whipped caramel mousse, orange and rosemary… all the chocolates are meticulously crafted and beautifully garnished.

I'd also like to buy you a classic chocolate block collection gift box at $29.90 as a reward when you complete the book (again, sorry, only on this page). The box contains two Creamy Dreamy White Blocks, two Moreish Milk Blocks, two More than Halfway Blocks, and two Pure Darkness Blocks – 20 g of each block. The chocolate percentage in the box for minimum cocoa solids is 28% (white chocolate), 34% (milk chocolate), 54% (more than half dark chocolate) and 80% (pure dark chocolate), respectively.

Here's a chocolate buying tip: cocoa should be the primary ingredient. High cocoa content in chocolate could indicate high-quality chocolate (Brianna Elliott, 2016). Look for chocolate that contains cocoa butter and not other vegetable fats.

Here's a chocolate storing tip: the premium temperature for storing chocolate is around 22 degrees or less. Avoid heat and light. [≈ Store away from direct sunlight.] Don't leave chocolate in a parked car on a hot weather day.

Finally, let's bite into it! Does the chocolate melt slowly on your tongue [≈ linger on your mouth]? What does it taste like? Is it bitter, roasted, fruity, earthy, woody, nutty or gooey [≈ sticky and soft]?

# DAY 345
# LET'S HAVE BEERS, CHEERS!

Are you keen on trying out beers sold at your local liquor stores (BWS, Liquorland, Dan Murphy's, My Bottle Shop…)? Well, please show me your ID (normally your driver's licence) first because it's an offence to supply alcohol to minors in Australia.

The bottle shop has a cold storage room where cold beer is stored in boxes. Feel free to go in there and grab whatever you'd like. Water, malts, hops and yeast are the four key ingredients in beer. I'll share my tasting experience with some popular brands in bold below.

A pale ale is a light-coloured beer and brewed with a top-fermenting yeast at room temperature. **150 Lashes** is so good. I instantly loved it after my first sip. **Coopers Pale Ale** is produced in South Australia. The beer has a fruity flavour. It tastes dry and earthy and is quite smooth. **Lazy Yak** has a citrus hop aroma and is light bodied with a moderate bitterness, and with a dry taste at the end.

A lager is a light-coloured beer and made with bottom-fermenting yeast at cooler temperature. **Victoria Bitter** (**VB**) is an iconic Australian lager. It's the best beer ever – hoppy and sharp. I also like **Furphy**, which is hazy and refreshing. It's deep gold in colour with fruity flavours and aromas. **XXXX Gold** is also *wow*! It's clean and crispy with a viscous body with subtle malt finish. **Crown Lager** has a creamy head [≈ the frothy foam on top], a creamy fruit taste and a rich palate.

Stout is strong dark beer made using roasted malts. **Sheaf Stout** is a lovely dark brown and smells like coffee. The initial light fizz soon settles. Trying a can of **Guinness Draught Stout** was my best experience, with a plastic ball inside filled with nitrogen. After the can is opened, bubbles will fizz as you pour the Guinness into the glass. This replicates the draught experience. Beer served from a keg is called a draught, and it's fresher than beer served in bottles or cans.

Cider is an alcoholic drink made from apples. **Somersby Cider** is my favourite – it's crispy and refreshing, perfect for a warm summer night.

Craft beer is beer that is brewed in a traditional way by small brewers. Many of these are worth trying as well.

Now let's grab a slab of beer or a six-pack. Crack open a cold one [≈ a coldie]. Put it in a stubby holder. Cheers!

< 'A slab of beer' is a carton of 24 bottles of beer. Six bottles in a carrying cartons are called 'a six-pack'. A 'cold one' or a 'coldie' refers to a chilled beer and 'stubby' refers to 375ml bottle of beer in Australia. >

# DAY 346
# WINE TASTING

Australia is one of the largest wine producing and consuming countries in the world. South Australia, New South Wales, Victoria, Western Australia and Tasmania have many wineries [≈ vineyards ≈ cellar doors ≈ wine regions] due to mild and moderate [≈ warm and damp] climates. When travelling to Australia, don't miss out on a wine tasting tour!

Below are five basic stages of the wine-making process. We'll not go into details on viticulture, which is a winemaker's job.

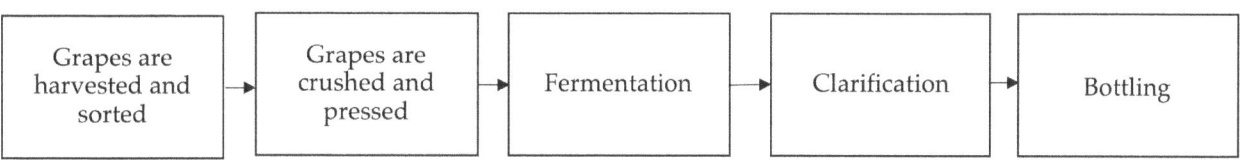

Let's taste three main types of wines, with its varieties, today.

First up, the white wines. **Chardonnay** is a dry white wine with fruity flavours of apple, pear and lemon. It's a great choice to have with fish and seafood in a lush [≈ rich] sauce. **Sauvignon blanc** goes well with proteins and nutty cheeses because of its light-bodied nature and high acidity. **Riesling** and **moscato** are dessert wines, sweet, light and refreshing with a heavy alcohol content – ideal for spicy food and salad. **Sparkling wine**, French **champagne** [≈ bubbly] and Italian **prosecco** have fruity (citrus, apple, vanilla), oaky and toasty flavours. White wines should be served chilled.

Now, for some red wines. **Pinot noir** is light bodied. It doesn't have too much tannin [≈ bitterness]. The name comes from the French words for pine and black (Pinot Nero (Pinot Noir), n.d.). It's a great match with salmon. **Merlot** is lighter and bolder, which pairs perfectly with lamb. **Shiraz** is well known for its full-body taste, strong tannins and high acidity, working well with BBQ fare. **Cabernet sauvignon** contains high tannin levels, making it the perfect accompaniment to steaks.

Next up, you're going to love a pinky rosé, which is crisp and fruity. It's made from red or purple grapes. Compared to red wines, fermenting time is reduced. The grape skins for rosé are removed after a short time in contact with the juice. This is why rosé doesn't turn into the red colour of red wine.

Lots of wines have a bittersweet taste. Quite like a life, isn't it?

# DAY 347
## FOUR TRICKS TO IMPROVE YOUR COOKING SKILLS

Who doesn't want to make a restaurant-quality dish or a dish from a Michelin star restaurant? Today, I'll show you four tricks to become a home cook guru.

**Trick #1:** Sharpen [≈ Restore] your kitchen knife and scissors regularly. If you don't have a sharpener, you can cut a few strips of aluminium tinfoil when they start to become blunt.

< **Warning** [≈ **Be warned**]: Don't microwave food covered in tinfoil. Putting foil in the microwave oven could lead to sparks and fire. >

**Trick #2:** Don't be shy with [≈ Don't be afraid of] salt and pepper. Flavour, flavour, and flavour is always the essence of a dish. You need to have a variety of seasoning [≈ condiments ≈ herbs and spices] in your pantry ready for use. Here are a few:

| All spice | Basil | Cinnamon sticks | Dried onion flakes | Fennel seeds |
|---|---|---|---|---|
| Garam masala | Hot Cajun | Italian herbs | Mustard powder | Nutmeg |
| Oregano | Parsley | Rosemary | Star anise | Turmeric |

The above list is not inclusive of every herb. Whether you're curing fish or seasoning beef, make sure you set them aside with the herbs for 15 minutes at least to develop the flavour.

**Trick #3:** Know different ways to cook fresh produce. Take a look at the SBS Food channel, a Jamie Oliver cooking show or *Poh's Kitchen*. Even cooking videos on YouTube can help inspire your cooking. Below are some tips that I found on YouTube:

- Five ways to cook eggs (poached egg, scrambled egg, shirred egg [≈ baked egg], hard-boiled egg, fried egg).
- Pantry pastas four ways.
- Every way to cook chicken drumsticks (30 methods).

**Trick #4:** Choose the right ingredient for the job. For example, there are three types of potatoes: starchy, waxy and all-purpose. Potatoes with high starch are best mashed or fried. Waxy potatoes can hold their shape well when boiled or steamed. All-purpose potatoes fall between the two types and are useful for roasting and stewing (Types of Potatoes and When to Use Them, n.d.).

# DAY 348
## GET TO KNOW THE RECIPE

In China, home-cooks don't normally use recipes. It's funny to see that some Chinese recipes don't state the exact amounts of each ingredient. Chinese recipes might say, 'use a moderate amount of flour'. So just put in as much flour as you please! It's not like western recipes that aim for exact amounts, like 'add in ¼ tablespoon (tbsp) salt and ½ teaspoon (tsp) vinegar'.

Cooking isn't rocket science. Just follow the recipe [≈ don't deviate from the recipe] and you should be able to make your dish appealing and with *bangs* of flavour.

I'll share one of my favourite savoury dish recipes with you here: spiced chicken wings with ranch dressing. This was taken from one of the Coles monthly magazines (which is free to pick up at the Coles supermarket check-out counter).

| Ingredients: | Ranch dressing: |
|---|---|
| <ul><li>1 kg chicken wing (RSPCA Approved, if possible)</li><li>1 tbsp (~15 g) brown sugar</li><li>1 tbsp tomato sauce</li><li>1 tbsp Worcestershire sauce</li><li>2 tsp sweet paprika</li><li>2 tsp dried oregano</li><li>1 tsp (~6 g) ground cumin</li><li>1 tsp garlic powder</li><li>1/2 tsp ground allspice</li><li>1/2 tsp dried chilli flakes (optional)</li></ul> | <ul><li>1/3 cup (100 g) mayonnaise</li><li>2 tbsp sour cream</li><li>1 tbsp white wine vinegar</li><li>2 tsp Dijon mustard</li><li>2 tsp finely chopped dill</li><li>2 tsp finely chopped chives</li><li>1/4 tsp sweet paprika</li></ul><br>Prep: 15 min<br>Cook: 45 min<br>Servings: 6<br>Easy |

One way to learn cooking is to know a bit more about each of the ingredients you're using. Here's some information on some of the ingredients above:

- **RSPCA Approved.** RSPCA stands for the Royal Society for the Prevention of Cruelty to Animals. RSPCA Approved means that the animal has been ethically treated during its life.

- **Worcestershire sauce.** This is a fermented condiment created in Worcestershire, England. Vinegar is the base ingredient, with anchovies, garlic, onion, molasses added to this sauce (Filippone, 2019).

- **Sweet paprika.** This is a ground spice made from sweet red peppers, with an intense bright red colour. It originated from central Mexico, but it's mostly seen in Hungarian and Spanish cuisine (Sweet Paprika, n.d.).

Now do some research on any of the other ingredients above that you're unfamiliar with and go get them from the supermarket.

# DAY 349
## LET'S COOK

Once you've gathered all the ingredients, let's roll up our sleeves and make some finger-licking good chicken wings together. The recipe is explained in detail below.

The first step is to preheat the oven to 200°C. Line a baking tray with parchment paper [≈ baking paper]. Combine the chicken, sugar, tomato sauce, Worcestershire sauce, paprika, oregano, cumin, garlic powder, allspice and chilli flakes in a bowl. Mix well. Allow to season for 15 minutes to develop the flavour.

< Back home, we don't have ovens in the kitchen. I'd never used one before I came to Australia. In Australia, an oven is an essential kitchen appliance for each household. It's normally installed right under the cooktop. Fan forced ovens are commonly used. This function heats up an oven faster, reduces cooking time and decreases energy consumption. It distributes heat [≈ circulates] evenly, so it's ideal when using multiple trays at the same time. Below are eight common oven symbols. Take a guess on the function each symbol represents.

        >

Now arrange the chicken mixture on the tray. Chuck it into the oven and bake for about 45 minutes or until the chicken is golden brown and cooked. Turn the chicken over halfway in the baking.

While the chicken is baking, let's take a look at some other cooking techniques and the names of some dishes in the table below. Write down two more cooking methods that you can think of below. Applying these methods can add variety to your home cooking!

| Cooking technique | Cooking verbs + ingredient | Final dish name example |
|---|---|---|
| **Braise** | Braise the green beans | Braised green beans |
| **Stew** | Stew the beef | One-pot beef stew |
| **Simmer** | Simmer chicken stock with kale and bacon | Simmered kale with bacon |
| **Steam** | Steam the pork buns | Steamed pork buns |
| **Sauté** | Sauté the vegetables | Garlic sautéed vegetables |
| **Fry** | Fry the calamari in batter | Deep-fried calamari |
| **Grill** | Grill the brussels sprouts | Grilled brussels sprouts |
| **Roast** | Roast the leg of lamb | Roasted leg of lamb |
| **Broil** | Broil the fish | Broiled fish fillets |
| **Barbeque** | Barbeque the chicken | Barbequed chicken |
| **Sear** | Sear the pork steak | Pan-seared pork steak |
|  |  |  |
|  |  |  |

# DAY 350
## COOKING CONTINUES

Let's continue cooking our chicken wings. The next step is to make the ranch dressing.

< Ranch dressing was developed by Steve Henson and his wife, Gayle. They developed this buttermilk dressing on a 120-acre dude ranch called the Hidden Valley Ranch. This dressing was popular among their guests. Steve first started to sell it to guests, then nation-wide as demand kept growing (Doss, 2021). >

Mix all ranch dressing ingredients (mayonnaise, sour cream, vinegar, mustard, dill, chives and paprika) together in a bowl. Mix until well combined.

< Mayonnaise [≈ Mayo] is a sauce made of egg yolk, acid (wine vinegar or lemon juice) and oil. It can be used in sandwiches, salads, on French fries and so on. Tomato sauce, tartar sauce, barbeque sauce, chipotle southwest, honey mustard, sweet chilli, sweet onion and aioli are also popular sauces in western eating culture. In general, a dressing is normally uncooked, while a sauce is cooked, adding flavour to another dish. >

About 45 minutes later, take the chicken wings out of the oven and arrange them on a serving plate. Sprinkle parsley leaves, chopped chives and chopped dill to add a bright green colour to the dish. Serve with ranch dressing and lemon wedges.

< Parsley looks similar to coriander. [≈ Parsley is similar in appearance to coriander [≈ cilantro].] Parsley is commonly used as a garnish. Coriander, also called Chinese parsley, is more pungent, and adds aroma and flavour to a dish (Morgan, 2019). There are also lots of fresh leaves and herbs that can make your dishes more appealing, such as basil, rosemary, thyme, oregano, mint, bay, chives, chervil, sage, tarragon, lime leaves, curry leaves, watercress, lemongrass, or even some edible flowers. >

I can't wait to try out the chicken wings with ranch dressing! Yum! It's simple and delish [≈ delicious]! See how easy it is to cook a restaurant-quality dish using a recipe, as long as you adhere strictly to it [≈ you don't read it wrong or deviate from it].

# DAY 351
## ANZAC BISCUITS

Hello home-cooks! Today, I'm going to share with you an Anzac biscuit recipe. When I cooked this for the first time, it unexpectedly ignited my interest in baking!

What are Anzac biscuits? These biscuits date back to World War I [≈ are associated with the First World War]. Soldiers [≈ Troops] were given these biscuits by their wives. Back then, these army biscuits were tooth-breaking [≈ rock hard ≈ firm and crunchy]. The ones that we're about to make are soft and chewy.

Here is a list of ingredients required to make Anzac biscuits:

- 1 cup rolled oats [≈ old-fashioned oats]
- 1 cup raw sugar
- 1 cup plain flour (sifted)
- 3/4 cup desiccated coconut
- 125g unsalted butter (melted)
- 3 tbsp boiling water
- 2 tbsp golden syrup
- 1/2 tsp bicarb soda [≈ baking soda]

While looking for these ingredients at your local supermarket, you might notice there are different types of each ingredient. What are the differences?

There are different kinds of oats: Rolled oats are made by the oat groats, which are steamed and rolled into flakes. It takes about 5–10 minutes to cook. Quick oats are thinner and smoother, and they can be cooked very quickly. Steel cut oats [≈ Irish oats] are chewier and take 20–30 minutes to cook – they are ideal for breakfast (Nut-Free Super-Seed Oat Bars, n.d.).

There are different kinds of dried coconut: Desiccated coconut is finely ground. Shredded coconut is shredded into thin strips, while flaked coconut is shaved into longer and wider flakes.

Salted butter has added salt, which is a preservative with a longer shelf life. Unsalted butter is purely the butter. It's often fresher.

As the qualified home cook, now it's your turn to tell us the differences between each of the types of sugar (white sugar, brown sugar, raw sugar, caster sugar, cane sugar, icing sugar) and flour (plain flour [≈ white flour ≈ all-purpose flour], wholemeal flour, self-raising flour, corn flour, rice flour).

# DAY 352
## MAKING ANZAC BISCUITS

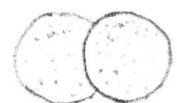

Roll up your sleeves now and let's mix up some ingredients to bake the yummy Anzac biscuits!

< Warning: don't call these cookie-like biscuits Anzac 'cookies'. It could cop you a fine because the word 'Anzac' is protected by the Department of Veterans' Affairs who sets out the rule that it must be called 'Anzac biscuits' not 'Anzac cookies' (Sutton, 2020).

What's the difference between cookies and biscuits? 'Cookies' is an American term. They're a type of biscuit that's normally sweet, heavy, chunky and rough. In contrast, biscuits can be sweet or savoury, and are flour-based bakery items. 'Biscuits' is used in British English (Difference Between Cookies and Biscuits, 2015). >

Let's cut the crap and do some baking, following the eight steps below:

**Step 1** Preheat the oven to 180°C (160°C if fan forced).

**Step 2** Line baking paper on two baking trays.

**Step 3** Mix the oats, coconut and sugar in a bowl. Sift in the flour. Stir the ingredients until they're mixed well.

**Step 4** Place the butter and golden syrup in a saucepan over low heat until the butter has melted.

**Step 5** Combine the bicarbonate of soda and boiling water in a separate bowl. Add this into the butter/syrup mixture. It'll foam up [$\approx$ fizz up]. Pour this into your mixed dry ingredients and stir.

**Step 6** Once the mixture is well combined, roll the mixture into golf ball-sized balls. Place them about 6 cm apart onto the tray. Flatten the biscuits slightly.

**Step 7** Bake for 15 minutes or until biscuits are golden brown. Turn the trays around halfway (180 degrees) during baking.

**Step 8** Remove from the oven and transfer biscuits to wire racks to cool down.

Once cool, put the biscuits in an airtight container. Their shelf life is long. But they probably won't stay in there for too long because they're so delicious and you'll just want to keep eating them.

# DAY 353
# FANCY COCKTAILS

A cocktail is an alcoholic drink made from a mixture of different drinks and ingredients. One of the stories is that a New Orleans apothecary served brandy with Peychaud bitters in a French eggcup (*coquetier*, which is pronounced in English as 'cocktay') (Foley, 2019). So 'cocktail' was just mispronounced (Where Does the Word Cocktail Actually Come From?, n.d.).

I'm always fascinated by the beautiful names of cocktail, such as those below:

| Sex on the Beach | Espresso Martini | Mojito | Old-Fashioned |
|---|---|---|---|
| Pina Colada | Aperol Spritz | Gin and Tonic (G&T) | Cosmopolitan |
| Tequila Sunrise | Love Potion Vodka | Margarita | Bloody Mary |
| Hurricane | White Russian | Negroni | Daiquiri |

I also like the story of how cocktails are invented. For Sex on the Beach, one version of the story is that in 1987, a Florida young bartender was participating in a bartending competition. He mixed up vodka, peach schnapps, lime juice and grenadine cocktail. The name was made up randomly because he thought people travelled to Florida for a holiday in summer for two reasons: sex and the beach (Rathore, 2015).

Now let's shake up the cocktail shaker and make a mojito like a mixologist.

**Step 1** Place **a small handful of fresh mint leaves, 1 tsp sugar**, and **30 mL lime juice** in the cocktail shaker. Muddle these ingredients with the end of a rolling pin to crush the mint. Pour it into a tall glass.

**Step 2** Add in **crushed ice**.

< If you don't have an ice crusher, just simply put all the ice cubes in a clean tea-towel. Wrap the tea-towel up. Smash [≈ Whack] the ice with a rolling pin for a while. Open the towel. Your crushed ice is now ready. >

**Step 3** Add in **60 mL rum** and **1/2 cup soda water**. Mix it up.

**Step 4** Garnish with additional **mint leaves**.

< A cocktail garnish doesn't just add appeal. It can also improve the balance of flavours in the cocktail. You can add a garnish using techniques such as cutting the lime into wedges and adding to your cocktail or using a peeler to get some lemon or orange rind to hang around the rim of the cocktail glass. >

Now, enjoy! If you're not a fan of alcohol, make a mocktail instead. A mocktail is a mixed drink like a cocktail, just without any alcohol [≈ which is non-alcoholic drinks that are made by mixing fruit juices].

# DAY 354
# MORE COOKING TIPS!

Today, I'll wrap up this chapter by teaching you four more secrets to bring your home cooking to the next level and teach you some verbs that a cook needs to know. What are we waiting for? Let's kill two birds with one stone right now!

**1.** Can you cut onions without any tears [≈ crying]? Chill them in the refrigerator or freeze them before cutting!

< What else can you do with a knife? Slice a pear up. Finely dice a tomato. Roughly [≈ Coarsely] chop [≈ hack up] garlic. French the rack of lamb… >

**2.** How can you peel tomatoes quickly? Cut a shallow 'X' at the bottom of your tomatoes. Drop them into boiling water for 30–60 seconds. Dunk them in ice-cold water! Then peel!

< What other ways are there to remove the unnecessary parts of an ingredient? Eggplants are deseeded. Avocadoes are stoned. Cherries are pitted. Prawns are deveined. Oysters are shucked. Fishbones are removed. Green beans are trimmed [≈ snapped off]. >

**3.** To make a dish more appealing, give it a final touch with a simple decoration. Here are some ideas. Spread the tomato sauce over the schnitzel. Dress the salad with olive oil. Top [≈ Dust] the sponge cake with icing sugar. Drizzle sauce over the plate. Pipe the cauliflower puree onto the plate using a pastry bag.

**4.** Follow the recipe to a T [≈ to a tee].

< 'To a T' means to follow the recipe precisely as written. >

As an amateur home cook, please interpret the below paragraph that uses idioms of 'cook'.

**What's cooking?** I hope you're **cooking with gas** in your English studies. If you're **cooking the books**, you'll probably **cook your goose** one day. Sometimes, **too many cooks spoil the broth** [≈ **the soup** ≈ **the stew**].

# DAY 355
## EXPLORING PERSONAL HOBBIES

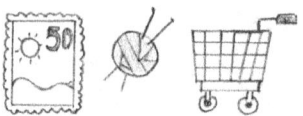

What do you do for fun in your free time? [≈ What do you get up to when you are free? ≈ What do you like to do outside of work?]

Here are a few things you might do as a hobby:

- I collect stamps.
- I really like writing a blog.
- I brew beer at home when I'm free.
- I'm a bibliophile. [≈ I'm a bookworm. ≈ I like books.]
- I'm an airplane-model collector.
- I enjoy exploring nature.
- Most of my free time is filled with doing all sorts of sports.
- I focus my spare time on embroidery, crochet and baking.
- I spend most of my leisure time singing.
- Learning English is what I do outside of work.

Hobbies don't have to make you money. They can be a great way to spend time, though – they can add spice to your life. List any hobbies that you would like to cultivate more of in your daily life in the lines below.

- 
- 
- 

If you are living abroad (not in mainland China), use YouTube to search for any hobbies (knitting, sewing, origami, beading, homecraft, drone flying, to name but a few) that arouse your interest [≈ stimulate your interest]. If you live in mainland China, you can use YouTube alternative, Youku (优酷) instead. Type in a few relevant words and a list of resources will be at your fingertips.

< People who make YouTube videos are called YouTubers. We call ourselves the 'YouTube Generation'. Instagrammers, bloggers and vloggers are also popular. >

Do something for fun and pleasure. No pressure. Hobbies should excite you, not feel like a burden. Let's now explore nine productive hobbies that could make you happier.

# DAY 356
## GRAB YOUR CAMERA

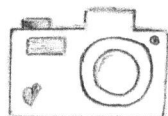

Nowadays, we all have a smartphone glued to our hands – these can deliver high-quality photos and video clips. You really don't need to spend hundreds and thousands of bucks on a professional camera. Why not become a self-taught photographer [≈ snapper ≈ shutterbug ≈ cameraman] or videographer just by using your phone?

First, turn on your phone camera. Get familiar with all functions: time lapse, slow motion, video, photo, portrait, panorama, flash, timer, live, filters…

Now I'm going to share some simple photography tips for you to practise:

- Keep your camera lens clean.
- Switch on the camera grid. In grid mode, the screen is divided into nine equal parts. This helps with mastering the most basic photography composition rule: the rule of thirds. That is, when placing the most important element along the gridline, you'll create well-balanced and eye-capturing shots.
- Get creative with angles. [≈ Seek out interesting angles.] Using eye-level position, shoot what you see. If you crouch down, shoot from the ground level, your subject will look strong and powerful. By doing this, you can make the person look taller [≈ elongate the person's legs ≈ make the person's legs thinner and longer]. Shooting from a high position, the object looks smaller and more vulnerable in a wider background.
- Look for the light source.
- Avoid shaky hands. [≈ Keep the camera steady.] Hold the phone firmly with both hands. Steady yourself by leaning on a wall or other solid object. Using a tripod is a good option too.

Would you like to take a portrait photo of your friend? Try out these words: 'Lean back. Push your face a bit forward, head slightly right. Tip your chin down. Look into my camera. Perfect. One, two, three. Shoot. You blinked! Let's take another shot.'

So the secret to become a shutterbug: never be shy in pressing the shutter! Shoot as much as you can as often as you can. You'll capture the perfect shot. As you go, you'll get more understanding on ISO, aperture, shutter speed, leading lines, fill flash…

# DAY 357
## RIDING A WAVE

Let's look for an outdoor hobby today: surfing a wave. The lesson is a simple guide for complete surfing newbies [≈ shark biscuits ≈ beginning surfers]. I would highly recommend getting an instructor to start with. Don't risk your precious life in the merciless ocean.

< 'Shark biscuit' is an Aussie slang for someone who is new to surfing. Because they are inexperienced, sharks easily eat them like a delicious biscuit ('Shark Biscuit' Meaning, n.d.). >

Do you have to be a good swimmer to become a surfer? The answer is a definite yes. You need to learn swimming beforehand, be it breaststroke, backstroke, butterfly stroke, freestyle [≈ front crawl], doggy paddle [≈ dog paddle]. At least, you need to be able to paddle and float and hold your breath under the water. Don't go surfing if you can't swim [≈ you swim like a brick ≈ you are a weak swimmer ≈ you can't lift your head out of the water to breathe].

Once you have enough confidence in swimming, let's choose the right paddleboard for you, and a decent wetsuit. For beginners, a longboard with volume is recommended, which should be easy to balance. Now put on the wetsuit and head out to the beach. Attach your foot to the surfboard leash. When you're ready, start paddling into the water to find your spot. When the wave approaches, stand on your surfboard. Catch a wave, engage with the wave, and ride the curl. Fall off your surfboard. [≈ Ditch your surfboard. ≈ Lose your board.]

It sounds easy, but it requires lots of practice! Bodyboard, speedboard and kitesurfing are also fun water sports that you can develop as a hobby.

< *Bondi Rescue* is a program filmed at Bondi Beach, one of Australia's most iconic beaches, just 7 km away from the Sydney CBD. The show depicts the work of lifeguards [≈ rescuers ≈ professional lifesavers] and their daily job routine to rescue swimmers, surfers, scuba divers and tourists who are in danger in the waters. Sharks sometimes swim near beach areas and are a danger. Lifebuoys and lifejackets can be life-saving at the 11th hour [≈ at the last minute ≈ in an emergency].

So safety is the priority when you're in the water. Don't become a victim of drowning. >

# DAY 358
# TIME TO SING

Let's make a bit of noise now. What kind of music might you put on?

| Song | Artist | Album |
|---|---|---|
| Blinding Lights | The Weeknd | *After Hours* |
| Peaches | Justin Bieber | *Justice* |
| Easy on Me | Adele | *30* |
| All Too Well | Taylor Swift | *Red* |

Are you considering making music your hobby? This is a great idea because singing releases endorphins. It's a hobby that makes you happy!

You might start singing by becoming a mic hog at a karaoke bar or becoming a candidate on *The Voice* (a singing competition TV show). Like any other skill, practice is crucial to learning how to sing flawlessly and beautifully.

Here are some tips to get you singing better: Listen to a song repetitively. Stay hydrated by drinking warm water to avoid your throat drying out. Now, stand up with your feet apart at shoulder width. Your shoulders should be in line with your hips and feet. Keep your abdomen flat and firm. Keep your body loose. Manage your breathing. Open your mouth and throat. Start singing. Keep your chin parallel to the floor. [≈ Make sure your chin doesn't point up or point down.] Don't lift your chin as you go up in pitch [≈ you sing higher [≈ high notes]]. Relax all the way through. Record your voice. [≈ Record yourself singing.] Analyse your singing afterwards to see what you could improve. (I probably shouldn't give you any tips here because singing isn't my thing.)

Now tell me: what type of music's your jam:

| | | | | |
|---|---|---|---|---|
| Pop music | Rock | Heavy metal | Country music | Blues |
| Classical music | Jazz | Musical theatre | Folk music | Reggae |

Are you crazy about any of the following bands? Put down your favourite bands in the last row of the table or in your notebook if they're not on the list.

| | | | | | |
|---|---|---|---|---|---|
| Muse | Oasis | Red Hot Chili Peppers | The Beatles | Green Day | Chicago |
| Devo | U2 | Fleetwood Mac | Coldplay | Pink Floyd | Guns N' Roses |
| Maroon 5 | Creed | Nine Inch Nails | Eagles | The Who | Supertramp |
| | | | | | |

(Music playing): 'Qing Hua Ci' ('青花瓷' 'Blue and White Porcelain') by Jay Chou, 'Seasons in the Sun' by Westlife, '365' by Katy Perry… Richard Wagner says music begins where the possibilities of language end. Let's stop talking now.

CHAPTER 41 - A Creative Hobbyist

# DAY 359
# PLAYING MUSICAL INSTRUMENTS

Are you interested in learning any of the instruments below?

| Flute | Electric/acoustic/bass/classical guitar | Piano/grand piano | Violin |
|---|---|---|---|
| Cello | Cucurbit flute | Drum | Oboe |
| Clarinet | Electronic keyboard | Trumpet | Harp |
| Erhu (二胡) | Chinese zither [≈ Guzheng (古筝)] | Accordion | Saxophone |
| Mandolin | Pipa (琵琶) | Ukulele | Trombone |

What would you call yourself when you play each of the above instruments? A flautist [≈ A flutist], a guitarist, a pianist, a violinist [≈ a violin player]…

Let's try picking up the piano…

Start with a good posture. Keep your fingers curved and relaxed. Keep your thumbs straight but loose. Align your head, shoulders, and hips for balance. Make sure your back is straight, not slumped, slouched, or hunched. Rest your feet on the floor or a footstool. [≈ Keep your feet flat on a surface.] Press the keys – and your fingers are dancing! Keep your wrists flexible.

Get to know some basic techniques [≈ fundamentals] for music notes [≈ sheet music].

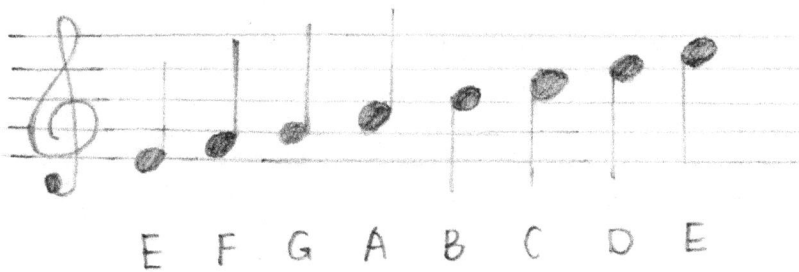

The musical alphabet is C D E F G A B C. Try practising this on your keyboard. How about going a bit faster? How about going backwards?

The next step is to make a habit of playing the piano regularly. Start with Do-Re-Mi-Fa-Sol-La-Si, 'Twinkle Little Star', 'Heart & Soul' or 'Fur Elise'. Watch some online videos. Make sure you are using the right fingers. Eventually, your fingers will do the work for you. You will start playing a few simple songs and work your way to more complicated ones – you will eventually sound bell-like, clear and crisp. If you're out of practice [≈ you haven't done it for a while ≈ you've dropped it ≈ you are losing your touch], you'll be rusty. This is the same with any hobby.

CHAPTER 41 - A Creative Hobbyist

# DAY 360
# GO BOLD WITH ART

You don't have to be Vincent van Gogh, Pablo Picasso, Claude Monet, Leonardo da Vinci, Henri Matisse or Salvador Dalí to make great paintings! Unleash your inner creativeness! Create a masterpiece!

Here's an easy way to start: take out a pen and draw the following emojis in the blank areas after the descriptions to start:

- Grinning face
- Drooling face
- Winking face
- Shushing face
- Zany face

- Face blowing a kiss
- Face savouring food
- Face screaming in fear
- Face with tears of joy
- Face with rolling eyes

Now, get some graphite pencils at the ready [≈ gather some pencils]. Let's sketch an object in front of you. Observe the object. What kind of shape does it have? Is it a circle, square, oval, rectangle, parallelogram, trapezoid, diamond, pentagon, hexagon, heptagon, octagon, nonagon or decagon? Make an outline of that object. Use different drawing methods (hatching, cross-hatching, scribbling, stippling, small circles, finger blend) to fill in the outline. Refine [≈ Finesse] the drawing to highlight and shade areas.

Next up: write neatly. Spend 10 minutes a day writing something to improve your handwriting [≈ hand lettering]. Hold the pen properly. The grip should not be too tight or too loose. Just relax. Mimic some of the below fonts from Microsoft Word on a piece of paper or in the space below:

English, *English*, English, English, **English**, *English*, English, ENGLISH

Our last activity: pick one of creative arts listed below and practise it regularly. Follow your intuition. Eventually you'll start to develop some skills in the art!

| Oil painting | Pastel | Watercolours | Chalkboard painting [≈ Blackboard drawing] |
|---|---|---|---|
| Acrylic paints | Crayon | Paper cutting | Brush calligraphy [≈ Brush lettering] |
| Clip art | Doodling | Casting | Stick figures |
| Graffiti | Sculpting | Moulding | Chinese brush painting |

# DAY 361
# FISHKEEPING 101

Check out today's title: what does '101' mean here? Something that's '101' means introductory. It comes from western university course numbering system, where '101' is the course for a beginner before they move to more advanced techniques. Plenty of 101 courses are available on YouTube, such as Toastmasters 101, Photoshop 101, or Salsa Dancing 101. These are all good hobbies you can start. Today, we'll focus on the basic knowledge of maintaining a home aquarium.

First things first, decide what type of fish you want to keep. Hardy fish are perfect for beginners [≈ are a good starter fish]. They are easy to care for and they can thrive in a wide range of water conditions (Price, 2021). Freshwater fish such as neon tetras, platies, guppies, barbs, tiger plecos and bettas are all great choices. They are communal fish that like to live in groups [≈ schools]. Such fish are not aggressive and get along well with other fish.

To start your aquarium, look for a 10-gallon tank. It takes effort to maintain the water balance in a small-sized tank. Once you have your tank, let's do some set up: Wipe clean the tank and place in some gravel. Then place in some ornaments: a Japanese shrine, marble rocks, pieces of driftwood, and so on. Install the air pump, heater and filter.

The rule here is not to fill the tank with water and add the fish on the same day. Wait for the nitrogen cycle to complete and to balance. You can use a testing kit to test the water for pH (many freshwater fish thrive between pH 6.8 and 7.8 (Douros, 2018)). You can also test for nitrates, ammonia, nitrites, chlorine and water hardness.

< One of the origins of 'testing the water' comes from bathing a baby where you dip your hand into a tub to make sure the water is at the right temperature [≈ not too hot or too cold] for the baby (Testing Waters, n.d.). >

Before putting the fish in the tank, turn your aquarium lights off so that you don't shock your fish. They will slowly acclimatise to their new environment [≈ surroundings].

As an aquarist, you need to take care of your fish. Don't forget to feed them. Don't overfeed them though. Your fish will also 'go potty' [≈ produce waste ≈ produce discharge ≈ defecate]. Change the tank water regularly to maintain the health of the water for your fish. Watch your fish swim around. Enjoy!

# DAY 362
## PETS ARE YOUR BEST FRIENDS

Keeping pets could be considered a hobby. But it's not one you can just give up on easily. In Australia, you're allowed to keep dogs, cats, rabbits, horses and some species of birds. Today, we'll talk more about keeping domestic dogs and cats.

Here are some popular cat [≈ feline ≈ kitten] breeds:

| British shorthair | Savannah | Maine coon | Russian blue | Birman |
|---|---|---|---|---|
| Persian | Sphynx | Himalayan | Ragdoll | Siamese |
| Burmese | Scottish fold | Australian mist | Devon rex | Snowshoe |

Here comes some breeds of doggies [≈ poochie ≈ puppies]:

| Siberian husky | Pit bull | Chihuahua | Pomeranian | Sausage dogs |
|---|---|---|---|---|
| Japanese spitz | Sniffer dogs | Greyhound | Pug | Jack Russell |
| Border collie | Australian terrier | British bulldog | Samoyed | German shepherd |

No matter if you're a dog person or a cat person [≈ you are a dog lover or a cat owner ≈ you like to be around dogs or cats], if you've got them at home, you must register them with your local council once they are 3 months of age and over.

Pet registration is a legal requirement in Australia. Registration must be renewed each year. Microchipping for cats and dogs is mandatory in most states. You'll need to get your pet implanted with a microchip, so if they go missing [≈ become lost], you can track them down through an app. You can get this done at the vet.

Pets can be affectionate, playful, naughty, placid, cuddly, furry, warm, clumsy or comforting. They are your companions. They give you a lot of laughs. It's said that pet owners have a lower blood pressure and heart rate.

Looking after your pets requires care and consideration. Here are a few tips for keeping pets:

- Build a pet house. Get the right food to feed your pet. Understand your pet's breed, lifestyle [≈ activity level], size and age.
- You need to walk your dog every day. Under new ACT laws, dog owners could be fined $4000 for not walking their pets (Dog Owners in Australia Face Fines for Not Letting Their Pet Out at Least Once a Day, 2019).
- Urine is hard to clean, and it is odorous. If your pet does a poo on the carpet, you need to figure out how to clean and deodorise it properly.
- You need to regularly take your pet for a hygiene tidy or for grooming and dental treatments.
- When pets fall ill or need an operation, you have to visit the vet.

If keeping pets is your hobby, treat them with compassion and give them a welcome home. Never mistreat your pet. [≈ Never abuse your pet.] You could be put in the jail. Also be aware that some dog breeds are aggressive and could attack people [≈ could be biters] if you're not careful.

# DAY 363
# BECOME A GREEN THUMB

Are you keen on growing plants at home? Take on this environmentally friendly hobby! Today's topic is for those who too often kill plants [≈ can't keep plants alive ≈ are lousy with plants ≈ are a brown thumb] but would love to become a green thumb [≈ become green fingered].

< A 'brown thumb' is someone who has poor gardening skills. Under their care, seeds don't seem to germinate. Their plants are droopy. Their flowers wilt and die. A 'green thumb' is a person who is very good at growing plants. What might a 'black thumb' be, then? >

First, decide on where to grow your plants: indoors, the courtyard, the backyard, a small plot of grass, flowerpots, or raised garden bed? What plants, flowers or vegetables do you want to grow? Maybe try one of the following:

| Herbs and beets | Bonsai | Radish | Eggplant | Kale |
| Sweet corns | Dwarf beans | Wildflowers | Camellia | Tulips |
| Love-in-a-mist | Lime tree | Climber | Hedge | Lavender |

< As its name suggests, a climber is a type of climbing plants. They can make your fence greener and prettier, screen the view, and save space in your garden beds. >

To start, pick low-maintenance plants [≈ those that are easy to grow and look after], and which are versatile [≈ have many different uses]. Here are some more tips:

- Select between plants that prefer a warm temperature [≈ thrive in sunshine or in bright light] and hardy plants that are drought resistant.
- Get seeds or plants from a nursery, or Bunnings, IKEA or even the supermarket.
- Understand your soil type. Is the soil too dry, rocky, deep, well-drained, soggy and wet, or moist? Add compost to the soil when necessary.
- Don't neglect your plant. Give them enough water, but don't overwater them!
- Your plants may attract a variety of pests. [≈ Pests might reside in your garden.] Below is a list of some different types of pests. Research how you might deal with them and keep them out of your garden.

| Caterpillars | Earthworms | Fungus gnats | Mealybugs | Whiteflies |
| Mites (red spider) | Scale insects | Snails | Citrus gall wasps | Slugs |

# CHAPTER 41 - A Creative Hobbyist

# DAY 364
## SET PEN TO PAPER

Do you love writing? Do you love playing around with beautiful words on the page? If so, I encourage you to put pen to paper (or put fingers to keyboard [≈ type on the computer]). Start with something short. Maybe try writing for just 15 minutes a day. But keep it up every day. You'll be surprised one day: you could create a masterpiece. You could be the next J K Rowling or Stephen King. Believe me. Now, put pen to paper [≈ start writing]. If you're stumped for what to write, here are a few ideas:

**Write about your day.** Wow, what a day! I was running late this morning, but I bumped into Mr President on the train. I recognised him straightaway. He was amiable and charming. I took a photo with him. It might become a collectable one day.

**Write down something new that you learnt today.** I crashed my car today. Luckily, no-one was injured. The damage was just a dent on the car door. I was in a big panic and didn't know what to do in that moment! I learnt a lesson though. Now I have to pay the excess of $600 to repair the car. I'll be more careful when driving next time.

**Write down where you spent your money today.** My morning coffee cost me $4. I spent $12 on soft-shell crab laksa for lunch. I bought a fluffy dog [≈ a plush dog] for $10 for the kids. Write down your daily spending habits and add the whole month up. You'll be surprised how much money goes out when you're not thinking about it.

< About one or two years ago, a takeaway laksa meal would be just around $12 in Melbourne. However, by 2022 it would cost you about $17 to get a laksa or fish and chips or any other takeaway meal because of the inflation seen in food, grocery and petrol prices. >

**Unleash your imagination and play with some fiction.** The last piece of ice on the Earth is melting. The oceans are submerging all the islands that humans live on. God blames us for damaging the beautiful Earth. He has decided to create new lives for us on another planet called HEART (which has the same letters with EARTH).

**Give some commentary on the news.** In February 2022, in spite of facing sanctions from other countries, Russia invaded Ukraine. The conflict is happening again between Russia and Ukraine after many years! Just within a few days, hundreds of people were killed, and thousands of Ukrainians were forced to flee to neighbouring countries. We are in a world that should be pursuing peace at all costs. Everyone on the planet deserves the right to a peaceful life.

**Try some spontaneous writing or drawing on some blank paper!** You never know when a great idea will just spark!

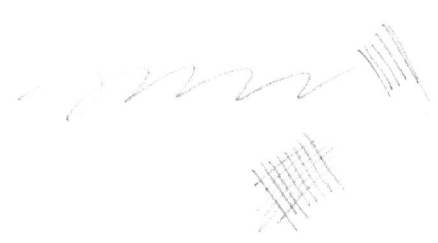

# DAY 365
# THE WORD - OVER

We've come to the last day. Hooray!

Do you still remember that sentence mentioned in the preface of this book: 'The quick brown fox jumps over the lazy dog'? What's the trick here? Let's reveal the answer!

This sentence is a pangram. It contains all 26 English letters in the one sentence! [≈ It is a sentence that contains all of the letters of the alphabet!] Can you believe we've come this far? What a terrific job!

**Go over** [≈ **Brush over**] **Day 29 Give It Your All** of the book and recap [≈ revisit ≈ revise ≈ rub up on ≈ review ≈ get a refresher] how to express 'hard work'. Here are other similar expressions:

- I have **bent over backwards** learning *The English Builder!*.
- I have spent a year **poring over** *The English Builder!*.
- I **sweated over** [≈ bashed away at ≈ **exerted** myself **over**] my English studies.

Now let's **jump over to** a short story.

I once dated a guy for 3 years, but he broke up with me for no reasons whatsoever. I'd fallen **head over heels** in love with him. I **bent over** as a feeling of anger **washed over** me.

I **tripped over** the footpath on the way back home. I **stayed over** at my bestie's place, and we **wandered over** to the park in the dark.

Since then, I've **mulled over** [≈ **ruminated over** ≈ pondered ≈ seriously considered] my future and living life without him. After a long period of time, I finally **got over** him.

My new life has **ticked over** for a while now. I'm so glad that I had my bestie to help **tide** me **over** the difficult times. Eventually, they were **over** [≈ The evil has left the building]. Everything's hunky dory now. [≈ Everything's fine and dandy. ≈ All is well now.] I've now found the love of my life!

End of story.

Congratulations! You've stuck with me to the end. This book might have taken you 365 days to read, or less if you read a few days at a time. Hopefully the writing has helped you to take your English to the next level. This book is coming to the end, but the game is not **over**. Your journey has just started. Embark on a new journey.

It's the beginning of a new chapter. Whatever you do, please do your best [≈ try your best]. Now, **turn over** the page [≈ **see over** the next page]. Now it's **over** to you!

# DAY 366
# YOUR TURN

From today onwards, it's your turn to start a new chapter. The ball is in your court now.

Do whatever you like on this page. Jot down any phrases or wisdom that you've learnt along the way. Make a little drawing for how your house is looking. Stick a photo of a memorable trip here. Tell me an anecdote about your English learning journey.

Imagine where you might go to from here. Just be creative!

# THE END

Congratulations! You've finished reading *The English Builder!!*

With all the effort you've put in while reading this book, how many 'bricks' have you laid down for your home? How good is your English now? What level of English would you like to reach moving forward?

- ☐ Intermediate
- ☐ Advanced level
- ☐ Proficient
- ☐ Expert

I hope that you've built up your own English 'house' (or skyscraper, bungalow, castle, cabin, cottage, fortress, hut, lighthouse, palace, yurt, farmhouse) with all the vocabulary, phrases and sentences I've included in this book. As a committed English Builder, you're now hopefully able to use what you've learnt to communicate better in English, verbal or written. It would be great if this book triggered further interest in your English studies or provided some guidance for your upcoming English tests. I guarantee the book will help to enrich your overseas experience and take you by the hand when you get into difficult situations in life. By reading it day by day, you developed new learning habits and used a bit of English every day.

Most importantly, what you should do now is to set up goals that matter to you and start to work on them. Goals on anything. Study. Work. Home improvement. New hobbies. Improving your English further.

Don't give it up easily. Even if you fall during the journey, you'll grow and learn from your experiences. You will accomplish [≈ actualise ≈ fulfill] your dreams. By then, it may feel surreal. It's true! There will be a big reward for tremendous effort and raw determination. When you succeed, savour the moment! If you desire to go further, I applaud you! Remember, no matter what your aim is: love, live and create a life that you desire. This is the ultimate goal for this book. I'm looking forward to hearing good news from you! Come on, buddies!

Here's one last question from me: What hurdle will you attempt to clear next? Are you thinking to build yourself another house?

# APPENDIX 1 COMMON BOY NAMES

- Howard
- Cameron
- Bishop
- Craig
- Santos
- Louie
- Randall
- Chad
- Gatlin
- Elliott
- Marley
- Agustin
- Lyric
- Markus
- Foster
- Shepard
- Marshall
- Muhammad
- Trevor
- Rory
- Clark
- Alexander
- Valentino
- Derek
- Wells
- Achilles
- Ronnie
- Darrell
- Duncan
- Alfred
- Jerome
- Adrian
- Billy
- Hugh
- Darwin
- Merrick
- Gerald
- Gordon
- Jordy
- Wayne
- Brentley
- Henrik
- Joey
- Jeffery
- Stefan
- Brett
- Kelvin
- Ford
- Tommy
- Eddie
- Terry
- Darrel
- Morgan
- Callan
- Morris
- Shawn
- Malcolm
- Kristopher
- Lennon
- Boston
- Legend
- Paul
- Lucas
- Kingsley
- Mitchell
- Harley
- Wilson
- Harrison
- Fletcher
- Douglas
- Carl
- Devon
- Curtis
- Jimmy
- Jerry
- Dennis
- Cannon
- Roy
- Ken
- Rodrigo
- Nathan
- Otto
- Ronald
- Bowen
- Dexter
- Connor
- Franklin
- Owen
- Austin
- Phillip
- Marcos
- Emanuel
- Alan
- Sullivan
- Phoenix
- Warwick
- Theo
- Cesar
- Desmond
- Edwin
- Troy
- Sergio
- Jose
- Zachary
- Maxwell
- King
- Ayden
- Warren
- Hayden
- Joel
- Dean
- Dawson
- Bryan
- Lukas
- Beckett
- Holden
- Griffin
- Leon
- Walter
- Lincoln
- Hunter
- Leo
- Lee
- Adam

# APPENDIX 2 POPULAR GIRL NAMES

- Helen
- Victoria
- Belinda
- Brooklyn
- Savannah
- Vivian
- Lillian
- Aria
- Sofia
- Evelyn
- Alison
- Chelsea
- Veronica
- Kira
- Heidi
- Angel
- Hayley
- Laura
- Nina
- Phoebe
- Francesca
- Sylvia
- Demi
- Frances
- Abby
- Rosemary
- Mackenzie
- Katherine
- Josephine
- Ivy
- Maria
- Hadley
- Kylie
- Faith
- Andrea
- Jasmine
- Margaret
- Caroline
- Amy
- Stella
- Lucy
- Rose
- Bella
- Mary
- Jada
- Sabrina
- Ruth
- Maggie
- Joanna
- Aubrielle
- Nicole
- Fiona
- Paige
- Nancy
- Raquel
- Cara
- Natasha
- Hana
- Christine
- Belle
- Joyce
- Lara
- Elora
- Simone
- Bridget
- Marissa
- Linda
- Jolie
- Mara
- Courtney
- Kristy
- Sandra
- Blaire
- Kristina
- Susan
- Beth
- Taliyah
- Florence
- Danna
- Remi
- Karla
- Gloria
- Tiffany
- Kelly
- Crystal
- Nicola
- Faye
- Rachel
- Brooke
- Catherine
- Camilla
- Diana
- Tessa
- Annalise
- Mia
- Molly
- Lauren
- Kimberly
- Nova
- Eva
- Gabriella
- Kinsley
- Melanie
- Teagan
- Elise
- Holland
- Karlie
- Vada
- Teresa
- Virginia
- Melissa
- Kate
- Izabella
- Kathy
- Amina
- Collins
- Mina
- Kori
- Elaine
- Logan
- Penelope
- Violet
- Valentina
- Madeline

# REFERENCES

- *6 Ways to Be a Better Neighbour – and Why It Matters*. (2019, March 28). Retrieved from News City of Sydeny: https://news.cityofsydney.nsw.gov.au/articles/6-ways-to-be-a-better-neighbour-and-why-it-matters.
- *7 Products You Didn't Know Come From Trees*. (n.d.). Retrieved from World Wildlife: https://www.worldwildlife.org/stories/7-products-you-didn-t-know-come-from-trees.
- *About Chinatown*. (n.d.). Retrieved from Chinatown Melbourne: https://chinatownmelbourne.com.au/about-chinatown/.
- *About SPF50+ Sunscreen*. (n.d.). Retrieved from Cancer Council: https://www.cancer.org.au/cancer-information/causes-and-prevention/sun-safety/about-sunscreen/spf50-sunscreen.
- Albright, D. (2018, May 15). *10 Email Facts to Impress*. Retrieved from Atmail: https://www.atmail.com/blog/10-email-facts-to-impress/.
- *All Around the World How Many Countries Are There in the World?* (2021, January 18). Retrieved from The Sun: https://www.thesun.co.uk/news/13732092/how-many-countries-world/.
- *All You Need to Know About Leather Doctor's Bags*. (n.d.). Retrieved from Mahi: https://mahileather.com/blogs/news/all-you-need-to-know-about-leather-doctor-s-bags.
- Allen, S. (n.d.). *What Is "Mea Culpa"?* Retrieved from Grammarly: https://www.grammarly.com/blog/mea-culpa/.
- *Animal Experimentation*. (n.d.). Retrieved from Animals Australia: https://animalsaustralia.org/issues/animal_experimentation.php.
- Ascott, E. (2021, November 19). *AI Will Create 97 Million Jobs, But Workers Don't Have the Skills Required (Yet)*. Retrieved from All Work: https://allwork.space/2021/11/ai-will-create-97-million-jobs-but-workers-dont-have-the-skills-required-yet/.
- Ashley. (2018, April 4). *Factsheet: Are You Entitled to Long Service Leave?* Retrieved from Professionals Austraila: http://www.professionalsaustralia.org.au/blog/entitled-long-service-leave/.
- *Asia Population*. (n.d.). Retrieved from Worldometers: https://www.worldometers.info/world-population/asia-population/.
- *Australia Powerball Prizes*. (n.d.). Retrieved n.d., from Lotto: https://www.lotto.net/australia-powerball/prizes.
- Baker, H. (2021, May 22). *Do Goldfish Really Have a 3-second Memory?* Retrieved from Livescience: https://www.livescience.com/goldfish-memory.html.
- Balfour, A. (2019, January 17). *Melbourne Grand Prix Circuit (Albert Park)*. Retrieved from Motorsport Guides: https://motorsportguides.com/melbourne-grand-prix-circuit/.
- *Ball of Fire*. (n.d.). Retrieved from Idioms.thefreedictionary: https://idioms.thefreedictionary.com/ball+of+fire.
- *Ball Tempering*. (n.d.). Retrieved from Wikipedia: https://en.wikipedia.org/wiki/Ball_tampering.
- *BC and AD, BCE and CE: What's the Difference?* (2017, December). Retrieved from Druide: https://www.druide.com/en/reports/bc-and-ad-bce-and-ce-whats-difference.
- *Behind the Eight Ball*. (n.d.). Retrieved from Grammarist: https://grammarist.com/idiom/behind-the-eight-ball/.
- Beurkens, D. N. (2020, July 21). *How Does Technology Affect Children's Social Development?* Retrieved from Qustodio: https://www.qustodio.com/en/2020/07/21/technology-child-social-development/.
- Bicks, B. (2019, July 11). *Do Cats Really Have 9 Lives? What You Should Know About Your Cat's Ability to Survive*. Retrieved from Pawp: https://pawp.com/do-cats-really-have-9-lives-what-you-should-know-about-your-cats-ability-to/.

# REFERENCES

- Biello, D. (2006, December 8). *Fact or Fiction?: Archimedes Coined the Term "Eureka!" in the Bath*. Retrieved from Scientific American: https://www.scientificamerican.com/article/fact-or-fiction-archimede/.

- Bishop, T. (2013, September 27). *The Rest of the Story: Control-Alt-Delete Inventor Didn't Expect It to Be Widely Used*. Retrieved from Geekwire: https://www.geekwire.com/2013/rest-story-controlaltdelete-inventor-expect-command-widely/.

- *Blah Blah Blah Day*. (2021, April 17). Retrieved from Days of the Year: https://www.daysoftheyear.com/days/blah-blah-blah-day/.

- Borji, H. (2016, July 25). *4 Global Economic Issues of an Aging Population*. Retrieved from Investopedia: https://www.investopedia.com/articles/investing/011216/4-global-economic-issues-aging-population.asp.

- Brianna Elliott, R. (2016, October 8). *Best Dark Chocolate: The Ultimate Buyer's Guide*. Retrieved from Healthline: https://www.healthline.com/nutrition/dark-chocolate-buyers-guide.

- Buddy the Elf. (n.d.). *Did Santa Claus Used to Be Green? Let's Learn About It*. Retrieved from Santa Claus and Christmas: https://santaclausandchristmas.com/did-santa-claus-used-to-be-green/.

- Burin, M. (2015, January 23). *Aussie Mateship: Tracing the History of a Defining Cultural Term*. Retrieved from ABC: https://www.abc.net.au/local/stories/2015/01/23/4167572.htm.

- Burrows, V. (2020, February 20). *Wait, Tempura Isn't Japanese? So Where Is Everyone's Favourite Healthy Fried Food Really From?* Retrieved from Style: https://www.scmp.com/magazines/style/leisure/article/3051515/wait-tempura-isnt-japanese-so-where-everyones-favourite.

- *Catcall*. (n.d.). Retrieved from Etymonline: https://www.etymonline.com/word/catcall.

- *Chicken Wing History*. (2017, January 24). Retrieved from National Chicken Council: https://www.nationalchickencouncil.org/chicken-wing-history/.

- *Civic Issues - Deforestation*. (2016, February 19). Retrieved from Sites at Penn State: https://sites.psu.edu/rcl2jacobsciosciaissues/2016/02/19/deforestation/.

- Clear, J. (n.d.). *What Happens to Your Brain When You Eat Junk Food*. Retrieved from James Clear: https://jamesclear.com/junk-food-science.

- Cook, E. (2017, October 3). *One Hour of Exercise a Week Can Prevent Depression*. Retrieved from UNSW Sydney Newsroom: https://newsroom.unsw.edu.au/news/health/one-hour-exercise-week-can-prevent-depression.

- *Cosmetics Testing FAQ*. (n.d.). Retrieved from The Hunman Society Of The United States: https://www.humanesociety.org/resources/cosmetics-testing-faq.

- *COVID-19 Coronavirus Pandemic*. (2022, May 04). Retrieved from Worldometer: https://www.worldometers.info/coronavirus/.

- Cox, L., & Butler, B. (2019, November 7). *Native Forest Logging to Be Phased Out by 2030 As Victoria Plans Timber Transition*. Retrieved from The Guardian: https://www.theguardian.com/australia-news/2019/nov/07/native-forest-logging-to-be-phased-out-by-2030-as-victoria-plans-timber-transition.

- *Cradle of Humankind*. (2021, May 24). Retrieved from Wikipedia: https://en.wikipedia.org/wiki/Cradle_of_Humankind.

- *Cream of the Crop*. (n.d.). Retrieved from The Free Dictionary: https://idioms.thefreedictionary.com/cream+of+the+crop.

- Croissant, M. (2021, June 7). *The Strangest French Superstitions*. Retrieved from Expatica: https://www.expatica.com/fr/moving/society-history/french-superstitions-579687/.

- Croxon, N. (2020, March 6). *Thirty-three Per Cent of People Report Workplace Sexual Harassment in Australia in Last Five Years*. Retrieved from Bendigo Advertiser: https://www.bendigoadvertiser.com.au/story/6665556/thirty-three-per-cent-of-people-report-workplace-sexual-harassment/.

# REFERENCES

- *David Bradley (Engineer)*. (2020, November 15). Retrieved from Wikipedia: https://en.wikipedia.org/wiki/David_Bradley_(engineer).
- *Difference Between Cookies and Biscuits*. (2015, December 11). Retrieved from Pediaa: https://pediaa.com/difference-between-cookies-and-biscuits/.
- *Differences Between British and American English*. (n.d.). Retrieved from British Council Foundation: https://www.britishcouncilfoundation.id/zh-hans/node/2623.
- *Dim Sim*. (2021, May 13). Retrieved from Wikipedia: https://en.wikipedia.org/wiki/Dim_sim.
- *Do Elephants Ever Forget?* (n.d.). Retrieved from Wonderropolis: https://wonderopolis.org/wonder/do-elephants-ever-forget.
- *Does Your Heart Stop When You Sneeze?* (2019, November 11). Retrieved from Library of Congress: https://www.loc.gov/everyday-mysteries/item/does-your-heart-stop-when-you-sneeze/.
- *Dog Owners in Australia Face Fines for Not Letting Their Pet Out at Least Once a Day*. (2019, September 26). Retrieved from Yahoo News: https://au.news.yahoo.com/dog-owners-australia-fine-not-letting-out-once-a-day-104929448.html.
- Doss, L. (2021, February 5). *The Surprising Origin of Ranch Dressing*. Retrieved from Mashed: https://www.mashed.com/328036/the-surprising-origin-of-ranch-dressing/.
- Douros, C. J. (2018, January 4). *How to Raise the Alkalinity in a Freshwater Aquarium*. Retrieved from Medium: https://medium.com/chuck-douros/how-to-raise-the-alkalinity-in-a-freshwater-aquarium-fb4a20895c9b.
- *Drake Passage*. (n.d.). Retrieved from The Solo Female Traveler Network: https://thesolofemaletravelernetwork.com/adventures/antarctica/drake-passage/.
- Dubé, D.-E. (2017, April 21). *This Is How Much Time You Spend On Work Emails Every Day, According to a Canadian Survey*. Retrieved from Globalnews: https://globalnews.ca/news/3395457/this-is-how-much-time-you-spend-on-work-emails-every-day-according-to-a-canadian-survey/.
- *Easy Peasy Lemon Squeezy*. (n.d.). Retrieved from Dictionary: https://www.dictionary.com/e/slang/easy-peasy-lemon-squeezy/.
- Ely, M. (2013, September 24). *History Behind 'An Apple a Day'*. Retrieved from The Washington Post: https://www.washingtonpost.com/lifestyle/wellness/history-behind-an-apple-a-day/2013/09/24/aac3e79c-1f0e-11e3-94a2-6c66b668ea55_story.html.
- *Excel Incorrectly Assumes That the Year 1900 Is a Leap Year*. (2021, May 17). Retrieved from Microsoft: https://docs.microsoft.com/en-us/office/troubleshoot/excel/wrongly-assumes-1900-is-leap-year.
- *Fat-Finger*. (n.d.). Retrieved from Merriam Webster: https://www.merriam-webster.com/words-at-play/fat-finger-meaning.
- Filippone, P. T. (2019, January 5). *Origin and History of Worcestershire Sauce*. Retrieved from The Spruce Eats: https://www.thespruceeats.com/worcestershire-sauce-history-1807686.
- *Fine Amounts & Demerit Points*. (n.d.). Retrieved from Cameras Save Lives: https://www.camerassavelives.vic.gov.au/fines-penalties/fine-amounts-demerit-points.
- *FIRB Approval*. (n.d.). Retrieved from Home Loan Expert: https://www.homeloanexperts.com.au/non-resident-mortgages/firb-approval/.
- *Flat as a Tack*. (n.d.). Retrieved from Idioms.thefreedictionary: https://idioms.thefreedictionary.com/flat+as+a+tack.
- *Fly Off the Handle*. (n.d.). Retrieved from Grammarist: https://grammarist.com/phrase/fly-off-the-handle/.
- Foley, M. (2019, February 15). *What's the Origin of the Word 'Cocktail'?* Retrieved from Chowhound: https://www.chowhound.com/food-news/54845/whats-the-origin-of-the-word-cocktail/.

# REFERENCES

- Funk, C. (2016, February 12). *Harassment: Effects on People and Organisations.* Retrieved from Bookboon: https://bookboon.com/blog/2016/02/harassment-and-its-effects/.

- G., P. (2020, May 25). *Performance Reviews Are Useless and Demeaning and You Shouldn't Do Them.* Retrieved from LinkedIn: https://www.linkedin.com/pulse/performance-reviews-useless-demeaning-you-shouldnt-do-patrick-gainer.

- Gandhi, L. (2013, December 23). *The Extraordinary Story of Why a 'Cakewalk' Wasn't Always Easy.* Retrieved from NPR: https://www.npr.org/sections/codeswitch/2013/12/23/256566647/the-extraordinary-story-of-why-a-cakewalk-wasnt-always-easy.

- *Gelato vs Ice Cream - What's the Difference?* (n.d.). Retrieved from Messina: https://gelatomessina.com/blog/gelato-vs-ice-cream-whats-the-difference.

- *Get Your Feet Wet.* (2019, February 25). Retrieved from Phrases: https://www.phrases.com/phrase/get-your-feet-wet_44704.

- Gilbert, B. (2019, July 31). *Almost 30% of Delivery Drivers Admit to Taking Food from an Order, According to a New Survey.* Retrieved from Business Insider Australia: https://www.businessinsider.com.au/uber-eats-delivery-drivers-eating-food-2019-7?r=US&IR=T.

- Goudreau, J. (2010, March 4). *Find Happiness at Work.* Retrieved from Forbes: https://www.forbes.com/2010/03/04/happiness-work-resilience-forbes-woman-well-being-satisfaction.html?sh=6f22d90e126a.

- Granero, K. (2019, August 28). *Everything You Need to Know About the History of the Scrunchie.* Retrieved from Purewow: https://www.purewow.com/fashion/history-scrunchie.

- Granic, I., Lobel, A., & Engels, R. C. (2014, January). *The Benefits of Playing Video Games.* Retrieved from Apa: https://www.apa.org/pubs/journals/releases/amp-a0034857.pdf.

- Greenwald, K. (2004, November 12). *Wordwizard.* Retrieved from Use Your Noodle: http://www.wordwizard.com/phpbb3/viewtopic.php?t=6956.

- Hanrahan, J. (2018, November 5). *Promising Rugby Player Who Became a Paraplegic After Swallowing a Garden Slug as a Dare at a Birthday Party Dies Aged 28 - After an Eight Year Battle with a Parasite Infection.* Retrieved from Dailymail: https://www.dailymail.co.uk/news/article-6352629/Sam-Ballard-dies-eight-years-swallowing-slug.html.

- Haridy, R. (2018, April 12). *Bad News Night-owls: Staying Up Late Could Be Killing You.* Retrieved from New Atlas: https://newatlas.com/night-owl-higher-risk-death/54196/.

- *Head Over Heels.* (n.d.). Retrieved from Dictionary: https://www.dictionary.com/browse/head-over-heels.

- Hersh, E. (2012, October 27). *How Happy Are Clams?* Retrieved from MentalFloss: https://www.mentalfloss.com/article/12846/how-happy-are-clams.

- Heventhal, B. (2021, May 10). *Renaissance Man: How Leonardo da Vinci Changed What It Meant to Truly Live.* Retrieved from AutoDesk: https://www.autodesk.com/products/fusion-360/blog/renaissance-man-leonardo-da-vinci-changed-live/.

- Hiskey, D. (2010, June 16). *What A.M. and P.M. Stand For.* Retrieved from Today I Found Out: http://www.todayifoundout.com/index.php/2010/06/what-am-and-pm-stand-for/.

- *History of the Yarra River.* (n.d.). Retrieved from Melbourne Boat Hire: https://melbourneboathire.com.au/news/history-of-the-yarra-river/.

- Houston, C. (2020, April 11). *Melbourne Uni Pays Out $700,000 to PhD Student.* Retrieved from The Age: https://www.theage.com.au/national/victoria/melbourne-uni-pays-out-700-000-to-phd-student-20200410-p54ixi.html.

- *How Was Australia Named?* (n.d.). Retrieved from National Library of Australia: https://www.nla.gov.au/faq/how-was-australia-named.

- Huber, C., & Bean, C. (n.d.). *Identifying Sexual Harassment Complaint Causes to Improve Workplace Safety.* Retrieved from BKS Partners: https://bks-partners.com/articles/identifying-sexual-harassment-complaint-causes/.

# REFERENCES

- Huesmann, L., & Taylor, L. (2006). *The Role of Media Violence in Violent Behavior*. Retrieved from Annual Review of Public Health: https://www.annualreviews.org/doi/pdf/10.1146/annurev.publhealth.26.021304.144640.
- Hutchinson, S. (2013, September 3). *Is It True That Elephants Never Forget?* Retrieved from Mental Floss: https://www.mentalfloss.com/article/52381/it-true-elephants-never-forget.
- *Inside Australian Online Shopping*. (n.d.). Retrieved from AusPost: https://auspost.com.au/content/dam/auspost_corp/media/documents/ecommerce-industry-report-2021.pdf.
- Jones, M. (n.d.). *Faux Pas Meaning & How to Use It*. Retrieved from SpeakUp Resources: https://magoosh.com/english-speaking/faux-pas/.
- Jones, N. (2020, October 29). *Will Robots Take Our Jobs If Accounting Is Automated?* Retrieved from Floqast: https://floqast.com/blog/will-robots-take-our-jobs-if-accounting-is-automated/.
- *Jump on the Bandwagon*. (n.d.). Retrieved from The Phrase Finder: https://www.phrases.org.uk/meanings/jump-on-the-bandwagon.html.
- *Jump on the Bandwagon*. (n.d.). Retrieved from Ginger Software: https://www.gingersoftware.com/content/phrases/jump-on-the-bandwagon/.
- *Jump Through Hoops*. (n.d.). Retrieved from Grammarist: https://grammarist.com/idiom/jump-through-hoops/.
- Kagan, J. (2021, April 19). *Glass Ceiling*. Retrieved from Investopedia: https://www.investopedia.com/terms/g/glass-ceiling.asp.
- Kelly, J. (2016, June 29). *The Origins of 19 'Skin' Expressions*. Retrieved from Mentalfloss: https://www.mentalfloss.com/article/81624/origins-19-skin-expressions.
- Ketchell, M. (Ed.). (2020, March 5). *Why Are People Stockpiling Toilet Paper? We Asked Four Experts*. Retrieved from The Conversation: https://theconversation.com/why-are-people-stockpiling-toilet-paper-we-asked-four-experts-132975.
- Kilmann, C. (2020, May 3). *Idioms Are Weird. Why Did Curiosity Kill the Cat?* Retrieved from Curiosity Never Killed the Writer: https://curiosityneverkilledthewriter.com/idioms-are-weird-why-did-curiosity-kill-the-cat-476ed762989d.
- Koerner, B. (2003, April 3). *Where Do "Cakewalks" Come From?* Retrieved from Slate: https://slate.com/news-and-politics/2003/04/where-do-cakewalks-come-from.html.
- Kyff, R. (2006, December 26). *Whence Origin of `Go South'? Look at a Map*. Retrieved from Courant: https://www.courant.com/news/connecticut/hc-xpm-2006-12-26-0612260438-story.html.
- Lammle, R. (2018, July 11). *11 Facts About 7-Eleven on 7/11*. Retrieved from Mental Floss: https://www.mentalfloss.com/article/51629/11-facts-about-7-eleven-711.
- Leahy, S. (2018, May 18). *How Zero-Waste People Make Only a Jar of Trash a Year*. Retrieved from National Geographic: https://www.nationalgeographic.com/science/article/zero-waste-families-plastic-culture.
- Lemonick, S. (2017, September 29). *Scientists Underestimated How Bad Cow Farts Are*. Retrieved from Forbes: https://www.forbes.com/sites/samlemonick/2017/09/29/scientists-underestimated-how-bad-cow-farts-are/?sh=2094c32a78a9.
- Lesiuk, T. (2021, May 14). *What You Should Really Know About Time Off in Lieu?* Retrieved from Factorial Blog: https://factorialhr.com/blog/time-in-lieu-explained/.
- *Life Is (Just) a Bowl of Cherries*. (n.d.). Retrieved from Idioms.TheFreeDictionary: https://idioms.thefreedictionary.com/life+is+(just)+a+bowl+of+cherries.
- *Like Gangbusters*. (n.d.). Retrieved from Grammarist: https://grammarist.com/usage/like-gangbusters/#:~:text=Originally%20it%20meant%20with%20great,lots%20of%20loud%20sound%20effects).
- *Lottery Mathematics*. (2021, May 16). Retrieved from Wikipedia: https://en.wikipedia.org/wiki/Lottery_mathematics.

# REFERENCES

- Lyall, A. (n.d.). *When Is the Right Time to Put Up and Take Down Your Christmas Tree?* Retrieved from 9Now: https://9now.nine.com.au/the-block/christmas-tree-when-to-put-up-and-take-down/1d589276-afd3-43c4-8951-2b3d67d16305.

- MacKay, J. (2021, February 9). *Context Switching: Why Jumping Between Tasks Is Killing Your Productivity (and What You Can Do About It)*. Retrieved from RescueTime:Blog: https://blog.rescuetime.com/context-switching/.

- Mangold, R. (2011, July 21). *A Decision in Due Season*. Retrieved from Serminutes – Sermon in a Minute: https://serminutes.com/tag/robert-schuller-story-about-cutting-a-tree-down-in-winter/.

- Martin, G. (n.d.). *Save One's Bacon*. Retrieved from The Phrase Finder: https://www.phrases.org.uk/meanings/save-ones-bacon.html.

- McCausland, P. (2019, Novenmber 10). *Self-driving Uber Car That Hit and Killed Woman Did Not Recognize That Pedestrians Jaywalk*. Retrieved from NBC News: https://www.nbcnews.com/tech/tech-news/self-driving-uber-car-hit-killed-woman-did-not-recognize-n1079281.

- McLean, H. (2020, August 31). *6 "Fun Facts" About Microsoft Excel*. Retrieved from New Horizons: https://www.newhorizons-jax.com/blog/6-fun-facts-about-microsoft-excel.

- Mejia, Z. (2018, April 29). *The No. 1 Thing Bill Gates Wishes He'd Done in College*. Retrieved from Make it: https://www.cnbc.com/2018/04/27/the-no-1-thing-bill-gates-wishes-hed-done-at-harvard.html.

- Meredith E. Gansner, M. (2017, September 6). *"The Internet Made Me Do It"-Social Media and Potential for Violence in Adolescents*. Retrieved from Psychiatric Times: https://www.psychiatrictimes.com/view/-internet-made-me-do-itsocial-media-and-potential-violence-adolescents.

- *Minimum Wages*. (n.d.). Retrieved from Fairwork: https://www.fairwork.gov.au/pay/minimum-wages.

- *More on Feeding Nine Billion People by 2050*. (n.d.). Retrieved from Agricultural Marketing: https://www.agmrc.org/renewable-energy/renewable-energy-climate-change-report/renewable-energy-climate-change-report/january-2012-newsletter/more-on-feeding-nine-billion-people-by-2050.

- Morgan, J. (2019, October 18). *Difference Between Parsley and Coriander*. Retrieved from Difference Between: http://www.differencebetween.net/object/comparisons-of-food-items/difference-between-parsley-and-coriander/.

- *Murder of Hannah Clarke*. (2021, June 2). Retrieved from Wikipedia: https://en.wikipedia.org/wiki/Murder_of_Hannah_Clarke.

- *New Zealand People*. (n.d.). Retrieved from 100% Pure New Zealand: https://www.newzealand.com/au/feature/new-zealand-people/.

- *Nine Things You Need To Know About the Michelle Payne Story*. (n.d.). Retrieved from Michelle Payne: https://michellejpayne.com.au/nine-things-need-know-michelle-payne/.

- *Nut-Free Super-Seed Oat Bars*. (n.d.). Retrieved from My Food Book: https://myfoodbook.com.au/tips/types-of-oats.

- *On the Wrong Foot and on the Right Foot*. (n.d.). Retrieved from Grammarist: https://grammarist.com/idiom/on-the-wrong-foot-on-the-right-foot/.

- Ortonsault. (2008, January 10). *Fuck the Heck*. Retrieved from Urban Dictionary: https://www.urbandictionary.com/define.php?term=fuck%20the%20heck.

- *Out of Sorts*. (n.d.). Retrieved from Grammarist: https://grammarist.com/phrase/out-of-sorts/.

- Patrick, N. (2016, August 28). *The Word "Checkmate" Derives From the Persian Phrase "Shah Met" Which Means "the King Is Dead"*. Retrieved from Vintage News: https://www.thevintagenews.com/2016/08/28/word-checkmate-derives-persian-phrase-shah-met-means-king-dead/.

# REFERENCES

- Payes, J. (2013, January 10). *Have You Kicked Your Tires Lately?* Retrieved from Livingston Church of Christ: https://livingstoncoc.wordpress.com/2013/01/10/have-you-kicked-your-tires-lately/.
- Payton, M. (2015, June 4). *8 Commonly Used Phrases and Their Interesting Origins.* Retrieved from Metro: https://metro.co.uk/2015/06/04/8-commonly-used-phrases-and-their-interesting-origins-5230002/.
- Peter Grinspoon, M. (2020, December 22). *The Health Effects of Too Much Gaming.* Retrieved from Harvard Health Publishing: https://www.health.harvard.edu/blog/the-health-effects-of-too-much-gaming-2020122221645.
- *Phonetic Alphabet: The Story From Alpha to Zulu.* (2019, April 17). Retrieved from The Week: https://www.theweek.co.uk/70110/alpha-bravo-charlie-how-was-natos-phonetic-alphabet-chosen.
- Picard, C. (2017, January 3). *If You Swear a Lot, You're More Honest — Science Says So.* Retrieved from Good Housekeeping: https://www.goodhousekeeping.com/life/news/a42172/swearing-honesty-study/.
- *Pinot Nero (Pinot Noir).* (n.d.). Retrieved from Italian Wine Connection: https://www.italianwineconnection.com.au/pages/pinot-nero-pinot-noir.
- *Poker Face.* (n.d.). Retrieved from Grammarist: https://grammarist.com/idiom/poker-face/.
- *Population.* (n.d.). Retrieved from Australian Bureau of Statistics: https://www.abs.gov.au/statistics/people/population.
- *Prevalence.* (n.d.). Retrieved from White Ribbon Australia: https://www.whiteribbon.org.au/Learn-more/Get-the-facts/Facts-and-Statistics/Prevalence.
- Price, L. (2021, March 27). *13 Best Freshwater Fish for Your Home Aquarium.* Retrieved from Fishkeeping Advice: https://fishkeepingadvice.com/13-best-freshwater-fish/.
- *Put On Airs.* (n.d.). Retrieved from Vocabulary: https://www.vocabulary.com/dictionary/put%20on%20airs.
- Rabe, T. (2019, July 9). *International Students Pushed Into 'Dark Corners' of Sydney's Rental Market.* Retrieved from The Sydney Morning Herald: https://www.smh.com.au/national/nsw/international-students-pushed-into-dark-corners-of-sydney-s-rental-market-20190708-p525aw.html.
- *Raining Cats and Dogs.* (2022, April 26). Retrieved from Wikipedia: https://en.wikipedia.org/wiki/Raining_cats_and_dogs.
- Rathore, J. S. (2015, July 3). *7 Interesting Stories Behind the Origin of Your Favourite Cocktail.* Retrieved from Storypick: https://www.storypick.com/famous-cocktails-origins/.
- *Record $71 Million in Prize Money for Australian Open 2020.* (2019, December 24). Retrieved from AO: https://ausopen.com/articles/news/record-71-million-prize-money-australian-open-2020.
- *Right Off the Bat.* (n.d.). Retrieved from Know Your Phrase: https://knowyourphrase.com/right-off-the-bat.
- Rocchi, J. (2015, November 10). *Six Practical Reasons to Save Old Buildings.* Retrieved from SavingPlaces: https://savingplaces.org/stories/six-reasons-save-old-buildings#.YLdoJS2r2qA.
- Roos, D. (2021, April 1). *What Are the Different Types of Cheese?* Retrieved from How Stuff Works: https://recipes.howstuffworks.com/dairy/different-types-of-cheese.htm.
- Ross, J. (2016, April 24). *4 Quotes That You Have Been Terribly Misquoting.* Retrieved from Student Voices: https://mystudentvoices.com/4-quotes-that-you-have-been-terribly-misquoting-6b2233d3212d.
- Rumana. (2019, March 4). *Advantages and Disadvantages of Watching Television.* Retrieved from Reel Run Down: https://reelrundown.com/tv/Advantages-and-Disadvantages-of-watching-Television.

# REFERENCES

- *Run Out of Steam*. (n.d.). Retrieved from Gingersoftware: https://www.gingersoftware.com/content/phrases/run-out-of-steam/.
- Saiidi, U. (2018, February 21). *Australia's Banknotes May Be the Most Advanced in the World*. Retrieved from CNBC: https://www.cnbc.com/2018/02/21/australian-banknotes-one-of-the-most-advanced-in-the-world.html.
- Sam. (2020, September 15). *The Surprising History of the Aussie Ugg Boot*. Retrieved from Everything Australian: https://everythingaustralian.com.au/blog/post/the-surprising-history-of-the-aussie-ugg-boot.
- Saurine, A. (2020, August 5). *The Surprising Truth About Pavlova's Origins*. Retrieved from BBC: http://www.bbc.com/travel/story/20200804-the-surprising-truth-about-pavlovas-origins.
- *Sexual Harassment*. (n.d.). Retrieved from Human Rights Library: http://hrlibrary.umn.edu/svaw/harassment/explore/3causes.htm.
- *Shanghai, China Metro Area Population 1950-2021*. (n.d.). Retrieved from Macrotrends: https://www.macrotrends.net/cities/20656/shanghai/population.
- Shapiro, S. (1998, April 17). *The Misunderstood 'Rule of Thumb' Misconception: Many Feminists for Years Thought the Phrase "Rule of Thumb" Referred to British Common Law's Tolerance of Wife-beating*. Retrieved from The Baltimore Sun: https://www.baltimoresun.com/news/bs-xpm-1998-04-17-1998107056-story.html.
- *'Shark Biscuit' Meaning*. (n.d.). Retrieved from Outback Dictionary: https://outbackdictionary.com/shark-biscuit/.
- Sheehan, M. (2018, December 19). *How Google Took on China—and Lost*. Retrieved from MIT Technology Review: https://www.technologyreview.com/2018/12/19/138307/how-google-took-on-china-and-lost/.
- Sherman, E. (n.d.). *More Women Are Managers Than Ever Before but There's a Big Downside*. Retrieved from Inc.: https://www.inc.com/erik-sherman/more-women-are-managers-than-ever-before-but-theres-a-big-downside.html#:~:text=Women's%20representation%20in%20management%20is,percent%20of%201980%2C%20suggesting%20progress.
- *Shoot the Breeze*. (n.d.). Retrieved from Grammarist: https://grammarist.com/idiom/shoot-the-breeze/.
- *Shoot the Breeze*. (n.d.). Retrieved from Dictionary: https://www.dictionary.com/browse/shoot--the--breeze.
- *Should We Bring Back Free Tertiary Tuition?* (n.d.). Retrieved from The Good Universities Guide: https://www.gooduniversitiesguide.com.au/education-blogs/education-news/should-we-bring-back-free-tertiary-tuition.
- *Sleep Like a Log*. (n.d.). Retrieved from Dictionary: https://www.dictionary.com/browse/sleep-like-a-log.
- Smissen, P. (2016, September 15). *Expression – To Hit the Sack / Hay*. Retrieved from Aussie English: https://aussieenglish.com.au/expression-hit-sack-hay/.
- Soniak, M. (2012, December 14). *What Does SOS Stand For?* Retrieved from Mental Floss: https://www.mentalfloss.com/article/31911/what-does-sos-stand.
- Soniak, M. (2012, October 18). *Why Is Abruptly Quitting Something Called "Going Cold Turkey"?* Retrieved from Mental Floss: https://www.mentalfloss.com/article/12798/why-abruptly-quitting-something-called-going-cold-turkey.
- Spaid, E. L. (1993, July 13). *`Sticky Floor' Keeps Many Women in Low-Paying Jobs*. Retrieved from The Christian Science Monitor: https://www.csmonitor.com/1993/0713/13122.html.
- Sutton, C. (2020, April 25). *Anzac Biscuits: Why Calling It a 'Cookie' Can Earn a Fine*. Retrieved from News: https://www.news.com.au/lifestyle/food/eat/anzac-biscuits-why-calling-it-a-cookie-can-earn-a-fine/news-story/3017910c019f84b3b1d2143dde37b98e.

# REFERENCES

- *Sweet Paprika*. (n.d.). Retrieved from The Source Bulk Foods: https://thesourcebulkfoods.com.au/shop/cooking/sweet-paprika/.
- T, B. (2021, February 15). *Why Domestic Abuse Happens*. Retrieved from Verywell Mind: https://www.verywellmind.com/domestic-abuse-why-do-they-do-it-62639.
- Tardi, C. (2020, May 25). *80-20 Rule*. Retrieved from Investopedia: https://www.investopedia.com/terms/1/80-20-rule.asp.
- Team, C. (2020, November 12). *Double 11 2020: Alibaba Tmall, JD Singles' Day Sales Exceeded US$116 Billion*. Retrieved from China Internet Watch: https://www.chinainternetwatch.com/31334/double-11-2020/.
- *Tennis "Love" and the Love of Tennis*. (n.d.). Retrieved from Dictionary: https://www.dictionary.com/e/love-tennis/.
- *Testing Waters*. (n.d.). Retrieved from The Phrase Finder: https://www.phrases.org.uk/bulletin_board/44/messages/185.html.
- *The Gender Pay Gap*. (n.d.). Retrieved from Workplace Gender Equality Agency: https://www.wgea.gov.au/the-gender-pay-gap.
- *The Great Pacific Garbage Patch*. (n.d.). Retrieved from The Ocean Clean Up: https://theoceancleanup.com/great-pacific-garbage-patch/.
- *The Origin of 'Proof Is in the Pudding'*. (2012, August 24). Retrieved from NPR: https://www.npr.org/2012/08/24/159975466/corrections-and-comments-to-stories.
- *The Origins of Pho*. (n.d.). Retrieved from Pho Fever: http://www.phofever.com/facts.php.
- *The Ugg Boot Story*. (n.d.). Retrieved from Melbourne Business Awards: https://melbournebusinessawards.com.au/latest-news-item/30933/the-ugg-boot-story/?type_fr=4.
- Thomson, J. R. (2016, July 13). *Can One Bad Apple Really Spoil a Whole Barrel? We Found Out*. Retrieved from HuffPost: https://www.huffpost.com/entry/bad-apples-rotten-good-ones_n_5784f23ee4b0ed2111d783ff.
- *Ticket Scalping FAQ*. (2019, June 7). Retrieved from Victoria State Government: https://djpr.vic.gov.au/ticket-scalping/faq.
- *To Bite Off More Than You Can Chew (Origin)*. (n.d.). Retrieved from Grammar-monster: https://www.grammar-monster.com/sayings_proverbs/to_bite_off_more_than_you_can_chew.htm.
- Townsend, A. (2020, August 3). *The 100-Year History of Self-Driving Cars*. Retrieved from OneZero: https://onezero.medium.com/the-100-year-history-of-self-driving-vehicles-10b8546a3318.
- *Tutankhamun Exhibition Breaks Records*. (2011, May 5). Retrieved from ABC: https://www.abc.net.au/news/2011-05-05/tutankhamun-exhibition-breaks-records/2706208.
- *Types of Potatoes and When to Use Them*. (n.d.). Retrieved from The Neff Kitchen: https://theneffkitchen.com.au/technique/types-potatoes-use/.
- *Union Jack*. (2021, May 29). Retrieved from Wikipedia: https://en.wikipedia.org/wiki/Union_Jack.
- Vital, A. (2013, April 29). *Why We Live – Counting the People Your Life Impacts [Infographic]*. Retrieved from Adioma: https://blog.adioma.com/counting-the-people-you-impact-infographic/.
- Vitez, O. (2012, July 4). *Brown Goods vs. White Goods: A Definiton and Brief Explanation*. Retrieved from HubPages: https://discover.hubpages.com/business/Brown-Goods-vs-White-Goods-A-Definiton-and-Brief-Explanation.
- Voss, C. (2020, September 2). *It's Official: Gabba to Host the 2020 AFL Grand Final*. Retrieved from Austadiums: https://www.austadiums.com/news/814/gabba-to-host-the-2020-afl-grand-final.

# REFERENCES

- Wasserman, T. (2019, February 5). *Tabitha Wasserman*. Retrieved from Medium: https://medium.com/@tabithawasserman/the-complete-saying-was-originally-a-jack-of-all-trades-is-a-master-of-none-but-oftentimes-5f4af01a72c6.

- *West Gate Bridge 50th Anniversary*. (2020, October 15). Retrieved from We are Union OHS Reps: https://www.ohsrep.org.au/west_gate_bridge_50th_anniversary.

- *What Does Earn Your Stripes Mean?* (n.d.). Retrieved from Writing Explained: https://writingexplained.org/idiom-dictionary/earn-your-stripes.

- *What Does Fight Tooth and Nail Mean?* (n.d.). Retrieved from Writing Explained: https://writingexplained.org/idiom-dictionary/fight-tooth-and-nail.

- *What Does Hem and Haw Mean?* (n.d.). Retrieved from Writing Explained: https://writingexplained.org/idiom-dictionary/hem-and-haw.

- *What Does Suck It Up, Butter Up Mean?* (2018, May 20). Retrieved from HiNative: https://hinative.com/en-US/questions/8177023.

- *What Is the Difference Between a Resume and a CV?* (2020, August 26). Retrieved from Indeed: https://au.indeed.com/career-advice/resumes-cover-letters/cv-vs-resume.

- *When in Rome, Do As the Romans Do*. (2021, March 10). Retrieved from Wikipedia: https://en.wikipedia.org/wiki/When_in_Rome,_do_as_the_Romans_do.

- *Where Does the Word Cocktail Actually Come From?* (n.d.). Retrieved from Taste Cocktails: https://tastecocktails.com/word-cocktail-come/.

- *Why Is Coffee Called "A Cup of Joe"?* (n.d.). Retrieved from Wonderopolis: https://wonderopolis.org/wonder/why-is-coffee-called-a-cup-of-joe.

- *Why People Abuse*. (n.d.). Retrieved from National Domestic Violence Hotline: https://www.thehotline.org/identify-abuse/why-people-abuse/.

- Wise, A. (2019, September 5). *8 Science-Backed Reasons to Read a (Real) Book*. Retrieved from Real Simple: https://www.realsimple.com/health/preventative-health/benefits-of-reading-real-books.

- Wood, M. (2020, February 10). *How Pink Collar Jobs Have Changed Since 1940*. Retrieved from International Women in Mining and IWiM: https://internationalwim.org/how-pink-collar-jobs-have-changed-since-1940/.

- Xiao, B., & Handley, E. (2019, November 2). *How Asian-Australians Are Struggling to Break Through the 'Bamboo Ceiling'*. Retrieved from ABC: https://www.abc.net.au/news/2019-11-02/asian-australians-struggling-to-break-bamboo-ceiling/11665288.

www.ingramcontent.com/pod-product-compliance
Lightning Source LLC
Chambersburg PA
CBHW081917090526
44590CB00019B/3384